Other books by George Boas include: *Our New Ways of Thinking, A Critical Analysis of the Philosophy of George Meyerson, The Happy Beast, Philosophy and Poetry, Dominant Themes of Modern Philosophy, A Primer for Critics,* and *Wingless Pegasus.*

THE PAUL CARUS LECTURES were established as a memorial to Dr. Paul Carus with the spirit and intention of his life work in mind. Dr. Carus became editor of the *Open Court* in 1888; he founded the *Monist* later in the same year, and he directed the editorial policies of the Open Court Publishing Company until his death at La Salle, Illinois, in 1919.

The purpose of the Lectures is to further interest and original work in philosophy. The lectures are held at the joint meetings of the various branches of the American Philosophical Association, and the lecturers are chosen by a special committee of the Association.

THE PAUL CARUS LECTURES
ELEVENTH SERIES

THE INQUIRING MIND

THE
INQUIRING
MIND

BY
GEORGE BOAS

THE OPEN COURT PUBLISHING COMPANY
LA SALLE, ILLINOIS
1959

Copyright 1959

THE OPEN COURT PUBLISHING COMPANY

Library of Congress Catalog Card
No. 58-6815

Printed in the United States of America
for the Publishers by
Paquin Printers

TO
JACOB LOEWENBERG

PREFACE

It may seem strange to find an historian of philosophy turning at the end of his career to systematic philosophy. But the very fact that philosophic ideas have a history is of philosophic interest. And since the invitation to give the Carus Lectures contains no restrictions upon subject-matter, I have felt free to put down on paper what I have learned from my historical studies about the way in which ideas are formed and developed. Hence these lectures are based upon history, though they do not trace the history of any one set of ideas.

The technique of thinking has always seemed of as much interest to me as the subject-matter of thinking. The criteria of intellectual satisfaction, the perception of problems, the basic metaphors which men have used in organizing their thoughts, their deafness to the voice of certain of their predecessors and contemporaries, the obsolescence of certain ideas and the rise of others, these incidents in history have perhaps occupied my attention more than dates, places, influences, and sources. It is useless to attempt to excuse this weakness, if it is a weakness, but it is just as well to confess to it.

It is also just as well to confess to other weaknesses of this book. I have always had a sceptical turn of mind which my colleagues have found distressing. An old man is more aware of his ignorance than a young one. He is more given to qualifying his assertions with such words as "perhaps," "on the whole," "for the most part," "as far as I can see." This is a dangerous practice, for sometimes one wriggles out of a difficulty in this way instead of meeting it head on. But I think my argument will show on what my scepticism rests and why my conclusions are phrased in a tentative manner. That, however, remains for the critics to decide. I am not rounding out a philosophic position in these lectures but laying the foundations for one. I have accepted more psychology and anthropology than is customary. I have used old-fashioned words like "mind" and "soul" without worrying much over precise definitions. I have also used dead authorities when possible, for a theory which is obsolete can often be discussed with less emotion than one which still has its adherents. For my purposes it made little difference whether the theory was true or false if only it illustrated a way of thinking.

Since what I have to say is addressed to philosophers and not to the general public, I have not felt constrained to load my pages with footnotes. I have tried to indicate sources for my quotations when they were not of the sort which is commonplace, but one can, I think, assume that certain ideas are pretty well known to the profession, and in such cases I have not hesitated to state them without citation. I am happy, however, to acknowledge my debts, even though most of them will be obvious. Thus the influence of A. O. Lovejoy will appear on almost every page, though there is much that he will not accept as true. The influence of Royce is perhaps not so apparent, though his course in metaphysics which I took in 1913-1914 made a very deep impression upon me. In revising my manuscript I was more aware of Dewey's influence than I was when composing the lectures, though, as in Lovejoy's case, I am afraid he would not be too happy at the use which I have made of his suggestions. When one has been reading and lecturing upon the history of philosophy for thirty-five years, one absorbs from the past a great many ideas without remembering where they came from. I have no doubt whatsoever that an historian could go over these lectures page by page and find anticipations of every assertion which has been made on them. But though I have at least the normal amount of vanity, I hope that I shall have profited enough from my studies to realize the futility of trying to be utterly original.

The debt which I owe to my friend Jacob Loewenberg, to whom I have dedicated this book, is very great. His dialectical skill, his philosophic insight, his great erudition, his ability to persuade me to study men like Hegel, whom I still find distasteful, have all proved decisive at certain moments of my career. It was he who gave me the courage to enter the field of philosophy seriously, and therefore I owe him some of the happiest hours of my life. But regardless of my special debt, no teacher of philosophy can forget the fortitude which he displayed in time of crisis, and it is gratifying to be able to say so in print, though he neither needs nor wants this testimony.

I have been singularly fortunate in my friends, both colleagues and students. I have been also fortunate in having been able to participate in events outside the academic field. My training in one of the arts, my classical education, my drifting about from one graduate school to another, my persistent refusal to confine my studies to any narrow field, an ability to pick up languages without much difficulty, a willingness to relax and let chance take care of me, have all contributed to making my career peculiarly agreeable. The greatest stroke of luck was my being called to the Johns Hopkins University where I have passed over half my life. As far as I can judge, it is unique in the latitude which it gives its faculties, in the informality of its organization, in its assumption that the professors are scholars and not bookkeepers. There may be other institutions in which this is also true, but I have not taught in them. It has always been a pleasure to acknowledge my debt to my university and I do so once more, even though it be the last occasion. I am happy to join to its name that of the Institute for Advanced Study whose guest I was in the autumn term of 1956. The Director and Faculty of the Institute have done everything possible to make writing this book easy. If it does not justify their hospitality, that is surely not their fault. Finally no Carus Lecturer can adequately express his thanks to the children of Paul Carus, whose generosity founded the lectureship. I can only say that the liberal spirit of their father still lives in them.

GEORGE BOAS

The Johns Hopkins University
1957

CONTENTS

CONTENTS

THE INQUIRING MIND

CHAPTER I

ASSUMPTIONS AND PRIMARY INFERENCES

It has been traditional in philosophy to consider the human mind as a sort of mirror reflecting a world which is alien to its nature. This world may be the world of common-sense objects, which swim in and out of our observation as in the fictitious doctrine called naive realism. It may be the world of primary and secondary qualities as in Locke, the world of ideas as in Berkeley, or the world of perceptions as in Hume. It may consist of the essences of Santayana, non-existent and eternal, which the mind somehow or other contemplates in moments of perception. It may be the Intelligible World of the Platonists which the active reason in rare moments catches glimpses of. It may be that which the mystic sees in his beatific vision. Whatever it is, it is always objects seen, observed, contemplated, enjoyed, apprehended, intuited, as if knowledge were a simple dyadic relation between two terms, the knower and the known. At times, as in the so-called empirical tradition, the known is the starting point of knowledge; at times as in Platonism and mysticism, it is the terminus. The purpose of these lectures is to suggest, if not to prove, that it is more fruitful to consider the human mind as a questioner, a doubter, a solver of problems, and that knowledge is always the answer to some problem. I am thus proposing nothing radically new, for something of the same sort was said by Peirce, and James and Dewey always took that point of view. To be anticipated in philosophy is not to be unexpected. But I hope that I shall have succeeded in presenting a philosophical standpoint from which old problems may be rephrased and for that reason alone to have unsuspected solutions.

I shall consequently first set down a few of my assumptions, for they may help to distinguish what I shall have to say from what my teachers said.

The first is the assumption that the human mind exists in time. This is in flat contradiction to the idea that we know only the specious present. I am rejecting the thesis that there is a psychic element which persists unchanged from moment to moment, the self-identical ego represented in personal pronouns. This is based upon introspection, to be sure, and psychologists tell us to beware of introspection. But the assumption is fortified by the consequences of assuming its contradictory. The premise of a permanent and self-identical ego leads one to believe that one ought to be able to discover in life some persistent certainties and that the history of philosophy ought to give us evidence of persistent and immutable methods of thinking. For if knowledge were the intuition of its objects and the intuiting ego never changed, how could it be expected to learn anything; why should it ever be forced to reject anything? But if there seems to be one thing certain about experience, it is that it changes, that we do learn to correct our thought, that we see problems where previously we had seen only facts, in short, that we can grow wiser as we grow older. Most of us do some reading, discuss things with our fellows, meditate in internal conversations with ourselves, act on principles which sometimes turn out to be misleading, discover that we are not the human race. That discovery may be as heartbreaking as an existentialist's discovery of existence, but it is surely normal and frequently beneficial. A mind which was a white piece of paper on which an unchanging world wrote its messages might be supposed to acquire a stock of such messages in childhood which would orient him through the rest of his days on earth. And indeed some minds, arrested in their development, never do proceed beyond childhood. Childhood may be retained by a variety of techniques, one of which is building a wall around one, so that one may never be contradicted either by the lessons of experience or by one's associates. But most of us soon learn that conflict is a striking aspect of experience, that history, in so far as it is our personal history, teaches us but the most shaky of lessons, and that learning itself is a process which never ends. The nineteenth-century idea of a mind acquiring facts, as a miser acquires gold, has little if anything to justify it. That little is seen in those impoverished lives which come about either by a kind of intellectual asceticism or downright incapacity. For if one does not wish to learn, one cannot be made to. One can always distinguish between subjects which are interesting and others which are dull. And so the dull remain unexplored. And it is also possible that some human beings simply cannot absorb certain lessons, no matter how hard they try.

My second assumption is that there is an existential and qualitative plurality of knowers. Existential plurality has never been denied, at least as far as our terrestrial life is concerned, but it has been traditional to speak of the subject, the knower, the ego, the mind, as if the various individual subjects had no noticeable differences. Presumably what could be said about one subject could be said about all, and whatever differences might be found to subsist among them have usually been held to be trivial. I cannot deny that any group of things may be found to have something in common, as Charles Peirce showed many years ago. But problems arise in various contexts, and one of the cognitive problems arises in the context in which minds differ from one another. These differences, I am maintaining, are as follows. (1) Historically people at different periods and in different places may and often do think differently. Their basic metaphors will change; their criteria of satisfaction or truth will change; their questions will change; their methods of investigation will change. I shall illustrate some of this in later lectures, but here I may be permitted to point out that these changes cannot be reduced or assimilated into a larger class of functions. It is of course obvious that all metaphors are metaphors, all explanations are explanations. But people who think in terms of teleology cannot harmonize their beliefs with those of people who think exclusively in terms of antecedent causation. They may be induced to change their minds, but that is agreement

only as a *modus vivendi.* (2) The extent of one person's information may be greater or less than that of someone else. This is
about as obvious as anything in philosophical discussion can be,
but since one's accumulated experience will always have some
effect on one's knowledge, even upon one's perceptions, its ob-
viousness is no sign of its triviality. (3) The orientation of minds
may vary so that one person will interpret an experience in a manner sharply different from the way another interprets it. One finds
the following situation: a given sensory datum may be the answer
to several questions, the corroboration of several hypotheses, the
stimulation of a new problem, or it may be cognitively neutral.
One sees, for instance, a red flag flying in front of a house. In
some cities this may mean that there is to be an auction in that
house, that it is the seat of a Communist cell, that it is the head-
quarters of the Harvard Club, or that it is simply a practical joke
played by some dull-witted boy. When one finds finger-prints on
a telephone receiver, one may choose to frame several hypotheses
about the significance of the find. Presumably only one person
could have put them there, but why they are there is problematical.
Until one learned that finger-prints vary with the people whose
prints they are and that no two sets are alike, the pattern of whorls
would have been indicative of next to nothing. The reason why
I emphasize this apparently innocent fact is that I am rejecting the
theory that there are cognitive perceptual units which are univalent.
Even to say that the smudges are finger-prints presupposes that
one knows what finger-prints look like.

In the third place, I am assuming that the growth of knowledge
is a sort of dialogue, either between a person and his past experiences or between two different people. This dialogue may proceed
by purgative steps, as some of Plato's do; may be progressive
clarification; may be the discovery of new questions previously unsuspected; indeed may turn into almost anything, ending in greater
doubt rather than in greater certainty. I am presupposing therefore
that no one learns anything unless he puts a question to experience
and that knowledge is a series of questions and answers. What is
this? What shall I do about this? How does this mesh in with

what I have believed to date? Why did it happen? Such are a few specimens of the kinds of questions which we put to experience. We do not add one by one new atomic truths to our accumulated store of truths. There is always the possibility that the whole edifice which we have erected on the foundations of the past may topple like a heap of jack-straws at any moment. Hasty generalizations, neglect of negative instances, fallacies in inference, wrong identifications, all are symptoms of the weakness of our knowledge. And I confess to being incapable of explaining this if knowledge is a complex of elementary sense-data.

My fourth assumption has to do with habit. Habit may be second nature, as Aristotle said, but we know enough about its formation and its effects not to neglect it. There could be no habits if we did not exist in time, but the fact that we exist in time is not proof that we can form habits. Habit has the following traits which are relevant here. (1) Anything which the human being is capable of doing may become habitual. Such things may be bodily acts, like eating, walking, dressing, talking in a certain dialect, playing musical instruments. But they may also be ways of thinking. We see this in the child who sometimes thinks as a Comtian theologian, endowing inanimate things with volition, with pleasant or disagreeable attitudes towards him, with feelings which should be appeased or flattered or sometimes punished. But we also see it in adults, who become habituated for instance to certain types of appraisal both of conduct and of works of art, who insist that there must be an unchanging substance beneath all appearances, that there must be an agent for every act, or who with equal dogmatism insist that there must not be agents or underlying substances. In fact, most dogmatism is intellectual habit, and one might hazard the guess that if an assertion of principle seems self-evidently true, it is because one is used to using it. Many of the persistent problems of philosophy persist because of the ritualization of thinking, and many of the usual answers have the same basis. (2) The time-span of action which has become habitual grows shorter and shorter until it reaches a minimum. That minimum is never zero, but at times it comes close to zero. Thus a

skilled pianist spends no time in transferring what he sees on the
score to what his fingers do on the keys; a skilled reader seems to
read off the words he sees instantaneously; and an actor repeats
his lines without having to recall what his text originally dictated.[1]
This reduction of the time-span gives us the feeling of immediacy,
and unless we could remember how laborious was the process of
learning, we should probably declare that most of what we do is
done automatically. For most of our daily living is ritualized. This
is specially true of perception, which often occurs so rapidly that
none of us can remember how we learned to perceive or even that
we learned to do so. But one has only to watch a baby manipulating things, trying to focus his eyes, exploring the material objects
of this world with his mouth, to realize that a process of learning
is going on. There is no more reason to think that perception is
ever immediate than to think that speaking a language is immediate. We forget the learning process, which may well be the
cause of infantile amnesia. The baby learns the most necessary
things at an early age and hence need not recall the process by
which he learned them. (3) As the time-span grows shorter, the
steps in the learning process drop out of consciousness, and we become unable to say how we proceed from what used to be called
the stimulus to the response. The signals which we obey in our
daily life, such as the red and green traffic lights, we obey unconsciously when we have learned the code, just as a soldier learns to
obey commands in close-order drill without remembering the steps
by which he learned them. We know in such cases that the code
has had to be learned, that it took time to learn it, and therefore
our unawareness of how it operates causes no illusions of inevita-
bility to arise in our minds. But, as I hope to show later, observation of the sensory world is also selective and learned; and those
perceptions upon which we mainly depend, such as the visual and
tactual perceptions, are much more quickly recognized and identified than those, such as odors, which count for much less in human
life. The rapidity of a judgment cannot then be said to be evidence

---

[1] It would sometimes be fatal to the smoothness of the act to try to remember.

of immediacy. Knowledge becomes immediate when habitual. (4) As a habit is formed, it takes on a compulsory force, so that the habitual way of doing something seems to be the uniquely right way. Now we know that harmful habits are just as compulsory as useful habits and that their victims feel just as guilty when they fail to complete them as others do when they fail to obey moral commandments or logical rules. It is only when a second person criticizes our judgments that we realize their peculiarity. A person who never encountered criticism, who was never frustrated in the fulfilment of his desires, would also never comprehend that ways of behaving other than his own were legitimate, or for that matter even possible. It is interesting to see how anthropologists will look for analogues to their own society's institutions in the cultures which they are studying, as if all societies must have the same institutions. Marriage, property rights, child-rearing, speech, religious rites, are all frequently supposed to be universal, largely on the ground, one imagines, that all tribes procreate children, have tools and weapons of some sort, communicate, and practice some form of magic, worship, or prayer. In fact, in the early days of anthropology it was not unusual to find writers blaming tribes which were polygamous for not being monogamous, clothing them if they went naked, and trying to put a stop to their religious ceremonies. Such diversities as those which I have mentioned ought to make people hesitate before talking about "the human mind" in the sense of universal cognitive principles in terms of which all people think, learn, and know.

In the fifth place, I am assuming that diversity is as normal, as "natural," as uniformity. There is no need to explain it away as if it were illusory. Uniformity might have some pragmatic value, at least for those who are uncomfortable in the presence of disagreement. But disagreement is more usual than consensus, especially in philosophy, and though we may understand why it arises, we need not expect to eliminate it except temporarily.[2] Dis-

---

2 Why there is disagreement has been explained as follows: (1) *Hegel,* because each philosophy is a "partial" statement of the whole which alone is true; (2) *Sheldon,* because of the inevitable strife of systems; (3) *Pepper,* because there are

agreement obviously may arise from the different meanings which a term has, one man using it in one way, another in another. Theoretically such disagreements could be eliminated by preliminary definitions, though frequently definitions are couched in terms which are also ambiguous. Moreover, there are some ideas which are so vague that one cannot express them in a manner satisfactory even to oneself. Berkeley's notions, it will be recalled, were introduced to take care of such beings. He had to distinguish between those things of which we could have ideas and those of which we could not, and though he had to use such signs as "myself, will, memory, love, hate, and so forth," he also admitted that they "do not suggest so many distinct ideas." They were mental activities which he was aware of but which since they were activities had to be caught on the wing.[3] But without going back to Berkeley, one can find plenty of terms in philosophic discourse which are notoriously ambiguous: "Being," "God," "matter," "spirit," "truth," being among the most prominent. One cannot eliminate such terms by fiat without first asking a man what he means by them, for whether a term has or has not meaning is not revealed in the term itself. But disagreement about the meaning of terms is only one source of discord. Two people obviously may disagree because they use two different authorities for their information or otherwise have two conflicting kinds of information. The Scholastic Method, as illustrated in the works of St. Thomas Aquinas, shows how authorities may disagree and how general rules must be laid down for

---

four root-metaphors, presumably equally good, in terms of which philosophy is expressed; (4) *Royce,* because of individual philosophers emphasizing either the internal or the external meaning of ideas or their logical relations; (5) *Montague,* because each great philosopher has his own vision of reality which he expresses in his philosophy; (6) *Lovejoy,* because philosophy is the testing of diverse hypotheses and also because of the influence of "metaphysical pathos"; (7) *Aristotle,* because his predecessors were groping towards his own philosophy or using only one of the four causes as their principle of explanation; (8) *Plato,* possibly because he thought of philosophy as the clarification of ideas rather than the solution of problems. But 6, 7, and 8 are highly dubitable statements. For Lovejoy has always thought that disagreement could be reduced somewhat by preliminary agreement on the meaning of terms; Aristotle and Plato were not writing histories of philosophy nor meeting the problem which I have suggested they were meeting.

[3] See the 7th dialogue of *Alciphron,* ed. Fraser, Vol. III, p. 327. I have treated of notions in my *Dominant Themes of Modern Philosophy,* N.Y., 1957, p. 269.

choosing between them. But for one who does not feel the necessity of following St. Thomas, how is he to choose between, let us say, St. Augustine and St. Gregory as authorities on Christian dogma? The method of authority is frowned upon today by all but Catholic philosophers, and we seem to have the hope of setting up irrefutable premises and procedural rules upon which all men will agree. But no argument can proceed without premises; and the premises, to say nothing of the rules, cannot in the nature of things all emerge out of a personal experience. Is the choice then to be governed by one's teachers, by some book in which one has confidence, by a supposed *consensus gentium?* All this is bad enough, but two people may also disagree because they draw contrary inferences from a common set of premises. Thus after Darwin there were people who said that the struggle for existence and survival of the fittest "implied" that we should close all hospitals and let Nature take her course. Others, like Kropotkin, maintained that we must correct the cruelty of Nature through mutual aid and also tried to show that animals, who were certainly "natural," did aid each other. Behind the dispute lay a more fundamental assumption concerning the role which the goddess Nature played in ethics, as well as a failure on the part of both sides to define what the term meant. Such disputes cannot be alleviated by asking their participants to look at the facts, especially facts as perpetual data, for there are no such facts in cases of this sort. How can one perceive *now* whether Nature—even granting that we know what we mean by the term—is or is not cruel, kind, or indifferent? One might as well argue that such debates arise out of temperamental differences and that the tough-minded will hold to one thesis and the tender-minded to the other.

Such then are my assumptions. Briefly and abstractly, they are (1) the temporality of the human mind, (2) the plurality of knowers, (3) knowledge as discovery rather than as exposition, (4) the influence of habit on knowledge as on other acts, (5) the normality of diversity. I should now like to pass on to what looks to me like a reasonable inference.

This inference is that the world of objects is a world of particular existents.

I say that this is an inference because even if a group of individual and particular minds were confronted with a matrix of universals, each man's perceptual apparatus would particularize elements in the field. It seems logically possible, though far from plausible, that there might exist an eternal mosaic of qualities and relations, such as the mosaic of subsistent entities which was described in E. B. Holt's early work, *The Concept of Consciousness*—a work which was later disavowed—from which individual minds selected certain items, as radio antennae might pick up certain wave-lengths or a search-light illuminate certain areas of the landscape. But unless the human minds were as colorless as white light, they would be bound to modify to some extent what they selected. They are not, however, so colorless. They do their selecting through their sense-organs, behind which lie almost innumerable prejudices, habits, anticipations, hopes, aversions, most of which have dropped below the level of consciousness. And what we see, to say nothing of hear, smell, taste, and feel—to name only the traditional senses —is to a large extent determined by these unconscious determinants. We do not automatically and universally attend to the same possible items in a field of perception. The tesserae of the objective mosaic themselves may vary from percipient to percipient. Thus the existential diversity of perceptual objects may in part be determined by the inquiring mind, rather than by a supposititious set of uniform objects. Again, the variations in acuity of perception are a well known factor in determining what qualities we perceive, a factor so well known indeed that it would be foolish to insist upon it here. In the third place, the affective fringe of many, if not of all, of our perceptions is explicable only by our past associations, unless we are to return to Watson's loud noises and the sensation of being dropped, about which there is no doubt. Fourth, the vocabulary which we have picked up in childhood and throughout our education directs our attention to certain features of the field and neglects others. Hence, even if Holt had been right in positing a uniform and eternal screen of objective existence, we should still have to admit that both the selection of the elements out of that screen and the actual qualities perceived would vary with the perceiver.

This does not, however, entail the conclusion that there is nothing out there, nor that what is there is a set of ideas in the mind of God, nor unknowable things-in-themselves. We are not projecting dreams or hallucinations into an external world, though my language might suggest something of that sort. When a light ray affects the optic end-organs or an air-wave the auditory, the resulting sensation is a function of both the physical stimulus and the physiological mechanism plus all the psychological determinants which we have listed and more. If knowledge were the neutral contemplation of eternal entities, there would be no more evidence of physical stimuli than of psychological determinants. But if we really learn through past experience, then we have to grant that our nervous systems operate in a world of material things. If that is so, then the resulting sensations are neither purely physical nor purely mental; they are clearly functions of both variables. There is no more reason to attribute causality to the light ray and consider the human being as the patient on which the light ray acts, than there is to attribute causality only to the human being. If, for instance, one mixes some blue and yellow paint on a palette, the result will be green, but the green is no more the effect of the yellow than it is of the blue, though if the yellow were put on the palette first and some blue were added later, we should be inclined to say that the addition of the blue caused the yellow to turn green. Introducing the dates in that way, one could of course argue that when one opens one's eyes in the morning after a deep sleep, the stimuli of the non-human environment causes us to see whatever we see. But a complete account of the matter would certainly have to include the human being as a whole, since without him there is no vision whatsoever. Again, when two billiard balls are in collision, the direction taken by either of them will be predictable according to the Law of the Parallelogram of Forces, but which ball is the agent and which the patient is a matter of convenience and interest. That we see a color rather than an odor, it will not be denied, is attributable to the light-ray. But what color we see, how clearly we see it, whether it is disagreeable or not, to what extent it predominates in our field of attention, are all functions of us, if by "us" we mean our total past experiences including our expectations plus our physiological structure. The totally neutral eye is a figment of the scientific imagination, a useful figment no doubt for scientific purposes but of little use philosophically. It serves the same function as the vacua through which falling bodies fall when we are trying to corroborate the Law of Falling Bodies. It is one of those things that have to be "equal," when we use the phrase, "other things being equal."

The perceptual objects might be individuated by the individual percipients then and need not be attributed to anything else, if we are willing to admit that percipients really are individual.[4] I am not arguing that this is the case; I am simply saying that it could be the case. The problem of individuation arises because philosophers have set up a system in which there ought not to be any individuals. And yet they find them. For we do not have uniform experiences, and one of our commonest difficulties in communicating our experiences arises from this fact. Tests can be made and have been made by psychologists to determine to what extent perceptual experiences are uniform, and there would be no reason to conclude that we are self-enclosed and totally unable to tell other people what we mean by "red," "loud," "sweet," "hard," and the like. If in laboratories individual differences are eliminated, as far as possible, and uniform external conditions of observation are constructed, then it would be expected that the results would be fairly uniform. At the same time we need not rush to the opposite extreme and conclude that we swim in a sea of common qualities, for, if we did, we should act like those material objects which seem to obey so docilely uniform laws. The degree of uniformity varies, and that is why no doubt we ask questions of one another about what we see and whether what we see is real and where it is and the like.

---

[4] The problem of individuation is discussed below in Chapter XII.

Moreover, there is a pragmatic factor which is often forgotten or overlooked and which determines our descriptions of experience. Questions of colors, for instance, cannot be answered absolutely, as every painter knows. Distance as well as light-rays, what was called aerial perspective, determines color. Is there a standard distance from which all colors should be seen? There is a distance, which is calculable, at which a certain color will be visible and another at which it will fade out, and a correct statement of the color of an object would include this detail as it would include the conditions of illumination. Such things are common knowledge, and I am not anxious to dwell upon banalities. But when we become entangled in puzzles about subjectivity and objectivity which arise because we have chosen premises which make them inevitable, we would do well to re-examine our premises. The color of an object will be settled by the use which we wish to make of the information we are seeking. A scene painter and a landscape painter learn how to color their scenery and their pictures in order, as they will say, to produce a desirable effect. They could not do this unless (a) there were certain general laws of color-perception and (b) those laws described variations in color-perception. If we assume as a premise that the percipient is like all other percipients and plays the role of patient, we shall phrase those laws in terms of non-human factors. The illumination, the distance, adjoining colors, sizes of objects, will all figure in such laws, and the human being will be reduced to the status of a neutral observer. But it is surely no heresy to point out that the observer is as distant from the object as the object is from him, that it is the observed size and shape, the observed adjoining colors, which enter into the operation. The way the laws are phrased depends upon the use to which we want to put them. It makes little difference to a landscape whether it is seen or not, though a Wordsworthian who believed in an *anima mundi* might project human pride into the natural order and express with eloquence and pathos its feelings on being observed or neglected.

If this inference is valid, a question will immediately occur to us all: how are the objects about which we ask questions constituted? Here the history of the idea of a natural world must furnish the evidence. At present the world of objects has become deeply stratified. We have the objects of common sense, clothed in all the variety of the secondary qualities; then we have the world of Galilean physics, endowed exclusively with the primary qualities; below this we have the molecular world, below that the atomic, and below that the sub-atomic. The use of stratification to describe this is obviously metaphorical. Presumably we ought to be able to begin with the sub-atomic world and from its nature infer the characters of the atomic, from these those of the molecular, and so on up. This of course is not the situation which obtains. For, to take but one case, color is described in terms of light-rays which are not explained on the basis of what is found in the Galilean world but rather on the basis of what is found in the sub-atomic world. In Locke the primary qualities were observed as they are, unaffected by the conditions of observation. They were the qualities which were sufficient and necessary for writing the laws of Galilean dynamics. They were no more below or above the secondary qualities than they were beside them. They were selected out of all the observed qualities, and it was found that on them alone as a foundation, a set of regular laws could be phrased. Similarly when Dalton set up his world of atoms, he argued from the observed properties of chemical substances to the properties of the parts which composed their mass. Laying it down as a fundamental principle that no matter could be either created or destroyed, he said, "All the changes we can produce consist in separating particles that are in a state of cohesion or combination, and joining those that were previously at a distance." He then, following the lead of Lavoisier, decided that the amount of matter present was indicated by weight. The weight of the "gross object" must be equal to the weights of the particles which composed it. If substances always combine according to the same relative proportions, that is if the same amount of oxygen always combines with the same amount of hydrogen to form water, then one can determine the relative weights of each. By assuming that each ultimate particle—the atom—must have ex-

actly the same weight as each other, and by assuming also that no
particle could change its weight, he was able to deduce from the
relative weights in combinations the number and weights of the
atoms. In his own words, it was his object "to show the importance
and advantage of ascertaining the relative weights of the ultimate
particles, both of simple and compound bodies, the number of the
simple elementary particles which constitute one compound particle, and the number of less compound particles which enter into
the formation of one more compound particle." He then set forth
the possible combinations mathematically: 1 atom of A plus 1 atom
of B equaling 1 atom of C; 1 atom of A plus 2 atoms of B
equaling 1 atom of D, and so on. If then the atoms combine in
the same way as the gross objects do, the relative weights and by
extension the numbers of the atoms could be inferred.[5] The
selection of properties of the common-sense world is clear and the
extension of the behavior of those properties into the scientific
world should also be clear. The results do not give us a world
consisting only of "ultimate particles" except on paper. This is of
course just where we need it most.

Galileo himself was in no doubt about this procedure. He knew
that the laws of motion could be expressed without reference to
color, sound, odor, taste, and texture. He knew, moreover, that
all material objects had the primary qualities though they might
lack some of the secondary. He could then say that the properties
in terms of which velocities and directions could be calculated were
more general than the secondary properties. But obviously they
were not so general that they could also be applied to a world
which included the secondary qualities. They were a select body
of properties to which certain assertions—those involving the secondary qualities—were irrelevant. He could also neglect our feelings about the objects and the values which we put upon them.
He could distinguish a realm of beings by pointing out that they

---

[5] See Sir William Cecil Dampier: *A History of Science,* 3d ed. rev. and enlarged,
Cambridge and New York, 1944, p. 227, where the quotation from Dalton is given
in extenso. Dampier also points out that the distinction between atoms and
molecules was made only after the time of Cannizzaro.

have no primary qualities, or that they have only some of them, or that they do not obey the laws which he had so beautifully expressed. But none of this was reason to decide that these beings were unreal in some other sense than that they do not follow the laws of dynamics. It is important for the sake of clarity to distinguish between various subject-matters, but we have no revelation to tell us which principles of description point to reality and which to unreality. One can call the most general properties of things the real, or one can call those properties from which all other properties can be inferred the real, but one must take the consequences. And one of the consequences is that some of the things which arouse the most baffling problems turn out to be unreal. But of that, more later.

All general statements obviously are made at the cost of neglecting specificity: so much is a tautology. It is no depreciation of them to point out that they have to be selective, that they apply only to a limited class of beings under laboratory conditions, and that they thus are a simplification of the empirical world. The scientist is usually careful to include all the necessary specifications when he phrases his laws, but sometimes when he writes what he believes to be philosophy, he attributes to his subject-matter an ontological status which there is no reason to believe it has. When a physicist says that a physical object is *really* mostly empty space, a good deal depends on what he means by "really." [6] He has the

---

[6] In the Introduction to his Gifford Lectures, *The Nature of the Physical World*, Cambridge, 1929, p. xii, A. S. Eddington gives his famous statement of the difference between the table of common sense and the scientific table. I quote the section on the scientific table. "My scientific table is mostly emptiness. Sparsely scattered in that emptiness are numerous electric charges rushing about with great speed; but their combined bulk amounts to less than a billionth of the bulk of the table itself. Notwithstanding its strange construction it turns out to be an entirely efficient table. It supports my writing paper . . . for when I lay the paper on it the little electric particles with their headlong speed keep on hitting the underside, so that the paper is maintained in shuttlecock fashion at a nearly steady level . . . There is nothing *substantial* about [this] table. It is nearly all empty space, etc. etc." Though this is quoted from a popular lecture in which the speaker could not be expected to be too precise, it looks as if the presence of empty space between particles dissolves the substantiality of the congeries of particles. But that would mean that a gas was not substantial. Moreover, is the word "bulk" used in the same sense when it refers to the particles as it is when it is referred to the table? Eddington was much impressed by the emptiness of matter and refers to it frequently, finally giving a rough histori-

right, of course, to use words as he will, but this "really" is not the "really" which distinguishes hallucinations or illusions from normal experience. It seems to mean that the world as described by sub-atomic physics is largely empty space. But the world as described in terms of tactile and kinaesthetic perceptions is a plenum in which the void is full of gases. Such a world has neither molecules nor atoms nor sub-atomic entities in it; they are derived from calculations made from quite different types of observation. It would be as great folly to introduce into the sub-atomic world the traits of the molar world as it would be to do the reverse. Clerk Maxwell many years ago in his article *Atom* in the ninth edition of the *Britannica* pointed this out in his discussion of Boscovich. "Boscovich," he said, "in order to obviate the possibility of two atoms ever being in the same place, asserts that the ultimate force is a repulsion which increases without limit as the distance diminishes without limit, so that two atoms can never coincide. But this seems an unwarrantable concession to the vulgar opinion that two bodies cannot coexist in the same place. This opinion is deduced from our experience of the behavior of bodies of sensible size, but we have no experimental evidence that two atoms may not sometimes coincide." Maxwell here clearly recognizes that the technique of observation helps determine the kind of world with which we are concerned. Our generalizations, then, if I am right, will themselves be limited in range by the same determinants.

If we are confronted with individual objects, then what has been called immediate knowledge is inarticulate. It can say nothing whatsoever, but furnishes the subject-matter for inquiry and

---

cal account of how matter was gradually, as he thought, dissolved. We find in the same lectures, p. 318 f., "The solid substance of things is another illusion. It too is a fancy projected by the mind into the external world. We have chased the solid substance from the continuous liquid to the atom, from the atom to the electron, and there we have lost it. But at least, it will be said, we have reached something real at the end of the chase—the protons and electrons [this was written in 1927]. Or if the new quantum theory condemns these images as too concrete and leaves us with no coherent images at all, at least we have symbolic co-ordinates and momenta and Hamiltonian functions devoting themselves with single-minded purpose to ensuring that $qp-pq$ shall be equal to $ib/2\ \pi$."

sometimes answers our questions. This stimulates a second inference from my assumptions, the inference that any judgment or assertion passes beyond the immediate. This again is no novelty, but was emphasized by both the English Platonists and Kant. The immediately given is Kant's blind percepts which act to fill up the empty concepts. This presents us with the problem so heavily accentuated by some existentialists of giving meaning to existence. I fail to see why the problem is so desperate as they seem to think, why it should cause nausea or gratuitous action. For nothing is more normal than interpreting what is before us. If we had no past and were suddenly projected like a bullet into this world, the experience might indeed prove disheartening. We can admit that judgment can never exhaust everything which confronts us. But then why should it? Knowledge is discriminatory, selective, and since we express our findings in common nouns and adjectives, in prepositions and verbs, in other words in universals, the choice is between applying general terms to particular things and events or saying nothing. This is not to deny our power of representing such things and events, if we wish, in art and loading them with affective auras, thus giving them a kind of significance which they do not ordinarily have. But such significance is not meaning in the sense that declarative sentences have meaning. A portrait can be called a true portrait, if one wishes to use terms ambiguously, when one recognizes in it a resemblance to its original, or when it evokes in one the same feelings of disgust or admiration which the original does, or when by emphasizing certain traits which the artist has spotted in the original it seems to pass judgment on him. But such significance is gained only by "saying something" in a derivative sense. The truth which a painting may be said to have is the truth of the judgments which we make after seeing it. But these are our truths, not necessarily the painter's.[7] Nor can we make a set of assertions which will ex-

---

[7] The confusion which has arisen in this field has reached such a point that it is probably impossible now to do much about it. Alexander Sesonske's article "Truth in Art" does about all that can be done in its distinction between "three kinds of truth," which means, I hope, "three uses of the word 'truth.'" See the *Journal of Philosophy*, Vol. LIII, no. 11 (May 24, 1956), pp. 345 ff.

haust everything in a painting, let us say, such as Piero's *Resurrection*. It simply has too many aspects for any two men to agree on all of them. Whatever we say about it will be based upon a preliminary selection of those aspects which happen to interest us: in the case cited, its subject-matter, its composition, its symbolic meaning, and so on.[8] But the situation here is like that of knowing anything. We have to analyse what is before us by first detaching from it certain features for which we have names, and then absorbing them into larger groups or classes. Even so simple an assertion as, "This is green," cannot be made until one has had previous experience of the color involved, and when one proceeds to more complicated judgments, more experience is needed.

Suppose one were to enter a room and try to observe without being told what to observe. In that case one's attention would be guided by one's habitual interests, and that which ran counter to them would probably strike him first. A philosopher might ask what he was being asked to look for, whether he was to observe the kinds of objects before him, the furniture and books, for instance, or the sensory qualities discoverable to the naked eye, or the aesthetic value of the objects as evidence of the taste of the room's inhabitants, or the materials out of which the objects had been made—wood, textiles, metals—or the tidiness or disorder of the room, or the economic value of the objects, or the architectural design of the room, or of course any of scores of other things. In fact, the possibilities which I have listed are simply evidence of their author's limitations. Undirected observation would be called utterly random, but even the randomness would have a concealed pattern, a pattern determined by psychological as well as non-psychological factors. In any event, it would be selective and would have to be expressed in those universals which appear to the observer to be relevant. It is not beyond the bounds of possibility that the observer would say that he observed

[8] As an example of how far interpretations of this type may go, the figure of Christ has even been interpreted as that of the god of vegetation. See Kenneth Clark's *Piero della Francesca*, 1951, p. 40.

certain sensory data, but such an observer, it may be surmised, would have had epistemological training. Be that as it may, his observations would be not a direct and unprejudiced reporting of a set of uniquely inevitable and standard data, but replies to questions which he put to himself as "right and proper," if no one else had put them to him. To state the matter differently, what a thing is, if the question is not to be answered by a proper name, means, what class does it belong to? And the class in question varies with the purposes of the inquiry.

Custom, not Nature, to use the old Greek formula, will settle the matter. But when custom has been followed for a certain time, it turns into nature. When we go to a zoo and ask what is before us, we expect the name, popular or scientific, of the animal in question. When we visit a botanical garden, we expect similar identifications. When we wander through an art museum and look at pictures, we either want to know what the subject-matter of a picture is, or its title, or the name of its author, or the school which authorities say it represents, or if it is, let us say, an abstraction, upon what principles of design it has been constructed. Museums usually furnish one with the name of the painter and the title of the picture and sometimes paintings of a so-called school or of a chronological period or style are hung together. But surely this sort of information does not exhaust the information which one is asking for. For pictures, one gathers from reading, are flat surfaces divided into colored areas, are literal representations of real objects, are idealizations of real objects, are symbols of abstract qualities such as vices and virtues, are emblems very thick with suggested meanings, and some pictures are all these things at once. One would scarcely satisfy the usual spectator who asks what is before him by replying, "A picture." All this raises the question of relevance.

Even when we report on our sensory data, the report is relevant to the assumption that sensory data are what we are being asked to report on. If one sees a statue of a winged horse and is asked what it is, one is not ordinarily expected to answer, "A winged horse," or "an equine shape with wings," or "a three dimensional object colored gray," or "marble." One is supposed to reply, "Pegasus." One knows that ahead of time, though no one says so. That all perceptual experience is relevant to something or other has probably been known ever since perception was distinguished from sensation. But not enough has been made of it. For the sensory data themselves have been distinguished by means of looking for them. Only assertions can be relevant to anything if by "relevant" we mean "logically related." And when a color or sound or shape or size acquires relevance, it is because it is believed to be the answer to a question previously put which makes it relevant. There is no more reason to answer questions of identification by sensory qualities than by anything else unless one knows beforehand that sensory qualities are being asked about. Relevance is an integration of present experiences into a context of past experiences and the integration cannot be made unless the observer understands what sort of answer he is being asked to give. One of the most familiar forms of misunderstanding is precisely misunderstanding the purport of a question. If there were only a few kinds of questions which could be asked, the situation would be more easily handled. But neither the categories of Plato nor those of Aristotle, nor those of Kant, limit the kinds of questions which might be put to experience. But even if they did, since they are many, no one would know which type was being required before being told. And to be told, one imagines, demands existing in time to be told. If the one question which could be asked were that of identification and if we knew that identifications had to be made in terms of perceptual experiences, then the illusion that ontology could be constructed out of sensory data would be excusable. The yellow patches and their fellow atomic experiences might suffice to do the work. But such is not the case. It might be the case if there were a standard observer observing under standard conditions and so ritualized—or restricted in curiosity—that he could never think of looking for anything but elementary sensa. Happily this is not our fate. The apparent simplicity of perceptual experience is explicable on the ground of our fourth assumption, that concerning the role of habit. Habit will explain why we ask the familiar questions and why we answer them, even when we are not aware that they have been put.

The question will now arise of why certain habits and customs are formed. Here we can give only tentative replies. Yet it is worth noting that psychologists have studied vision extensively, audition less extensively, olfaction, taste, and touch very little. Boring in his *Sensation and Perception in the History of Experimental Psychology,* certainly the most thorough study of the subject, gives over two hundred pages to vision, half as much to audition, and twenty-one pages to taste and smell combined. This is not because he is not interested in taste and smell, but because they occupy so little space in history. When one asks why, the answer may be twofold: first, that most scientists follow the routine of their teachers; second, that vision and audition play a larger role in our reaction to the environment than the other senses. We can neglect the former, important though it is, and turn to the latter. We are visual, auditory, and mobile animals. We are not primarily olfactory. Our physics derives from a visual and kinesthetic pattern, not from an olfactory pattern. We have erected a visual and mobile world with objects moving about in space, and we have assumed that this space has no influence on their "inner natures." This is reasonable enough and, though a dog might have more use for an olfactory physics, we are not dogs. But though we may recognize this fact as needing no explanation, we might be asked to use caution in projecting the Idols of the Tribe into metaphysical laws. But this, like so many other matters, must be postponed for later discussion.[9]

---

[9] See Chapters II and XIII. It will be recalled by students of Freud that he explained the small part played by olfaction in our lives through our erect posture which makes it next to impossible for us to follow scents on the ground. Olfaction, as everyone who ever watched the beasts knows, plays a dominant role in their lives. It is the one sense possessed by the terrestrial animals—which excludes the birds—which permits them to smell things which have disappeared from vision. We do of course smell things and we can, when necessary, recognize things by their odor. But we are more likely to recognize things by their looks.

The whole problem of relevance is so great that it cannot be settled in a few words. But it will not be useless to say that I am using the term in this place to indicate the relationship between evidence and that of which it is the evidence. Such a relationship will be found only in strict implication. Thus if p strictly implies q, then q is relevant to p, and if it does not, then it is irrelevant.[10] According to this usage, only assertions or judgments or propositions can be relevant and all things, events, qualities, and properties are non-relevant. My reason for emphasizing this is that we use things and qualities to prove propositions and do this as if they themselves asserted something. If they are in themselves without relevance, then only assertions in which they are embodied can take on relevance, and such assertions are always made in the form of judgments pronounced by a human being. We have to know what is relevant before we can make any inferences whatsoever, and though we often make them with the speed of lightning calculators, and therefore are unaware of the inferential process which is going on, we are none the less reasoning and not intuiting. The most common instance of failure to make the proper inferences is that of perceptual illusions. No one to the best of my knowledge has ever denied that we see bent sticks and converging railroad tracks, nor has anyone denied that if we make no judgments about them, we shall never be mistaken. Similarly if we never eat, we shall never suffer from food-poisoning. If we take a vow of silence and never say anything, we shall never lie. Error consists in the judgment that the partial immer-

---

10 This should be qualified in that a number of propositions may together strictly imply another. Thus m, n, o, and p together may imply q, in which case q is relevant to the group. The sight of a ship disappearing over the horizon may be evidence of the rotundity of the earth, not that a small shape disappearing would in itself be evidence of anything other than its disappearance, but that its disappearance when explained by the laws of perspective could be used to prove the rotundity of the earth. In other words, the sentence, "I am seeing a ship shrivel to a point and disappearing," in itself could not imply that the earth is round, but if the earth is round, then we can use the sight of the disappearing ship as partial evidence of its rotundity. This is partial evidence only, since the ship would disappear if the earth were flat, but its hull would not first disappear and then the tips of the masts.

sion of a straight stick in water will bend it at the water-line. The evidence that such a judgment is wrong is clearly not in what we see when the stick is bent, but in what we discover when we take the stick out of the water. From the purely visual evidence all one could conclude is that sticks regain their straightness when they are removed from water. But if we are going to argue about this problem and not simply forget it, then each step will have to be expressed in sentences, and in this particular case two sticks are involved, the visual-stick-in-water and the visual-stick-out-of-water. A standard stick is assumed and it is also assumed that this standard stick is not exclusively visual. The standard stick looks bent when partly immersed, and the common-sense expression is extraordinarily accurate. If our acquaintance with sticks was on the whole that of sticks partly immersed in water, then they would become the standard sticks which looked straight when withdrawn from water. No one could maintain that the visual illusion in question was relevant to the ordinary shape of the stick, for no one probably would say that the test of straightness was the illusion of bentness, though in fact the angle of the bend would be in part a function of the straightness. So long as illusions are accepted as normal, few will pay any attention to them. One has only to think of the history of painting as evidence of vision to realize how little even careful observers have actually seen. For instance colored shadows, decrease in size with distance, linear perspective, are modern developments. They came into fashion as painters became more interested than their forebears in literal representation. To see something in the sense of expressing what one sees or, if this is preferable, in the sense of realizing what one sees, is always dependent on making a comparison between what one sees and what one ought to see if certain things are true. We expect a kind of historical uniformity such that the evidence of one set of perceptions will be corroborated by that of another. But the set which will establish the norm is bound to be the set which serves us most in our daily life.

If the general tenor of this chapter is correct, we shall be forced into a discussion of perception itself in order to have a clearer notion of what part judgment plays in it. I shall consequently turn to that problem immediately.[11]

---

[11] Since writing this lecture, I have read Bruner, Goodnow, and Austin; *A Study of Thinking,* New York, 1956. This study, though it corroborates much of what I am saying, does it on an experimental basis. It is thus much more acceptable than anything which I have written, and I am glad to admit this.

CHAPTER II

THE PROBLEM OF PERCEPTION

Perception became a problem for philosophers when it was recognized that it might deceive us. The assumption was that there must be some sort of primary experience which would always be valid, and the so-called Plain Man was supposed to rely on his senses for guidance through the maze of total experience. The very words used to distinguish between appearance and reality indicated that what appeared was not to be relied upon and that presumably most people did rely on it. It may be granted that when Thales announced that all things were really water, he also announced that they were water whether they seemed to be or not. And it did not take philosophers very long to widen the gap between what seemed to be and what really was. Nevertheless it was also clear that there must be some perceptual or apparent experiences which could be trusted, and even Plato, whose admiration for the sensible world was not excessive, was willing to grant that perpetual beings copied, though imperfectly, the eternal archetypes after which they had been modeled. In the Democritean tradition, it will be recalled, these beings threw off images of themselves which entered the sensory orifices of the psychophysical organism and, thus received, became the building blocks of all knowledge. Though Democritus, like so many other ancient philosophers, survives only in tantalizing fragments, it seems likely that his theory of knowledge was itself the archetype of most theories which today predominate, theories in which perceptions or sensory data are the elements of all cognition.[1] But

---

[1] There is, however, a growing reaction against this. Cf. Charles F. Wallraff; "On Immediacy and the Contemporary Dogma of Sense-Certainty," *Journal of Philosophy*, Vol. L, no. 2 (Jan. 15, 1953), pp. 29 ff.

even the most faithful adherents of such epistemologies still admitted that some such elements might turn out to be misleading. Hume, for instance, when he distinguished between simple and complex ideas, distinguished also between valid and possibly invalid experiences, and it was the possibility of the invalid which led to a critique of pure experience. Knowledge in all such theories was imagined to be a pattern of elementary sensory data, qualities, shapes, sizes, and the like. Some, like the English Platonists and after them Rousseau and Kant, refused to admit that relations could be directly perceived, largely on the ground, anticipated in the *Theaetetus,* that the objective existence of relations would lead to objective paradoxes which would be intolerable. There was little justification for this unless relations were turned into "things," and "things" were held to have invariable characteristics. For if we can see that a cube is red and six-sided, then we might also see that it is on a table or to the right of another cube or smaller than a third. The trouble arose out of the ambiguities in the verb "to see."

Regardless of the terminology employed by the English Platonists and the Kantians, they saw these ambiguities. "To know" might either mean sensory apprehension, the simple awareness of a color or shape or what-not, or judging what is before one, identification. The former sense need not have entailed any belief whatsoever, for the apprehension of a sensum might be accompanied by nothing more than astonishment or curiosity. Such philosophers were not bound by logic to deny Mr. Lewis's terminating judgments, but they were bound by the exigencies of their theory to insist that terminating judgments were judgments. These judgments might be based on the best of evidence, but they were not immediately given for all that. Even if one's knowledge is reduced to nothing more than recognizing as familiar what is before one, familiarity itself demands previous experience. And when such testimony is invoked, there is always the possibility, if no great probability, of error. No one to the best of my knowledge has ever made a statistical study of the incidence of error, but

surely there is enough error in judgments about immediate perceptions to warrant some scepticism when their invariable validity
is pronounced. For if one confine oneself to what is before one,
one has no evidence whatsoever of whether one is looking at an
externally aroused sensation or an image, a veridical experience or
an illusion, something which has occurred just now in the specious
present or something which is the end-term of a process which
started hundreds of years ago. In fact, one has no evidence beyond the datum which is there. And even "there" becomes un-
localizable. There is no reason to confine experience to the immediately given unless one is anxious to deprive the mind—or
experience if one is afraid of the word "mind"—of its temporal
dimension. Much of our life is given over to correcting present
guesses and rapid decisions on the basis of past experience. So
common a matter ought not to be tossed aside as of no importance.

Moreover, not only is the immediate frequently incorrectly interpreted, but it seems to be largely a personal matter, like the
mystic vision, ineffable and incommunicable. If what is seen is a
function of an individual psycho-physical organism and a material
stimulus—such as light rays or air waves—then the only possibility
of communication would depend on the homogeneity of the various perceiving organisms. But we have reason to believe that such
homogeneity is not found. And even if it were, and we must admit to a high degree of similarity among human organisms, there
are enough variations in the answers to such questions as, "Do
you see what I see?" as to give one some doubts about the necessity of everyone's seeing precisely the same datum. Existentially
it would follow that everyone's data are individual and different.
Qualitatively they might be, and probably are, alike. But we are
all too familiar with the self-refuting arguments which are derived from theories of immediacy to trust to sensory data as that
which makes communicable knowledge possible. We need a
theory which will allow for inter-personal statements. A set of
postulates which inevitably leads to the solipsism of the present

moment ought for that reason, if for no other, to be rejected.[2] Even the demand for an escape from solipsism would seem evidence that people believe in the existence of other men's minds, though their own theories make the demand unreasonable. But we need spend little time on this for the very tenets of solipsism cannot be expressed in terms of the immediately given. Such a sentence as, "I alone exist now," contains terms which differentiate what is before one from what is not now given. How could the equivalents for "I," "alone," and "now" be found if there were nothing other than oneself? To distinguish between oneself and something else, being alone and being accompanied, now and then, requires more than a qualitative datum. Not even animal faith can construct a world for which there is no model.

Contemporary psychology has given a new and more fruitful interpretation of perception than that which was current in nineteenth-century psychology. Allport in his *Theories of Perception and the Concept of Structure* (1955) gives us a succinct account of one such theory, that of the Transactionalists. I shall list his summary, hoping not to distort his findings if I translate some of them into my own terms. They run as follows.

(1) The nature of what is perceived is determined by "the combined operation of the subject and the *perceiver*." This operation is called a "transaction" to distinguish it from reaction in the mechanical sense of that term and from an effect produced upon a passive perceiver by a material stimulus, as in the Lockian theory. It will be noticed that this makes the percept a function of both the stimulus and the perceiver and thus it cannot be attributed to either the traditional objective or subjective realms.

(2) "In this process of perceiving, the past experience of the organism plays an important part." This fits in with my assumption that the mind has a temporal dimension.

(3) The past experience of the perceiver contributes what are called "assumptions" about the world in which he lives. Such as-

---

[2] For the record let me say that I have gone into this matter in more detail in "The Truth of Immediate Knowledge," *Journal of Philosophy*, Vol. XXIII (1926), pp. 5 ff.

sumptions are usually unconscious, and I have assumed that they are the effect of habit. In Allport's words, they "represent the 'weighted average' of the individual's past experience." In statistical language they might be called the modal interpretations which the individual makes in the presence of a given thing or event.

(4) Regardless of their truth or falsity, the percept will always be "in accordance with them." "As the organism assumes, so it will also perceive."

(5) Through their resulting percepts, these assumptions provide a "basis for action in the present and future." We rely upon them as guides for our behavior; we interpret the meaning of what we observe in the light of what we have learned. In short we not only learn what the world is like but also what to do about it.

(6) At times the percept formed turns out to be a bad guide to action. It prevents successful action. It is the false note, the misstep. It is a misreading of the stimulus. This is analogous to Dewey's principle that so long as action proceeds without a hitch, no problem will arise.

(7) The individual differences in various persons's past, experiences cause differences in the "assumptions" which individuals will make. But insofar as past experiences are alike, to that extent the assumptions will be alike.

(8) "All the presently existing assumptions of an individual, taken together, constitute what may be called his 'assumptive world.' It is the only world he knows, and it determines the way he perceives the (physicalistic) world at any particular time." To what extent this assumptive world can be described in a set of consistent assertions is unknown, nor is it important, except to the extent that some philosopher might question the propriety of calling that a world which could not be so described. My own impression, and it is only an impression, is that the assumptive worlds of most people are far from being logical wholes and that the correcting of past experience is more normal than abnormal.

(9) The action which is guided by our percepts is always purposive and "perception is the process by which an individual

attributes to his immediate environment the significances which he has found from previous experience to *have furthered his purposes.*" But of course the individual may be wrong, may change his purposes, and, I should add on my own, may live a life of frustration and even become habituated to it.

(10) An individual's purposes may be absorbed from the social groups with which he has become identified, and the values which he attributes to the achievement of these purposes may be taught him in the various ways social groups have of educating their members.[3]

The student of the history of philosophy will see in these principles psychological confirmation of philosophic theories which go back at least to Schopenhauer and which were restated in our times and in very different terms and in greater detail by Royce and Dewey. Royce's theory of the internal and external meaning of ideas, as well as his definition of an idea as a plan of action, Dewey's theory of thinking as problem solving, are both capable of being accommodated to transactionalism.[4] As for our own purposes, the theory appears to confirm the assumption that the human mind exists in time and that perceptual data are functions of both an external material world and a human being. They have characters which differentiate them from either the physicist's conception of a material object or an image, dream, or hallucination. They are a third kind of thing or event. The assumptions which the individual makes and which are so often unconscious can easily be interpreted as habitual judgments made on the occasion of a stimulus, for that would explain why they are unconscious, why they are compulsive, and why they are immediately made. The theory also explains why people differ even in their normal perceptual experiences and by introducing the social

---

[3] The quotations cited are from *op. cit.,* pp. 278-280. I have omitted an eleventh principle since it is largely a repetition of the first, a justification of the term "transaction."

[4] In fact, the term "transactionalism" was first used by Dewey and Bentley in "A Terminology for Knowings and Known," *Journal of Philosophy,* Vol. XLII, 1945, pp. 225-247.

factor gives proper weight to the value which we all put upon
perceptual normality.

The orientation of the observer or, if one prefers the technical
language of the transactionalist, his assumptions, can be viewed
as a complex of the following items.

(1) *Speech habits.*[5]

The influence of our habitual language surely must be of some
importance in determining what we shall look for, what we shall
consider to be right and proper, what we shall see. Our language
is as if it were based upon a protophilosophy in which the thing
and its attributes are fundamental. Our use of nouns and adjectives throws us into an attitude of expecting to find things which
are more or less permanent, or which have a permanent substantial core, and which move about in space-time without noticeable alteration. This, it will be obvious to all students of the
history of philosophy, is derivative from Aristotle's theory of substance and attribute. Meyerson in his various books has shown
how change is always explained as the acquisition and loss of
properties which seem to float about and come to anchorage on
various self-identical subjects. These properties are themselves
probably descendants of the qualitative atoms of Anaxagoras,
though whether they are or not is not essential to our exposition.
In any event they are atomic in the sense that they retain their
nature or character wherever they appear. In the Middle Ages
they were the sensible species;[6] in Locke they turned into the
primary qualities; in Hume they were the impressions; in Avenar-
ius and the James of radical empiricism they were neutral en-

---

[5] Lest anyone conclude that I am maintaining that metaphysics is always a projection of linguistic habits, let me emphasize my disagreement with that thesis. My
general point of view about the relation between language and philosophy is that
expressed by Lewis S. Feuer in his article, "Sociological Aspects of the Relation
between Language and Philosophy," *Philosophy of Science,* Vol. XX (1953). I do not
agree, however, with his opening historical comments, though that is of little importance, nor do I think that he has sufficiently acknowledged the influence of linguistic
habits upon thinking. It may be, of course, that he thought Bacon had already
finished that job.

[6] For an excellent account of the sensible species written by one who accepts
them, see Etienne Gilson; *The Christian Philosophy of St. Thomas Aquinas,* N. Y.,
1956, pp. 203 f.

tities; in Santayana and Strong they were essences. Since there seemed to be no way in which direct apprehension of anything else could be discovered, philosophers hit upon the conclusion that the whole universe consisted of nothing more than these floating qualities and that whatever we thought of as permanent substance was in reality a complex of them, selected out of the totality of qualities in accordance with laws which were never clarified. When, as in the case of Auguste Comte, it was seen that they themselves changed as the conditions of observation changed —the illumination, the distance between observer and observed, the age, health, acuity of perception of the observer, and above all the instruments of observation—a rule had to be laid down in accordance with which certain conditions of observation had to be set up as correct and others as incorrect. Thus Comte himself deprecated the use of the telescope and microscope, for no one could deny that what one saw through these instruments differed greatly from what one saw with the naked eye. The innocence of the naked eye was assumed and the nineteenth century was keen on innocence. But the eye, whether naked or clothed, was itself an instrument, and its contribution to what was observed should never have been discounted.

The value of the theory of atomic qualities was that it gave the philosopher a set of beings external to human interests and above all conforming to our language. Each adjective could be said to name one or more of them. It did not do so well when it came to tackle the nouns. The things which those parts of speech named had to be Aristotelian subjects, and, as one could never reach them by direct perception since one could perceive only attributes, a number of evasions were required. They could, as we have suggested above, turn into constellations of qualities, and in such a work as Russell's *Analysis of Matter,* that is what they were. In Locke they had been the material in which the primary qualities were resident, and, again as we have suggested above, these qualities were the properties which were sufficient and necessary for the construction of Galilean dynamics. The Lockian tradition has never died out, and today we are accustomed to the theory that whatever physics decides are the necessary and sufficient terms of its fundamental equations remain as the properties of the material substantial world. In the long run these are its indefinables, whether they are mass or energy or something else. Even in such a tradition as that which derives from Malebranche and Berkeley, though the two men differed on many points, there was something permanent and indifferent to human cognitive needs and interests, ideas in the mind of God. It was of small importance whether they were directly apprehended, as in Malebranche, or represented by their effects in us, as in Berkeley; in both men the mind of God performed the function of a permanent external world which stood there as the ultimate test of truth and about which all propositions were ultimately made. I say "ultimately" since no philosopher said that all assertions were equally true. Some were made about beings which were not part of God's mind.

Even in such a subject as biology, where the subject-matter is obviously in a state of constant change, it was assumed that something must be found which would correspond to the nouns and thus be that which did the changing or underwent the changes. In the theory of preformationism, the whole animal or plant was believed to be present in the seed or egg and growth was simply its exfoliation. As Pearson had said that the ether was invented to provide a subject for the verb "to undulate," so something had to be provided as a subject for the verb "to grow." Preformationism by putting the whole animal or plant back into its seed, did just this. In Nägeli the permanent subject was the idioplasm which in turn became Weismann's germ-plasm, for which genes were later substituted. The permanent "thing" in all these cases satisfied the need for something which might be that which did the developing, for whether the biologist was consciously philosophical or not, he had to have something for his nouns to name. The animal or plant then became the idioplasm or the germ-plasm or the bundle of genes which were transmitted from generation to generation, and everything else was to be correlated with the changing conditions under which these permanent things lived.

In psychology the nouns named the soul, the subject, the Ego, or the person which had experiences but which was presumably never itself experienced. The biologist had the advantage here over the psychologist, for he could point to fertilized eggs whose material substance could be said to be pre-existent in the parents of the individual organism and again to unicellular organisms whose substance pre-existed in the cells which had divided. The soul in Aristotle was the form of the body, that for which the body existed, and its permanence might be thought of as permanence of function. Yet when he had erected a psychical structure which seemed able to perform all the functions which the human being needed for life, he then divided the reason into two parts, one of which was active and which was later believed to be the permanent agent of all psychical activities.[7] In Descartes the permanent substance became the Ego which was the agent of all thinking, and thinking for him meant all the psychic functions. In Locke and Berkeley it was the active mind just as it was in the English Platonists. And in Kant and the Post-Kantians, though they differed greatly in what powers they granted to it, it was always there as the one reality of which we can be certain. It was Hume who threw the gravest doubts upon its existence, for he maintained that such a being could not exist, since its properties were such that there could be neither an impression nor idea of it; and furthermore introspection, at least as far as his own introspective powers went, showed none such. To deny its existence was to assert that there could be thinking without a thinker, consciousness without anyone to be conscious, acts without an agent, and this appears to have been repugnant to most nineteenth-century thinkers.

But the thirst for substances was so great that workers in all fields tried to quench it. Historians talked about nations, civiliza-

---

[7] In Aristotle's *De anima* the paragraph on the active and passive reasons is one of his most obscure. There is no longer any way of telling just what he meant by the immortality of the active reason or, for that matter, its separateness from the body. But in such a philosopher as St. Thomas Aquinas, its substantiality and eternality are clear.

tions, cultures, which were unchanging in their inner natures but which somehow or other expressed themselves variously through time. Sometimes an actual *Geist* or spirit or collective self was asserted to exist; at other times scholars used equivalent terms without definition. Writers were said to be perfect expressions of their times or their culture or their nation, as if the latter could be described without reference to those men who expressed their nature. Aestheticians talked about the spirit of tragedy, of comedy, of the epic, the lyric, the ballad, of the mediaeval mind, the Renaissance mind, the modern temper and mind, to say nothing of the Collective Unconscious, all of which lay behind or below or above the multiple observable features of these permanent beings. Sociologists talked of social minds which somehow or other explained the peculiar properties of various societies. And in our own time we have heard of larger agglomerations of permanent and hidden cultural beings known as the East and the West. I am far from denying that the technique of discovering or of constituting these various entities differed widely and I am not identifying Professor Northrop, for instance, with Swammerdam. Both may in fact be right in their several theories. But I think it will be granted that their thoughts were directed to the discovery of a permanent subject which might suffer the changes or even create the changes because our linguistic habits demand that our nouns actually name something. In short I am not saying that it would not be possible to find complete homogeneity in a set of societies or cultures, but to attribute that homogeneity to something permanent within the culture seems to be nothing more than satisfying a need for meeting the demands of language.

But our language also encourages us to reify abstractions as well as material things and to handle them intellectually as if they were things. The whole debate about universals and particulars as it arose in the Middle Ages was an attempt to invest logical beings with the properties of substances. Like substances, universals were so permanent that they were said to be eternal, outside of space and time, but they too could appear here and there and now and then without suffering any change whatsoever. In some cases it was they which caused the changes to appear. Thus when a bad man became good, the universal goodness appeared in him exactly as Aristotle's floating quality of heat passed out of the masseur's hand, as he said, into the body of the person being massaged. The heat was a permanent being and in Aristotle was irreducible to anything else. But as late as Carnot, though he knew that heat was not a substance, it was spoken of as if it were a fluid running downhill, so strong was the potency of the caloric theory. Though logical realists insisted that their universals were not material beings, yet they had to admit that they behaved like material beings, for they could be found incorporated in material form (as when circularity was found in a wheel) or in a person's bodily acts (as when a wheelwright makes a wheel) or abstracted from material substances (as when a philosopher discovers that wheels, millstones, the orbits of the planets, or cross-sections of columns, are all circular). These operations showed that just as material substances retained their self-identity regardless of apparent changes in them, so these eternal substances retained theirs. Some of the most eloquent and moving passages of philosophic rhetoric play on the pathos of the eternal beings, whether they are situated in the Intelligible World of the Neo-Platonists or incorporated in the Sensible World of the empirical scientists. And just as matter in Locke possessed solidity, extension, figure, and mobility,[8] so the universals were indestructible, distinguishable from one another in character, and, though capable of spatio-temporal incorporation, immutable. One realizes more clearly how they were modeled on material beings when one reflects on these three traits alone. Their indestructibility was analogous to the solidity of the material beings, their capacity for incorporation to the various states which material beings might manifest, and their individual characters— their specificity—which made them discernible, to Locke's figures. Figure in Locke could not be eliminated because every material object has some shape, whether that shape can be named or not.

---

[8] In the first three editions of the *Essay*, as Fraser points out in his edition, Vol. I, p. 169, note 1, the primary qualities were listed as solidity, extension, motion or rest, number and figure. The reduction to four was made in the fourth edition.

These shapes were geometrical figures, and the geometrical figures were universals in logical realism. A final analogy will be found in the fact which no logical realist could deny that certain universals could be logically generated from others, as when logicians define certain terms by more primitive terms. But similarly material things could be compounded out of smaller parts which might disappear in the larger wholes, as when physical copies of logical archetypes are compounded to make molar objects. Materially, I imagine, one could say that straight lines are represented by rods and planes by boards, and any carpenter could be described as embodying the precepts of plane geometry in his work. But one could with equal plausibility say that the geometrical entities are themselves modeled upon or derivative from the work of the carpenter. When a carpenter moves a ruler from one plank to another, he is transposing a straight line and when he smooths down a surface he is producing a plane. The modern geometer would howl in indignation at this, and it has no more than historical relevance, if that much. But nevertheless the interplay between pure and applied geometry is as stubborn a fact as any with which the philosopher has to deal. Idealization or purification of experience is common enough to cause no surprise. The question which concerns us is the direction in which the process of purification moves. And that direction seems to be that established by the idea of the thing. For if universals are not modeled on things, then it becomes absurd to discuss their properties, their appearance and disappearance, their generation in the logical order. It would seem to be more reasonable to admit a distinction between the words which symbolize them and the universals themselves and not attribute to the latter properties which more reasonably are attributed to the former.

(2) But our language also possesses verbs, and verbs always denote relations. Nobody any longer reifies relations, but the symbols for verbs are always individual words or groups of words when we have to use auxiliaries. Consequently when an idea is thought of in terms of the symbols which express it, it looks as if there were at least two terms externally related to each other by the verb. It will be recalled that in Aristotle two of the categories

were the two voices of the Greek verb, the active and the passive. These correspond to our notion of a relation and its converse. They either gave rise to or accompanied the rise of our notions of activity and passivity, action and passion. In order to give sense to action and passion, agents and patients had to be provided, and these beings had to be substances, which, since frequently they were not observable, turned into those metaphysical beings which became the laughing stock of Molière. In many instances men were tempted to analyse the relation without its terms, as when we discuss love, fatherhood, justice, truth, and even being. This has become standard operating procedure and it may be presumptuous to satirize it, since it has the prestige of long standing tradition. But just as there can be no fatherhood without a man and his children, no love without a lover and a beloved, no truth without a proposition and that which it expresses, no being without something which *is* something, so there can be no relations whatsoever without relata. Relations have been classified in a very general way by Whitehead and Russell, according to the number of terms which they relate, their symmetry, and their transitivity. This is a purely logical analysis. But no one would maintain that because both fatherhood and motherhood are intransitive and asymmetrical dyadic relations, they have no important differences. To be a father and to be a mother are two different experiences, and the great differences which exist between the terms involved throw the logical similarity into the background when the relations between parents and children become a problem for the psychologist or ethicist. That only certain terms can sustain certain relations makes one suspect that the complex of terms in relation is more subject to verbal than to existential analysis. I am far from deprecating the study of logic, but I am deprecating projecting its findings into existence. When one is studying an existent relationship, such as love, parenthood, truth, justice, or any of the others with which we are familiar in books on ethics, aesthetics, and metaphysics, it is not the purely logical properties which interest us and create the problems, but rather those complexes in which such relations are found. One has but to think of all the space which has been given to such discussion as that of the good, obligation, instrumental and terminal values, the right, to see how a little more concreteness, (such as is found in works on moral casuistry) would clarify the questions, if not produce the answers. When a philosopher admits that circumstances can modify moral values, he is asserting, whether he knows it or not, that the values are found in systems of relation and that their nature cannot be discovered outside the system. Within the system we find a certain person or thing or event doing something or other to another person or thing or event. What the relation is called will be determined in part by the terms involved. To abstract the relation and give it a name, is to deal with it as if it could have the same characteristics in isolation from the terms as it had when conjoined to them.

As an example of what I am driving at, let us take the case of brotherly love, or charity. This is said to be the greatest of the theological virtues. But one cannot manifest it unless one knows who one's brother is and one cannot love someone whom one does not know, even if told that he is one's brother. Charity is said to begin at home, but when it is extended beyond one's immediate home, the problem is precisely to know how to limit the frontiers of the home and one's family. For ethical purposes I suspect that all who believe in brotherly love will also believe that home is the whole earth and that all men are brothers. This Stoic principle can be applied up to a certain point, but somewhere or other a person is going to say, "This man is not my brother." In the Christian Church that point was where heretics and schismatics were to be found; in the Southern United States it was the point at which a certain degree of pigmentation was discoverable in one's neighbor's skin. On the other hand, in Buddhism all living beings, except vegetables, were brothers. Now the serious person will wonder whether he is manifesting charity on certain occasions, for he finds that the love he bears to his biological brothers does not appear to be identical with the friendship he has for his neighbors, and that too seems different from the charity which he bestows on starving or otherwise suffering Koreans whom he does not know. Such remarks may seem frivolous and pedantic, but whether they

do or not, they suggest the limiting cases which cause inner questioning and a sense of guilt or self-approval. If charity could be
defined simply as a dyadic and, let us hope, symmetrical relation—
though that is far from certain—then such questions ought not
to arise. One of the errors of Luther, damned in the bull *Exsurge
Domine,* was his insistence on the need of perfect charity if one was
to be saved.[9] The question was how far a man could approach such
perfection. The idea of perfection was elaborated by lifting the
relation out of the complex in which it is found and treating it
as if it were a term. This is not a book on ethics, but I am frank to
say that I have never yet come upon a moral problem which did
not arise out of a man's ignorance of whether he was or was not
committing a sin, or in the more usual language doing what he
ought to do. Unfortunately the "ought" in such cases is debatable
in terms of the right occasion, the right reasons, the right purposes,
the right persons. When Aristotle wrote down these restrictions,
he was apparently pointing to some of the relations in which
moral acts are to be found. Nevertheless he too abstracted the virtues from the relations in which they arose, except when he was
considering cases. But the cases always include the terms as well
as the relations.

What I am asserting then is that there is no such thing as love,
there is only loving; no such thing as acts, there is only acting. I
am saying that turning relations into terms leads to the contrary
conclusion and is at best only a logical device.

(3) Besides linguistic habits, there are expectations, motivations,
what Bruner and Postman have called "hypotheses." To use the
language of every day, we see in part what we expect to see or have
reason to believe will be there. The discovery of the influence of
expectation upon perception was anticipated by the Würzburg
School when it emphasized the importance of the *Aufgabe* and the
Einstellung. The *Aufgabe* was of course simply the problem set to
the subject, and the *Einstellung* became his attitude towards that

---

9 See Denzinger's *Enchiridion Symbolorum,* 1921, no. 744. In the *Index systematicus* of this work, XI d, this passage is under the heading, *Caritas imperfecta
non est inhonesta.*

problem, an attitude which produced results which ran contrary to the rules of the association of ideas and which at times obscured some features of the objects to be perceived and, naturally, heightened others. Thus there was no way of interpreting the percept exclusively in terms of material stimuli, unless one were willing to include the instructions of the experimenter among the material stimuli. But even if one did, they were not identical with the physical object before one, the light rays or air waves or whatever it might be which presumably was being reported upon. The percept could not be understood apart from the total complex of the psychophysical organism plus the stimulus taken together, and the search for a purely objective stimulus which somehow or other would be reproduced or represented in the percept turned out to be vain. In fact, in such experiments as those in which a series of sounds given in rhythm is interrupted, the observer failed to observe the interruption, once he began to expect that the rhythm would continue. Hence he was perceiving something which was not present. But we need not go into the laboratories to discover this phenomenon. When we knock on a door and hear a voice saying, "Come in," and enter the room to find no one there—or for that matter mistake a voice over the telephone for that of someone to whom it does not belong—or make similar perceptual errors, are we not also operating from expectation? Such occurrences are in flat contradiction to any theory which holds that there is a field of sensory data which we perceive directly and which can therefore serve as the ground for true judgments. It is through our mistakes that we discover the truth, as the truth turns out to be in conflict with what we have habitually believed. There could be no error, as Royce said years ago, unless there was some truth to err about, but that truth might be the ideas held to be true by the person who is in error. One might of course assume the objective subsistence of erroneous percepts, as Montague seemed to do, but, like negative facts, erroneous percepts which are objective cause more trouble than they are worth.

(4) Along with expectation is to be found the factor of value-

judgments. Bruner and Postman have found, for instance, that what is valued looks bigger than what is not valued. In their well-known experiments on the size of symbols, they found that a symbol of what is liked would appear to be bigger than one which is disliked. [10] This can be phrased, if one wishes, in terms of a "hypothesis" that there is a linkage between size and value, but we need not for our purposes go into that. If our likings and dislikings can influence the look of things, that is all we need to know. And it begins to seem likely that they can. If then these findings are correct, we can assert that what is seen will depend in part on what is approved or disapproved of by the perceiver. He may not emphasize one side or the other at all times, for he may have a tendency to perceive above all that of which he disapproves or that of which he approves. And indeed one of the predominant traits of what we call a man's personality is just that sort of tendency. Or it might be possible that in certain areas, but not in others, he will perceive objects of which he approves and not those of which he disapproves. Thus a critic of art who is for one reason or other fond of purely formal characters of a painting or poem will spot those characters or their absence and fail to see anything else. In fact, unless my experience with critical essays is peculiar, he will get to the point of defining a work of art as an artefact possessing just those characters of which he approves and no others, and he will become annoyed when some other type of critic points to others. We are all familiar with the man who in most things sees no evil as well as with the man who sees no good. But I doubt whether any of us have ever run into a man who sees only evil in everything or only good in everything.

The business of the psychologist can be carried on only by testing for each of these determinants in isolation from the others. But we are not pretending to be psychologists here and are interested only in indicating some of the factors which could reasonably be called the psychic, rather than the objective, determinants

---

[10] See J. S. Bruner and L. Postman; "Symbolic Value as an Organizing Factor in Perception," *Journal of Social Psychology,* 1948, Vol. XXVII, pp. 203 ff.

of our perceptions. For by indicating these factors we may be able to persuade our colleagues that they will never be able either to develop a theory of truth or a metaphysics on the basis of a world which is directly absorbed, as by a blotter, in perception. I doubt whether any psychologist would deny that the human being acts as a complex in his perceptions, and the various determinants, language along with expectation and valuation, usually are all intertwined. Nor are we driven to setting up a unified person, completely integrated, if we talk in this way, for we can still maintain that no one acts consistently. The *intermittances du coeur* of Proust may be found to express themselves in our perceptions as well as in our judgments of value.

The question must now be faced of the source of our "hypotheses," or "assumptions." Why do we expect certain perceptual experiences rather than others? What determines our *Einstellungen,* our attitudes, our emotional sets, our linguistic habits? Some features of what used to be called the apperceptive mass[11] may easily be explained as the accumulated experiences of the individual which have become compulsive, but others must have a social or cultural source. Thus no one invents his own language. Children do occasionally make up words and phrases of their own to name and to interpret events going on in their environment, but they soon learn, even when their inventions are greeted as charming and delightful, to amend them and to adopt the language of their more mature associates. If Piaget's studies have contributed nothing else to philosophy, they have taught us that there might be a great variety of ways of both thinking and perceiving, if people were not disciplined into thinking in terms of a traditional matrix of ideas which are crystallized in speech. I

---

[11] It is interesting to note that this term which was introduced by Wundt and Herbart does not appear either in Boring's *Sensation and Perception in the History of Experimental Psychology* or in Allport's *Theories of Perception and the Concept of Structure.* Yet in psychological studies in the nineteenth century it occupied an important place as an explanation of how we understand or interpret our experiences. Its use and obsolescence are interesting examples of how a concept is formed to fit preconceived ideas—in this case that of a permanent subject of all consciousness —and of how substitutes for it will be sought after it has been discarded. See Karl Lange's *Ueber Apperception* for a classic example of its former use.

am not urging my colleagues to turn into babies, for I recognize the value of a common speech, but I am urging them to observe the growth of the inquiring mind in order to see how the basic notions which we believe to be essential for what we call correct thinking are acquisitions and neither rooted exclusively in the inevitable ways of thought or in the structure of the non-human universe.

That language may "work" without mirroring the structure of the world it describes is seen clearly enough in our compound verbs where the auxiliaries are no longer taken seriously. When we translate, "I have gone," into the French, "Je suis allé," no one is worried about whether the French auxiliary or the English is a more faithful reflection of what happens when one goes somewhere. *To have* might by some fantastic scholar be said to mean possession and *to be* to mean *to exist* or even *to be equivalent to.* He might then puzzle over the problem of how one could possess *goneness* or even to be it. But such fantasies are fruitless, and we have come to accept idiomatic turns of speech as needing no other than an historical explanation. But again, as my colleague, Leo Spitzer, once pointed out, the song of the barnyard cock is *cock-a-doodle-do* in English, *cocorico* in French, *kikeriki* in German and in Italian.[12] Would anyone propose a debate on which is right or whether cocks in different countries sing different songs? Some languages give tenses to nouns as well as to verbs. Some make nouns out of verbs by adding a nominal ending. German seems to have a trick of turning nouns into both verbs and adjectives, a trick which we Americans are beginning to imitate. Whatever may have been the origin of such practices, they are accepted now as normal. And though they cannot be said to give us a picture of an objective world, they do not misguide us as we wander through that world unless we insist on constructing a metaphysics out of language.

Language will, as we have suggested earlier in this lecture, di-

---

12 See "Language—the Basis of Science, Philosophy and Poetry," in *Studies in Intellectual History*, Baltimore, 1953, p. 70.

rect our attention to certain features of the landscape so that others
are obscured. If we speak a language with few general terms—
and primitive languages do not have the same general terms that
more developed languages have—then in those cases where no
general terms are to be found, it is unlikely that a person will look
for common traits in all the things which we name by one word.
On the contrary, he will accept diversity as normal. It is plati-
tudinous to point out that the Eskimos have no single word for
snow and in rural English speech dozens of obsolete terms are
preserved for things which urban dwellers call by one name. It is
important for some people to perceive the differences between
mares, studs, geldings, foals, colts, and fillies, but for others the
word *horse* will do to cover them all. A landlubber will call every
vessel a boat, whereas a sailor will sneer at him for doing so. The
main importance of these remarks is to point to the influence of
terminology on conceptualization. The sciences always begin and
have to begin their classifications with generally accepted similarities and differences, and these similarities and differences are
those to which one's attention has been called by the language of
his social group. We can see why animals were once classified
into aqueous, terrestrial, and aerial, and why a search for an
igneous one was also made. The reason was not purely linguistic,
but once the linguistic distinctions were made, zoologists were set
on a course which it took centuries to change. The first chapter
of *Genesis* anticipates these distinctions, and for all I know its
prestige may have been one of the causes of preserving them so
long. But though common speech retains them as birds, beasts,
and fishes, the zoologist of today is more interested in morphological similarities than in similarities of habitat and even that basis
for classification is giving way to a functional one.[13] Now if a
man is educated in the speech of a certain cultural group, the
group of countrymen or of urban dwellers, of contemporary scientists or of dead scientists, he may to be sure learn to change his

---

[13] Cf. E. Mayr; "Concepts of classification and nomenclature in higher organisms
and microorganisms," *Annals of the New York Academy of Science,* Vol. LVI,
pp. 391-97. Other references will be found below in Chapter III.

language, but the changes as well as the tradition will be induced in him by other people with whom he is associated. He may also learn to use one form of speech in one social group and another in another. When he is talking to horticulturalists he may use the word *Philadelphus* and when he is talking to his neighbor next door he will speak of the syringa or mock-orange. Similarly when he is talking to a fellow fisherman, he may speak of minnows and mean by the term not the British *leuciscus phoxinus*, but any little fish of the *Gambusia* and *Notropis* genera. To say that only the *leuciscus phoxinus* is really a minnow is to be excessively pedantic. The adverb "really" can mean only that the speaker prefers to use the term in that way or that originally it was used in that way, unless he thinks that British usage is based on Revelation.[14] But only lexicographers have the power as individuals to impress their wishes on the linguistic habits of society and even they fail in their efforts as far as large groups are concerned. Linguistic usage changes in a very complicated way; some words are indeed invented, and some which are invented take hold and are incorporated in common speech. But in general we do not invent a complete vocabulary and syntax of our own, and if we did, no one would understand us. We absorb them from the people with whom we grow up. Consequently insofar as language determines perception, to that extent we have an inter-personal determinant of perception.

If I speak of this as inter-personal or social rather than as cultural, it is because I wish to preserve the possibility of society's being composed of social groups which have little homogeneity as a collection. I wish also to permit the possibility of a single individual's belonging to several social groups in which not merely his speech but also his system of values will change. I am not denying the possibility of completely homogeneous societies, such as those studied by Mrs. Benedict in her *Patterns of Culture*. But contemporary urban societies, as Lloyd Warner and David Ries-

---

[14] In fact a thorough going pedant might say that any tiny fish is really a minnow since the word comes from the Indo-European root *min* which appears in *minor*, *diminutive*, and the like.

man have shown, are stratified and possess not only diversity but also inner conflict. Their conclusions are borne out by the study of intellectual history which cannot fail to weaken the older idea that ages and periods have pervasive traits. At best such traits are the most frequent traits found by the historian, but even they emerge usually out of debate or dialogue between individuals who hold differing views. No one, as far as I know, has ever been able to devise a method for uncovering a baby's system of values. Whether all babies like and dislike, approve and disapprove of the same sorts of things is still a moot point. Where individual preferences make themselves first known can be decided only by experiments not yet elaborated. There is always the possibility that people differ at birth to a degree which makes any future harmony a matter of convention. It may be that body-types, which I imagine are determined by one's genes, always have the upper hand and that the man who prefers Mozart to Tschaikovski can never be brought to change his mind until he changes his body. If this is so, then all moral and aesthetic education is futile and there is no reforming recalcitrant members of a society. We normally get hold of people when their minds are pretty well made up. They may not be adults, but they have already suffered the influence of hundreds of other people to an uncalculated extent. If it is true that the first few years of life set the course of the future, then it is clear that most sermonizing is a waste of time, except for the preacher. One can speak only for oneself where there is no generally accepted rule, but I may say that in my own case it looks as if I had learned things from my teachers, my reading, and from rubbing up against people very different from myself in genetic antecedents and education. This may of course be an illusion and I may well be one of those weak-minded people who find their salvation in submission rather than in rebellion. But again, I may have been guided to people whose ideas I found congenial and to whose influence I enjoyed submitting myself. One often transfers one's admiration and affection for a person to the things which he admires and is fond of and one also transfers one's dislike of a person to the things which he likes.

Since one cannot hope to answer this question finally in the present state of our knowledge, one has to make a guess. It certainly looks as if our prejudices, our emotional attitudes, our likes and dislikes, our approbation and our disapprobation, were inculcated in us by the various social groups with which we have been identified. I think it will be granted that the overwhelming proportion of the human race grows up in some sort of family, either our small group of biological parents and siblings or the more extended families of other peoples. Foundlings for that matter grow up surrounded by adults and their contemporaries who act as parents. But one cannot grow up without being disciplined, rewarded and punished by others, even when those others have neither a consistent system of values nor any consciously accepted set of rules. The notion of right and wrong may be identified merely with that which is praised and blamed, though some individuals may and do learn to correlate the right with what is blamed and the wrong with what is praised.[15] But even recalcitrant members of a group are influenced by what the group believes and the action it takes to enforce its beliefs: these are the very rules to which they are recalcitrant. This seems to be a general rule, for we see it in the lower animals as well as in human societies. Hierarchies of powers are common enough to have been found in the barn-yard; witness the system of peck-dominance among domestic fowl. If one learns to accept the group's system of values for reasons which need not be examined here, and if one's emotional set is in part determined by that accepted system, and if it in turn partly determines our perceptual judgments, then there is again no denying the conclusion that perception is partly determined by social forces.

The society to which one belongs may be the society of scholars. The scholarly tradition has established intellectual rituals which are just as compulsive as individual habits. The history of philosophy is eloquent proof of how the problems to be treated—periodization, the importance of certain philosophers as contrasted with

---

[15] See the fictitious but persuasive case of Ernest in *The Way of All Flesh*.

others, the condensation of their views, the selection of which of their views are representative of them—are determined by tradition and little else. It can easily be shown, and Wolfson has shown it, how ancient Greek philosophy gradually developed into Patristic philosophy. Philo Judaeus, it cannot be denied, was interested in problems which could not have interested Plato. But his solution of these problems was couched in Platonistic and Aristotelian terms, tinged with Stoic coloration. His theory, for instance, that the angels moving up and down Jacob's ladder were Aristotle's *dynameis* did not arise out of Aristotle who had no angels, unless one thinks that the planetary intelligences were angels. But the identification of the Hebraic angels with the *dynameis* did come out of Aristotle. When Philo said that Plato was Moses speaking Greek, he obviously meant either that Plato had read the Pentateuch and accepted its philosophy, expressed as it was in allegorical language, or that the same ideas which were to be found in Revelation could also be found in Plato. The whole doctrine of a God Whose influence upon earth is propagated through the Logos and thereafter through the angels, the hierarchical universe, the interpretation of the stories of the three patriarchs as the education of the *Nous,* are as Platonistic as the *Life of Moses* is Stoic. What has happened then is a shift in attention from the literal metaphysics of the Ancients to an allegorical interpretation of Scripture, but the literal metaphysics turns into the correct interpretation of the allegory. Philo was free in a sense to rewrite the Bible in any way he pleased, but he was looking for literal truth and literal truth to him could only mean what it means to all of us: the accepted ideas of the scientific world. These ideas were a fusion of the various current doctrines which I have mentioned. Regardless of tradition then, a modern historian of philosophy could refuse to break off Greek philosophy before Philo. He could, if he wished, carry it on to the point where the Pagan elements were outnumbered by the Christian. But historical ritual is against it, and few can read Philo now with minds unprejudiced by that ritual.

Just how free a scholar is to set up his own basic metaphors, procedural rules, problems, premises, is a matter of dispute. Probably no laboratory scientist today would think of doubting the efficacy of the experimental method, though few would be aware of what it presupposes. He would insist in all probability that no scientific thesis could be demonstrated without experimental corroboration, and he would be perplexed and annoyed if a philosopher were to ask him on what assumptions the method itself was based.[16] The use of the term as well as the constitution of an experiment has become ritualized, and it sometimes looks as if scientists were unaware that problems other than those which can be integrated into an experimental device have meaning and can be discussed. We all know now that Galileo's experiments were largely rhetorical and were never carried out[17] and Newton's, as recorded in the *Principia,* are thrown in after his proofs *more geometrico.* Like Spinoza's examples in the *Ethics,* these observations are a sop to the irrational reader who has too little confidence in logical demonstrations to give them more than notional assent. There are, to be sure, many kinds of experiment, from those which are performed just to see what will happen, as boys with new chemistry sets mix different substances together, to those which are devised to corroborate a conclusion reached by rational demonstration. We all know that corroboration is not proof. If p implies q, the discovery of q is not proof of p. That is learned in Freshman logic. If this were not so, no perception would be

---

[16] Even Dampier sees no problem involved in the use of this term. See his *History of Science,* 3d ed., 1944, p. 98: "That which marked [Roger] Bacon out from among the other philosophers of his time—indeed of the whole of the European Middle Ages—was his clear understanding that experimental methods alone give certainty in science;" p. 141: "Galileo is the first of the moderns; as we read his writings, we instinctively feel at home; we know that we have reached the method of physical science which still is in use today. The old assumption of a complete and rationalized scheme of knowledge, the characteristics of mediaeval Neo-Platonism and scholastic philosophy alike, has been given up. . . Each fact acquired by observation or experiment is accepted as it stands . . . irrespective of the human desire to make the whole of nature at once amenable to reason;" "[Boyle] carried on the experimentalist tradition of Gilbert and Harvey, and he accepted the theory of experimental method set forth by 'our great Verulam';" "Galileo had . . . proved experimentally that no continual exertion of force was needed to keep a body in motion."

[17] To those who may think this assertion too bold, we recommend a reading of A. Koyré's *Etudes Galiléenes,* Vol. III, *Galilée et la Loi d'Inertie,* esp. p. 74, n. 3.

ambiguous. But nevertheless within a given field, which term must include a whole logical matrix, certain observations can be used as proof. In that matrix will be certain rules for demonstrating general laws. If they lead us to expect certain observations and if those observations are made, they must be admitted to be consistent with the rest of the system. On the other hand we can make observations which are consistent with two or more sets of premises. It is no discovery of mine that we can all see the sun rise in the east and set in the west. What could be more self-evident than sunrise and sunset? In itself this observation might be used to prove that the sun moves and the earth stands still. But we have learned to reject this self-evidence in favor of notions which are more harmonious with other and more general notions. This is not said in deprecation of the search for more general notions. But the point is that we accept this search as self-evidently justified, just as we use such terms as simplicity, the uniformity of nature, universal causation or regularity, as principles which we must not question. But have we forgotten the hundreds of books written by men our equals in intelligence, in which other principles, which are now rejected as superstition or nonsense, were pronounced with equal assurance? I refer to such principles as, "Nature does nothing in vain," "Nature abhors a vacuum," "Nature always follows the simplest course," "Everything which has a beginning must have an end," "There is nothing in the intellect which was not previously in sensation," "Action at a distance is impossible," "Every act must have an agent," "Entities must not be multiplied beyond necessity," to mention only the more ordinary. The rituals of intelligence seem to be as compulsive as those of the muscles, and we must investigate the procedures of the inquiring mind more critically if we are to understand its operations. We can no longer accept the data of perception as absolutely impersonal records of objective proof; we can no longer use them to construct the universe as if they were given by a supernatural architect. The human equation, as well as the personal equation, must enter our calculations at this point. If we neglect to profit from its lessons, we shall never understand why we ever ask questions or why there is ever disagreement.

If on the contrary we think of the mind as a questioner, as asking *how* and *why*, we must find a solution of the problem of why the world is itself a problem.

APPENDIX TO CHAPTER II

Some Meanings of the word "idea"

In view of the confused situation in epistemology and the habit of treating something known as ideas as the elements of cognition, I am appending some common meanings of the word "idea." This list is neither supposed to be exhaustive nor is it arranged in historical order.

1. The shape or "look" of something.
2. That which is named by the common characters of a group of things or events.
3. The common pattern or structure of such characters, in distinction to the common qualities.
4. The supposed original or archetype or plan according to which a group of things or a thing is made.
5. The pattern existing in the mind of a human artisan in accordance with which he makes his artefacts.
6. The Divine thoughts, ideas in the mind of God, in accordance with which the world was made. These are sometimes said to be mathematical in nature.
7. The most perfect exemplification of a species or genus or class.
8. The standard in terms of which the perfect exemplification will be found.
9. The statistical norm—mode, median, or arithmetic mean.
10. An intention or plan of action of anybody for anything, regardless of value.
11. The right intention or plan of action: what one *ought* to plan.
12. An image existing in the mind of someone.
13. A memory-image as contrasted with a sensible datum.
14. A concept as contrasted with a percept.
15. The subjective as contrasted with the objective.

16. Hence, the mental as contrasted with the physical.
17. Any thought, image, notion, way of thinking, as contrasted with the non-mental.
18. Any object of knowledge.
19. Representations [*Vorstellungen*] of other things.
20. The external shell of reality, as in Schopenhauer: the idea vs. the will.
21. That towards which all history is tending, as in Hegel [Cf. no. 10 above].
22. Any generalization, scientific law, or mathematical formula. Cf. Natorp's interpretation of Plato's ideas.
23. An exclamation, as, "The very idea!"

Each of these definitions may take on normative significance. Thus it may be assumed that the ideal is better than the non-ideal; the general, the common, the archetypal, the purpose, better than the particular, the singular, the derivative, the means to attain a purpose; the goal better than that which is moving towards the goal. But sometimes the pattern is reversed, as in some "Romantic" writers who believe that the striving is better than attainment, the individual better than the class, and so on.

Chapter III

WHAT IS A PROBLEM?

We have so strongly emphasized our belief that all knowledge is an answer to a problem, that we should now turn our attention to problems and ask what they are. We shall maintain that a problem arises when one becomes aware of a deviation from the rule. To become aware of a problem then demands first that one know the rule. This requirement is easily met since there is a kind of humdrumness to daily life in any event and furthermore our modes of perception are so limited that they set up regularities of pattern and quality which we accept as normal. A person who depends almost entirely on his eyes will never see irregularities of sound, odor, taste, or texture. Not to observe is much easier than to observe, and since we can get along pretty well without much sensory discrimination, we usually do not go out of our way to look for more than what is superficially apparent. Nowadays we know that shadows are not gray or brown but have other colors. We also know what rules determine those colors. But only a hundred years ago painters had not observed this. For that matter Aulus Gellius tells us that his Latin contemporaries had some trouble understanding the color vocabulary of the Greeks, probably because it was so limited in range that some color distinguishable to Aulus Gellius had no special name in Greek.[1] In fact, our modern color vocabulary dates largely from Bernardin de Saint-Pierre and his immediate predecessors. Two conclusions may be

---

[1] For ambiguities in Greek color adjectives, see Liddell and Scott under, e.g., ξανθός ἐρυθρός, χλωρός. But such ambiguities are not unusual. We use the same adjective, *red*, for hair, sunsets, poppies, noses, blood, as well as for such various colors as scarlet, crimson, and vermilion in common speech. When finer discrimination is wanted, we name our colors after the things which are recognized as having them: olive, bottle, Nile, grass-green; golden, butter, straw, lemon-yellow, etc.

drawn from this: (1) that people with a poor color vocabulary cannot distinguish colors; (2) that they are not interested in distinguishing them. In any event we cannot jump to the conclusion that the existence of a deviation from the norm is always going to be noticed. The compulsion to see the world as regular may drown out the irregularities.

But the moment we define a problem as the awareness of a deviation from the norm, we are forced to refine the notion. If we set up gross enough rules, there will never be any noticeable deviation from them. As long as a man is willing to stop at the point where he will say that all visible objects are colored—and is also willing to classify the grays as colors—he will never have to worry about why some things are red, some green, some yellow, some blue. We do not see color, we see colors. There is no visual similarity between the various colors which we can draw off and then call "color." For qualitatively each color is unique. The abstraction, "color," is reached not by removing sensory qualities but by a quite different process. The word itself in English is connected etymologically with the Latin *celare,* to conceal; color was a form of covering. Now one cannot argue much from etymologies and I shall not attempt to do more than say that the word must have meant originally no more than what one could *see* on the surface of things. It seems to have been a sort of functional term. In our time we find that we have to resort to the manner in which color arises in our experience if we wish to define it. We refer at once, as the dictionaries will show, to the effect of light reflected from physical objects upon the optical end-organs. But this is precisely what we do not see. It is a definition derived from the way in which color-sensations are produced, not from the way they look. And if we did not know that white light was a composite of all the spectral colors, the differentiation between the colors would not be the same kind of problem which it is today. But knowing beforehand, not perceiving, that white light is so composed, then we can raise the problem of why some things look red, some green and so on. At this point a new rule has arisen, and, once it is accepted, a new deviation from it may be observed. We know that a given object usually—that is, nearby—looks red. But we also observe that it loses its redness at a distance and becomes gray. We have the problem of aerial perspective on our hands. Or we notice that an object which looks red when in front of us becomes gray when it is moved to one side and seen, as we say, in peripheral vision. We may also notice that at different times of the day the relative intensity of colors changes, the greens becoming brighter than the yellows, the Purkinje phenomenon, now a commonplace but first noted only in 1825. The rule is becoming more and more complicated, and we begin to realize that to state the color of an object is to hedge it in with all sorts of limiting conditions, conditions which may include not only the illumination, but also the part of the eye which is seeing the object, and the distance from the eye. We can ask why the color is as it is only if we have reason to believe that it ought to be something different. We ask why the apple looks gray when it is moved to one side because we have come to believe that it ought to look red and the "ought" in this case means simply that it usually does look red. Such reasons are to be sure the rule, but only the rule as known or accepted up to the moment when the deviation is spotted. This moment may be dated either in the biography of the individual noticing the deviation or in the history of the science concerned. The latter obviously can be reduced to the former.[2]

The only reason why this is important to us is that we have a variety of ways of avoiding the recognition of problems. We may first maintain that the deviation is trivial. How trivial a deviation may be without becoming troublesome is a matter of dispute. Thus the deviation in the secular perihelion of Mercury does not seem to have caused much trouble until the time of

---

[2] It could be maintained, on the ground that several people independently raise and answer problems at about the same time, that there is a kind of law according to which the sciences evolve, that if Newton had not elaborated his theory of optics, someone else would have. But the fact remains that out of the hundreds of people who were working in Newton's time and had roughly the same education as he had, it was Newton and not someone else who wrote the *Opticks*. Scientific theories are not precipitated out of the air, however heavily charged with information the air may be. They are formulated by people.

Einstein and variations within animate species until that of Lamarck. Aristotle was able to explain such variations away as due
to matter; incorporation distorted the eternal forms, though how
matter could do anything whatsoever, especially to the immutable, remained problematic. One could also introduce the concept
of the monstrous, the accidental, the contribution of the instruments of observation, the exceptional. Such concepts are seldom
defined and in reality all they do is to exhibit the weakness of our
generalizations. But they might also be used as ground for the
belief that existent things, individuals, confront us and that universals are at best a practical device for handling them in groups.
Where the statistical group replaced the Aristotelian class, variation within the group was accepted as normal, though the drive
towards uniformity continued. It continued since knowledge is
impossible without universals, and universals are rooted in our
language. One cannot argue from the demands of method to the
nature of that upon which it is used. But the point at which a
given method becomes more trouble than it is worth always seems
to arrive sooner or later, and the basic illustration of this will be
found, as is inevitable, in the primitive classifications upon which
our rules are founded.

At the risk of repeating the obvious, let us take the case of the
doctrine of the four elements. In Aristotle this doctrine asserted
that each element was a combination of two properties, heat and
moisture, the absence of which was cold and dryness. The possible combinations of these were the hot-dry, the hot-wet, the
cold-dry, and the cold-wet. The combinations were chosen by logic
but the selection of heat and moisture was determined by historical considerations. For we find the four elements already
distinguished in what is left of Empedocles. To the four possible
combinations of the primary qualities and their privations corresponded the four elements, and each element was utilized in physics
to explain local motion, the hot-dry (fire) always moving out to
the periphery of the world, the hot-moist (air) to a position just
below that of fire, the cold-moist (water) to a position between
that of air and that of earth, the cold-dry (earth) to the center.

But Aristotle also had a primitive idea which was the distinction between the natural and the unnatural. An example which he gives of the unnatural is "the production of a mule by a horse."[3] One gets the impression from reading his works that if Nature were left to herself, that is, if men and other disturbing forces did not interfere, if violence were not introduced into the natural order, all the fire would be at the periphery, all the air below that, all the water between the air and the earth, and all the earth at the center. Now, as it happens, this was a very beautiful theory within the limits of ordinary observation. It was the triumph of common-sense. Whenever we light a candle we see the flames pointing upward and whenever we drop something heavy, it falls to earth. Water when drawn up into the heavens in the form of clouds falls upon the earth as rain, and when it is imprisoned in the earth, it shoots up in the form of springs and geysers. And air, too, when beneath the surface of a basin of water, bubbles up out of the water into the sphere of air. But the four elements, which composed all material things also composed the human body. Within the human body they were known as the four humors, air corresponding to the blood, fire to the yellow bile, earth to the black bile, and water to the phlegm. When these humors were in equilibrium, a man was healthy; when unbalanced, he was sick. To each of the humors corresponded a temperament: to the blood, the sanguine; to the yellow bile, the choleric; to the black bile, the melancholic; to the phlegm, the phlegmatic. Hence a man's character could be predicted from his physiology. It was in fact a theory something like that which was so fashionable a few years ago, according to which character was explained as due to the influence of the endocrine glands. Finally the zodiacal signs, the seasons, the ages of life, the winds, and even four colors were all tied in with the theory, and the planets were seen to be predominantly of one humor rather than another, and we have retained, as everyone knows, such adjectives as saturnine, jovial, mercurial, martial, and no doubt venereal. Now when one has a

---

[3] *Metaphysics*, 1033 b, 33.

theory which covers everything from dynamics to psychology, one cannot but admire its generality and simplicity. The only trouble with it was the concept of the unnatural. The unnatural could be nothing other than the unusual, and when too many things become unusual, trouble ensues. Any student of the history of physics or astrology or medicine will know the enormous number of exceptions which piled up and the complications which had to be introduced to keep the generality stable. But even at that the doctrine of the four elements lasted roughly until the time of Lavoisier and that of the humors until a generation later. At the risk of over-simplification one might say that too many sub-species had to be introduced to be scientifically tolerable. And there were also demands for greater precision in measuring time and weight which made the old theory unviable.[4]

An analogous situation occurred in biology. Omitting the Aristotelian classification of plants and animals, made on the basis of their normal habitat, we find that Linnaeus grouped his specimens exclusively on morphological differentiae. These differentiae were primarily the kind of hearts which animals had and whether their blood was hot or cold. The results gave him six divisions, of mammals, birds, amphibia, fishes, insects, and worms.[5] Each of these on the basis of other morphological peculiarities were further divided until one reached the varieties within species. This was accomplished by disregarding small variations. But then the question arose of how great a difference

---

[4] For a table showing the correspondences between the various elements and other things, see Jean Seznec; *The Survival of the Pagan Gods*, Bollingen Series 38, N.Y., 1953, p. 47. For the multiplication of sub-species of temperament, see Burton's *Anatomy of Melancholy*.

[5] For the sake of curiosity, we give his primary schema from the *Systema Naturae*, 1758, p. 11. Divisio naturalis animalium ab interna structura indicatur:

Cor biloculare biauritum	}	viviparis — mammalibus
Sanguine calido rubro		oviparis — avibus
Cor uniloculare uniauritum	}	pulmone arbitrario — amphibiis
Sanguine frigido rubro		branchiis externis — piscibus
Cor uniloculare inauritum	}	antennatis — insectis
Sanie frigida albida		tentaculatis — vermibus

The whole introduction, however, should be read if one wishes to see the more complete method he used in classification.

was important enough to differentiate a species from other species. From this in turn there arose what Ernst Mayr has called the splitters.[6] The splitters, as contrasted with the lumpers, divided and sub-divided species by morphological differences, "even though they consisted only in the presence of an extra bristle or slightly different body proportions."[7] This procedure, if continued to its natural end, he continued, would eventuate in giving a name to nearly every individual.[8]

Now the presence of individual morphological differences is accepted by Mayr and, I should imagine, by all taxonomists as normal. The species, therefore, insofar as it names a group of individuals, each with its own characters, must point to something which they have in common and that something by Darwin's time became their phylogenetic origin. Darwin's observations of the finches in the Galápagos Islands suggested to him that if there was so much variation in a single group of individuals, it must have been produced historically; that is, it was too great to be normal. *Prima facie* the birds were all finches, but they varied significantly from what was to be expected of *finch-hood*. One of the important distinguishing characters of genera of birds is the form of the beak.[9] Darwin's finches have beaks running from the stubby beak to the long and curved. Their color ran from "almost white" on Barrington Island to "olive green" on Chatham and "rather more olive" on Albemarle (p. 40). Moreover the various specimens of Darwin's finches from any one island do not form a continuously graded series from large to small, thick-billed to thin-billed, or dark to pale (p. 125). Instead they fall into distinct, segregated groups. The problem here arose from the abnormal morphological variations within what was supposed to be a single species. But then it was found that the pattern of be-

---

[6] Ernst Mayr; *Systematics and the Origin of Species,* 1942, p. 280.

[7] *Op. cit.,* p. 286.

[8] *Op. cit.,* p. 105. He adds, "This, of course, is exactly what some extreme authors have done," but does not name them.

[9] See David Lack; *Darwin's Finches,* Cambridge, 1947, p. 12. My discussion is based on this very illuminating book. Page references are given in parentheses in my text.

havior in courtship and the postures adopted, nesting habits, incubation, and care of the young were also similar throughout the group. Which was the more important character or set of characters, the observable morphological differences or the similarities of behavior? By introducing the historical factor, that is the hypothesis that all these birds must have come from a common ancestor, Darwin concluded that he could explain the differences and retain the similarities. Lack suggests (p. 159) that the ancestral finch became differentiated into various forms in geographical isolation on the different islands. After a "sufficiently long period of isolation," some of these forms had become so different that when by chance they met on the same island, either they were already intersterile, or hybrids between them were at a selective disadvantage so that intersterility was evolved. A new distinguishing character is now introduced, that of intersterility, a character which is, however, more functional than morphological.

We thus have two different fashions of setting up classifications, the morphological and what amounts to the phylogenetic. The former rests upon observations of what we have before us, the latter on a dynamic element which in the nature of things could not be observed. Nevertheless since the rise of modern genetics biologists have observed the rise of species in certain animals, such as *Drosophila*. Though both *D. pseudo-obscura* and *D. persimilis* originate in a common ancestor; they form two distinct races. On what then is their distinctness based? On intersterility. The fact that different species will not produce fertile offspring is an old story, but since the general acceptance of some form of evolutionism, it became a principle of radical differentiation. Yet, as Mayr points out (p. 118), it is not an infallible method. In fact this author quotes Dobzhansky as giving us five different ways of distinguishing between species which are worth noting if only because they throw so much light on the methods of inquiry. They run as follows.

(1) The *practical.* "A species is a systematic unit which is considered a species by a competent systematist" (p. 115).

(2) The *morphological.* "A species is a group of individuals or populations with the same or similar morphological characters" (*ibid.*).

(3) The *genetic.* "A species is a group of genetically identical individuals" (p. 118).

(4) The test of *intersterility.* "All forms belong to one species which can produce fertile hybrids" (p. 119).

(5) The *biological.* "That stage of the evolutionary process at which the once actually or potentially interbreeding array of forms becomes segregated into two or more separate arrays which are physiologically incapable of interbreeding."

To these may be added Mayr's own definition: (6) "Species are groups of actually or potentially interbreeding natural populations, which are reproductively isolated from other such groups" (p. 120).

Each of these definitions provides a rule not merely for classification, but also for the determination of problems. Only the morphological definition could be based on simple perceptual observations. Yet even these depend upon measurements, and, though one may be determining color by the naked eye, the instrument of determining it cannot be left out of consideration as if it were neutral. A deviation from the rule in each of these cases could result in one of two conclusions: either that the deviation is big enough to indicate a new classification or that it is not. But the bigness is determined by what one wishes to do with the classification after it is made. The Linnaean classification, or the natural system as it has been called, did very well so long as a cross-section of the biological world was taken at a certain date and no question was asked about its past. Linnaeus saw no problem there because he believed that God had created the species as he, Linnaeus, had found them. The question of how they arose could not be put since he did not believe that they ever had arisen; they always were. But Darwin when he visited the Galápagos Islands found it hard to believe that God had created so many species of finch. Yet on the Principle of Plenitude, he might very well have argued that God, seeing the possibility of such variety in finches, actualized it. On the simple basis of what he observed, unsupported by palaeontological evidence, he could not have reached an hypothesis of evolutionary speciation.[10]

Now we have a similar situation in epistemology today. We make a cross-section of the objects of acquired knowledge and classify them, if we see fit, into species, genera, and the higher categories. But we then argue as if they had always been as they are now and as if none of them had a history, either in the life of the individual or in the traditions of the group. We overlook the fact that sensory data are precipitated into objectivity and isolated from both their antecedents and their neighbors. No one looking at a patch of red can be aware of how redness is caused nor of all the conditioning relations under which it must be observed to be red and not, let us say, gray. The temporal dimension came into serious consideration through historical studies, including embryology, entomology, geology and all fields in which the past must be taken into account. Such a cross-section of the data of sensory perception can certainly be made if one wishes, and I am debating simply its utility. If one wishes, one can also begin a study of mankind with men at the age of twenty-one and stop with men at the age of fifty. In which case it becomes reasonable to overlook the historical aspects of experience as they appear in learning and the formation of habits. So the primitive entomologists failed to see the historical or genetic connection between larva, pupa, and adult, and one suspects that common-sense today thinks of caterpillars and butterflies as separate kinds of animals. Just looking at them without looking at them through time would never reveal their historical connection, and one would never look at them through time unless one first suspected that something might be learned by doing so.

The rule then will always be determined as of a certain date and within the limitations of an individual's knowledge. This

---

10 In the *Origin of Species* four groups of data were brought to bear on the hypothesis: data from taxonomy, from comparative anatomy, from embryology, and from palaeontology. Though all these data were observable, they were not in themselves and isolated from one another relevant to anything. Darwin and his predecessors first had to put a question to them.

being so, deviations from the rule will be measured also by individuals at that date, and a man will push his investigations forward only if he has reason to expect that further deviations will be found. But this rests upon a methodological assumption, seldom overtly expressed, that deviations ought not to occur, that they are "contrary to nature," that there must be discoverable not merely individuals with stable characters but also groups of individuals. The object which is red here and now ought to stay red, and if it changes its color, then some reason must be given for that change. The bird which is a finch ought to be a small passerine bird of the family *Fringillidae* with heavy, conical, seed-cracking bill. If one finds a bird which looks like a finch but has a long curved bill, then either it is not a finch or the rule must be revised or a reason given why some finches have long curved bills, which means that we have some further reason to include the specimen in question in the family of finches. No *a priori* rule can be given for telling a man how far he ought to go in the direction of generalization or how far he ought to go in the opposite direction. Such rules have been assumed at times: Nature always follows the simplest course is one; the Principle of Parsimony another; the Uniformity of Nature a third. All three have led investigation towards further and further generalization. But along with that type of drive one also finds the Principle of Plenitude, a principle which also has had its followers and not among the least respectable of philosophers.

The overlooking of perceptual differences is not simply a psychological fact; it is also a methodological necessity. Anyone with training in the art of painting knows that he never actually sees two patches of red which are identical and that all that is required to prove it is to look carefully. But there are several reasons why he paints them as the same red. One is that he is provided with a set of pigments which themselves limit the variety of colors which he can put upon his canvas. Another is that painters like to simplify a color-pattern for purposes of "unity." A third is that the painter sets up a standard set of relations in which the objects are to be painted, and two of the factors involved are a stable illumination and an unfatigued eye. The first is purely instrumental—or perhaps economic, the second aesthetic, and the third conventional. If we are to discuss things, we must use universals, as we have constantly reiterated, and to make the universals applicable we are forced to overlook whatever differences may be perceived even under the standardized conditions. The naked eye has no more authority than the microscope, and it gives no more truth; but its findings may be accepted as one of the conditions under which observations will be made. One surmises that if its findings were as reliable as they are sometimes said to be, no instruments would have been invented to correct them. That is only a surmise, and we shall not dwell upon it, important though it may be to find out just why instruments were invented. Similarly there is no ontologically justified reason for calling the appearances of things nearby, whatever that may mean, their real appearance, deviation from which requires explanation. But one of the tasks of knowledge is organization, and it is obvious that without overlooking differences no organization would be possible. At the same time I trust that one will grant the impossibility of overlooking differences if there are no differences. We soon learn to overlook them as we are given the names for our various qualitative experiences. The process itself obscures the conditions which make its discoveries compulsive. Though we can no longer perhaps recall whether we were or were not astonished to learn that two apparently different colors or smells or tastes are the same—that is, given the same name—all of us can recall when we learned that there were only ninety odd elements, that the air is a mixture of gases, or even that adults were once children. Let us then ask how an apparent diversity is really unified.

The unity we are looking for may be found in a variety of ways. (1) There is the unity of perceptual qualities. Here the universals are the colors, sounds, tastes, the more easily recognized geometrical shapes, such as squares, triangles, and circles. But these are more useful in setting up sub-classes within larger groups than in setting up the larger groups themselves. That is, we do not usually find it as useful to talk about red, blue, green, as to talk about color; or triangles, circles, and squares as to talk about plane figures. But the word "usually" must be included in such an assertion. (2) There is a sort of teleological unity, as is found in edible and inedible things, right and wrong acts, useful and harmful things. The Biblical distinction between animals with cloven hooves which chew the cud and those which do not is a case in point. (3) There is unity of stuff, as when we classify compounds on the basis of the elements which compose them, or speak of carbon compounds as a group, or of woolen and cotton and silk clothing. (4) There is a unity of structure which may or may not be perceptible to the naked eye. If vertebrates are distinguished from invertebrates exclusively on the basis of the presence or absence of a spine, this would be purely structural unity. Aristotle's classification of governments would be another case. The differentiation of styles of architecture is sometimes made on the basis of structural similarities and differences. (5) There is a unity of origin, as is found in genealogy or phylogeny or embryology. It is seen in histories of philosophy which speak of schools emanating from the teaching of one man: Platonists, Peripatetics, Stoics, Epicureans. (6) There is a unity of order or law, as is found in the normal curve of distribution or for that matter any regular curve of distribution. Thus we find that the possible numbers of two dice or the variation in temperature throughout the year in countries well beyond the Equator in specified localities, or the growth and decline of populations in a geographical region, illustrate describable orders. The relation between the tides and the moon or the orbits of the planets or the life-cycle would be other examples of this kind of unity. In short, every category which we use can serve as a standard of unification, whether we go back to the categories of Aristotle or prefer others of our own devising.

Though we have distinguished six types of unity, nothing in our opinion precludes the possibility of any group's manifesting several kinds of unity.

But now what is common to all these various types except the word "unity"? In some cases one kind of material is present with a differentiation of quality, structure, purpose, origin, and possible laws of behavior. We have only to think of the difference between, let us say, molecular oxygen and ozone to see how this might be possible. Similarly it is conceivable that any of these implied systems of order could be discovered regardless of the presence or absence of the others. Any group of individuals which manifest traits in common, even when the manifestation occurs under highly artificial conditions, will form a set and therefore will be said to be unified.[11] The important thing is to establish an order which can be symbolized in easily read symbols and frequently this is done metaphorically. Hierarchical orders are a case in point. Here the origin of the concept is levels of power, as in the armed forces, the higher ranks having power over more groups than the lower. But the very use of the terms "higher," "lower," and "levels," is itself metaphorical. It has been extended from a system of more inclusive power to levels of value, of logical inclusiveness, and even of "reality."[12]

Which of the categories one uses will be determined prior to its use, as is inevitable. The fundamental problem turns out to reside in the perception of deviation from a previously accepted rule. Something is where it ought not to be; why? Something is moving in a direction in which it ought not to move; why? Something is behaving as it ought not to behave; why? Something is heavier or lighter or more voluminous or less voluminous than it ought to be; why? In the eternal realm there are no such questions since everything in logic is as it should be. By assuming that the temporal world is a moving image of eternity, one attempts to fit the diversities of time to the unity of eternity. Eternity gives us the pattern which we imagine that temporality ought to exemplify. Gilson points out one of the difficulties in

---

[11] For an extension of this idea, see John R. Gregg; *The Language of Taxonomy,* 1954, in which the question of classification is analysed in terms of symbolic logic. Membership in a set, however, is not defined in more primitive terms, though it is illustrated. Ordered pairs and hierarchies are skillfully defined and the logical problems which they introduce ingeniously presented.

[12] Hierarchies are discussed below in Chapter VII.

such a doctrine when he says that St. Augustine "in order to make a philosophy of history out of [the] theology of history . . . had to explain what is always other through what remains immutably the same."[13] And he concludes, "The only reason for the choice of this particular universe is the pure and simple will of God."[14] "Such is the will of God," is the answer to all questions. It is analogous to saying, "Such are the facts." What ought to be, it will appear, is that which always has been, but since there is no way of determining what always has been except in terms of what we know about the past, what ought to be is what the rules say it is. The unity sought for is a uniformity or conformity to some eternal law. But that there is such conformity to be found is an assumption.

I should now like to cite one or two examples, one or two since this is not a history of scientific method and, furthermore, an exhaustive investigation of the matter would carry us too far afield.

One of the most impressive examples of what I am driving at will be found in the opening pages of Faraday's *Experimental Researches in Electricity*.[15] Up to the time of Faraday investigations into electrical phenomena had been conducted as if they were to provide the solutions to separate problems. Thus Gilbert had worked on the magnet and amber, Franklin on lightning, Lémery on tourmaline, Bancroft on the torpedo, Cavendish on electrical measurements, and Galvani on animal electricity. Along with such investigations went the invention of such machines as the Leyden Jar and the Voltaic Pile. But though these various phenomena were usually given names suggestive of a "unity of nature," disputes did arise over whether or not they all had common enough characteristics to entitle them all to be classified together. The opening of Faraday's *Researches* is called "Identity of Electricities derived from Different Sources." Faraday classified

---

[13] Etienne Gilson; *The Christian Philosophy of St. Thomas Aquinas*, p. 134 f.

[14] *Ibid.*, p. 149.

[15] An inexpensive and easily procured edition of this can be found in the *Everyman Library* with an excellent introduction by Tyndall. I quote from this edition.

all the kinds of known electricity as "electricity of tension" and "electricity in motion." "This distinction," he went on to say, "is taken at present not as philosophical, but merely as convenient." His problem was aroused by the differences; his purpose was to reduce these differences to uniformity. To accomplish this purpose, he set down the effects of electricity, thus separating electricity from its effects. The effect of electricity of tension, at rest, "is either attraction or repulsion at sensible distances." Those of electricity in action, or electric currents, he listed as (1) the evolution of heat, (2) magnetism, (3) chemical decomposition, (4) physiological phenomena, (5) spark. He then proceeded to make experiments to show how far electricity produced from different sources would produce these effects in common. Readers of the *Researches* will recall that he took up Voltaic electricity, "ordinary" electricity, magneto-electricity, thermo-electricity, and animal electricity in order and applied the same tests to each, the tests of attraction and repulsion and the five tests of the presence of an electric current. He then drew up a table to show clearly to what extent all five kinds of electricity agreed in meeting the same tests, and though there were gaps in his table, he was later able to fill in some himself, and needless to say, they were all filled in later. His conclusion ran, "The phenomena in the five kinds of species quoted, differ, not in their character but only in degree; and in that respect vary in proportion to the variable

	Physiological Effects	Magnetic Deflection	Magnets made	Spark	Heating Power	True Chemical Action	Attraction and Repulsion	Discharge by Hot Air
1. Voltaic electricity	x	x	x	x	x	x	x	x
2. Common electricity	x	x	x	x	x	x	x	x
3. Magneto-electricity	x	x	x	x	x	x	x	
4. Thermo-electricity	x	x						
5. Animal electricity	x	x	x			x		

circumstances of *quantity* and *intensity* which can at pleasure be made to change in almost any one of the kinds of electricity, as much as it does between one kind and another" (par. 96).

What was actually shown in the many experiments which Faraday carried on was that eight kinds of effect could be produced by the five kinds of electricity indifferently—or almost indifferently. To conclude from this that all five kinds are really one kind is obviously to assume that the similarity of effect must be attributable to one cause. But clearly all that Faraday had on the empirical or perceptual level was a set of diverse causes which had been given the same name because of the similarity of their effects. But so strong was the methodological assumption of a difference between a "thing" and what it does, that Faraday can be found to say in a later passage of his *Researches,* "Though we are . . . unable to say whether [electricity] is a particular matter or matters, or mere notion of ordinary matter, or some third kind of power or agent . . ." (par. 587), as if somewhere behind the observable phenomena there was a self-identical agent producing the observable effects. This distinction between what a thing is and what it does is of course common to everyday speech, and we shall not press the point here. It suffices to say that Faraday found uniformity in the behavior of an apparent multiplicity of kinds and thus established a common nature. The subsequent history of electrodynamics need not concern us here, but it will be admitted that for Faraday, once his position was entrenched, no problem could arise until, for instance, electrolysis would not break down water, or certain metals when heated to different temperatures would not manifest an electric current between them, or no spark would be seen in a Leyden Jar until the proper condition to produce one was created. But the outstanding problem after Faraday had published his work was why there were gaps in the table. And Tyndall in his edition reprints a later note by Faraday to the effect that all but five had been filled by 1838 and that there was every reason to believe that they too would be filled in time.

There is one other feature of these conclusions of Faraday's which should be noted, though they are obvious. And that is that his interpretation of what he saw was far from being identical with a set of descriptive statements in terms of sensory data. To avoid the introduction of diagrams, let us quote the simplest of these interpretations. He is discussing magneto-electricity.

"Par. 79. *Tension.*—The attractions and repulsions due to the tension of ordinary electricity have been well observed with that evolved by magneto-electric induction. M. Pixii, by using an apparatus, clever in its construction and powerful in its action, was able to obtain great divergence of the gold leaves of an electrometer.

"80. *In motion:* i. *Evolution of heat.*—The current produced by magneto-electric induction can heat a wire in the manner of ordinary electricity."

Such phrases as "due to" and "the current produced by" are inferences, not simple observations. If Faraday had anticipated the operationalism of Bridgman, he would have had to write down merely what he saw, and the meaning of the words "electric current" would have been no more than what he saw under the conditions in which he saw it: the fluttering of the gold leaves and the heat. This would not have explained why he rigged up the apparatus in question in order to see gold leaves flutter, and indeed if all he had wanted was to see the gold leaves flutter, he could have held them up by pincers and blown on them. The flutter became of relevance to a theory which he was interested in and it was of relevance only in the total experimental situation under consideration. He was not interested in producing certain effects as of importance in themselves, as a silversmith might be interested in electro-plating or a psychiatrist in electro-therapy. In the language of common-sense, the observed results were results because they came after the experiment was set up, and that constituted in the terms of the experiment a corroboration of the hypothesis that magneto-electricity could do everything that other kinds of electricity could do. This hypothesis itself was derived from a methodological rule, that different things are identical or have an identical "nature," if under specified conditions they manifest the same behavior. The nature is hidden, according to this rule, and appears to observation in the form of overt action.

I should like now to introduce a second example of the identification of apparently different things and again choose one from nineteenth-century science. Romanes in his book on *Animal Intelligence*[16] makes a distinction between reflex action and action which he is willing to call in his own terms a mental adjustment. "All that we can mean," he says (p. 4), "by a mental adjustment is an adjustment of a kind that has not been definitely fixed by heredity as the only adjustment possible in the given circumstances of stimulation. For was there no alternative of adjustment, the case, in an animal at least, would be indistinguishable from one of reflex action." If then, given a single stimulus, an animal reacts in a variety of ways, the reaction can be called mental, however we ourselves should call it today. In his own words, the criterion of mind is phrased in the following question: "Does the organism learn to make new adjustments, or to modify old ones, in accordance with the results of its own individual experience? If it does so, the fact cannot be due merely to reflex action . . . for it is impossible that heredity can have provided in advance for innovations upon, or alterations of, its machinery during the lifetime of a particular individual" (*ibid.*). The ability to learn is then the criterion of mentality.

> "A dog has always been accustomed to eat a piece of meat when his organism requires nourishment, and when his olfactory nerves respond to the particular stimulus occasioned by the proximity of the food. So far it may be said, there is no evidence of mind; the whole series of events comprised in the stimulations and muscular movements may be due to reflex action alone. But now suppose that by a number of lessons the dog has been taught not to eat the meat when he is hungry until he receives a certain verbal signal: then we have exactly the same kind of evidence that the dog's actions are prompted by mind as we have that the actions of a man are so prompted."

Had the dog belonged to Pavlov instead of to Romanes, learning to wait for the signal would have been called a conditioned reflex, and the Russian would have continued until the animal had

---

[16] I use the edition of 1886 in The International Scientific Series.

snatched at the signal whether any meat was there or not. But it would have violated all the instincts of an Englishman to carry the experiment that far when his subject was a dog.

Now as Romanes says in so many words, the arguments which he is going to use are all analogical. He cannot directly perceive mentality, though he thinks he can in the case of his own mental processes. But since, he maintains, we cannot directly perceive the mentality of other human beings but assert its presence only from analogy, there is no reason why we should not attribute minds to other animals if they behave in certain circumstances as human beings do when we attribute minds to them. He immediately proceeds to show how even the lowest animals, the protozoa, learn from experience. He then continues moving upward in the scale of evolution and demonstrating by example how all animals learn and therefore have minds. Since he was an ardent evolutionist, he was only too happy to admit that minds existed in various degrees, though not in various kinds, and that the higher animals showed more skill, learned more easily, were more intelligent, if one will, than the lower. In all cases learning was present and therefore mind was present too. It was not enough to say that animals learned how to do things with varying degrees of skill; the ability to learn had to be attributed to an inner source.

We have here then in the field of biology a set of demonstrations similar to those of Faraday in physics. Romanes, too, was interested in showing that a variety of phenomena could be reduced to unity, that when a protozoon learned to do something, it was acting exactly as a dog does when it learns to do something. And again, the interpretation goes well beyond the sensory observations, and furthermore the sensory observations isolated from the total problematic complex are trivial. No one watching a dog do a trick, if he did not know that dogs have to be taught to do tricks, could possibly see the relevance of the tricks to Romanes' thesis. One must first know that dogs do not in an undomesticated condition sit up and beg or play dead or roll over, and must also know that the dog in question had to be put through a course of training before he could do the tricks. Once more we are face to face with the fundamental decision which all philosophers have to face: do we or do we not include the temporal dimension which is resident in all facts in our calculations? The identity of that which is said to be the origin of learning is demonstrated by identity of behavior tempered by degrees. The most that could be observed was the behavior itself.

That identifications are primordial is nothing which I pretend to have discovered. It was the cardinal principle of explanation, according to Meyerson, and as early as 1881, the too much neglected American philosopher, J. B. Stallo, in his *The Concepts and Theories of Modern Physics,* had said the same thing.[17] He says in that work (p. 105), "Phenomena are explained by an exhibition of their partial or total identity with other phenomena." And he quotes such writers as Sir William Hamilton, Bain, and Jevons in support of his views. The question which the scientist puts when he asks, "What is this?" can be translated, he says (p. 106), into the question, "Of what known, familiar fact is this apparently strange, hitherto unknown fact a new presentation—of what known, or familiar fact or facts is it a disguise or complication? Or, in as much as the partial or total identity of several phenomena is the basis of classification (a class being a number of objects having one or more properties in common) it may also be said that all explanation . . . is in its nature classification." But, unless I do Stallo an injustice, he did not appreciate how different might be these properties which identified objects.

Thus it cannot be denied that water and hydrogen peroxide are identical in that both are exclusively composed of hydrogen and oxygen, or that similarly steam, liquid water, and ice are identical in that they are all forms of H_2O. But such identities are of interest only in special contexts. The contexts themselves are not given, except in the sense that our reading or our teachers or someone else give them to us. We have to accept them as right, as we accept most of our usual names for things and classes of things. We cannot repeat too often that history no longer tells

---

[17] I must not give the impression that Meyerson shared in the neglect of Stallo. He knew his work and quoted from it.

us why we have lumped together certain elements of experience as we have, but there is enough etymological evidence to show that in a great many cases the answer is a pragmatic one. This is clearer in the newer sciences such as chemistry where a nomenclature has been artificially contrived to answer certain needs of which we have a literary record. But we no longer know why the ancient Greeks classified the elements as earth, water, air, and fire. Why not add a fifth element, metal? Or wood? Or why not mercury, sulfur, salt, and earth as some of the alchemists did? Why not include heat and light as elements as even so great a chemist as Lavoisier did? The answer to this question is our preference for a single formula in terms of which we can describe a great number of observations. We may say either that Dalton's law of multiple proportions is the reason for the fixation of the elements as we had them in the Periodic Table or that it is verified by the Periodic Table. Both statements would be misleading. But nevertheless the concept of a chemical element by the end of the nineteenth century had to be such that the law would apply and at the same time the law itself was elaborated by Dalton on the assumption that all material things were composed of elements. The elements themselves had to be immutable, and after Lavoisier's time the unchanging property of all matter was to be found in its weight. If it be asked why the notion of "amount" was so vague, when, after all, people had measured things by scales ever since the days of the Egyptians, the only answer is another question: how is it possible for people to disagree? Once the Periodic Table was set up on the basis of atomic weights, the idea spread abroad that all elements had precisely the same atomic weight. But then when isotopes were discovered, atomic weight was seen to vary; and when isomeres were discovered it was found that even when two substances had the same elemental composition, they might have different properties. The identity between ammonium cyanate and urea is their substantial unity, not their structural. The identity between two or more isotopes lies in their chemical properties, that is in their reactions with other substances.[18]

---

[18] Though this requires much qualification to be precise.

As we have said, any category may provide the context in terms of which identifications may be made. The extraordinary feature of all this is the custom of transforming the categories themselves into things which have metaphysical priority. Thus we abstract from the category of causation the notion of a First Cause or a Universal Cause, though every cause of which we know anything is itself an effect. Moreover, causes are discovered through generalization, and it is meaningless to ask for the cause of any individual, localized, and dated event, if we include in our problem the individuality, location, and date. It is only as an event is an example of a class of events that its cause can be assigned. We can ask for the cause of, for instance, the Civil War insofar as it was a war and to the extent that we have rules to help us determine the causes of wars in general. We can also raise the question insofar as it was like other rebellions. But as the historians will tell us, if we do not already know, it was different both from other wars and rebellions in so many ways that only a detailed narrative will do justice to its complexity and individuality. But a First Cause by definition is neither the effect of anything else nor is what it causes a sample of a larger class of events about which generalizations can be made. What we have done is, as was suggested by Kant, to remove the temporal factor from causal sequences and to imagine a first moment of time, at which point we tumble into the abyss of the antinomies.

In a similar manner the Neo-Platonists abstracted the grammatical relations of action and passion and set up that which is always active and never passive, the One, and that which is always passive and never active, Matter. Though it might have been obvious that an agent can do nothing unless there is something to serve as patient and that a patient which is non-being could hardly be expected to be even acted upon, Plotinus and his disciples worked out elaborate schemes which would connect the two. The metaphor of emanation was invoked to explain the relation between the two and by introducing the notion of degrees of reality a hierarchy of existence was established down which the reality of the One might flow and up which the unreality of Matter might climb. Neither

Plotinus nor any member of his school ever satisfactorily explained how something which was so thoroughly one as the One could ever become multiple. And the procession of the Cosmic Intelligence and after it the Soul of the World out of the One were simply asserted without proof. But in the nature of the case no proof could be given, not that there was no evidence for such a process, but because the One was indescribable and thus no proposition could be asserted about it—or him—from which anything whatsoever could be deduced. But this would be true of any category which was generalized and erected into a universal principle, the *fons et origo* of all existence. Time, Space, Eternity, Life, Purpose, and their fellows could all be treated as Plotinus treated activity and passivity. One could argue, for instance, that since everything we know is temporal, Time is the universal predicate and the timeless simply that whose rate of change is imperceptible. It would thereupon become the Principle of Change, the ever-living Fire whose ashes are the physical universe, but which itself is never consumed. Hobbling on the crutches of the Heraclitean fragments, the imagination could sing a hymn to the Cosmic Fire which feeds itself out of its own being, self-destructive and self-preserving. To prevent the complete annihilation of the cosmos, one would introduce cycles of flaring up and dying down, just as some physicists, worried by the Second Law of Thermodynamics, attempted to evade it by maintaining that somewhere in the universe energy was being built up instead of running down.[19] But should some doubting Thomas ask how a fire could feed itself, the answer would be that this is metaphysical fire, the principle or quintessence of fire, not the crude process of oxidation which we see about us. If then the question were raised of how this metaphysical fire resembled crude terrestrial or empirical fire, the answer would be that it was a name for the observable process of destruction and creation, analysis and synthesis, or whatever terms would be used for genesis and destruction.

---

[19] Meyerson in his *Identité et Réalité* (p. 302) discusses several of these hypotheses. See also his *de l'Explication dans la Science* (p. 206) for the statistical evasion.

What the nature of a set of things is will always be determined by the uniform reaction of these things to certain tests, as in the example from Faraday cited above. Unless it is forgotten that even looking and seeing are tests, using organic instruments of detection instead of manufactured tools, it will be agreed that no nature is ever discoverable outside of a complex including the conditions of observation. It is always hoped that by keeping these conditions constant, one will arrive at invariant observations, and when that end is reached, one will assert that a nature has been found. But this cannot imply that a thing which has the nature in question has been found. What has been found is a set of situations in which constant observations can be made. When Newton was asked what was the nature of gravitational force—was it the will of God exerting itself upon matter?—his reply was that he was measuring the attraction and repulsion of material bodies and not discussing what the nature of gravitation was, though in the General Scholium he put the question differently. He might as well have said that the nature of gravitation was given in the Law of Gravitation; it had no other nature. The Law of Gravitation expresses in mathematical terms a set of relations which subsist between masses. To ask what it is that makes bodies attract each other directly as the product of their masses and inversely as the square of their distance from each other, is like asking why a product is always bigger than either the multiplier or the multiplicand. I do not say that the question is meaningless, for the person who asks it has some meaning in mind. It is simply unanswerable. In short a law such as this states what might be called indifferently the Will of God, the Ways Things Are, the Nature of the Case, or the Facts. What then are facts?

CHAPTER IV

FACTS

I shall assume for the purposes of this chapter that all declarative assertions refer to something beyond themselves and that what they refer to may be called facts. In place of the word "refer to" one may substitute "express," if one wishes. Such sentences, I assume, are made to communicate to other people one's beliefs, that which one says one knows, and therefore they may be true or false. But even a false sentence may refer to facts or contain expressions which refer to facts. The first clause of my sentence, "that all declarative sentences refer to something beyond themselves," is in agreement with the theory of types. The second is simply a statement of my verbal usage. Facts, then, I am saying are whatever is verbally symbolized in judgments by subordinate clauses which normally begin with "that." Thus in the sentence, "I see that it is raining," the clause "that it is raining," expresses the fact. In such a sentence as, "It is raining," the introductory clause is omitted, but since every assertion made by a human being is a judgment, the introductory clause is, as the grammarians used to say, "understood." It might be maintained that whether assertions are judgments or not is irrelevant to logic which is interested only in the formal properties of sentences and, indeed, of certain kinds of sentences. With this I am in complete agreement. But whether it is relevant to logic or not, it is indubitably relevant to epistemology, for unless sentences expressing beliefs are made by human beings, the whole problem of truth and error becomes trivial. What is called truth in logic is systematic consistency and that, as everyone knows, may exist between false propositions. I am assuming that some statements are true and some false in another sense. It is the sense in which someone says that a statement is true to fact, can be verified by some kind of experiment or experience. Whether all such statements form a single set of logically consistent statements may be assumed, if one wishes, but it has never been proved. What consistency is there between any two existential propositions? They presumably include references to dates and places, and until someone sets up a logical system in which dates and places at which historical events occur can be deduced, there is no reason whatsoever to insist that all such statements be internally consistent. It may turn out to be the case that they are, but that might depend upon the existence of a universe not only with a limited number of kinds of events which might occur but also upon the constant repetition of those events. The fact that certain things and events are given the same name may lead us to assert that they have common natures, and if one talks about nothing but their common natures and omits everything which differentiates them, then to that extent one will have a set of consistent propositions, or at least could have one. But the problem is not one of saying things which are true of everything in general, but that of saying things which are true of everything as a collection of individuals.

In one of the common uses of the word "fact," my own usage is wrong. I refer to the dictionary definition which runs, "What has really happened or is the case." We have of course tests which are more or less reliable for determining what really happened. But I am dealing here with epistemology, and for my purposes it is better to modify this definition to read, "What is believed to have really happened or to have been the case." For I want to be able to admit the possibility of error as well as truth. Moreover, such a modification permits constant amendment of our beliefs, constant correction in the direction of greater precision. Thus to say that the United States flag is red, white, and blue, is true, but we should add the conditions of normal illumination and normal eyesight and a traditional distance if we mean by "the flag" the visible flag. Just what "normal" and "traditional" mean in this sentence we can disregard. But now suppose we want to make this more precise and therefore to state as correctly as possible the conditions

under which the flag will appear to be red, white, and blue. However pedantic this may seem, if the flag is to be shown in a theater,
a knowledge of how colors change under artificial lighting and of
how to provide the right kind of lighting will be necessary in order
to make the flag appear red, white, and blue. But we may not be
interested so much in the colors of the flag as in its official design,
dimensions, arrangement of stars and stripes, and so on, information which is given in Army Regulations. Any statement containing the words, "the United States flag," turns out to have a great
many meanings. Few flags bought commercially have the official
dimensions and design. What are commonly called flags may be
ensigns, standards, symbols, signals, and so on. To state that the
flag is red, white, and blue does not distinguish it from the British
Union Jack or the French tri-color. So that before one knows it,
one begins to extend his statements in a variety of ways. If one
grant that the judgment, "That is the United States flag," is made
on an historical rather than a logical occasion, one must then ask
why it should be made. One sees it flying from the mast of a ship
but upsidedown. Someone asks, "What's that?" The answer,
"The United States flag," is correct, but it may very well be that
the answer which is wanted is, "A ship in distress." The position
at which the flag is flown here must be taken into account just as it
would be if it were flown at half-mast. In all such cases the context determines the meaning of the question as much as the
physical objects or qualitative perceptions do, and since the meaning of a question determines the right answer, one has to grasp the
context. Contexts are grasped automatically from custom in most
cases, but if one is to be very careful for theoretical purposes, then
one should take note of the influence of custom.

It is my thesis then that beliefs or judgments may be true or false,
and that their "correspondence with fact," as it is usually called,
determines their truth. But I see no way of reaching primitive
judgments which will somehow or other always be true. This is
what C. I. Lewis would call a silly thesis. His doctrine of terminating judgments is, if I understand him correctly, based on the
premise that in our reports on simple perceptions we cannot go

wrong, and that somehow or other these reports may be elaborated into the more complicated judgments about which there may be some doubt. That there are terminating judgments it would indeed be silly to deny. But they terminate inquiry and always terminate it temporarily or until for some reason or other they are corrected. If this were not so, why should opinions have changed so much since men began to record them? That most people see red under the same conditions of stimulus and medium and so on, is probably true. But seeing red has relevance to knowledge only as it answers a question; as we have insistently repeated, it is inarticulate in itself.[1] A person who went about saying, "red," "sour," "hard," would be saying nothing; the reason why he seems to be saying something is that we assume that he has asked himself, or someone has asked him, what he is perceiving. But such questions are only a tiny fraction of the questions which one has to answer, and even they are questions. To maintain that perceptual assertions of that sort are true or expressive of the facts only in complicated systems of relation is not to deny that they do terminate inquiry; so much only says that the inclusion of the system of relations makes our judgments more accurate. Let us omit what we mean by "accurate." My protest is against the establishment of a kind of judgment as final and basic to all others. What is final and basic is the method of inquiry, not the answers given to our questions. Thus if our method is that of "ordinary" sensory perception, sensory perception will terminate all inquiry. But if a magnifying glass or a high-power microscope or an infra-red camera is introduced between the human eye and the object being observed or takes the place of the eye, then ordinary sensory perception is not final but actually irrelevant.

Suppose, however, that we take ordinary sensory perception as our standard. We cannot in that case erect an external and non-human invariant world out of its data. Leaving out of considera-

---

[1] There is no science of red things. There is of course a science in which an explanation of why we see red on certain occasions and other colors on others is given. But neither red things nor round things nor any other things classified on the basis of their sensory similarities exclusively form a science. This was not always the case. See Hélène Metzger; *Les Concepts scientifiques,* 1926, p. 21.

tion the Ten Tropes of Aenesidemus,[2] since they are well known, and clinging conservatively to the traditional five senses, we shall find that we cannot make the objective frontiers of our objects coincide. A purely visual object is in the long run known by our reaction to light rays. We have already seen that much more than light rays are needed, but we are trying here to simplify. If one asks exactly where a visual object is, the only answer is that it is where the light rays are, and they may extend through millions of light-years in space. When we say that we are now seeing a star which was extinguished x-million light years ago, what do we mean by the star? Obviously not the visual star. We may assert that the center from which the light rays started out on their journey to us was located in such and such a part of the heavens; but we are not seeing that center; we are seeing the light. It is possible that we have erected a star on the model of a tangible object, like the material objects which surround us in daily life. And if we were to touch the star as that kind of object, we should have to travel so many million miles outward into celestial space. But that is not what we are supposed to be talking about. And if it makes any sense to ask where a visual object is, the answer is, "Wherever you see it." The tangible is wherever you touch it. And similarly the auditory object is wherever you hear it and the gustatory and olfactory objects wherever you taste and smell them. There is no *prima facie* evidence of the coincidence of all these places. If visual objects are light rays, they extend very far through space; if auditory are air-waves, they extend next farthest; the olfactory come next, and the gustatory and tangible objects must be where we are or in contact with our bodies.

But there are further complications. By staring at a visual object one can keep it pretty stable and permanent; but by continually smelling an olfactory object, one loses it. Whether through fatigue or adaptation, an olfactory object vanishes after a certain amount of time. If we were purely olfactory beings, such a principle as that of the conservation of matter would be nonsense.

---

2 See Aristotle's *Metaphysics,* IV, 5, 1009 b for a discussion of the questions raised by individual differences in perception, antedating Aenesidemus.

Olfaction gives us no definite boundaries; odors pervade certain regions of space and most of us would be hard put to it to tell exactly where an object is, if all we had to guide us were our sense of smell. We know roughly whence an odor comes, just as we know roughly whence a sound comes, but such roughness is far from reliable, and we usually do not rely on it. We happen to be more dependent on our eyes and muscles and finger-tips than on any other organs, but we also know that some animals rely more on their sense of smell than on their eyesight—witness dogs—and some, the birds, more on their eyesight than on their tactile organs. To a hawk there are visual objects which simply do not exist for us, and consequently what would be a terminating visual judgment for a hawk would not be one for us. Such remarks are commonplace in non-philosophic discourse, and though we are neither dogs nor hawks, it is my hope to persuade people to take them more seriously in philosophy.

For this is not a question of degrees of perceptual acuity; it penetrates more deeply than that. It is the question of the contribution of the instruments of investigation to the facts. We have to use some instruments, even if they be only the naked sense-organs. And it will be found that the testimony of our perceptual instruments is inconsistent. One does not see an object where and when one feels it, smells it, tastes it, or hears it. And even if one admitted that one could be aware of the reports of all our senses at one moment—which is of course dubitable if not impossible—we might conclude that five objects were present to our senses simultaneously, but not that they were all in the same place. Now we do not get into such difficulties because we seem to have taken the tactual object as standard and to have attempted to fit the visual, auditory, and other perceptual objects into it. This has worked very well on the whole. But it has also given rise to the hoary problems of bent sticks, moons which break in two when an eyeball is pressed, railway tracks which converge in the distance, and so on. We have also recently learned that if we generalize the behavior of the tangible object and use it as a model for all objects, we shall never be able to make sense out of such a science as quantum mechanics. This is fundamentally the trouble with the nineteenth-century procedural method of mechanical models. Mechanical models are constructed out of bodies moving about in free space and colliding. The laws which are exemplified by the parallelogram of forces or by the three laws of motion, have been so well demonstrated that they certainly require no apology here. But there is no more reason to accept them as universally true than there is to deny their universal applicability. The choice has to be made on grounds other than that of self-evidence. They have no relevance to psychic phenomena or to phenomena such as works of art, except insofar as such phenomena can be identified with macroscopic material particles in motion. It may very well turn out that even our dreams are as they are because of biochemical events which may then turn out to be deducible from quantum mechanics or something similar. But whatever they are grounded in and whatever the biochemical causes of dreams may eventually be proved to be, once the dreams come into existence, they can be described in their own terms, just as works of art, political constitutions, economic systems, or religious ritual may be.

The facts then as the physical facts are simply the facts of physics. Each kind of fact is discovered within a cognitive context, and outside the context it will not exist. For if facts are that in which people believe, it must be admitted that beliefs are not indeterminate but are oriented in one direction or towards one subject-matter rather than another. When a term is absolutely unambiguous, it naturally must name something which one knows how to recognize. It is a fact that Mars is a planet and Sirius a star, and the two nouns mean definite and specifiable things. But planets and stars, though defined without reference to the means of detecting their differentiae and their existence, are nevertheless distinguished by means of certain instruments of observation. And though the planets were first recognized and named through procedures which are not our procedures and were part of a system of astronomy which is not ours, that in itself does not constitute a nature transcending the methods of observing them, for just as the beliefs about these planets varied, so did the facts which were believed and the methods of justifying the beliefs in question. Again until the time of Lavoisier the notion of the amount of matter which one had was vague, and it was he above all others who maintained that all matter is ponderable and that the presence or absence of matter could be detected only by weight. The amount of matter in his system was what a bit of matter weighed, and that was the end of it. But there have been occasions when it was more important to measure in terms of volume. Does this imply that the real amount of matter is its weight? Or volume? Such questions seem to me to be futile. I do not say meaningless. They are futile because they give no indication of the meaning of *real*. One can never be sure in cases where such questions are asked, but one may guess that the people who ask them are excessively given to "monadolatry" and think that all ambiguity can be eliminated by finding a single meaning to any group of terms.

Does this entail the doctrine known as operationalism? I fail to see that the belief in the contribution of instruments of observation to the results of observation is equivalent to the belief that the meaning of a term or sentence is the operation by means of which one detects the presence of the object named or the truth of the sentence uttered. Our belief that Caesar crossed the Rubicon and cried *Jacta alea est* is based on Suetonius's *De vita Caesarum,* I, 32. But does the sentence, "Caesar crossed the Rubicon etc." mean, can it be substituted for, the sentence, "Suetonius says in *De vita Caesarum,* I, 32, that Caesar crossed the Rubicon"? I doubt it. My reason for doubting is that either sentence might be true or false without the truth or falsity of the other being affected. If this were not so, then it would be impossible for a man ever to give a false report of anything. For if the meaning of his report is the report itself, no sentence would ever have reference to anything outside itself. All sentences would be, so to speak, self-contained. There might be a selection of them to be made which would be consistent, but there would be no existential propositions possible. But the proposition about Caesar is precisely an existential proposition. Since it speaks of something which happened two thousand years ago, we have to rely on indirect testimony to prove it. It may of course be false, for it is quite possible that Suetonius was in error. But no one is going to confuse, one hopes, false propositions with meaningless propositions. "Caesar" is the name of a man and "Rubicon" the name of a river and "crossed" is the name of an act. We may use Suetonius's testimony as evidence for the act and we may be wrong in doing so, but we are not thereby identifying the meaning of the sentence expressing the historical fact with the meaning of the sentence or sentences describing our sources of information about it.

Moreover, we cannot tell the meaning of the existential proposition simply by looking at the words or hearing their sound. We already know—or are supposed to know—their meaning ahead of time. If we did not, we could not interpret the sentence. Similarly when we say that someone talks nonsense, if he is using words in their traditional sense and is following traditional syntax. If he says something which does not make sense, as we are likely to say, then we had better first ask him what he intended to say, to define his terms, before charging him with speaking nonsense. If there are no people who speak sentences or who make judgments, then clearly what I say is absurd. But in my first lecture I assumed that there were people and that judgments were made by them. Experience, in the form of debate and of asking these people what they had in mind when they said what puzzled us, might convince us that it is not the symbols themselves which have any meaning but that they acquire meaning through the use to which they are put. Thus there are many areas of speculation and indeed of experience which it is hard to speak about. If by fiat one assumes that all sentences must be translatable into the language of sensory data or that of physics, then it follows that those which cannot be so translated are nonsensical. We have learned in recent years that all talk about God, the immortality of the soul, the inner life, and I should imagine dreams, is nonsensical for the simple reason that it cannot be put into either of these languages. It is true that if I have dreamed of something or other last night—and recent investigations into dreams make one chary of being more precise—there is no sure way of knowing what I dreamed about. I shall be asked to relate my dream, but of course one's memory is notoriously faulty about such experiences. For psychoanalytic purposes it makes very little difference whether my story is correct or not, but even though my evidence in proof of its correctness is weak, my account is not necessarily meaningless. The facts in such cases are based upon the assumption that dreams fall into certain typical classes, dreams of flying, of falling, of domination, of self-humiliation, and so on, but that assumption is founded on generalizations made from reports of dreams given by hundreds of people. Are we to say that the meaning of the sentence, "I dreamed last night that I was Aristotle," is, "I am reporting now that I dreamed last night of being Aristotle"? But a report of the dream is made now, during one's waking life, and the dream itself occurred during last night's sleep. Do these dates make no difference to the meaning of the sentences in which they occur? Now unless there is no difference between having a dream and reporting it to someone else, the two statements must mean different things, and as in the case of Suetonius and Caesar's crossing the Rubicon, one may be true or false without reference to the other. That is, it may be either true or false that I dreamed of being Aristotle, regardless of whether it is true or false that I reported the dream. Yet the report is the only way another person has of discovering what I did dream. Since neither I nor anyone else can go back in time and re-enter my sleep and have my dream, is one to conclude that the word "dream" is meaningless and that sentences in which it occurs are nonsensical?

As for the supernatural references, they may again all be false or founded on such vague evidence that they have little plausibility. It is undoubtedly right that philosophers should insist on people's defining their terms as far as they can, and the word "God" in philosophy has no privileges. But even if one talks nonsense in theology, that is not because the meaning of theological statements is identical with the means of verifying them—unless of course one so decides—but because they contradict each other or are internally self-contradictory. But before pronouncing judgment, it is always prudent to ask the theologian to tell you what he has in mind, for it is not self-evident that he has only nonsense in mind. I admit that much theology strikes me as nonsense, but for reasons other than those which operationalism or its similars propose. For if one identifies meaning with the technique of verification, one finds oneself in the awkward position of not knowing how to verify a sentence until one knows its meaning. If one says, "Dit-dot-dit is a letter of the alphabet," it sounds nonsensical, but as soon as one knows that dit's and dot's are names for dots and dashes in the Morse Code, then one can discover whether or not dit-dot-dit is a letter of the alphabet. The fact in this case is easily seen to be dependent on information about a certain convention; the convention is partly responsible for determining the facts. One believes that dit-dot-dit is a letter if one knows the code; if one does not, one may doubt it, may deny it, or simply shrug one's shoulders and walk away.

If this is so, facts should not be considered in isolation from the method of determining them, from the system of belief in which they arise. But they actually are isolated in conversation, as we isolate the color of a picture, or its size and shape, or its symbolic or other meaning, and forget for purposes of discussion that all its characteristics occur together and are as they are because of the reciprocal influences of one on the other. For instance, the reason why the Blessed Virgin is given a blue gown in many old pictures is that blue became symbolic of the Virgin; it was her color, just as red was often associated with Mary Magdalen. But someone, let us say an interior decorator, could discuss the blue without reference to the personage wearing it in the picture. Yet if we ask why the personage is in blue, the answer is that the Blessed Virgin is supposed to wear blue. The blue may be that which determines our identification of the personage, though as a matter of fact it would be pretty thin evidence to go on if that were all there was to go on. But the additional fact that the Virgin wears blue can only be the result of a great deal of investigation which carries us far beyond looking at the picture before us. If we then proceed to ask why she wears blue, the fact would emerge from a study of color-symbolism in the

Middle Ages. That would in all probability lead us into a study of the mediaeval lapidaries and thence into the Book of Revelations. The facts appear all along the line and what we shall call *the* facts are simply those at which we stop. Thus judgments do terminate inquiry, to be sure, but the point of termination is not necessarily in the non-human world. It may very well be in us, in the sense that we are satisfied with the information we have achieved. If our preliminary question is, "What color is the robe of that personage in the picture?" the answer is of course, "Blue," a sensory datum. If then the question is, "Why is it blue?" the answer is no longer a sensory datum at all, unless we maintain that there is nothing in a book—a lapidary in this case—other than little black marks on white paper.

By a natural association of ideas, we may turn to the use of indicators in chemistry. Since at least the time of Robert Boyle, changes in color have been used to detect the presence of acids and alkalis.[3] Litmus, as we all learn in elementary courses in chemistry, is turned red in acids and blue in alkalis. The sensory data in such cases are clear: red or blue and the change from one to the other. In an epoch when vegetable dyes were the rule, it must have been a common experience to spill a bit of acid fruit juice or vinegar on a blue robe and see a red spot appear. What are the facts in such a circumstance? The red spot or the presence of an acid? If one confines oneself to naked sensory observation, the fact is a red spot, and that is relevant simply to sensory experience. It may become relevant to judgments about the carelessness of the wearer of the robe, or it may be a warning to people not to dribble fruit juice on blue clothes. But surely no one will deny that a student of chemistry using such indicators is not so much interested in the sensory datum itself as in its significance as an indicator. There is no longer much mystery about why litmus turns red in acids and blue in alkalis—at least we are used to it. But training suffices to lead the young chemist towards making the

---

[3] For the acid-alkali dispute in the seventeenth century, see Marie Boas; "Acid and Alkali in Seventeenth Century Chemistry," *Archives Internationales d'Histoire des Sciences,* January-March, 1956, pp. 13-28.

test, and he need not know the theory behind it when he makes it. He need merely know that blue litmus paper turns red and red litmus paper blue when dipped in acids and alkalis respectively. I doubt, to take another example, whether anyone knows why each person has his own unique set of finger-prints for that matter, and even if he does, he does not use that knowledge when he identifies people by their finger prints. The proper correlation has been made for him by other investigators, and that is enough for what we call practical purposes. Whether we call the finger-prints the facts or that a certain person must have made them depends entirely upon the context in which we use them. There is, finally, I suppose, some theory to explain why the *rosaceae* have flowers of five petals and lilies of six, but the average person identifying a flower counts the petals—among other things—and is satisfied with that as a significant fact.

This isolation of facts from their methodological context is thus normal enough to arouse no perplexity. We are accustomed to cutting out one cross-section of an event and isolating it from its past and future. Birds and most insects are customarily referred to by their adult names, though we know that a long previous history brought them to maturity. It is only entomologists and ornithologists who are careful about such matters. Yet the perceptual differences between the immature and mature forms sometimes have led people to differentiate between the young and the mature as different kinds of animal. Witness the *leptocephali* and eels. So a countryman distinguishes between the various stages of his animals' growth and gives them each a separate name, if only for economic reasons: you can't substitute a foal for a horse nor a shoat for a hog. But we do run into trouble when we are dealing with historical events, for popularly they have dates which are different from the dates which professionally are given them. We have to begin somewhere, and when we are dealing, for instance, with wars, a brief introduction seems to be all that is needed before we begin our story with the shooting. Yet if we were interested in the prevention of war, we should probably begin several years before the shooting began. We might not, following Horace's warning, begin the Trojan War with the twin-egg, but still we would begin before Homer did. When did the First World War begin? Must one start with the assassination of the Archduke Ferdinand? Or should not the earlier Balkan Wars be seen as prelude to that assassination? But before them, there was the Italo-Turkish War which it is next to impossible to lop off from the Balkan Wars. For there was a continuity of international conflict which has only begun to end today—if it has begun to end—and since it is impossible to go back to the Flood, we have to cut off our events where there is enough observable novelty to warrant the assignment of a new name. Yet even this is not clear. We have to decide what kind of novelty we want, whether it is to be purely military—the type of weapon and tactics used, the alliances, the formal declarations of war or lack of them, the armistices and surrenders, economic rivalries, power-politics, ideological clashes, or something else. This, I imagine, would be granted by most historians. When, however, we ask why certain features are selected rather than others, to help us cut off the beginnings of our historical events, the answer is very uncertain. Today we raise questions about international relations which were not usually raised before the nineteenth century, though they might well have been. From the time of Thucydides to that of Gibbon, it was customary for historians to ask about political and military matters and to let others drop into the background, even when religious quarrels were the supposed causes of the wars. Such a statement requires serious modification, for the *City of God* is a history beginning with the first appearance of man on earth, and its program is defined by the reasons why nations flourish and decay. But it is fair to say that economic forces, as described by a Marxian, never figured largely in pre-nineteenth-century histories. We happen to be more conscious than our ancestors were of economic and cultural changes, and the role of great men as the steersmen of destiny has diminished. However great the role played by a man like Churchill in the Second World War, it is doubtful whether most historians of the future will center their stories about him or Roosevelt or Stalin or even Hitler. Mussolini has already dropped out of the picture, and at the time of writing these words Stalin too is being pushed into the background. The parts which these men played cannot be changed now, but the parts which they play in historical accounts of the events in which they participated can be and is being changed. But again that is because historians are asking questions to which the personalities of leaders are not the answers.

Now if facts terminate inquiry and if the methods of inquiry select certain facts as relevant and reject others as irrelevant, then the facts themselves are inextricably bound up with the process of inquiry and their separation from that process falsifies the epistemological question. For several such separate facts with the same name and the same observable qualities will become that which a variety of propositions may express. One has only to think of a landscape as viewed from a hill to see this point. It in itself as so much brute matter does not change because of our point of view or our intellectual attitude towards it. But it signifies one thing to a painter, another to the farmer, a third to the real estate operator, a fourth to a geographer, a fifth to the geologist, and a sixth to the theologian. It might be possible, though hardly likely, that each would "see" the same sight, but each would interpret it differently when he was acting in his professional role. Rivers, I assume, run downhill whether they are being looked at by a painter or by a geographer, and sedimentary rocks "look" the same to both a geologist and a farmer. But how inevitable it is that such words as "see" and "look" be put in quotation marks, for the minute we use them, we realize that they are being used in a variety of senses. The perceptual data are charged with relevance to questions, most of which are forgotten by the questioner. Each has his habitual attitudes and the attitudes are overlooked since they are habitual and hence compulsive. The compulsions are of course sometimes overcome, though I have never taken a walk with a geologist or a geographer who seemed able to overcome his. But so a man who knows two languages overcomes his compulsion to read one as if it were the other.[4] These ambiguities cause no great trouble since some of us fit ourselves into appropriate contexts without struggling. Thus the fact that *Voi che sapete* opens with the same notes as *Adeste fideles* does not make us think that the *Marriage of Figaro* has anything to do with Christmas. And surely few of us hearing a group of carolers singing *Adeste fideles* think of Cherubino. Nevertheless I have seen a child standing before a Fragonard ask why there were little naked babies in the sky. Both the child and the adult see the same perceptual pattern, but they do not assert the same facts.

If there were neutral facts which arose independent of inquiry, then it would be impossible, as far as those facts were concerned, for anyone to err. There would be then a one-to-one correspondence between facts and propositions expressing them. We could be trained to see the facts and learn the appropriate propositions. We should be even less imaginative than Peter Bell looking at his primrose. We do learn a given discipline, whether scientific or not; we do learn to make certain correlations from the moment when we are taught the right name to give the birds, beasts, and flowers to the time when we learn the simple operations of arithmetic and the formulas of algebra. We learn rules of grammar and syntax and rules of experimentation in elementary courses in science. Thus a body of knowledge becomes hardened, and facts are precipitated out of the rough and tumble of daily life. Material substances become classified as gases, liquids, and solids; animals are grouped into felines, canines, and so on; works of art turn into samples of the mediaeval, renaissance, baroque, rococo, and "modern." And the world becomes a collection of specimens. It is then that we wake up—if we do—to the importance of James's remark that water is not merely hydrogen oxide but wet. And that remark, or one like it, causes us to question whether our collections and groupings exist, to use the Greek phrases, "by nature" or "by custom." Unfortunately we also frequently decide that existence by custom solves all our difficulties, and we overlook the stubborn

---

[4] I have, however, caught myself when talking in French trying to interpret English words spoken by my interlocutor as if they were French.

refusal of some experiences to adjust themselves to certain of our customs which we would like to impose on them. No one as yet has succeeded in teaching a fish to live out of water or a plant to get up and walk. Why must we always be pouring water over it and giving it nitrogen? No one has succeeded in collecting the heat given out by a steam boiler, then reversing the process to recapture the fuel which was burned to heat the water. We may be as pragmatic as we wish; there are certain ideas which not only do not work but apparently cannot. And we can usually tell which can not, in spite of the continued existence of people who try to invent perpetual motion machines and proofs of the squaring of circles. Why does this seem to be peculiar?

One of the reasons, it would seem, is that the moment one points to relativistic situations, one meets the objection that if something is so, relative to something else, then anything can be true. Thus if one says that aesthetic values are always determined in a cultural complex, part of which is human beings, one is immediately told that everyone in that case would be free to believe anything he wished about aesthetic values. This of course is nonsense. One is free to calculate the orbit of Mars from the center of the earth, as was done before the time of Copernicus, or from the center of the sun, or for that matter from the center of anything he pleases. But once one has chosen his system of relation, one is no longer free to do whatever he wishes. The compulsions of a cultural complex are strong as long as one is not aware of them, but if one chooses to discriminate virtue and vice on the basis of the Decalogue, one is not then free to call adultery virtue and chastity vice. The questioning of the utility of the system arises not within the system, unless it is seen to be inconsistent or to give rise to inconsistencies, as when, for instance, one attempts to guide one's life by proverbial philosophy. It arises when two systems are in conflict and that conflict arises when a man grows out of the system in which he was educated into another. In ethical matters it looks as if most ethical systems were corrections of man's natural impulses. It could be maintained that no one would seriously doubt the legitimacy of his own desires unless someone else first ques-

tioned them. This is not self-evident, to be sure, but it pretty well
accords with what one would expect from one's own experiences.
But taking this simply as an imaginary case, one can see that
whether a person questions his own desires or not may be determined by the moral complex in which he lives. If so, moral judgments are far from indifferent but are theoretically predictable.
I am simply saying that an assertion may be true or false without
necessarily being true or false of things or events whose character
is an independent variable. Thus certain standards of social groups
may be predictable on the assumption of their determination to
survive as social groups, and one such is the rule that behavior must
not be detrimental to the survival of the group. Thus it is a safe
guess that all groups will insist upon obedience to those rules for
living and for thinking which custom has made binding. The fact
that custom is a dimension of the group's history in no way makes
it less compulsory or domineering. Its traits will be described in
great detail and may even be petrified into a set of divinely or-
dained laws. But whatever they may be, and however much they
may irritate the people who have to live under them, the values
which they prescribe will tend to have inner consistency, analogous
to the consistency of a set of mathematical theorems, and error
will be departure from the road they have surveyed.

Moral and aesthetic laws in the opinion of the writer of these
lines are neither laid down by *notre grande et puissante Mère
Nature* nor by God. Nor are the laws of thought so laid down.
The human equation can be detected in all of them, for after all
they are our ways of doing things, and if Nature is to be brought
in, she had best be Human Nature. For two things in themselves
cannot be inconsistent, though statements about them can be. But
the moment we make statements, we begin to talk about classes and
not about individuals except insofar as they are members of classes.
It is inconsistent to say that mankind is both rational and irrational in the same respect and it is also inconsistent to say that a
given man is rational and irrational in the same respect and at the
same time. But respects and dates have nothing to do with classes.
If consistency is a feature of assertions, then it is to be determined

by essences and not by existents. It is unfortunate that, for instance, there should be so many kinds of triangles; it would be simpler for all of us if there were only right triangles. But right triangles and scalene triangles and equilateral triangles are all geometrical possibilities, and whatever their differences may be, they are forced upon us. Even if we had developed our idea of triangularity from collecting material shapes and purging them of their spatio-temporal characters, as long as a triangle is defined as a plane figure bounded by three straight lines—and we know what the terms mean—we can understand why some should have sides of three unequal lengths and some should contain one right angle and some should have three angles which are equal and so on. But when we are dealing with the objects of experience as distinguished from those of logic, we neither know whether all possibilities are realized, nor how many are, nor whether any are, nor what determines which are and which are not. We have, for instance, been given some clues in the studies of D'Arcy Wentworth Thompson to certain limiting factors of growth and form, but even so ingenious and painstaking a student has been able to do no more than point out why a given animal has a certain form in view of the physical pressures under which it must live. Nor is his great work depreciated if one points out that he cannot prove that certain forms must exist for logical reasons. I have no doubt that he could have invented an animal or plant which would have been viable in any statable environment; but the invention in spite of his genius would have lived only in a book.

The pressure which is put upon us by *The Facts* is felt only after repeated observation and experiments when we are proceeding from the facts to generalizations. No single experience could possibly tell us anything except insofar as it corroborated an idea or hypothesis or general law or theory or simple guess. It gains relevance as the answer to a question, and it is its relevance which is compelling, not its raw existence out there in isolation from any inquiry. We may forget or overlook the questions which have been put to it in our past, just as we forget the rules of grammar or the rules for the performance of any bodily act like eating with a knife and fork. Children, it seems likely, spend a good deal of their time learning how to identify things, learning their names, and their identifications are made by means of such rudimentary and often misleading experiences as prominent colors and sounds. Thus a fruit, flower, or bird, a dog or kitten, may be identified by some fragmentary aspect, such as its redness or softness or twittering or shape. But no one would say that an apple was identical with redness or a bird with its song. It is precisely because we do substitute these fragments of perceptual experience for that which we are identifying that we make so many mistakes. And the reason why we have to look again, to have another look, as we say, is that we are confident that, if no mistake has been made, the object will not have changed its color or its sound in time. We assume that all real objects are changeless, and one of the differentiae of the real, as opposed to the apparent, is its immutability. But this is far from being a discovery; it is an assumption. It tells us what to look for and what we may neglect. That is why no logical rules for induction have ever been successful in the eyes of logicians. They all presuppose the very thing which induction is trying to establish.

As soon as we discover that some of the object's attributes do change, the following conclusions will be drawn: (1) either that the changing attributes are unreal, merely subjective, apparent; or (2) that they change regularly. We may conclude that Rhode Island Red hens are red and then learn that their chickens are yellow. Thereupon we set up a rule which correlates the color of the feathers with the age of the bird. But if each time we looked at a Rhode Island Red we saw it as of a different color, we should in all probability put down its color as irrelevant, unless we could also find some rule in accordance with which the color changes took place.[5] But we soon find out that in most cases of sensory qualities there is change rather than permanence. When it is a question of living things, we can elaborate rules for ourselves or

---

[5] Audubon, for instance, mistook the change in color of the pelage of some quadrupeds as indicators of different species. He failed to discover that the changes in color were seasonal.

find them in books, and these rules regularize the changes. But at this point we establish a class of certain types of objects, physical objects whose properties do not change in time. I refer to such things as the colors which we see when light rays are reflected or sounds which are produced when air-waves hit our ears. But it is obvious that in such cases there is no way of telling whether the constancy is due to the permanence of the objective stimulus or to the stability of our sense-organs. For we have reached the stimulus through the sensory impressions which they are supposed to make on our minds. If we accept the classical interpretation of sensory experience, the sensory quality can no more be referred to the human organism than to the stimulus, for both are required to produce it. It occurs only when both are in a specific relation. We can assume for purposes of experimentation that it is we who do not change; or we can assume that if a variety of observers report the same thing, then their individual differences cancel out. But if on the other hand the *Aufgabe,* the expectation, the *Einstellung,* the anticipation, or the transaction—call it what you will—has any effect upon what is perceived, and if in order to purify our conditions we give each observer the same directions, who can tell to what degree the directions are responsible for the results? Strictly speaking, all we have is a number of similar reports from one observer or a variety of reports from several observers on one occasion. The facts gain their compulsive power from their repetition. They become, whether we are aware of it or not, examples of a rule.

To have found ways of getting constant results is a great triumph of scientific method and one should not denigrate it. But one should see exactly what is taking place. We want regularity and we have devised methods of obtaining it. But the regularity is purchased at the price of depriving normal uncontrolled experience of its complexity and individuality, which render it inarticulate and dumb. For no localized or dated experience is likely to be exactly like another unless it has become so purified that its date and location are nullified. The nullification of spatial and temporal location is prerequisite to classification, unless one is going to set up a class of those beings which are in the same place at the same time. Is it not of the very nature of a universal to be indifferent to dates and locations? One could call an accurate description of what is taking place at a certain spatio-temporal location a law, if one will, but usually we should call it at most a description, a biography or perhaps a history. In any event it would be different from the laws to which we are accustomed in the sciences for they state general propositions. These propositions are expressed in terms of variables, of "all" and "any," and their possibility is predicated on the ancillary possibility of repeatable observations. But the minute one asserts the possibility of repetition, one has discounted the space and time. In common speech we do speak of returning to the same place at a later date, but the usage is questionable. For if we are dealing with point-instants in space-time, then no place can be imagined without date. Dates may be negligible, as colors, sounds, weights, shapes, and almost any other property of things may be in certain circumstances. But whatever is neglected impoverishes experience, whatever good it may effectuate. We clearly do not have to discuss times when we are speaking, for instance, of the chemical constitution of the stars, unless it varies with time. And we do not have to discuss location when we are dealing with the difference between hexapods and quadrupeds. But this does not establish a "realm" of spaceless and timeless beings any more than our ability to distinguish between colors without actually having the colors before our eyes sets up a realm of unseen colors. Thinking proceeds by abstraction; that is its difference from sensory perception. One can think about redness without seeing it at the time of thinking, and one can see it without thinking about it. But to think of it as if it existed in a special realm of chromatic beings would be like thinking about the colors of the infra-red and ultra-violet rays which are invisible to human, if not to apian, eyes. Perception sets limits to our thoughts in the old-fashioned sense that we cannot imagine anything whose parts were not once perceived. But nevertheless thought can proceed by imagining the very opposite of what we perceive, meaning by "opposite" that which lacks the sensory properties which experience tells us are essential. Thus if experience tells us that no elephants are pink, we can still imagine pink elephants. Or if we know that vision is limited to a certain range of light, we can nevertheless think about light which lies beyond that range and which is invisible. But we cannot imagine what colors it would stimulate if it stimulated colors. This will, I suppose, be granted by everyone. But when we talk about invisible light, we deliberately abstract something from the totality of what we know, and by doing so we can elaborate principles and laws which turn out to be of great theoretical importance. As long as we can state in intelligible fashion the constancy of these laws, it makes no difference whether every feature of that which they describe is corroborated by perceptual experience or not. A scientist would like to have such corroboration, one imagines, but sometimes he gets it by inferring that if the law is true, then certain observations ought to be possible. If it were not possible for us to make inferences from laws or general statements, thought could never transcend experience in the narrowest sense of that term, that is, in the sense of *my* experience, *your* experience, *his* experience. One of the demands which we make upon thought is that it extend beyond anyone's experience, and it does so the moment we give a common noun, instead of a proper name, to whatever confronts us.

It is much easier to verify the physics of Aristotle than that of Galileo, for it corresponds more closely to uncontrolled observation. Galileo's law of falling bodies is true only under laboratory conditions: the bodies must fall in a vacuum. But outside the laboratory bodies fall through some medium such as air or water. We have learned to calculate the resistance of the medium—or to the medium, if one prefers—but one could maintain with some justice that in doing so one has departed from experience. This departure, which is always found when laboratory conditions are introduced as the limiting conditions of our laws, is essential if we are to have any laws at all. For a law is by its very nature no one man's experience, whereas all experience belongs to someone. The discrepancy between thought or science and experience is ineradicable, the former being a corrective of the latter. That is its beauty. On the other hand, when we establish an ontology as the image of our thoughts, then we fall into the trap of the Idols of the Tribe. There is constant interplay between thought and experience, to be sure, an interplay of which the Post-Kantians made a good deal. Unfortunately they seem to have concluded that the interplay was within the frontiers of the mind, whereas there was no evidence that such was the case. Science does not appear to be introspection, though it does stimulate lyrical expression. I do not deny that the history of science could be interpreted as the evolution of collective thought, each man's thinking resembling to some extent every other man's, and the whole progressing according to some formula of internal growth. But that would involve such complications to smooth out the conflicts between mind and mind, to explain how something which seems to be the polar antithesis of thinking can act as the corrective of thinking and of everyone's thinking, to make room for error, to justify experimentation, to give any ground for choosing between one set of ideas and another, that it seems undesirable to move in that direction.

Whatever one's final account of fact may be, it must be such that the facts are expressible in general terms, not individual; that they may corroborate declarative sentences; and that they may be believed by a variety of persons. That being so, they cannot be physical or psychical beings or combinations of them in single isolation. They must be recognized as signs which have relevance to inquiry. Their relevance has to be learned; it is not—at least normally—revealed. Facts always occur in categorical systems, whatever the categories may be which are used to set up the systems. Whatever certainty we have about them is acquired, not given. That certainty may be vested with immediacy, but knowledge becomes immediate thanks to constant repetition or to careful application of corrective measures. It is of course true that we do rely upon our immediate experiences, but the "we" in question is the adult who has already built up a mass of reliable knowledge and absorbed a whole technique of correction. If now someone asks how we know that we have any past, I can reply only that if we deny it, it would be impossible to understand why the problem of the past should ever arise. If Hume's theory of knowledge was correct, we could not only not prove the previous existence of any past experience but, I am saying, no one could dream of raising the problem of how to prove it. No proofs of the reality of the past have ever been drawn out of the immediate data of consciousness, though sometimes epistemologists have been willing to grant us a tiny bit of memory, and indeed how could there be? If there were any such thing as time at all, it would sputter and sparkle from conscious moment to conscious moment, and the word "moment" would mean nothing.[6] Is it not better to start with premises which do not give rise to insoluble problems?

The establishment of the facts then demands the following: (1) a system of categories within which facts are to be found; (2) a method of investigation which will remain constant and which will permit repeatable observations; (3) a clear understanding of what problems the facts are supposed to answer; (4) as a consequence of 3, a knowledge of the rule, deviation from which has given rise to the problem; (5) a recognition of the kind of answer which will serve as a satisfactory explanation of the deviation from the rule, that is, which will answer the question.

We shall now turn to types of explanation.

---

[6] But see A. O. Lovejoy, in *Contemporary American Philosophy*, N.Y., 1930, Vol. II.

CHAPTER V

EXPLANATION — BY CAUSE AND EFFECT

The purpose of the next four lectures is to expound a fourfold ambiguity in the word "because," or, if one prefers, in the word "why." Aristotle had already pointed out a similar ambiguity in his own time, but he seems to have believed that all events must be explained in terms of all four causes, and his causes are not identical with those which I shall be discussing here. There will appear to be, however, certain similarities between his doctrine of causation and the views which I shall discuss, but that is because the latter in part derive from his theories. It may be well to say at the outset that I am neither maintaining that every event can be assigned all the causes which I discuss nor that one should try to assign them all. Moreover I am not maintaining that there are not still other types of answer which may be given when the question of why something happens is raised. Finally, I am not attempting to do again what Emile Meyerson did with such brilliance in his *De l'Explication dans les Sciences* and to reduce all types of explanation to one.

The ultimate answer to the question of why something occurs is, "These are the facts." This may be disguised in a variety of ways depending upon a man's philosophical position. The answer may also be given at a variety of times, depending on how much intellectual stamina a man has. If he is a theist, he will sooner or later announce that things happen as they do because such is the will of God. And if he is an anti-theistical naturalist, he will substitute the laws of nature for the will of God. It makes little difference except connotatively which of these statements he makes; the epistemological function of whatever it is which is denoted by his phrase will be the same. It is that which puts an end to his questioning. As Parmenides says to Socrates in Plato's *Parmenides* (135 B), when he is talking about the Ideas, without them one would have no fixed goal upon which to turn one's thoughts.[1] That there is such a fixed goal is an article of faith justified by disciplined thought, but it rests upon certain assumptions which should be clarified. These assumptions, as I see them, are three in number.

(1) The possibility of formulating a sentence such that it will express a state of affairs relevant to the question being asked and at the same time irrelevant to date and place. Such statements need not be and, I think it can be shown, usually are not inductive generalizations from uncontrolled observation. Thus if it is raining and I raise the question of why it is raining or what causes it to rain, I may mean, (a) Why is it raining now and here rather than yesterday or tomorrow? or (b), What is the general cause of rainfall? I may answer the first question by pointing out that the inhabitants of this region held a rain-dance last night with appropriate sacrifices, or that the congregation of the village church prayed for rain, or that the clouds bearing rain were seeded from airplanes, or that the water-vapor of the atmosphere has condensed in contact with a cold front. But sooner or later I shall have to introduce a general statement on the cause of rainfall of which this instance of rainfall will be an example. For insofar as a particular event is unique, it is either inexplicable or self-caused or an accident, all of which are synonyms, except for their emotional charge. Moreover, neither rain-dances, nor prayers for rain, nor seeding the clouds would be initiated unless a previous correlation between some such practice and rainfall had been made. For note that when the rites fail to produce rain, a significant account of their failure is given. The incantation was not properly sung; the enemy had frustrated one's power with counter-magic; one's ancestors or the gods were angry; one did not deserve the rain; the wind changed and drove the clouds away; the seeding was not heavy enough. The very fact that an explanation can be given for

---

[1] Jowett translates, "He will have nothing on which his mind can rest," which would be better for my purposes, though not for Plato's.

the failure of a cause is in itself evidence that a general rule has been invoked. It is reasonable to suppose that if the Dieri of Central Australia were asked why they select two wizards who are bled in their rain-making ceremonies and their blood allowed to flow upon the old men of the tribe while the two wizards throw handfuls of down into the air, they would reply that the blood was the rain and the down the clouds. (It is furthermore probable that visiting anthropologists would believe them.) But it is also probable that if they were asked why all this was done, they would more truthfully reply that this is the way to make it rain, just as if one were to ask an American why he always addresses God in the second person singular, he would reply that such is the correct way of addressing the Deity. And in both cases it would be impossible to make any experimental checks because of the sanctity of the rites.

(2) That every event has at least some properties identical with those of other events such that the events as a group may be given a name or descriptive phrase in common. This name does not change with date and location and the characteristics upon which it is based also remain permanent or are at any rate only trivially mutable. Trivial mutability is the name for such changes as one wishes to neglect or which do not fall under the categories which are the principle of the classification. Farmers and meteorologists are more interested in the amount of rain which falls than most urban dwellers, and any amount is a blessing to a cab-driver.

(3) Because of this second assumption we can speak of any particular event as an example or illustration or instance of a class of events. We are forced to talk of classes, and we learn in time that, except in mathematics, nothing is a perfect example of any class. This is inevitable since the differentiae of a class have to be observed by human beings with instruments, and both the human beings and even the instruments vary from moment to moment. Also any character, such as a color or shape, that is, any quality observed by our sense-organs, has to be observed under standardized conditions, and these are next to impossible to obtain except within certain limits. It is the duality of classes and their members

which is partly, but far from entirely, responsible for the problem of the relation between universals and particulars. For since we talk about things by class-names, we expect all things of the same class-names to have all characters in common, whereas they are always discovered to have characters of their own as well. For instance, those of us who live on the East Coast have in recent years learned that each succeeding hurricane has its own personality, that the Hazel of 1955 was different from Alice and her sisters, and we should have little patience with someone who shrugged his shoulders and said that they were all simply hurricanes. We should grant that they were all hurricanes but not simply hurricanes. The only reason for accentuating this is that Neo-Platonists and one type of Empiricist assume the contrary. The former maintain that the individual differences are merely apparent, the latter that they are as good as non-existent. Now it is true that for intellectual purposes we have to overlook them, or, when they become troublesome, we have to explain them. But the type of empiricist who says that all generalizations are abstracted from experience is forced by the dialectic of his standpoint to assert that the general characters are there in experience—for otherwise they could not be abstracted from it—and presumably they are only externally related to whatever other characters are also there. The other characters are not part of the events being discussed. This is analogous to the Aristotelian distinction between essential and accidental properties, though the whole Aristotelian metaphysics is far from being empirical.

What is essential and what accidental is determined by definitions.[2] But the author of the distinction believed that his definitions were real and not nominal and that for that reason essences were determined not by logic alone but by logic as a reflection of ontology. I am taking the position that all definitions are nominal; that is, they state how one wishes to use a term. If then we define "man" as a rational animal, then the size of his head— *pace* Sherlock Holmes—is accidental, though in fact either a

---

[2] Cf. Aristotle's *Metaphysics*, 1030 a.

microcephalic or macrocephalic individual will probably be far from rational. The various definitions and pseudo-definitions of "man" are good illustrations of how use influences the distinction between essence and accident. When we hear that man alone laughs, or that he alone has a sense of estrangement from God, or that he alone is self-conscious, or that he alone has erect posture, or that he alone has a history, we see at once that each differentia arises out of a special context which is logically independent of the others. Thus a man's sense of humor does not follow from his rationality, his erect posture, his selfconsciousness, his historicity, or his feeling of estrangement from God. These various differentiae, it will be granted, are noticed when men are compared with other animals in respect to certain traits which they might, for some reason or other, be expected to share with him. It is then essential in the class of animals-in-relation-to-the-Creator that man feel his estrangement from Him, and in the class of animals-as-psychic-beings, man be differentiated from the others by his rationality. But nothing forces an investigator to indulge in one set of comparisons rather than another. If the essences were determined by Nature, as Aristotle thought, then these other traits would all be accidental, and one might or might not have them and still be a man. But if they are determined by definition, then each is essential within one class of beings and can be accidental in others. Thus one might be a laughing animal and irrational, unselfconscious, unhistorical, unreligious, even stooped like a beast with face to the earth, and nevertheless be human. This of course is simply playing with concepts, and in reality the possibility of heaping up so many essential characters rests upon the complexity of the class whose essence one is trying to define. Man's rationality may distinguish him from all the other animals and so may the other features listed. What used to be called the universe of discourse will determine what characters are essential and what not.

A universe of discourse—or a context—looked upon from the point of view of inquiry, is a collection of information which is believed and which is also believed to be consistent. The information is about something. What it is about is the problem or problems which started the inquiry. This can be illustrated in the history of a science, but only in its history. Physics begins in Aristotle, let us assume, in spite of the inaccuracy of the assumption. In him the main question is motion. This is still given as one of the differentiae of physics in such a dictionary as Webster's Collegiate.[3] Problems of statics were introduced by Archimedes, and his problems could be solved without having recourse to the dynamics of Aristotle. Had Archimedes been living in an American university, he would have been told that what he was doing was not really physics at all, for only the science called physics up to that time would have been deemed worthy of the name. But coarse jokes are not in order, and the point of my remarks is simply that sheaves of questions are raised and answered, and the answers become the science. Any of them can be viewed with scepticism under sufficient provocation, but as long as they are not questioned, they will determine what an investigator will accept as essential and what accidental. The essence then is the problem turned into a fact. We notice that man alone laughs, and notice it presumably by comparing him with the other animals. Strictly speaking, we should ask why he alone laughs, but can do so only if he is so much like the other animals in other respects that this similarity is disturbing. We come, however, to this observation with a long set of preparatory ideas about man in the back of our minds. We are educated to think of him as rational, religious, erect, and so on; in fact, so unlike the other animals, that we find it hard to classify him among the beasts. What might seem primitive to the biologist is derivative—has to be demonstrated—for the general run of us. We had to learn of our animality, and indeed up to the time of Linnaeus it is unlikely that anyone would have classified man among the primates. In Linnaeus for that matter he was given a very special place,[4] a place so remote from that of the other primates that his animality was almost nullified. Hence the differentiae of man

---

[3] See the 5th edition, 1937, s.v., "The science which deals with those phenomena of inanimate matter involving no changes in chemical composition; more specifically the science of matter and motion."

[4] See his *Systema Naturae*, ed. cit., p. 20, note on *Nosce te ipsum*.

have usually been neglected by philosophers, though not by biologists or theologians. If we wander in this domain at all, it is probably to ask why the beasts are not more like us rather than why we are not more like them. Our differences from the beasts may be used for satire when writers prefer them to men, or for self-approbation when the reverse is found. But when we come to establishing classes of things, we have to accept their differences as fact and not as problematic.

Here then there is no more possibility of explanation than there is in the case of individuals and the classical identification of individual propositions with universal propositions works out well. It makes little if any difference whether we say that man's rational animality is inexplicable or that it is his essence, assuming that it is his essence.[5] But when one notices that some men are more or less rational than others and that some men's rationality appears to have reached the vanishing point, then a problem arises and one can ask why this is so. But the moment this question is asked, it is agreed that the members of a class have characters which are not those of the collection as a whole and that this requires explanation; that the non-temporal and non-spatial nature of classes distinguishes them from their members; and that if we are talking of classes, we are not necessarily saying things which will be equally true of their members. This is both anti-Platonic and anti-Aristotelian. It entails a complete duality between ideas and their subject-matter, though I fail to see that it entails a duality of substance.[6] The class becomes a group of individuals which have a range of properties more or less similar, the similarity increasing as the methods and conditions of observation become more stable. This is just the common-sense conclusion that so long as I and my instruments of observation and the conditions under which I make the observations do not change, then what I observe will remain constant. It is usually assumed that the objects of my observation

---

[5] The "little difference" might be psychological, that is, one term might be more agreeable than the other.

[6] Cf. A. O. Lovejoy's distinction between epistemological and psychophysical dualism in the *Revolt against Dualism*.

do not themselves change, though if they did and no one observed
the change, clearly no account would be given of it. Much of the
universality noted in intellectual histories may be attributed to
crude observation. As long as we cling to the naked eye, we can
have a fairly stable world. And what escapes the naked eye will
be said to be not worth seeing.

One can then reach universality in two ways: either by eliminating within a collection of things all individual differences or
by including in one's judgments all the restrictions which make
them true and limiting oneself to whatever particular thing is under observation. Aristotle in combating the sensationalists of his
time, says, "Those who ask for an irresistible argument, and at the
same time demand to be called to account for their views, must
guard themselves by saying that the truth is not that what appears
exists, but that what appears exists *for him to whom* it appears,
and *when,* and *to the sense to which,* and *under the conditions
under which* it appears."[7] If the italicized portions of this statement may be said to define the whole matrix within which the
individual is found, then, as Aristotle goes on to say, the statement
is perforce true. It is true only of that particular experience but
it is logically equivalent to a universal proposition. Whether
Aristotle saw that much more was involved in this than the
straightforward apprehension of qualities, I do not know, though
it is indisputable that he did not believe such apprehension to be
knowledge. In any event one must know before making this or
any other judgment what framework will be used to express it.
The relativity of the proposition, as distinct from the judgment,
to the person, the time, the sense-organ, and the conditions, is a
discovery which is certainly not made automatically. If it were,
Aristotle would not have had to point it out. Where does one get
the evidence that certain persons—as distinguished from others,
certain sense-organs, at certain times, and under certain conditions,
will observe certain things or make certain judgments? Not from
a single experience. Its only ground could be a comparison be-

---

[7] *Metaphysics,* Gamma, 6, 1011a,21 f, Ross's translation.

tween what one is now observing and what one has observed in
other circumstances. No matter how many conditions one introduces in one's "statement of the case," that statement can be true
only because the knowledge of the influence of those conditions
is sound and tested. Hence to say, "This apple is red," and sur-
reptitiously to introduce the observer, the time, the sense-organ,
and the conditions, is not to avoid the use of universals in order to
particularize. The class really is not so much the class of one
member which is "This apple," as the whole range of visual perceptions as defined. Within that class, as within any other, variation will demand explanation, though the nature of the class will
demand none. I am not inferring that species cannot be grouped
in genera and genera in families and families in orders and so on.
Nor am I inferring that the differences on given "levels" are inexplicable. But once the level of classification is established, the
class-characters are not problematic. They are accepted as facts.

Variations are problems only if they conflict with the facts as
established, or with accepted beliefs. The two phrases are interchangeable. It is assumed that no class of beings ought to manifest
variation other than as described in the rule. Things, as the
Ancients said, must "maintain their own natures." And in those
men who used to be called with a bit of contempt the hylozoists,
regular changes were part of the natures of things. It is not until
we come to Empedocles that we find a philosopher introducing
something which will account for the change. His predecessors
seem—and we must say "seem" since they exist now only in scraps
of what they said, torn from their contexts—to have thought that
their first principles had a right to change without violating any
metaphysical rule. Indeed, Cherniss has shown that as far as the
Ionians were concerned, "there appears to be a steady and swift
development of the problem of change starting with Anaximander's theory of separation and commingling, developing through
Anaximenes's notion of a quantitative mechanism reduced to a
single simple law and making the nature of all physical bodies
relative to the degree to which the mechanism has been applied,
and ending with Heraclitus's radical thesis that all distinctions are

merely superficial phases of the universal process of change besides which nothing exists."[8] But in Empedocles, the four elements do not change "of their own accord"; Love brings them together, and Strife pulls them apart. Love and Strife thus become active causes while the elements are the patients upon which they act. The elements cannot change internally: earth always remains earth, water always water, and so on. It is their combinations which change, much as in modern chemistry, the elements forming different groups and thus producing compounds. In our own times the changes consist in changes of location. The elements which enter the compounds appear to be differently disposed in space and the molecular formulas which organic chemists have devised are, so to speak, maps of their spatial dispositions. What actually was supposed to have happened in the system of Empedocles, we do not know. All that we can say is that he seems to have introduced the notion of change as composition and dissolution and the further notion that the composition and dissolution was brought about by two agents. That he gave these agents such poetical names may or may not indicate their highly anthropomorphic character. But it is not without interest that Love and Strife were chosen, for the choice established a paradigm for all later causal explanation. For it is clear that he did not mean by using the term *Love* to denote merely the fact that the elements combine and the word *Strife* to mean that they also break apart. On the contrary, they are what Aristotle was to call "efficient causes." And since they are also represented in the human being by two recognizable feelings, one might say that Empedocles was especially empirical in his theory.

But to the modern reader it would seem inevitable that Love is "nothing but" the fact of composition and that to call such a fact by so biological a name, to personify it, is to avoid the issue. So Boyle objected to his alchemical predecessors who also explained chemical combination by the love which the elements had for one another. He preferred the less anthropomorphic term of "affinity,"

---

[8] Harold Cherniss; *Aristotle's Criticism of Pre-Socratic Philosophy*, Baltimore 1936, p. 382.

as Stahl also did. Whether "affinity" is a less objectionable word than "love," I leave to others. In both cases it is assumed that to state the conditions under which two or more elements unite is not sufficient explanation of their union. One must introduce an external agent to bring about the union. The origin of this type of thinking can no longer be discovered, though it looks as if Comte were right in attributing it to thinking in theological terms, by which he meant thinking in terms of human behavior deified. *Homo faber* makes things, put things together, pulls them apart, and in his sexual life feels the power of something which does not seem to be his own power and which compels him to action. Even so sophisticated a philosopher as Whitehead believed that we have a direct apprehension of causal efficacy in the action of our own organs.[9] If this is so, then efficient causality is a projection of one of our customary feelings into the world of nature. Since we make things, then there must be agents, external to us, who do likewise. And causal explanation is the discovery of such agents.

When we come upon them, they turn into forces, affinities, powers of attraction and repulsion, principles, or their embodiments in various *things*. We need not go to the length of Molière's physician; we need not say that aspirin reduces a fever because it is a febrifuge. But we will say that the aspirin is the cause of the drop in our temperature. This conclusion is based on the contrary to fact proposition that if we had not taken the aspirin, our temperature would not have dropped. The aspirin becomes an external agent introduced into a series of events. After the introduction of the external agent, the series of events changes from its normal course. Now even the earliest Greek physicians knew that sometimes morbidity disappeared without medication. An illness, whatever its name, might develop according to a regular curve and then subside. But so accustomed were they to the use of the causal

<hr/>

[9] This is a commonplace, but should references be wanted, see *Process and Reality*, N.Y., 1929, pp. 125, 177, 184 and especially 361, where we find the words, "A simple physical feeling is an act of causation." Cf. Victor Lowe's presentation of the matter—in language easier to understand than Whitehead's—in his essay, "Whitehead's Philosophy of Science," in *Whitehead and the Modern World*, Boston, 1950, p. 19.

concept of agents, that they invented the term, the *vis mediatrix naturae,* the curative power of nature, to serve as a cause. At the same time the Hippocratic Corpus contains a celebrated number of case-histories in which the course of disease is related in some detail.[10] And we see in these case-histories the establishment of the normal development of a disease, what occurs even when no medication is used. They are beautiful examples of the recognition that without such norms no modifications in the course of events are discoverable. They establish the rule which the physician hopes to break. The diseases are of course themselves a break in the normal course of events, and when one is trying to establish the cause of the disease, one must discover another agent which caused the patient to swerve from the path of health. To take but one example, if the theory were held that health is a balance of the humors, then some account must first be given of how the balance was upset. A balance, however, could be upset only by a superfluity or deficiency of one of the factors which were originally in balance. Consequently the physician could either supply the deficiency or remove the superfluity. But since one could not in those days introduce into the bodies of patients such things as blood, the two biles, and phlegm, one could at least purge the patient of his superfluities. Bleeding, expectorants, sweatings, coolings, could do the trick, and all the physician had to know was when to stop—not in itself the easiest task. The causal agent could be either the physician or the drug.

But now the question arose—logically if not historically—of why some things were effective causes and others not. We then find speculations on causation which are of great interest since they involve general principles which illuminate the whole principle of causal efficacy. Most of the Ancients seemed to hold that only similar things could stand in the causal relation.[11] In medicine this was phrased in the famous dictum, *Similia similibus*

---

10 See among other works in the *Corpus, Epidemics.*

11 According to Theophrastus, this was extended even to epistemology. See the distinction between the likeness-school and the unlikeness-school in the opening of the *De sensu.*

curantur, a kind of rudimentary homeopathy. We find the same idea in folk-medicine, especially in such proverbial wisdom as using a hair of the dog which bit you to cure dogbites. But the idea is more sophisticated than that and eventually emerges as the principle of which Lucretius made so much, the principle *ex nihilo nihil.* We all remember his verses in the *De rerum natura* (I, 149-50)

> Principium cuius hinc nobis exordia sumet,
> nullam rem e nilo gigni diuinitus umquam.

The target of this couplet is to be sure divine intervention and behind it, as the earlier lines in praise of Epicurus show (I, 62 ff.), lay the dogma of the uniformity of natural law, law which limited the power of the gods. Epicurus, says Lucretius, showed mankind

> quid possit oriri,
> quid nequeat, finita potestas denique cuique
> quanam sit ratione atque alte terminus haerens.

The principle *ex nihilo* meant two things (1) that which the nineteenth century called the reign of natural law; (2) the possibility of discovering in antecedent conditions that *out of which* the effects arose. The two principles were confused and, though the second was possible only if the first was sound, the first might be sound without the second's being possible. For it all depended on how literally one took the preposition *ex.* Oddly enough, instead of its becoming more obviously metaphorical, it became more literal, and the general drive was to show how effects literally pre-existed in their causes. This drive was what Meyerson called identification, and, as he showed in detail, it could never be complete.

As far as the uniformity of nature is concerned, to invoke it either as an explanatory principle or as a justification of universal causality would be equally unsound. Its use as an explanatory principle is a *petitio principii,* for to say that C is the cause of E in the sense that all C's always cause E's on the ground that Nature always acts uniformly, is clearly to assume what one is trying to prove. Empirically, it is true, one is limited to particular propositions, and, if one so desires, one can go on collecting a number of them and thus extend their significance to universality. But it is no news that a complete induction is impossible in most cases; that when one is possible, there is no need to invoke the principle of the uniformity of nature; and that when one is not possible, one might just as well hold that until a case in which C does not cause an E to appear is brought forward; the generalization will hold. In other words, such generalizations can be considered as tentative hypotheses. Moreover, the methodological problem is to so purify situations that one has something approaching *C-hood* and *E-hood*; for otherwise one has a case or an example or a specimen of nothing but itself. But *C-hood* and *E-hood* are analogous to Platonic ideas, or, if one prefer, class-concepts, and whatever conclusions one draws from their relations, will hold true of the abstraction and not necessarily of the concrete cases or examples. One need not deny that there is a high degree of uniformity in laboratory results to make this assertion. But one should notice that the experiments are set in order to obtain uniformity, for otherwise only particular or historical propositions could be made.

To speak of universal causality is also misleading, except in the sense that causal statements are always universal. One cannot discover the cause of a particular event except insofar as it is a fair sample of a class of events. This is the justification of the French proverb which says that there are no diseases, there are only sick people. This should be obvious, but apparently, if one may judge from current discussions, it is not. No scientist ever denies that his laws are true, other things being equal, or under laboratory conditions. But the things which have to be equal are precisely those things which occur in history as distinguished from logic. No physicist can predict what actually happens, any more than a statistician can predict individual histories. Consequently the notion of a first cause of everything, or a cause of the universe as a whole, is nonsense, unless the word "cause" is used in some peculiar sense. The establishment or discovery of causes requires repetition, and whatever else a cause is, it must be something after whose appearance the effect follows. But events unique in kind cannot be repeated. It is perhaps for this reason that when one invokes the principle *ex nihilo nihil,* one is driven to relegating those aspects of the effect which cannot be discovered as having pre-existed in the supposed cause to the realm of appearance, thus reducing both cause and effect to permanent substrata which turn out to be identical in kind: in mass, weight, amount of energy present. But this technique too evades the issue. For sometimes, as in chemical reactions, causes are set to work to produce effects which are wanted expressly because they do not pre-exist in their causes. It would be tedious and fortunately unnecessary to point out again and again how chemical compounds have characteristics which are not those of their elements. But the epistemological lesson of their appearance is clear: they arise *ex nihilo.* We know what preceding conditions are required to obtain them, but that is far from saying that they either *are* those conditions or exist *in* those conditions. Some such characteristics are notoriously the secondary qualities, which are secondary simply because they cannot be traced to their causes. But the fact that they are secondary or even the fact that they are subjective does not entail their non-existence. If material causes lacking them cause them to appear, the principle *ex nihilo* has to be seriously amended.

To take another example of what I am driving at, though the law of the Parallelogram of Forces states a geometric sum of two directions, the resulting direction obviously does not pre-exist in either direction singly; to say that northwest is the sum of west and north may make sense, but it does not make sense to say that it pre-existed in either of these two points of the compass. Any vectorial statement will be as good an example, though there would probably always be a tendency to mistake an equation for a statement of identification. And here as elsewhere by stripping the phenomena of what differentiates them, one can usually find something permanent "underlying" the change in question.

Sometimes the difficulty is avoided by the doctrine of potentiality, another doctrine which the Occident owes to Aristotle. But even in the originator of the doctrine, a potentiality was only a possibility. He asserts himself, in contradiction to Plato, that all possibilities are not realized, thus rejecting the Principle of Plenitude.[12] The potential was sometimes described as if it were the germ in a seed, sometimes as if it were the power (δύναμις) of a drug, but in every case that which is potential in anything can only be determined after it has become actualized. No one by just contemplating an egg or reflecting upon the meaning of ovality—if the neologism is permissible—can learn what is potentially in it. We have to have learned that processes of a certain type always or on the whole develop in a certain fixed manner. To say that a hen's egg is potentially a chicken might mean simply that if it is fertile and if it remains at a given temperature for twenty-one days, it will hatch into a chicken. It does not mean that a real chicken is discoverable in the egg. The closest which anyone came to saying that was the preformationists, who did believe that everything found in the adult animal or plant was actually folded up within the germ and that the process of growth was simply an unfolding. But they too must have known that an unfolded germ was at least bigger than the germ itself, occupied more space, weighed more, ran about and pecked—when it was a question of chickens—and in short manifested hundreds of traits which the germ did not manifest. So today when a geneticist points out that all adult traits are in the genes, he does not mean that a high powered microscope would actually find down, bill, spine, intestines, heart, and so on, in the packets of chemicals. In fact, the main reason why the doctrine of potentiality was needed was because so many discoverable characteristics were not to be found in the germs of things but developed later. It was a verbal invention made to preserve the literal meaning of *ex nihilo*. Yet as Meyerson's works have shown, the search for permanent substances which could be found in both cause and effect, which could be identified, which could be passed on from one term of the equation to the other, persisted.

The principle moreover was used in provinces well beyond that of natural science. In logic, in metaphysics, and in epistemology it flourished and brought about some of the most interesting argu-

---

12 See *Metaphysics*, Beta, Ch. 6, 1003 a, 2.

ments which Western philosophers have indulged in. Thus the conclusion of a syllogism was seen to be potentially in the premises, just as a whole system of geometry was sometimes said to be in the axioms, definitions, and postulates. The metaphors used to make syllogistic reasoning intelligible play upon the figure of speech so often that they become wearisome to the historian of philosophy. Nothing must be in the conclusion which was not previously in the premises, it was said, though opponents of the syllogism pointed out that, if this were so, then every syllogism would be a *petitio principii*.[13] But it could be only in a figurative sense that the conclusion to even a syllogism in *Barbara* is in the premises. If it were, then one might conclude that in the argument, A is greater than B, B is greater than C, therefore A is greater than C, that the "size" of C is literally in A and B.[14] But no one would be so stupid as to assert any such doctrine, though many might assert that it was in both A and B composed in some way or other. All that one has before one is the undeniable fact that if the premises are true, then the conclusion follows. If one takes an aspirin tablet, then one's fever will drop. But the drop in temperature is neither in the aspirin nor in the patient until he has taken the aspirin. By the seventeenth century Leibniz had begun to argue that unless all logical arguments were tautological, illicit conclusions would be drawn from them, an argument taken up again by D'Alembert in the *Discours Préliminaire* in the *Encyclopedia*. And we now know from the work of some of our contemporary logicians how the same idea has been revived. The desire here, however, seems to be that of reducing formal reasoning to Poincaré's "cascade of equations." And when genuine equations are utilized, it is clear that at least the meaning of them all is identical, however different the symbols in which an identical meaning is expressed.

It is foolhardy for one who is neither a logician nor a mathe-

---

[13] See W. D. Ross's introduction to his edition with commentary of the *Prior and Posterior Analytics*, p. 38. According to Ross, the first of the Ancients to attack the syllogism on this ground was Sextus Empiricus.

[14] It is of no importance that my example is not a syllogism.

matician to discuss mathematical problems. But there may be some value, should any competent person read these words, to point out the difficulty in identity of meaning as it appears to a philosopher. Proof by substitution we all know is a valuable device and we have all used it profitably since adolescence. But if the right-hand side of an equation means no more than the left-hand side, one cannot help wondering what new information has been acquired by writing it down. No one doubts that the square of the sum of two numbers is equal to the square of the first plus twice the product of the two plus the square of the second. No one doubts furthermore that, if there is any reason to do so, one may substitute the shorter statement for the longer or the longer for the shorter wherever they occur. Similarly in Kant's famous equation, 7 plus 5 equals 12. If these equations are symbols for operations, and not simply definitions, then obviously something new has been learned. But if they are simply definitions, then all that has been learned is a tautology. We have here, it would seem, a telling illustration of the difference between history and eternity. On the level of history we shall use these formulas to perform certain acts; on the level of eternity, they simply stand there. But on the former level the conclusion is not in, but follows from, the premises. On the latter there is no such thing as *following* since all is a *totum simul*. The mathematizing of knowledge is the elimination of history and consequently the elimination of causality, if in all instances of causality there must be a temporal sequence.

In metaphysics the principle *ex nihilo* was used in so many ways that one has an embarrassment of choices. One of the most interesting is the search for some sort of identity between God and Creation or some evasion of that identity. If God is really the primordial cause of the universe, creating it out of nothing, then there ought to be some likeness between Him and His works, for otherwise there would be no more reason to believe He made it than that He did not. (One could in spite of lack of reason believe it on faith or through private or common revelation.) Just as man was made in the image and likeness of God, so must the universe have been made, though the similarity might well be dimmer in the latter case. For though the principle *ex nihilo* says that nothing must be in the effect that was not previously in the cause, it does not say that everything in the cause must also be found in the effect. This in spite of the transformation of the principle in natural science. We find St. Bonaventura insisting that the created world is a reflection of God's being in the sense that, for instance, the order and beauty of the universe reproduce the order and beauty of its Creator. In an earlier thinker, Erigena, this argument is developed to the point that the distinction between God and Creation is purely verbal. Nature as creating and non-created, as creating and created, as non-creating and created, and non-creating and non-created, all turn out to be fused into one being, that is, God. This was indistinguishable from pantheism and therefore unacceptable to the Church. Moreover, one of its implications was the absolute determination of man's will, condemned as coming from John Scotus at the Council of Valence (855).[15] It was a delicate question of how much of God's being and nature could be found in His works, for the Church had to maintain both the absolute perfection of God and the goodness of His Creation, while at the same time keeping the transcendance of the Creator unimpaired. Natural theology, though insufficient for religious purposes, nevertheless was useful, and natural theology was based on God's manifestation of His goodness and power in Creation. There must therefore be clear traces *(vestigia)* of God's hand in the universe, but somehow or other—never satisfactorily explained—the traces must not be so clear that faith would be rendered superfluous. Creation itself was of course *ex nihilo;* in that respect it differed from fabrication or composition or production. But nevertheless the eternal Creator was also the First Cause, and when metaphysicians began to speculate about His relations to His effects, they were tempted—and few resisted the temptation—to find more and more of God in Creation until the point at which they

---

[15] The text of this condemnation deserves the closest study by philosophers. It can be conveniently found in Denzinger's *Enchiridion*, nos. 320 ff.

stopped before identifying the two was fixed, it would seem, solely by caution.

The use of the hierarchical metaphor—which will be discussed at greater length later—was a great help in solving this problem, for as one went down the ladder of existence and goodness, one retained some of the qualities which were on the upper levels but not all. The notion of degrees of reality, vague though it was, need not be examined here; suffice it to say that it has always appealed to some metaphysicians as an escape from the many puzzles which their presuppositions gave rise to. In Plotinus, whose God was not a Creator, the scale of being descended into complete Non-Being and rose again to the *ens perfectissimum,* the One. But no Christian could accept such a solution wholeheartedly, for he could not believe the material world to be absolutely unreal, absolutely ugly, and absolutely bad. Otherwise how could the heavens declare the glory of God and the firmament show His handiwork? There were some Platonizing Christians, like St. Augustine, who could identify evil with the absence of reality, but they had to attribute to this absent reality so much vigor that it might just as well have been present.[16] But not even St. Augustine, after his Manichean period, maintained that the material world was unreal and evil. In fact, St. Isidore of Seville quotes St. Augustine in speaking of the beauty of the human body as saying; "In corpore nostro quaedam tantum utilitatis causa facta sunt ut viscera. Quaedam, et utilitatis et decoris, ut mamillae in viris et in utroque sexu umbilicus. Quaedam discretionis, ut in viris genitalia, barba promissa, pectus amplum; in mulieribus leves genae, et angustum pectus, ad concipiendos autem et portandos fetus renes et latera dilatata."[17] But almost all mediaeval philosophers who survive follow Boethius in echoing the speech of Diotima, mounting the scale of beauty from that of corporeal

---

[16] Students of Thomism will recall that St. Thomas also sees evil as the lack of reality. For a short account of the problem of evil in St. Thomas, see Etienne Gilson, *The Christian Philosophy of St. Thomas Aquinas,* pp. 155 ff.

[17] *Etymologies,* XI, 24.

beings to the Absolute Beauty which, in their case, is God's. As Boethius says, addressing the Creator,

> Tu cuncta superno
> ducis ab exemplo, pulchrum pulcherrimus ipse
> mundum mente gerens, similique in imagine formans
> perfectasque iubens perfectum absolvere partes.[18]

But the beauty of Creation as a reflection of God's beauty is a commonplace of the Middle Ages, and it is unnecessary to cite a variety of texts to prove this.[19]

But the metaphor of degrees of power, as well as that of reflection, was not entirely satisfactory even in the Middle Ages. For if this world is to any extent less perfect than its Maker, to that extent it might appear to be unworthy of Him. The Christian world could not accept the doctrine of emanation—though the word was used—which might have remedied matters in that it was one of its cardinal principles that the creator is always better than the creature. If the creature was worse than the creator, some explanation was demanded for that lack of goodness and, as in Leibniz, the most one could say was that at least it was as good as possible. To attribute the loss of perfection to the influence of matter would not do, for an Omnipotent Deity might have been expected to overcome the limitations of the material world, even if terrestrial artisans could not do so. In all Christian writers the existence of evil remains mysterious, if not a Mystery, and the general tendency was to look upon the bright side of the picture rather than upon the dark. But for our purposes it is the dark which is the more important, for we have to inquire how the power or the goodness or any other property of a cause can be lost when one also asserts that the cause and effect must be equal.

In physical science the problem was more easily solved by such principles as that of the conservation of energy. The intellectual

---

[18] *Consolation of Philosophy*, III, met. 9.

[19] Moreover it has been thoroughly explored along with other questions concerning mediaeval aesthetics in the three volume work of Edgar de Bruyne; *Etudes d'Esthétique médiévale*, Bruges, 1946.

equivalent for causal power was energy and when investigations into change were pushed to their limit, it always turned out that all change was a change in motion. As early as Bacon even such apparently "subjective" phenomena as heat were guessed to be modes of motion, and we know how successful the kinetic theory of heat became. Motion could be measured and its course plotted in time and space; it could be found to occur at different rates; but best of all, it could be interpreted as a force transferred from one moving body to another. If one such body collided with another, it could be maintained that it passed its motion over to the other, and by setting up closed systems, one could infer that no motion nor energy was ever lost. The third law of motion in particular was useful in preserving the causal postulate—namely that there was nothing in the effect which was not previously in the cause—for if action and reaction were equal and if they could be measured in terms of identifiable motions, we could see that there was nothing after the collision which did not exist before the collision. The changes in direction could be predicted on the basis of the law of the Parallelogram of Forces. In this field of investigation the causal postulate could be applied with a certain rigor.

In Spinoza the postulate is stated overtly and results in his psychophysical parallelism. For as Höffding has pointed out in his *History of Modern Philosophy* (I, 304 ff), there was no distinction made by Spinoza between cause and ground, and even the temporal sequence between cause and effect disappeared as he formulated the relationship between the two. One must be able to deduce the existence of the effect from that of the cause, and consequently he was more interested in what was involved in certain concepts than in the supposed objective "natures" of things. Thus he lays it down as an axiom (I, Axiom IV) that "the knowledge of an effect depends upon the knowledge of [its] cause and involves the same," following this by Axiom V, "Whatsoever have nothing in common between them cannot be understood through each other, or the concept of the one does not involve the concept of the other."[20] It follows then that since matter has no modes which are those of mind and mind has none that are those of matter, matter being determined exclusively by extension and mind by thinking, there is no way of deducing the existence of one from that of the other and for that reason alone one cannot be the cause of the other. In fact, when Spinoza argues in this fashion it looks as if his very conception of deduction were the drawing out of a concept consequences which were already in it, so that the parallel between deduction and causality becomes exact. The involvement of which he speaks is the possession of a trait which is common, and that trait does not change in time. The principle *ex nihilo* applies both to the mental and to the material worlds. As in preformationism the adult animal had to be already in its germ; so here the last lemma of a deductive system had to be implicit in the premises of the system, and all motion had to be somehow or other in the first moving cause.

It was in vain that Malebranche in the seventeenth century pointed out that the very concept of a transfer of energy was unviable. Malebranche was a metaphysician, and the people utilizing the concept were scientists. By his time the split between the natural and the moral philosophers was beginning to make itself felt like the first intimations of a rupture in conjugal felicity. The scientists went their way without too much regard for the opinions of philosophers, and there can have been no great number who changed their mode of explanation because of the criticism of Malebranche. For that matter Hume himself had little influence until the eighties of the last century when Mach published his *Beitraege zur Analyse der Empfindungen*. Scientists when they felt philosophical might say with some pride that they described and left explanation to the metaphysicians, making a distinction between what they—fatuously—called the *how* and the *why*. In reality they utilized causation just as their predecessors had, and

---

[20] In Latin these two axioms run respectively, "Effectus cognitio a cognitione causae dependet, et eandem involvit;" and, "Quae nihil commune cum se invicem habent, etiam per se invicem intelligi non possunt, sive conceptus unius alterius conceptum non involvit." I have translated *involvit* as *involves* rather than *implies* because of the restricted meaning of *imply* in contemporary logic.

even today when they can talk in causal terms they do. It is notorious that even so great a figure as Einstein felt uncomfortable when he was confronted with scientific situations into which causality did not seem to fit. But insofar as causality is reduced to an equation, whether between forces or masses or anything else, that which is equal is never on the level of perception but is reached only after intellectual manipulation, either mathematical or logical. Could one perceive the equality without such manipulation, no question of causation could arise. For if our interpretation of what is a problem is correct, then the question of what caused a given effect would arise only when a different effect was expected. And that would presuppose a series of events which suddenly swerved from its anticipated course. No one would raise the question of why sugar tastes sweet until he discovered that the taste buds are located in various places and that the stimulation of certain taste buds will produce the taste of sweetness. But when he learns that the four elementary tastes can be stimulated in four different regions of the palate, he no longer asks why each region produces its peculiar taste. Is he then to say that those which produce sweetness are the cause of sweetness? They are no more its cause than the material which stimulates them. The search for an explanation here will be the search for the kinds of things which will be effective in stimulating the taste buds, and if the stimulation turns out to be purely mechanical, then the causal equation will be phrased in mechanical terms. But at that point we reach a level well "below" that of tasting. We taste sweetness, not stimulation. From the perceptual level all that we can say is that when sugar is placed on a certain area of the gustatory surface, it will taste sweet.

Thus causal explanation varies with the method which we use to determine it. It is no less sound to say that coffee tastes sweet because sugar has been dissolved in it than to say it tastes sweet because certain taste buds have been stimulated. When we talk in terms of coffee and sugar, we are establishing a constant relation between two perceptual objects. When we talk in terms of taste buds and mechanical stimulation, both the coffee and the sugar become irrelevant. For by that time we have simplified our gustatory experiences by the discovery of the four elementary tastes: sweet, sour, salt, and bitter, and have explained the additional factors, those which subdivide the four, by means of odor. But the problem of how taste is stimulated—or produced if one prefer—is different from the problem of what sugar tastes like or what coffee plus sugar tastes like. And to maintain that the coffee plus the sugar is not "really" sweet can mean nothing more than if one is asking a different question, one will get a different answer. Many a puzzle might be eliminated if this were clearly seen. Thus we sometimes explain an event by the absence of something, as when we say that the coffee is bitter because there is no sugar in it. Philosophers with sophistic inclinations might well ask how non-being could cause anything. Like all such sentences, this one too can be translated into other terms. "Coffee without sugar is bitter," or "Coffee is bitter," will do as well as, "The absence of sugar makes coffee bitter." Note that no one would say, "The absence of sugar makes beer bitter," for what we say is determined by custom, and we remark on the absence only of that whose presence we are accustomed to. If now we go on to ask why sugar imparts its sweetness to the coffee, we make an existential separation between the sugar and one of its qualities. This is as if one were arguing that the sweetness which was "in" the sugar was transmitted to the coffee, much as Aristotle speaks about the passage of heat from one body to another.[21] But the theory of floating qualities with its affinity to that of sensible species, is too full of difficulties to be of much use except as a figure of speech. Yet it is based upon the same postulate as that from which the identity of cause and effect is based.

It cannot have failed to be observed that the postulate of an identity between cause and effect nullifies any qualitative change. What remains in the equation is precisely everything which does not change except in position. The energy, for instance, which

---

[21] See *Metaphysics,* 1034 a, 26.

was here is now there; the mass which was here is now there. The origin of this technique may well be that passage in Aristotle's *Metaphysics* (Zeta, 7, 1032 b, 30 f), where he says, "It is impossible that anything should be produced if there were nothing existing before. Obviously then some part of the result will pre-exist of necessity; for the matter is a part; for this is present in the process and it is this which becomes something" (Ross's translation). The concept of matter underwent profound changes after the time of Aristotle, to be sure, but the compulsion to find a stable something which could suffer the changes without itself changing remained. Hence the very aspects of experience which gave rise to the problem are eliminated in the answer. Bacon, for instance, in his Table of Essences and Presence lists the many occasions on which one has the sensation of heat, but when he comes to explain the occurrence of heat, we are left with motion and no sensations at all. He is not so much interested in why moving particles should feel warm as he is in what is always present when we have that sensation and whether, when it is absent, we have it or not. He thus finds something common to a great variety of experiences and checks his conclusion by noting that in its absence the experiences are also absent. But he has not established an equation between motion and a perception. Nor did he attempt to. But having made his correlation between that which is on the perceptual level and a something which is also always present though not perceived, he could then proceed to investigate the modes of the latter to his heart's content. His heart, it is worth noting, was easily contented, and he carried the investigations no further.

When we arrive at problems in which identities between causes and effects cannot be set up, we have either to elaborate a new technique of explanation or to decide that no answer can be given to the question. That is, we have finally reached the facts. There are cases, vectorial cases as we have suggested above, in which no such identity can be found and the metaphor of the result coming out of the cause is inapplicable. The fact that a direction can be predicted or, in reverse, that given a direction one can calculate how it was reached, does not allow us to infer that the product pre-existed in the multiplicand and multiplier. We can state the conditions essential for the development of a seed into a plant, but we cannot find any identity between the habit of a plant and those conditions. If then causation always operates on the principle *ex nihilo nihil*, we must conclude that there are some problems to which no causal answers can be given. Nothing in this statement means that we cannot give the sufficient and necessary conditions for producing the kind of effect we are interested in. But the *ex* becomes purely figurative. The philosopher of science as well as the epistemologist is faced with the necessity of making a decision, the decision of either extending the notion of causality to include changes in which identities cannot be discovered or admitting that some events are not caused.

One of the great achievements of those who utilized causal explanation was the suppression of the human equation. Even when it was obvious that a problem—such as that of the nature of heat—arose out of human feelings, an answer was sought which could eliminate all such feelings. When heat was thought to be a fluid substance, passing from one body to another, it was also thought to be a substance isolable from our perception of it. The primitive evidence that something was warm was, it cannot be denied, our thermal sensations. But as early as Aristotle the hot was believed to perform its various functions independently of those sensations. In this way certain events could be thought of as existing well beyond human experience. In fact, one of the lessons of the history of the sciences is found in the extrapolation into the extra-human world of equivalents for our own feelings. The point has now been reached when in a great many fields the observer may be left out altogether, though it is interesting to notice that in quantum theory the observer has been reintroduced. If he is left out of macroscopic physics, it is by convention. The personal equation is not of enough importance to count. But as soon as very fine measurements are wanted, the observer is always brought back on the stage. Of course, he is really never absent, but just as in conversation several people can understand each other by neglecting each person's particular accent, intonation, pronunciation, so in scientific investigations the routine of research may cancel out personal differences.

In the second place, causal explanation as we have understood it, created the idea of a world which was non-human not merely in the sense that it extended beyond the limits of experience, but in the sense that laws could be formulated about it which were not the laws of human experience. The Laws of Motion as stated by Newton are descriptive of nothing which occurs in experience. And that is no doubt why they could be formulated mathematically.

CHAPTER VI

EXPLANATION—BY THE FULFILLMENT
OF PURPOSES

Though teleological explanation as a general scientific technique would appear to be outmoded, we still revert to it when explaining some conscious behavior. For when we ask a person why he did or did not do something of interest, we mean by "why" what was his purpose. Even though it may turn out to be true that all purposes can be correlated with physiological states which themselves demand causal explanation, the existence of purposes is not denied on that ground alone. Their existence is at least as well attested as that of sensory data, and it ill behooves a philosopher who prides himself on his empiricism to deny any efficacy to purposes, ends, final causes, goals, or whatever other name they go by. The fact that one can pursue a phenomenon analytically to the point where it is no longer recognizable does not entail its unreality before analysis. To use a familiar example, we do not rightly say that because table salt is a compound of a poisonous green gas and a gray metal that bursts into flame when dropped in water, it is not a white crystal which is neither poisonous nor inflammable in water. But similarly when a man doggedly follows a course of action in order to achieve a certain goal, it may well be that he does so because of the peculiar functioning of his endocrine glands or even because of his suppressed incestuous love for his mother. But that still does not mean that on the conscious level the goal which he is seeking does not orient his conduct quite as efficaciously as his glands or his repressed desires. We put salt on our food because of its taste, not because of its chemical composition nor our biochemical need of it. If this is denied, then the adversary should explain why people ignorant of both chemistry and dietetics, to say nothing of the animals, want salt and eat it. Again, one can do nothing whatsoever without using the body, unless Aristotle was right in believing that thinking went on without organic instruments. But there is a context in which the body does not have to be considered when we are discussing human behavior. We may grant that a man could not solve a mathematical problem if he had no body or were dead. But he solves the problem without introducing into his solution any mention of his body. Even if he is at the stage of counting on his fingers when doing additions, the length of his fingers, their agility, the color of his skin, the prominence of his knuckles, and so on, can all be discounted.

It would, to be sure, be misleading to say that a man's aims were a cause in the sense that his glandular structure—or whatever it might turn out to be—is a cause. The physiologist who is studying the endocrine glands can neglect the purposes of people when he does so and usually does neglect them. If a cause is to be identified with the conditions in the absence of which an event will not occur and in the presence of which it will—other things being equal—then it is necessary to make a sharp distinction between two sets of conditions. We can call the one the set of causes and the other the set of reasons. Of the former a man may be and often is unaware. Of the latter he must be aware when they exist. One can have reasons which are not causes and causes which are not reasons. This is illustrated by reasons which cannot be carried out, and they are plentiful enough. We often struggle to move towards a goal which is unattainable and which we know is unattainable. We comfort ourselves with the thought that any progress towards it is that much to the good. We can state the goal in words and we can sacrifice pleasures in our struggle; we can even go without biological necessities in the hope that we shall have furthered our purpose. We need no consciousness of why we behave in this way, if we mean by "why" the unconscious causes of our behavior both psychic and somatic. Investigations of the two realms are carried on in different fashions, but all one has to do to discover why a man acts as he does when one wants his reasons, is to ask him. These reasons may be determined by that very complicated system of events which is resident in the human psychophysical organism, but we are not talking about what determines their appearance. We are talking about *them*. A painter may have his own reasons for depicting a scene in a certain way, and it is undoubtedly true that he would not have those reasons if he were a different person. But to deny the efficacy of his reasons, is like denying that we often recognize things by their looks rather than by their chemical constitution. We are aware of the looks; we are not aware of the physiology of vision. Similarly some causes have to be unconscious if they are to be effective. If we knew enough about the causes of artistry, scientific endeavors, religious aspirations, we might well turn aside from them. For often what charms us in a program evaporates when we know more about its aetiology. But that simple fact is proof enough of the difference between the two things. The nucleus of the tradition that virtue is its own reward is in all probability the belief that one should think neither of the rewards of virtue nor of the causes which have placed virtues on so high a level, if one wants the Sage's palm. If there are true causes of a virtuous life which are not the reasons which a man believes in when he strives to be virtuous, then ethics can be discussed from two points of view—that of causes and that of reasons. Much traditional ethics and, I suspect, untraditional too, is in a state of conflict here, in that the ethicist on the one hand urges his disciples to be rational, to be aware of the reasons for their conduct, and at the same time to seek the final good in loyal and unquestioning devotion. When a man insists that he will be loyal to his friends regardless of the world's opinion of him, the cause of his behavior may be his dependence on them for support, his need for admiration, his frustrated sexuality, his lack of imagination, his childish need for "belonging." But nevertheless his purpose may well be loyalty, and he will maintain it through thick and thin, and any evidence of disloyalty in his conduct will eat into him as a worm into an apple.[1]

There are obvious differences between causes and purposes which we must now try to clarify. The most familiar is that resident in the temporal sequence of events. Causes are held to be anterior to their effects, whereas purposes are posterior. It would be more accurate to say that a purpose must be before one as a plan of action if it is to be taken seriously, but that it is not achieved until the end of the action is attained. The purpose as an idea or plan of action or program now before one acts like a cause in that it may be assumed that were it not before one the action would not be carried out. But unlike a cause, it may operate through a variety of means to achieve its end. Like a cause also, it may not eventuate in its end at all but wither away in despair. Regardless of that, we recognize our ability to devise several ways of meeting our goals when one ends in frustration, and, as far as we know, causes do not do this. A billiard ball propelled from behind may be said to be seeking the direction in which it is moving, should such a phrase give anyone satisfaction. But if it were blocked, its resultant path would be calculable according to the law of the Parallelogram of Forces. A man trying to move from point to point and finding himself blocked, may look about for another path, jump over the obstacle, or remove it. Military tactics are a good illustration of this. The commander is given an objective but is also given the freedom of planning how to attain it. It is assumed that within his range of operations several courses of behavior are open. He then prepares his plan but, if he is normally intelligent, he knows that the plan must not be so rigid that it cannot be modified as the enemy counter-attacks. Only purposes the means of attaining which are variable would be accepted as genuine purposes, for if

---

[1] Cf. Bruner, Goodnow, and Austin; *A Study of Thinking*, p. 79. "Psychology has been celebrating the role of 'emotional factors' and 'unconscious drives' in behavior for so long now that man's capacity for rational coping with his world has come to seem like some residual capacity that shows its head only when the irrational lets up. . . Man is not a logic machine, but he is certainly capable of making decisions and gathering information in a manner that reflects better on his learning capacity than we have been as yet ready to grant."

we stubbornly moved about in a certain direction regardless of circumstances, and stopped when opposed, we might be engaged in rudimentary purposiveness, but would be approaching the mechanical. In causal events we demand not only that a definite effect be produced but that the way in which it is produced be always as closely identical as possible, the latter phrase being equivalent with "other things being equal." There are of course things which have to be equal also in purposive behavior. And frequently we accept these limiting conditions as part of the game. An artist has to cope with his materials, just as a writer has to cope with words, and part of the game is meeting the challenge which they present. In ethical matters we are urged to achieve our ends regardless of the obstacles, and the man who fails to overcome them is usually condemned as a weakling. Hence though purposes may be frustrated and though their attainment does depend on material instruments and though success and failure vary both in relation to the goal and to the means chosen to reach it, nevertheless it is admitted that the regularity of purposive behavior is not so great as that of causal.

There is another important difference between causes and purposes which should be mentioned here, since it is part and parcel of teleological explanation. As we pointed out in our previous lecture, it is theoretically possible to express causal relations in equations. In fact that which cannot be absorbed into the causal equation is usually relegated to the world of appearance. But there is no possibility of equating a purpose and its accomplishment even though the intention is the imaginary anticipation of the end. I may now dream of writing a great epic, of composing a perfect fugue, of painting a fresco as marvelous as those of Piero della Francesca at Arezzo. But until these things are done, they remain nothing but dreams. We may speak of the incorporation or realization of our plans, and it is perhaps possible that their incorporation may be no more than the perfect embodiment of what we dreamed of doing. But the duality of intention and achievement is not only existential but also generic. The intention demands a means for its realization, some matter in the Aristo-

telian sense of that ambiguous term in which it can be made
actual, whereas the cause is already embedded in some material,
is in fact some material. Even when purposes are used to explain
events in which we have only analogical evidence for intentions,
as is the case in animal behavior, to say nothing of God and the
angels, they are always at the mercy of means. These means may
vary, as we have said, but they are necessary if the end is to be
reached. The fact that we can foresee the limitations of our means
does not weaken the argument. On the contrary, it strengthens
it, since it shows that purposes, unlike causes, cannot be self-
actualizable. In Aristotle where the purpose was potentially
present in the matter, a greater regularity in actualization was also
found. But upon investigation it turns out that all that is purposive
here is precisely the regularity of the course of events. Consequently a statement of purposive action to be complete must include the means by which the action is fulfilled, however diverse
these means may be. They differ from causal conditions in that
the latter are not instruments or tools which lie ready at hand
to be utilized. This is perhaps one of the reasons why the Hebraic
God had to have ways which are beyond understanding. His purposes were perforce unintelligible for the simple reason that He
was not only a creator but that He created *ex nihilo.* Even after
His world was made, no rational limits could be set upon the
achievement of His purposes. Miracles had to be possible lest
His utter sovereignty be conditioned. But in this situation He was
no more purposeful than causal, and His action was in essence
mysterious. That the creation followed immediately upon His
command was a necessary conclusion for there was nothing with
which He could work, no matter, no instruments. Indeed there
was nothing which He needed, as the Christian Platonists were
accustomed to say, and He could have had no intelligible reason
for creating the world at all.

The wishes of such a being are identical with their fulfillment,
so that we have here an important difference between purpose
in the human sense and in the divine. But there is another im-

portant difference. In what sense of the word could an omnipotent being have any purposes whatsoever? We make plans
not merely because the future is largely unknown but also because we know that it is a natural obstacle to the fulfillment of
our desires. A stone does not need plans since there is only one
thing that it can do. But a human being has to make plans for
he is not sure that he can do what he wants to do. Which means
that he has to prepare for success. But an omnipotent being is
like an impotent being: his actions flow out of his nature. We
do not make plans for our hearts to beat and our lungs to breathe;
nature takes care of that. The dream of omnipotence is an extension to be sure of our experience of relative impotence; we
can imagine situations in which we would have more power than
we now have. But as we grow more and more powerful, choice
is indifferent to our future and should we reach the point where
all desires were inevitably fulfilled, choice would be unnecessary.
But where there is no choice, there is no purpose. We can choose
to die, but we cannot choose to be born. We can plan our death
but not our birth. Surely these assertions will be accepted. And
so ought the assertion that if we know that a certain course of
action is forced upon us, whether by our own nature or by external forces, it is foolish to say that we have planned it that way.

In this respect, if in no other, the Demiurge of Plato's *Timaeus*,
though he became the model for many Christian theologians, is
the polar antithesis of the God of *Genesis*. The *Timaeus* is no
doubt familiar to anyone likely to read these lectures, but at the
risk of repeating the obvious, we shall examine for a moment
or two the passage in which the creation was described in that
dialogue. After invoking the help of the gods, it will be recalled, Timaeus raises the following question: What is that which
always is and has no beginning, and what is that which is always
being born and never is? (27 D). The distinction here is clearly
that between the timeless and the temporal. The first, he continues, is grasped by the intellect according to reason, and is always self-identical. The second is thought about by opinion

according to irrational sensation, being born and dying, and never really existing. This distinction is common to the Platonic dialogues which always equate real being with eternality and rationality and persisting self-identity. If then the Demiurge is timeless and unchanging and purely rational, the sensory temporal mutable world could not emerge from his being as an effect from a cause since there is no similarity between the two. Had Plato really been Moses speaking Greek, as Philo said, he might have made his Demiurge command the world to appear *ex nihilo*. But there was a variety of traditions which made such an outcome unlikely, if possible. The two main popular cosmogonies posited at the beginning of things either Chaos, a grand mixture of everything—not unlike Anaxagoras's mixture of the seeds—and the primordial being of Earth, Erebus, and Eros, Eros emerging from the egg of Night which floated on Chaos. As far as we know, there was no myth according to which the world appeared *ex nihilo*. There was no creation in the Biblical sense; there was production. Moreover, the duality between maker and that which was made appeared over and over again in Greek thought, in the distinction between the two forces and the elements of Empedocles, the *Nous* and the primordial mixture of Anaxagoras, form and matter in Aristotle. The possible exceptions to this were the philosophies of the Milesians. Change, as we have said before, always seemed to be envisioned as the action of one being upon another, as in the active and passive voices of the verb. Plato in the *Timaeus* is faithful to that manner of thinking, and his Demiurge has something to work with. Everything, he says (28 A), which comes into being is born of necessity from some cause, for it is impossible for anything to be born without a cause. The Demiurge then must be the cause of the world of becoming, but before making it, he must have a model, and that model must also be eternal and self-identical. The Demiurge is not identical with the eternal and self-identical archetype, nor does he create it. It is there before his mind and he strives to copy it. And it is interesting to observe that since he makes copies of this eternal model, it is "beautiful from necessity." Whereas, Timaeus continues, if he had fixed his eyes on the changing, that which comes into being, his work would not have been beautiful.

Timaeus's Demiurge then is purposive in that he wished to make the most beautiful world and took a model for it. His behavior, therefore, is intelligible and rational and not an affair of caprice or unguided will. The identity between the beautiful and the logical, the rational, the intelligible, is overtly stated (29 A). Thence it follows that all details of the cosmos can be explained as exemplifications of these characters. And purpose becomes the realization of the orderly, as the orderly becomes conformity to an eternal and rational pattern. Now even this is not quite the same thing as human purposiveness, for the Demiurge did not choose his plan in partial ignorance of its feasibility. He chose a plan which was harmonious with his own nature and one from which logical inferences could be drawn. Since the eternal model must be mathematical in kind, Timaeus proceeds to infer the reasons why even the details of the visible—the sensory—world are as they are. I say "infer" since the whole exposition of Timaeus's story is inference, not history. Thus (31 B) if something is to come into being, it must be corporeal, and if corporeal, visible and tangible, and if visible, it must be igneous, and if tangible, solid and terrene. Like all such reasoning, the general principles, such as that only the igneous can be visible, are ultimately reflections of experience; they are not self-evident axioms. But it is questionable whether any purely formal reasoning which neither reflects the structure of things as experienced nor contradicts it, is possible. Even the primitive ideas of formal logic, such as "either," and "and," and "not," reflect ordinary language. Once they are accepted as primitive, the logician can do all sorts of tricks with them which reflect nothing but his own fantasy. The general principles of the *Timaeus* are quite as logical as the first principles of any rational discipline can be, or at any rate Plato seems to use them as if they were. If I am right, then we have a special type of teleological explanation in this dialogue, a type in which purpose is guided by logic rather than desire, the only desire being that of conforming to logic. The eternal para-

digm furnishes the logical structure in accordance with which the
Demiurge operates. Though Timaeus is not made to distinguish
between the will and the reason of his Demiurge, we shall not
be distorting his thought to say that his reason is the guide to
his will.

Whether such a state of affairs is psychologically sound need
not concern us insofar as we are expounding Plato. But if we
are interested in justifying teleology as a type of explanation, it
must concern us. For purposive behavior, like causal, originates
in a projection of human psychology into the non-human universe
and if it turns out that, as in Schopenhauer and Freud, the reason
is always subordinated to the will, then a purely rational universe
will be one which is ultimately impossible. Bits of it might be
explicable in rational terms, as we were able to correlate strands
of existence with rational sequences. But the intellectualism of
both Plato and Aristotle, as well as that of St. Thomas Aquinas,
Descartes, and Spinoza, demands our ability to calculate what we
should do to achieve our ends and then to do it. Minds of that
type could not stop short of accomplishing their decisions. In
Spinoza (*Ethics*, II, 49, corr.) will and the intellect are one and
the same: *voluntas et intellectus unum et idem sunt.* They are one
and the same, since the will is concerned with affirming and denying, and the only thing which can be affirmed or denied is a
sentence. That propositions—or sentences—might be so forceful,
so clearly expressive of fact, that we should accept them as self-
evident and that their self-evidence might be simply their harmony with our primitive desires, however these might be identified, does not seem to have occurred to any member of the school.
Even the innate ideas of Descartes and the intuitive truths of
Spinoza might have been thought of as expressions of what we
might like to believe, what would reassure us of the validity of
our moral standards, what would be useful otherwise. But I find
no evidence that such notions even occurred as early as the
seventeenth century. These men were aware of the conflict between the passions and the reason but they also believed that
the reason could control the passions. Spinoza's denial of freedom,

or perhaps it would be better to say his equating of freedom with acting in accordance with our nature, follows directly from his identification between *voluntas* and *intellectus*. For however free a will may be if it is activated by appetite or desire, the reason is certainly not free from the chains of the laws of thought. The intellectualistic theory of action demands that we act rationally, and if we are able to, which no one seemed to doubt, then there was only one course of action possible.

Whatever the language employed, this doctrine gave us a cosmos in which universal laws are possible and which, if discovered, would be quite as binding as the causal laws of Democritus. The Principle of Plenitude, of which we have already spoken and whose subsequent history has been so thoroughly explored in *The Great Chain of Being,* is applied step by step by Plato when he sets forth the kinds of being which were made and it is itself the reason why the various kinds were made. It is a program for the Demiurge to fulfill. Thus after describing the genealogy of the gods, Plato goes on to have the Demiurge say to the gods (*Timaeus,* 41 B), "There still remain three kinds [*genera*] of mortals yet unborn. And while these are unborn the heaven will be unfinished. For it will not contain within itself all kinds of living things. But it must contain them if it is to be perfect enough." To make a perfect universe is the goal; and perfection can be attained only if all kinds of possibilities are realized. But the determination of what is possible is a matter of reasoning. The two main possibilities are named in the general terms, the Same and the Other, that is, that which is unchanging and always self-identical, and its antithesis, that which changes and is never self-identical. Time may be the moving image of eternity, but it is a distorted image. Plato—or at any rate the fictitious Timaeus—lays down as his pattern of reasoning the principles of affirmation and negation, and as soon as one concept is affirmed, its negation has to be considered. Thus if there is eternity, there must also be the non-eternal, and the non-eternal instead of having an unlimited connotation, is limited to connoting whatever is antithetical to eternality. The Other, thus, is not simply the Not-Same; it is that which under no stretch of the imagination can ever be the Same. Such a dichotomy gives the reason an ancillary guide to the Principle of Plenitude, a guide which is needed since before one can deduce the occurrence of all possibilities, one has to know in advance what the possibilities are. With those two principles in hand, even the more fantastic physiological details of the *Timaeus* become plausible. The dialectic of teleology demands certain preliminary conditions, which themselves are, to be sure, taken from the conditions of human success. One must have a plan; one must be able to realize the plan. The plan is timeless, neither here nor there. Its realization requires some means of individuation, and that means on the universal scale is called by Timaeus with some hesitation the Receptacle. It is analogous to Aristotle's substratum, without character in itself but capable of receiving characters. In the thirteenth century it became St. Thomas's *materia signata*.[2] Such details, however, are of no interest here; what is of interest is Plato's technique of discovering the prerequisites of purposive success. And that technique is properly called mathematical, or logical, since it operates by means of reasoning alone.

It might well be maintained that Plato was first confronted with the problem of the reality of time. Once permanence and eternality are accepted as criteria of the real, then temporal things would have to be jettisoned. But since Plato seems incapable of imagining events which reveal a pattern but do not conform to a previously formulated pattern, purpose for him became the striving to realize the perfection of the eternal ideal. This to his way of thinking was order and in the long run it was the only kind of order which he was willing to recognize. This order could be expressed in dialectical terms as a set of logical possibilities permitted by one's analytical method. In his case the method, as we have just said above, operated through the Law of Contradiction. This is illustrated throughout his works. The Same and the Other, the One and the Many, the eternally immutable and the tem-

---

[2] For the history of this term, see Roland-Gosselin's edition of St. Thomas's *De ente et essentia*, Bibliothèque Thomiste, VIII, Le Saulchoir, Kain, 1926.

porally changing, reason and sensation, knowledge and opinion are all familiar antitheses in the *Dialogues*. Once this pattern was developed, it became simply a question of introducing the means by which alone such order could be made manifest or concrete. Consequently the outcome of the *Timaeus*, as far as our special interests are concerned, is that purposive events are those which follow from the most general laws of the rational universe as distinguished from the sensible.

In Aristotle the situation is somewhat different. He does not assume teleology; he tries to prove it. In the famous passage of the *Physics* (II, 8; 198 b), he presents the case for natural teleology after making certain distinctions which are fundamental to his concept of Nature. First this passage shows that not everything which we might call a natural event was a work of Nature, so that in order to avoid ambiguity in English, we shall simply transliterate the Greek *Physis* where we are speaking of Nature in this context. *Physis* then is seen to be the whole order of the cosmos, working so to speak behind the scenes, pulling the strings of the marionettes which we see when we are not philosophers. Second, he distinguishes between acting for the sake of things (purposively) and working through necessity, a distinction which would not do for a man like Spinoza to whom necessity was logical necessity. "What then," asks Aristotle (198 b, 16), "prevents *Physis* from not acting for the sake of something or because it is better, but as Zeus rains not to make the grain grow, but from necessity? For what is drawn upward must cool off, and the cooled, turned to water, falls down. And this having taken place causes the grain to grow. And similarly if the grain rotted on the threshing floor, not to this end did the rain fall, that it might rot, but this simply happened." Why again should we not say that our teeth emerge from our gums because of necessity, with their special function of biting and grinding? Why should we not maintain that we bite and grind food as we do through necessity, as if, having no other way to chew, we chew as we must? In fact in this passage Aristotle poses as a sort of Proto-Darwinian, asking why we could not conclude, "Whenever things happen as if they had come about for the sake of something, some survive automatically because they have an appropriate constitution, whereas those which are not so constituted, have died out and will continue to do so, just as Empedocles says of the human-headed oxen?"

Such a view, he says, is impossible. And the reason, oddly enough, is that the works of *Physis* are invariable or almost so: "All the things which are in accordance with *Physis* either happen always in the same way or for the most part, but not so with chance or automatic things" (198 b, 35). The contrast here is obviously between the invariable and the occasional. The invariable follows *Physis* or what might be called the Order of Nature; the occasional is a matter of chance. But there are only two possibilities open: purposive or chance events. Hence if the acts of *Physis* are not chance events, they must be purposive. And one of the differentiae of purposive events is their invariance. To which category necessary events belong, he does not say in this passage, but that is just one of Aristotle's many oversights. One might imagine that something which happens always or for the most part must happen necessarily. But he does not draw this conclusion.[3] Necessity might characterize a peculiar event, such as frequent rain in summer or heat in winter, to use one of his examples of chance events. When it rains in the dry season, it is both a chance and a necessary event, a chance event in this context being one which is rare but quite explicable.

Not only are purposive events those which always happen, but they are also those in which there is an end. The word "end" here means an inevitable termination towards which each preceding step leads. Aristotle uses the example of housebuilding to illustrate his point. If a house, he says (199 a, 12), were made by *Physis,* it would be built in exactly the same way as it is built by man. Such processes are like mathematical progressions in that a direction is given as well as the steps which must be taken. In

---

[3] The whole matter is discussed at some length in my "A Basic Conflict in Aristotle's Philosophy," *American Journal of Philology,* Vol. LXIV, 2, April 1943, pp. 172 ff.

art the artist imitates *Physis,* and we can fill in the gaps in our knowledge of *Physis* by observing the processes of artistry. We know that the reason why the builder moves as he does, laying the foundations, raising the walls, putting in the beams and the roof, is because he is looking forward to a completed house. He is not operating in a random fashion. Consequently when events in the world about us always move in a given direction step by step and end at a certain point, we can conclude from what we know of art that *Physis* too is working towards an end. The best illustrations of natural teleology are to be found in the making of animal artefacts, where there is no question of art or deliberation or inquiry. As we observe the working of the animals in building nests and spider-webs and honeycombs, we notice that they too are always built in the same way and have a termination. Indeed, says Aristotle, the same is true of plants. Now *Physis* in such cases is both matter and form, and the form is the end, that for the sake of which the transformation takes place.

Aristotle's discussion in this passage is unambiguous. Purposiveness can be of two sorts: natural and artificial. In natural teleology one finds processes which constantly manifest a given pattern in time, a pattern which is growth from seed to maturity, or indeed any other process which is constant. In such processes the final cause is the essence. Artificial purposes do not always occur but may happen once in a while by chance. In them an accidental property becomes the final cause. It is natural for an acorn to turn into an oak; it is artificial for it to be eaten by a pig. Once this is grasped, one sees that such a slogan as, "Nature does nothing in vain," amounts to no more than the assertion that the natural scientist should look for those constant series of events as the laws of nature and give them a primary position in his system. As every reader of Aristotle knows, he recognizes the existence of chance events and also of failures and monstrosities. When he says, as he does in the Metaphysics (1076 a, 4), that things do not wish to be governed badly, he means, as his discussion of this axiom shows, that there must be one final cause or end for all events in the cosmos. That end becomes the Unmoved Mover which is equivalent to the cosmic order. Unfortunately the cosmic order is not a series of events with a given direction. It is not like growth from acorn to oak, but is rather an unchanging cycle of events of which the circular orbits of the planets are the paradigm. In the superlunary world there is only invariable repetition and no change from matter to form. Even if one could set down a formula for everything which happens in the cosmos, a formula which would hold good for the movement of the spheres, the motions of the elements, and for the growth of plants and animals, one would have no process of actualization for the world as a whole, but simply a static picture. The Platonic division between eternity and time would be revived, and purpose would be found, as it actually is found in Aristotle's examples, only in the temporal world. Teleology might be useful then in explaining vectorial changes, but as a universal principle of explanation it would be sterile.

Actually Aristotle's only attempt to apply teleology on a universal scale is in his vague assertion that the Unmoved Mover moves the world as the beloved moves the lover. This is the love that moves the sun and all the stars, but when one seeks a concrete example of it, one comes up against the prosaic fact that scientific laws are invariable. There is no cosmic process in Aristotle's universe, and all the Unmoved Mover stands for is a symbol of its inventor's faith in cosmic order. But when he is dealing with events this side of the moon, then teleology in the sense expounded above is of course his dominant principle. But there again, if a plant or animal is the whole process from seed to adult, to say that the seed grows because of its entelechy—the immanent form which is potentially in the matter—is to say nothing more than that seeds grow into plants of a given kind, though occasionally sports and failures occur. The emotional overtones of the theory are quite different, and the Peripatetics used the formulas of their master to different ends. As was seen at least as early as Bacon and ridiculed as late as Heine, it makes little difference whether one say that we have eyes in order to see or that we see because we have eyes. Teleology became a greater force in Occidental thought when man was made the center, if not the measure, of all things, and natural events were given a purpose determined by man's needs. At that point one could raise such questions as why there are poisonous insects and answer it seriously by saying that they exist to try man's stamina. So later it was possible to argue that fossils had been planted in the earth to tempt men not to believe in *Genesis*. Such purposes are intelligible because they are strict analogies to the only purposes which we know concretely, human purposes. It is not characteristic of human purposes to do everything in the same way. On the contrary, it is characteristic of human purposes that they be achieved in various ways, and we should be more likely to call a man whose behavior was as invariable as that of *Physis* in Aristotle, a machine whose mechanism would be completely frustrated once its operations were blocked. The introduction of human purposes into the cosmos as a whole, though adumbrated by the Stoics and Plotinus, was a contribution of those Christian thinkers who fused the Biblical God with Plato's Demiurge and the Unmoved Mover.[4]

But before touching on Christian theology, we should note in passing that Plotinus, who prided himself on being an interpreter of the Ancients (*Ennead* V, i, 8), amended Aristotle's cosmic picture so that there were two processes always going on, each of which was vectorial. I refer to the cosmic katabasis and anabasis. The emanations from the One formed a constant series down to matter, from which there arose a constant series in reverse back to the One. The two in combination had no more purpose, and obviously could not have, than the cosmic good government of Aristotle. But again within the whole one could plot two sets of events into which human behavior could be integrated and yet the pattern of which transcended human behavior. The Plotinian hierarchy was teleological in Aristotle's sense, and many of its details were reproduced by mediaeval Christian philosophers. But

---

[4] The profound differences between Plato's Demiurge and the Biblical God are clearly expounded in F. M. Cornford's *Plato's Cosmology*, London, 3d imp., 1952, pp. 35 ff.

it was far from being harmonious with one of the fundamental tenets of Christianity, the personality of God as Creator and Judge. But we shall reserve the Principle of Perfection for a subsequent lecture and turn now to Christian teleology.

Since man was made in the image and likeness of God, it was possible to project into God at least some of man's traits. God could have purposes analogous to man's; He could be good, wise, rational, loving, punitive. And though it was and still is customary to keep the analogies as loose as possible, Christian philosophers seldom if ever give their readers a measure of how loose they are. We may be said to know what we mean when we judge a man to be good; he fulfills all the ethical commandments in which he believes. But there can be no commandments for God to obey. We may be said to know what we mean by the other adjectives of praise usually listed; but in each case the best we can do when applying them to God is to say that He is the highest or most perfect or ultimate exemplification of the trait in question. We, for instance, are defective in our wisdom, our charity, our understanding; God is never defective. But each of these terms acquires its meaning in contrast to its complement or correlative or "opposite." We recognize goodness by contrasting it with evil, not merely with non-goodness. A world, as was said by Plotinus and after him by Saint Augustine, in which there was no evil would be a world in which there was no good. If that be true of a person, too, namely that a person incapable of doing evil, who had never encountered evil, had no temptation to do evil, could not be rightly called good, then it would be impossible for God to be either good or evil and the analogy would break down. Yet it was essential for Christians to retain an anthropomorphic God and when one robbed God of those traits which made Him somehow similar to man, one fell into the danger of transforming Him into a metaphysical principle who could neither create nor judge, to say nothing of rewarding or punishing His children.

There were, it must be admitted, two Gods in the Christian tradition, the religious God of the Bible and the metaphysical

God of the philosophers. The former appears in the first verse of *Genesis* and in the last verse of *Revelations*. He is presented in a variety of ways, as every reader of the Scriptures knows, but whatever else He may be, He is always a person with whom men can enter into communication through prayer, Who has revealed certain truths, Who can send pestilence and floods and other disasters upon this earth, Who loves mankind as a father and not in some bloodless analogical manner, Who has created man and begot a son, Who has performed miracles, and Who has actually appeared to certain prophets and spoken to them. Such a God is not the answer to the "question implied in being."[5] He is more like Zeus. Moreover the religious God was not, as far as we know, discovered by reasoning to the necessity of His existence. Men accepted Him because they were educated to accept Him, because they had faith in Him, had been converted, had seen Him in a vision. He was there long before the first philosophers began to write, just as Kronos and Rhea were there. When He reappeared in philosophic form, it was because the philosophers sought reasons for accepting Him, not satisfied with the credibility of the absurd. To prove His existence was like trying to prove one's own existence or the existence of an external world: we know that we exist and that a world external to our minds exists, but we want to prove it. But when we reach the end of our proof, the God we find is far from being the God we sought.

The God of the philosophers was entirely different except in name. Not even the Demiurge of the *Timaeus* was the God of Greek mythology; he is not Kronos nor Zeus. He is introduced as the *Nous* of Anaxagoras was introduced, to explain why the world is as it is. Critias outlines his role. Timaeus is the best astronomer of the group and should therefore begin with the origin of the cosmos and end with the nature of man. The Demiurge is needed because an eternal cause is needed for the temporal and changing world. Reason demands Him; the dia-

---

[5] See Paul Tillich; *Systematic Theology*, p. 166.

logue is not an exercise in apologetics. But similarly in the twelfth book of the *Metaphysics* Aristotle argues to the necessity of an Unmoved Mover from the existence of motion and reaches the first heavens. Assuming that nothing moves without being moved by something external to it, he concludes that there must be a mover who is not himself moved. He then points out that the desired and the subject of thought move in just this fashion. They attract us. Again Aristotle does not have a religious myth on his hands which he has to make rational; his theology is itself a rational structure. The God of the Stoics, called Zeus in the *Hymn* of Cleanthes, was a closer approach to the religious God. But in spite of His name, he is reached by Cleanthes because a lawgiver is needed to explain why the cosmos exhibits law. Such Gods are not persons in the anthropomorphic sense. They are not intimately associated with men. One may, and should, admire them and sing their praises, but they can take no direct interest in human affairs. Divine beings who may take such an interest are the traditional gods, and they too were given their place in the philosophies of all ancient schools. Socrates did not hesitate to pray to Pan and the nymphs or to remember the cock which he owed to Asclepius. Aristotle was not unwilling to locate divine intelligences in the planets. And though Lucretius thought the influence of the gods upon human beings unfortunate, he nevertheless believed in their existence. But these Gods were of no significance to the Christian philosophers. Pascal was unanswerable when he criticised Descartes's God for giving merely the first impetus to the world and then stepping back and letting it run itself. "It is a thing of wonder," he says,[6] "that never does a canonical author make use of nature to prove God. All strive to bring about belief. David, Solomon, etc. never said, 'There is no vacuum; therefore God exists.'" What he wanted was a personal God for Whom the traditional religious services might be performed and such a God so far transcended the laws of logic that it was futile to seek him through dialectics.

---

6 *Pensées,* ed. Pleiade, p. 1090, no. 6.

It is the religious God Who makes natural teleology intelligible, since those who believe in Him also believe that He has given man a special place in the universe. This place entitled us to certain privileges, one of which is the coincidence of our values with those of the Deity. The coincidence was made by God Himself: the world was made for man, however much it may declare the glory of God, and since it was made for man, man has every right to interpret its happenings in terms of his own welfare. This would have been nonsense in a universe in which there was only a metaphysical God. In Aristotle God is as much interested in minerals, vegetables, and the beasts as in man, and the closest approach one can make to defining Him is the Form of the World. Such a definition would be only approximate, since forms usually in Aristotle are not separate from their matter, and the Unmoved Mover is separate. In traditional Christianity the plants, beasts and even the sun and other stars are made for man. It therefore could be argued that if water runs downhill, it does so to enable man to turn mill wheels, and extravagant as some of Bernardin de Saint-Pierre's examples of teleology may seem, they are quite in keeping with the general tenets of the Bible. In fact they are the natural outcome of a belief that man's place in the cosmos is privileged. It is true that there are at least as many natural events which run counter to human desires and ends as are consonant with them. The same water which turns mill wheels also floods houses, and the same insects which fertilize fruit trees also sting people. The alternation of drought and rain does not always occur as farmers would plan it, and we have it on good authority that the rain falls on the unjust as it does on the just. But theistic teleology can absorb these apparent anomalies easily enough by introducing, as the Stoics sometimes did in similar circumstances, the moral effect of withstanding misfortune, or by speaking of the hidden sins of man and finally of the ultimate mystery of God's motives. To them God's will, as we have suggested earlier, is "the facts." Just as the facts are inexplicable, being that which explains everything else, so is God's will. Just as they must be accepted with resignation, so must it.

It will seem to be wilful perversity for a philosopher to discuss this matter seriously, but it rests on a doctrine by which millions of people have lived, and one cannot decently maintain that they were all stupid. My point is that if we are to follow the teleological cue, we must do so in such a manner that purpose will be the only kind of purpose of which we have any concrete acquaintance. It will not do to posit purposiveness in so vague a fashion that it will comfort us when we are depressed and annoy us when we are elated. When people ask what is the meaning of life, why are we here, or even why there is anything rather than nothing, they are voicing the last faint echoes of this type of teleology. The answer to the "why" in such cases is a purpose. If we reply that the purpose of life is the love for God, then clearly God must be the kind of being who desires or at least knows about our love for Him. The Ground of Being or the Principle of the Conservation of Values or the Principle of Concretion can no more desire or know anything than the binomial theorem can. We cannot swing from the metaphysical to the religious God as it suits our convenience and also maintain that both are identical. The purpose of the former is uniform scientific laws; of the latter distributive justice. The former are contrasted with unusual events and necessary events; the latter may be both unusual and necessary. The effort will always be made to systematize the divine purposes, for if there is no general rule, there is no explaining anything. But often the purposes of the religious God must remain beyond explanation. If we maintain that disasters, for instance, happen only to the wicked, we run into cases like that of the Lisbon earthquake which so excited the ire of Voltaire. Hence we usually retreat to the unfathomable purposes which we assert are the expression of a sense of justice, though we are unable to determine wherein the justice lies. "Though He slay me, yet will I trust in Him."

The most intelligble attempt to rationalize the divine purposes was, as far as I know, that of Leibniz when he used the Principle of Sufficient Reason. This principle appeared in various contexts but when Leibniz was trying to justify the ways of God to man, he attributed to God the power of choice between two or more possible ends. Since his God was rational and since He always chose the best possible course, one could confidently assert that whatever came about was good. It was not only good-in-itself but good for mankind. That which is good-in-itself is usually considered to be the purpose which a course of action is designed to achieve. This is easily enough identified in ordinary behavior, as when we say that we eat to sustain life or drink to quench thirst or paint pictures to express ourselves or fight to protect our rights. In such cases we may be wrong about our "real" purposes and may substitute for them our ostensible purposes which, we are told, often justify in our own eyes ends which society would reprove. Here we have a definite choice—or think we have—and one of the conditions of a choice of acts is an ultimate distinction between past, present, and future. Another is the possible indeterminacy of the future, an indeterminacy which is reduced by the act of choosing. Our end or purpose is usually called our reason for making the choice. And it is called our reason presumably because we can lay before our imagination two or more courses of action and choose one of them. This obviously cannot happen unless there is a real future not as yet realized. Moreover, if that which we choose is an inevitable consequence of some present condition, it is hard to see in what sense of the word we are making a choice, participating in the determination of our future, except as a present cause or group of causes participates in the determination of the future. If it follows necessarily that a person of a given nature always must choose a predictable course of action, and if there is no future but time is a *totum simul,* then choice is an illusion and the course of history a logical or causal network.

But when we make God a timeless being, we make Him a being who cannot choose, regardless of what Leibniz may present Him as doing. His reasons can be nothing more than an expression of His nature and any attempt to read into His acts an historical series of events must be a perversion of the truth. One could to be sure interpret divine action logically, as one lays out the theorems of Euclid, and it would be possible for human beings to begin with the premises of such action and proceed to the conclusions in a series of demonstrations which would take time. But it would be a misinterpretation to think of such a God as proceeding from step to step as we are forced to do. Yet that is what Leibniz, because of his desire to weld the story of Creation into a metaphysical system, tried to do. Hence he had to present God as having not yet made the world—though there could be no "not yet" in the divine life—and moreover as considering various possible worlds before the act of Creation and choosing between them. But the choice is at most analogical, as Leibniz admits in his *Theodicy* (section viii) when he is arguing about the freedom of the divine will. This is not the only obstacle towards a clear comprehension of what he was aiming at. For in what sense of the word "good" is the world good? It cannot be good for God, for reasons which need no explanation. It is presumably good for man. But that good is not the terminal good which would characterize human choices. When Leibniz admits the existence of some evil in the universe, he is clearly talking about things which human beings would not choose. But, as everyone knows, such evil he thinks to be a necessary feature of any possible world. The world thus becomes good for man in the instrumental sense of "good." And it is not to be wondered that Leibniz resorts to Stoic principles at this point and holds up acceptance of the universe as the wisest ethical program. "To the sage," he says, *"necessity* and what *ought to be* are equivalent things."[7] Indeed one might add that in a world of strict necessity the distinction between what is and what ought to be disappears. For though there is no reason why what ought to be is not, unless there is a possibility of its not being, there is no point in introducing the concept of the ought whatsoever.

To project teleology from human life into the universe as a whole, if it is to be done on a theological basis, demands that God like humans have a future which His purposes can modify.

---

[7] I quote from the admirable edition of Leibniz by P. P. Wiener in the Scribner Modern Student's Library, p. 521.

This would remove God from eternity and relocate Him in history, as He is in the Bible. The analogical method will not work here until at least one feature of human purposiveness is retained in the analogy: the possibility of two conflicting choices' being fulfilled by Him and at least of their beginning to be fulfilled by us. One can of course use words as one will, but it makes little sense to say that there is any purpose in the sequence of theorems, and similarly there would be no purpose in an eternal mind. If one prefers to use "purpose" to apply to such incidents, then another term should be chosen to name human choice and purpose. This does not entail the belief that human beings cannot rationally plan the future. We can obviously argue that if we wish to accomplish something, the way to do so is such and such. If we wish to travel from New York to Paris, the shortest route is a great circle, and if we wish to remove the salt from sea water, the best way to do it is by distillation. In such cases we can define what we mean by "best" and experience will tell us how to achieve it. But the very use of "better" and "best" rests upon the belief that several courses of action are open to us, though we may be mistaken about this as about a number of other things. It makes no sense, for instance, to argue that the best way to survive is by breathing oxygen since there is no other way to survive. We have no way of knowing how God could have created the world otherwise than as He did create it, though we can imagine a different kind of world. In fact, we know of a world which was different, namely that in which there were no human beings or even any life whatsoever. We can raise the question of why God decided to create human beings, but all such speculation is making God's mind more similar to our own than is customary in metaphysical circles. But whether metaphysicians like it or not, the one way to reason in a straightforward manner is to follow the rule of unambiguity during discourse. If purpose is primarily human purpose, then however far we may desire to extend its meaning, we must never lose sight of its original and primary meaning. When one has so far extended it that it is attributed to acts which lack the differentiat-

ing characteristics of purposiveness, then the term would appear
to be misapplied. And the acts of a metaphysical God insofar as
they are not capable of nullification through a change of will and
design do lack these characteristics. Purposes of this kind are
like the imponderable matter of the phlogiston theory; it was
supposed to be matter, but it lacked the differentiae of matter.

We sometimes find the term "purpose" applied to situations
in which means are discovered to lead to certain ends though no
personal will is found. This is common in biological research,
especially in physiology. Henderson's classic study, *The Fitness
of the Environment,* is an excellent example of this type of reasoning, for it attempts to show how our organism and that of other
animals and plants are wonderfully suited to the specific environment in which they are found. We are far from belittling the
wonders of adaptation and we recognize that the intricacies of
organic systems must always excite the admiration of poets as
well as that of philosophers. Nevertheless, the anatomy of an
organism presents limiting possibilities of so strict a type that one
might just as well wonder at the obstacles they create as at the
purposes which they permit to be achieved. It is indeed wonderful that a plant can absorb nourishment from the chemicals dissolved in the soil in which it grows, but the argument cuts two
ways. The plant may be what it is because of the limitations of
its environment. If it could get up and walk, it would not necessarily die in times of drought but could look for water when it
needs it. One could of course argue that the immobility of plants
was planned so that the animals might have a greater chance to
get at the water in the water holes. As for the wonders of our
own organism, it would be just as well if we could swallow our
food without chewing it, as snakes do, or could squirt hydrochloric acid at it after it had been ingurgitated. Such arguments as
that based on the fitness of the environment, like those found in
the Bridgewater Treatises, do give us detailed pictures of a complex of means and ends, but again they do not prove that any
choice was exercised in our formation. They do not show that the
human body was designed beforehand to do certain things; they

show just as well the things which it is not equipped to do.

Hence it is the point of view of this lecture that teleology had best be used where it can be used literally and that if it is to be extended into cosmic planning, the God that rules the cosmos had best be the God of Scripture rather than the God of metaphysics.

CHAPTER VII

EXPLANATION — BY THE PRINCIPLE
OF PERFECTION

The universe of Plotinus was not only teleological in detail but was also teleological as a whole. All things aspired both to their own good and to the good-in-itself. By fusing the three hierarchies of logical classes, values, and reality, Plotinus was able to construct a system in which there were no gaps between the levels of reality, though there were, of course, gaps in the realm of appearance. Everything was not only related to everything else but everything *was* everything else. For all things participated to a greater or lesser extent in the One, since all things had their ultimate source and their ultimate goal in the One. The aspirations of the mystic for beatific union were different only in degree from the growth of plants and animals and even of stones.[1] The katabasis was a steady loss of reality, goodness, and generality, the anabasis a steady gain. The cosmic cycle was everlasting, and from an external point of view it might be maintained that there was neither purposiveness nor lack of it in the ebb and flow. For if everything is dominated by a universal law in accordance with which it has to act, then why should it be called a purposive agent? It was, however, impossible to take a point of view external to all being; the philosopher like everything else was in it. And from within the cosmos events were always to be explained as either in a state of degeneration or of perfection. Oddly enough, there was almost a superfluity of examples of perfection, for from the Aristotelian tradition alone Plotinus could conclude

[1] For the growth of stones, see *Ennead,* IV, iv, 27, 9.

that minerals were the matter of vegetables, vegetables of animals, animals of men, though no one ever saw a stone turn into a vegetable or a vegetable into an animal, and in Aristotle himself it was the vegetative soul which clearly stood for vegetation and the sensitive soul which stood for animality. But where were there to be found examples of degeneration? Again, only in the myth of incarnation or in human life where men might be found who let their reasons degenerate in order to live the life of beasts or plants. Hence on the cosmic scale Plotinus was pushed into finding metaphors which would illuminate his basic idea and, as we all know, he found his metaphor in the streaming of light into darkness and the overflowing waters of the *fons vitae*. He was, so to speak, in the position of the eighteenth-century comparative anatomist, who could illustrate the similarities of animal structures and arrange them in the fanlike tree of life from simple to complex but who could not point to the genetic affiliation of his various forms. Plotinus too could lay out a cosmic map from the One down to material particulars, but he had no evidence of a genetic link between them.

The anabasis had long been established as a possibility by Aristotle, as we have said, in his theory of matter and form coupled with the notion that the lower functions of the soul were matter to the higher. The ladder of nature was clearly indicated in his writings, but he gives no demonstration of any genetic relation between the things on the various rungs of the ladder. In fact, with the exception of the zoophytes, there were definite gaps between the rungs: it was a ladder, not a ramp. It is more likely that the first place where such a conception is clearly suggested is in Philo's interpretation of the dream of Jacob in which the angels, interpreted as Powers, move up and down between Heaven and Earth. But as far as we know, it was Plotinus who first gave a detailed interpretation and application of the metaphor to the realm of science. Because of the influence of Neo-Platonic ideas upon the subsequent history of scientific explanation and the use of the Principle of Perfection to explain growth, the interrelationship of classes of beings, and even the moral life of humans it is worth while to spend some time on it here.[2]

There are two kinds of science, according to Plotinus (v, ix, 7), one of which deals with sensible things and which ought more properly to be called opinion, the other which deals with the Intelligibles, which have no images of sensible things within them. The second type of science apprehends the Ideas directly, does not create them, and in one theorem contains all the others *in potentia* (IV, iii, 2, 53).[3] It should therefore be possible to deduce from one theorem—or law—all the others or, if one preferred, to return to the first theorem from any later theorems, thus reproducing in thought the cosmic cycle. But whether this could be done in the Sensible World as well as in the Intelligible is problematic, and, though Plotinus may well have believed it possible, he also believed that opinion would have to be transmuted into the higher type of science before it could be accomplished. For he stoutly maintains (VI, ii, 20), that Intelligence refuses to become particularized and that its science is anterior even to the various categories, genera, and species. It contains within itself all the special sciences, though it is not fragmented in them, an idea which we might paraphrase by saying that all special sciences use the same categories and the same logical devices, though they use them on distinct subject-matters. This primary science, which is the peculiar property of Intelligence, is simply the contemplation of these means of reasoning reduced to one. But what that one is, is left obscure. Nevertheless it is an article of faith with Plotinus that what he calls the true scientist can move in either direction, up towards unity, down towards multiplicity, as he will. Here, he says in a striking parallel to Saint Paul, these things are darkened because of our weakness and our body, "but yonder each and all are clear" (IV, ix, 5).

---

[2] It was coupled with the Principle of Plenitude as Lovejoy has shown in *The Great Chain of Being*. We are not here so much concerned with that principle, however, and moreover it would be absurd to attempt to do a second time what has already been done with such great skill.

[3] This is repeated almost word for word in III, ix, 2 and IV, ix, 5. These tractates, according to Porphyry's chronological list, are much earlier than IV, iii.

The science of which he is thinking is of course geometry (V, ix, 11) which to him is the paradigm of all mathematics, though neither he nor anyone else has ever succeeded in deducing all the theorems of plane geometry from one premise. Yet it is clear from various statements of Plotinus that he thought it could be done. But the kind of deduction, like the kind of science, has its peculiarities. For he was convinced that Intelligence when contemplating Ideas did not engage in discursive thought but saw the consequences in the premises and saw them without making distinctions or "taking steps." The unity of thought and being had to be preserved and though we now know that it is impossible to move from a conclusion back to a unique set of premises, since even in the syllogism an indefinite number of premises may imply a given conclusion, he apparently was not aware of this. "By a natural necessity," he says (III, iii, 1), "all starts from unity and returns to unity." And to Plotinus the return was even more important than the departure. For through the return human beings may liberate their souls from their bodies and live a purely contemplative life. The cycle of thought, as we say, runs parallel to the cycle of being, and the cycle of being parallel to that of logical classes. In his second tractate on *Forethought* (III, iii), he points out how individuals, no matter how diverse and how antagonistic, form a single and unique genus which is their unity. And he goes on to say (*ibid.* 1), "One must combine again all species into one species, that of animal, then again those which are not animals into one species, then once more the [animal] and the non-animal, and then similarly, if desired, reduce them both to being, and then into that which possesses being. And again, after having bound them all together into this class, one descends by division." Thus one sees unity dividing itself after it has been formed. This is of course what was later to become the Tree of Porphyry and, though Plotinus does not tell us where to make our divisions, it is clear from the context that, as in the *Phaedrus*, the joints are determined by Nature. And later in the same passage, he points out that in the hierarchy of classes there is an order of inherent excellence, since the producer is always better than the product.

There is then obviously running through the *Enneads* a general principle which attributes to all things a unique end. This end has two aspects, division and unification, the Way Down and the Way Up. Hence all change, whether it occurs on the human, animal, vegetable, or mineral level, is to be interpreted as an example of the cosmic cycle. But since the scale of values is fused into the scale of being, the levels themselves have inherent values, values which in the Middle Ages will be called *dignitates,* and it is literally, not figuratively, true to say that it is better to be a man than an animal, and an animal than a plant. And the whole Sensible World taken together is worse than the Intelligible World which in turn has its own scale of dignities mounting up to the One. This reading of value into reality is never disputed by Plotinus. It is one of his presuppositions. And it will be retained throughout the Middle Ages as one of those self-evident axioms which can be applied to discussions about Heaven, Earth, the Kingdom of God and the Kingdom of Men. He does not even reason as Victor Hugo did in his *Contemplations* (VI), that if the Creation had been perfect it would have been indistinguishable from the Creator.

> Dieu n'a crée que l'être impondérable.
> Il le fit radieux, beau, candide, adorable,
> Mais imparfait; sans quoi, sur la même hauteur,
> La créature étant égale au Créateur,
> Cette perfection, dans l'infini perdue,
> Se serait avec Dieu mêlée et confondue,
> Et la création, à force de clarté,
> En lui serait rentrée et n'aurait pas été.
> La création sainte où rêve le prophète,
> Pour être, ô profondeur! devait être imparfaite.

So Plotinus might have argued, but did not, that if the Sensible World had been as perfect as that from which it emanated, it would have been indistinguishable from its source.

For perfection in the eyes of Plotinus was unity.[4] The source of all being was the One; all souls were united in the Soul of the World; individuals were united into species and the species into genera; theorems were united into one in which they were implicit; knowledge of the best kind was simple contemplation without discursive thought; and matter, the principle of individuation, was also the principle of evil. But when one comes to examine a bit more closely just what this unity was, one is at a loss. In the logical hierarchy it was clearly the class-characteristics, or equality, which defined it. All members of a class must have one thing in common. And if there is a class of all classes, that class will possess the one quality or, if a more non-committal term is preferable, one trait resident in all things whatsoever. But it would also possess a trait which nothing else whatsoever possessed, namely the trait of being the class of all classes. Even if it is given that colorless but very popular name, Being, it must have a very special kind of being, for if it did not, its status in the hierarchy would be different. To take a more *terre-à-terre* example, we are accustomed to classify the data of all five senses as sensory data, which is tautological and hence indisputable. We can argue reasonably that all sensory data are alike in that they are all apprehended by sensory organs. But that in no way confers any sensible quality upon the class of sensory data nor does it eliminate the very real differences between colors and sounds or between the various colors or the various shades of a single color. To achieve complete qualitative unity through classification, every member of a class ought to have all properties except existential singularity in common. And not even Plotinus believed in that. Unification through classification is bought at the price of overlooking precisely those differences which are stubbornly present except to thought. This denies neither the possibility nor the utility of classifications, nor does it deny the possibility and utility of a hierarchy of classes. But it does deny the elimination of multiplicity through classification. To prove

---

[4] This does not conflict with the idea of measuring excellence by self-sufficiency, lacking nothing.

that several things have something in common does not also prove that they have lost their individuality.

The unity which was perfection was a universal trait. And therefore the highest class would appear to contain within it more members than any other class. But since it is a class of classes, it does not contain the members of the member classes unless the class-concept is interpreted in extension, which is hardly likely in Plotinus. "Animality" as a class-concept would include "vertebrateness" and "invertebrateness," but it would not necessarily include all the actual flesh and blood vertebrates and invertebrates which are specimens of classes but not classes. Otherwise, though I do not find this problem discussed by Plotinus for obvious reasons, there would be no class-concept for the various species of extinct animals, to say nothing of the dead specimens of the non-extinct. Since Plotinus was dealing with knowledge and not with the beings about which we know something, the hierarchy of classes is based upon the abstractness of the ideas involved. And since he was definitely of the opinion that the logical katabasis could be mapped by reasoning alone without the aid of observation, it is doubtful whether he realized the difficulty of the problem of demonstrating existence from essence. He says himself in one place (V, ix, 5) that being and thinking are both one and the same and that the science of the immaterial is the same as its subject-matter.[5] It is one of his reasons for maintaining that there can be rightly only opinion about sensible things. Another of course is his fidelity to Plato. The hierarchy of being then is a purely logical hierarchy, and strictly speaking there no more ought to be any things exemplifying the logical essences in his system than in any other of a purely rationalistic type. To complete the hierarchy, there must be a *summum genus,* an *ens realissimum,* but that is the One, not Being (V, v, 5). "Should anyone say that [the word] being [εἶναι] comes from [the word] one [ἕν], he would probably have hit upon the truth." For the One is utterly without differentiation, and every individual

---

[5] This should be recalled when historians discuss Saint Anselm's ontological proof.

being, whether a thing or a class of things or a quality or anything else of which one may speak, is a unit. But Being is not one, since there are several kinds of Being (VI, ii, 1). Hence there must be a level of perfection higher than that of Being.

Should one ask why the abstract is any better than the concrete, he would find no answer in Plotinus. Unity, eternity, immutability, were by his time signs of perfection and presumably philosophers thought that a genus was more unified than a species and a class of genera more unified than a genus. But it does not require great intellectual exertion to see that unity, eternity, and immutability do not admit of degrees. Even on the level of sensory qualities, "redness" is no less a unity than "color." And as for eternality and immutability, how can anything be more or less timeless, more or less unchanging? Rates of change may vary to be sure, and a very slow rate of change might be said to approach immutability. But if there is no change whatsoever, one might reasonably conclude that two immutables have equal immutability. This is child's play. To argue against this would be like arguing that though sound, taste, and smell are colorless, sound is more colorless than taste or smell; or that since triangles, squares, and hexagons are not circular, triangles are less circular than squares.[6] And I think that we can assume the absurdity of such an argument. If perfection is equivalent to unity, then there can be no levels of perfection. The notion of an *ens perfectum* would be viable, but not the notion of an *ens perfectissimum*.

But perhaps the measure of altitude in the hierarchy is not so much unity as the values, goodness and beauty. No one denies the significance of comparative degrees of these two terms. But here, too, certain difficulties arise which have persisted into modern philosophy. Comparisons of value in human life are usually made

---

[6] Lest anyone think that hexagons are more circular than triangles, on the ground that a circle is a regular polygon with an infinite number of sides, we can only reply that though things can be more or less close to a limit, that does not confer upon them a degree of whatever character is inherent in the limit. Are we to say that because a series is approaching 0 as a limit, the later terms are more zero-like than the earlier?

either on the basis of human preferences or on the basis
of the inherent worth of two objects, events, acts, or pursuits.
We can omit the former since the Neo-Platonist is not concerned
with human preferences, for he is convinced that the valuable is
not determined by what people value. It is rather an inherent
trait of beings. It is common knowledge that in Plotinus and
his disciples the true, the good, and the beautiful fuse as we
pointed out in our opening sentences. The true is not the adequacy
of an idea to a particular thing, but to another idea or class-
concept. That is why, as we have already said, there can be only
opinion about sensibles. One can have knowledge only about
universals or, if one prefer, by spotting the natural class into
which sensibles fall. And the adjective "natural" is of fundamental importance here. Thus the apprehension of a red object
through the senses, just seeing it, is not knowledge but simply
sensory experience. That was pretty firmly established by Aristotle.[7] But the moment one wakes up to the fact that the object
in question is, let us say, material, then one can have some
knowledge about it, make inferences from its materiality, as in
physics, compare and contrast it with other material things, and
so on. But now it should be observed that in Plotinus as in
Aristotle the natural class to which a thing belongs is its essence
and that its essence is its form or final cause. To see it is to see
its unity with other members of its natural class. But, according to
Plotinus, this is just what the experience of the beautiful is. As
he makes clear in his famous tractate on Beauty (I, vi), an object
is beautiful insofar as its form is clear to us. Our souls too are
forms and by the attraction of similars, we are attracted to the
forms of other things and this is the aesthetic experience.

But if this is so, then how can one thing be more beautiful than
another thing? Can one form be more of a form than another?
Only in the sense that it is a more inclusive class, a class of
classes. In that sense color would be more beautiful than red,
green, and blue, animal more beautiful than any man, bird, beast,

---

[7] This pervades the Corpus, but there is special treatment of it in *Metaphysics*,
Zeta, 15, 1039 b, 20 ff.

or fish, and Being more beautiful than materiality and immateriality. It is this in fact which justifies his notion of Intellectual Beauty (V, viii). Here he returns to his other master, Plato, and follows the lead of Diotima in the *Symposium*. He sees the problem of contemplating such abstractions as one looks at a beautiful object and that is why he introduces the idea that the Egyptian hieroglyphs were concrete perceptual manifestations of Platonic ideas.[8] We must confess that we find the notion of a form of a class being more of a form than a form which is not the form of a class too obscure for us to discuss sympathetically. The application of "more" and "less" to qualities is a transfer from quantitative measurements to a subject-matter which is in no sense of the word quantitative. Is scarlet any redder than pink? Only in the sense that one puts more red pigment and less water—or white lead—on one's palette to produce scarlet than one does to produce pink. Pink resembles red to be sure but, as a color sensation, it is whatever it is. It will be found, we believe, that whenever such comparisons are made, they rest upon quantitative measurements of the stimulus which gives rise to the sensation or of the amount of material needed to produce the sensation. Most of our qualitative experiences have been handled by the sciences only after they have been correlated with some measurable quantity or set of quantities. We can recognize what we mean when we say that the bath is too hot, but when we come to say how hot it is, we have to put in a thermometer and measure the height of the mercury. Similar remarks may be made about another favorite of the value-theorists, duration. A value which is more permanent than another is usually said to be more valuable than one which is less permanent. But no one surely would maintain seriously that a red barn is redder than a red sunset, though the former may last for years and the latter but for a few moments. And would one maintain that a beautiful picture which

---

[8] For hints of the subsequent history of this, see the introduction to my translation of the Hieroglyphics of Horapollo which has numerous references, the various iconological studies of Erwin Panofsky, and the files of the *Journal of the Warburg and Courtauld Institutes*.

was destroyed became because of that accident less beautiful than
it was before? Since it has been destroyed, it is not beautiful at
all, nor ugly. It has ceased to exist. But for that matter the
aesthetic experience is an experience, and since no one is immortal, and since each repeated hearing of a piece of music or
viewing of a picture is different from its predecessors, not merely
in date but also in character, no aesthetic value can last longer
than the experience plus the memory which one has of it. But
someone will reply that duration is not the same as timelessness.
That is certainly true, though usually value-theorists overlook the
difference. If then we are to measure values by their eternality,
how can anything be more or less timeless than another? But we
confess, we repeat, to our inability to understand the Neo-Platonic
theory of a scale of beauty, and in such a situation it is the course
of wisdom to retire from the field.

Since beauty and goodness are identified in the Intelligible
World, what we have said about beauty could be applied to its
associated value. Goodness is what everything seeks when acting
in accordance with Nature. In the Sensible World the realization of the potential is the pattern of excellence. Plotinus identified forms with Plato's ideas and thus was able to find parallels
to human excellence through the universe as a whole. The animal
realizing its natural potencies was doing exactly what a man was
doing who tried to be more of a man and less of a beast or
vegetable. Each class of things had its own excellence. If one
stopped at this point, there would be no possibility of comparing
the relative values of the various kinds of goodness, for there
would be no greater goodness in being a man than a cow or
an ant or even a cabbage. But by developing Aristotle's classification of beings and the principle of matter and form into a cosmic
hierarchy, Plotinus was able to conclude to an absolute scale of
goodness embedded in the structure of the universe. Vegetables
could be excellent vegetables, but as a class they existed for the
sake of animals. Animals again could be excellent cows, horses,
dogs, and cats, but they too as a class existed for the sake of
human beings. The form of vegetation was nutrition and reproduc-

tion, of animation was sensitivity, of humanity was rationality, as
we all learn early in our careers as philosophers. But just as one
could not be rational without being, or having been, also sensitive
and vegetative, so one could not be sensitive without being vegetative. This was in beautiful agreement with the Macrocosm-Microcosm metaphor (II, i, 5). This ingenious solution of the
problem presented by degrees of goodness worked very well—
regardless of the truth or falsity of its principles—but it gave
rise to conclusions which should not be neglected. One of these
was that there was only one end to man; that no individual could
be good except to the extent to which he realized the potencies
of the class *mankind*. The "romantic" program of being true to
oneself was an impossibility, for the only self one had was the
form of the class. Yet Plotinus (V, ix, 12) also maintained that
there were ideas of individuals and thus made it possible for each
man to fulfill his own destiny by his own means. This was a flaw
in his system, corrected by his disciples.

The only way in which one man could be better than another
was that he was more of a man than the other. The value of a
good will or of pure motives or of self-sacrifice or of consequences
to the welfare of society need not even be mentioned. Regardless
of the Stoic elements in Neo-Platonism, Plotinus is not bothered
about the Cosmopolis.[9] Every man can find salvation for himself
as an individual by first discovering what human nature is and
then by seeking to realize it in his own life. In Aristotle, where
the same principles are laid down—at least in the *Nichomachean
Ethics*—due attention is paid to the vegetative and sensitive functions. But curiously enough in Plotinus these functions, which
might have appeared to be the foundations of a rational life, turn
out to be impediments to it. The asceticism which he preached
and practised too—if Porphyry is telling the truth about his
master—is antithetical to the Aristotelian ethics, so that in spite
of the Peripatetic elements in his theory of value, he rejects them
as a clue to a program of living. The division of the cosmos into

---

[9] He does, however, discuss the cosmos as an animal. See *Ennead* II, iv, 35.

two worlds is duplicated by the division of man's nature into soul and body, and though the body exists only for the soul, which is its form, as a means to an end, he seems to believe that one can attain the end without the means. He swings between considering the body as an inevitable step in the scale of being and considering it as the enemy of the soul which must be conquered. The fusion between Platonism, in which ideas were separate from particulars, and Aristotelianism, in which they were never separate, could not be effected.[10] Though the doctrines which he took over from Aristotle are numerous, no philosophy in which the Way Up was so heavily accentuated could accommodate the central theses of Aristotle.

The ultimate explanation of any change in Plotinus lies in the attempt on the part of sensible things to exemplify the universal laws of generation and regeneration. Though the Intelligible World is timeless, nevertheless there is a kind of change which occurs in it, change which is instantaneous, as he imagines the transmission of light to be instantaneous. This of course is emanation. It was to find an echo later in Christian theology in the spiration of the Holy Ghost. The three persons of Plotinus's Trinity—the One, the Intelligence, and the Soul of the World— manifest the same generation and regeneration as things in the Sensible World do, but they manifest the process eternally. One gathers that the model for this process was mathematical implication. Spiration also occurred without temporal sequence, but it goes without saying that the persons of Plotinus's Trinity were not all identical as well as distinct. It is, says Plotinus (IV, viii, 6) a universal law that all things must produce something and produce something "lower than" themselves, and the process of production or generation must go to the limits of possibility. But once generation has been completed, the movement upwards begins, a movement which in the Intelligible World is exemplified in the longing of the souls for Intelligence and of Intelligence

---

10 Nor was it in Aristotle. See my *Basic Conflict in the Philosophy of Aristotle,* cited *supra,* p. 146.

for the One. Cosmic teleology, or the Principle of Perfection, must be envisioned then as a double process, though the word "process" can be used only metaphorically in the Intelligible World. And, as we have said, every change whatsoever must be located either in the process of producing something lower or mounting to something higher.

If one ask what is the good of all this, the end, the purpose, the answer is simply, "a manifestation of cosmic order." The cosmos as a Great Animal has its own life to live, and all things which compose it must contribute to its life. That is why, according to Plotinus (III, i, 5) there is a kind of sympathy throughout all the parts of the cosmos, making prediction possible and exemplified in the rhythmic growth of plants and animals according to the seasons. No explanation of anything then is sound which does not interpret events in these terms. And hence it follows that explanation is always the integration of a description into one of the two universal laws. Nevertheless, since Plotinus and his disciples were always more interested in the anabasis than in the katabasis, values were to be attained in the former rather than in the latter process. Thus the human soul must sooner or later inhabit a body, but the good which is to be attained by this act is a release from the body. Its descent from the Intelligible World was necessary, and moreover once it had descended, it would engage in a struggle in which it might be worsted. It might have to inhabit several bodies before it could regain the Heaven which was its home. But its good was a final and total rejection of the corporeal life, in spite of the fact that part of its destiny was incorporation. This was far from being the only consequence which Plotinus could have drawn from his basic theory. He could have maintained that incorporation was in itself a good and that living the terrestrial life had its own values. But again here he turned away from Aristotle to follow Diotima. Here too there was a parallel with the philosophy of many Christians. His fellow pupil, Origen, even went so far as to accept reincarnation so that all souls might eventually be saved. But the pre-existence of souls was condemned under Pope Vigilius;[11] their post-existence was an integral part of orthodox Christianity and has remained so.

This is the more curious in that, as far as Plotinus was concerned, the good was the complete realization of the form of humanity, and since he had neither a sacred text to go on nor a special revelation, the only evidence he had of what that form was—aside from tradition—was terrestrial life. To maintain that man was a rational animal could be based only upon a comparison between him and the other animals. In fact, the very duality of soul and body insofar as it was not merely a rhetorical flourish, must have been rooted in an observed conflict between the two or, as in Descartes, upon the logical discovery that one could be defined without involving any of the attributes of the other. Even when the duality was accepted, that in itself was not proof that the good of the soul was better than the good of the body and it might just as soundly have been argued that the soul existed for the sake of the body as that the body existed for the sake of the soul. This conclusion with certain modifications was the conclusion of Schopenhauer and might well have become the conclusion of the Neo-Darwinians. The escape from sensualism, corporeal hedonism, even the identification of the good with the preservation of the species, were provided for in the cosmic hierarchy. But that, as I hope we have seen, is as obscure a notion as any which have appeared in the history of philosophy. To call better things higher things is an ancient custom, as E. R. Bevan pointed out in his *Symbolism and Belief,* but it is only a figure of speech. For the pyramidal structure of the universe is in itself no more intelligible than any other metaphorical structure which has been attributed to it. For all anyone knows, the universe may be a flat reticulated system, in spite of the logical technique of ordering things into classes and classes into classes of classes. The animal kingdom at present is divided into five classes of which gastropods are one. This class is divided into four orders of which the

---

[11] See *Enchiridion,* 203. The text is from Justinian's *Liber adversus Originem.*

pectinibranchiata are one, and these into five families. The process continues until we come to species and sub-species. But no one surely would assert that there could be animals which were simply gastropods and neither aspidobranchiata nor pectinibranchiata nor opisthobranchiata nor pulmonata. Nor would anyone urge one of the Neptuneidae to be a good mollusk but not to bother about being a marine snail. Yet when one argues that the highest classes are inherently the best and that their traits constitute absolute goodness for all members of lower orders, one overlooks the fact that one cannot simply be a member of the higher classes; one is an individual of the *infima species* and there is nothing which can be done about it. Surely one of the problems of the value-theorist is how to meet this obstacle to moral purity.

It must be obvious that the main block to reaching a higher class is one's existence. If John Doe and Richard Roe find it a problem to be men, it is because their existence as individual men stands in the way. They must first eliminate their individual differences, purge themselves of all that makes them Doe and Roe, dated and localized beings, and they soon wake up to the fact that their moral problem is insoluble. Trite though the remark may be, it is essential that it be repeated: this side of mathematics we find only things and events; we do not find pure ideas. But we demand that the things and events become pure ideas. One cannot ask the question why there is existence; but one can ask the question of how to rephrase problems so that they will be relevant to existence. We begin our answer as soon as we make judgments about the world of existence, for judgments are always framed within a universal matrix whose terms and relations are represented by our common nouns, adjectives, and verbs. This is an immediate transmutation of existence into essence, whether we know it or not, and the transmutation is always bound to be imperfect. Thus the identification which Meyerson saw as the solution of all explanatory problems was, as he also saw, never quite realizable. An existent being is always something more than that which it is supposed to exemplify. The eternal or logical man may be a rational animal, but the temporal or historical man is also a passionate, sensitive, appetitive, and reproductive animal. In order to achieve the status which logic demands of him—assuming that he is converted to this type of ethics—he can only repudiate a large part of his nature and the way is open for some form or other of asceticism. It may not be so extreme as that of Plotinus who, we are told by Porphyry, so loathed his body that he would neither bathe nor permit his birthday to be celebrated. But in Nietzschean language it must be a Nay-saying to something. Am I too fantastic in suggesting that this might be an apology for phrasing laws and commandments as prohibitions?

An analogous situation is to be found in aesthetics. Here, too, we are confronted not by eternal ideas but by individual works of art. But the books of criticism talk in terms of classes: tragedies, comedies, lyrics, epics, portraits, landscapes, illustrations, emblems, fugues, sonatas, rondos, minuets. What else can their authors do? If they are to think and to say something, they must do so in language and the moment they speak, unless they are to emit cries and moans and sighs and cheers, they have to use general terms. When the child asks, "How do you draw a man?" he is talking as if there were a standard or essential man which can actually be represented on paper, a sort of universally understood hieroglyph. He is fortunate in having a simpler, if more obscure, vocabulary than that, but if he had become an aesthetician, he would immediately begin writing about the eternal, universal, immutable essence, *mankind,* which it is the artist's task to put into visible form. It is not surprising that people write in this way; there is no other way in which to write. But it is surprising that they should think that they are talking sense. The very notion that an ideal being can be represented in visible or any other type of sensory form, is in itself paradoxical. And it may be the charm of the paradoxical mystery which has seduced so many writers on art. One can, to be sure, look at a picture and attend only to what one believes it to have in common with all other pictures, or with all other pictures of its kind (landscape), just as one can read *King Lear* and attend only to what it has in common with other tragedies, *The Persians, Antigone, Medea,*

Hercules Furens, and *Le Cid.* Thinning out the content of an idea in this way, one can find essences galore and admire them if one so wishes. The fundamental question is in what sense the essence explains the individual.

Insofar as an artist is actually trying to exemplify a general rule, his work may be judged by its success in doing so. It has been assumed that artists do try to exemplify rules and in some periods, as well as among some groups of artists, one can discover what those rules are. We know, for instance, what the rules for a sonnet are in a vague way and we know what fugues are and what the rules for perspective are. If we assume that such rules actually guide the artist whose work we are examining —and this is only an assumption—then we are faced with the problem of why the individual work of art deviates from them. The sonnets of Shakespeare resemble in some ways the sonnets of Petrarch or, better, Drayton. But even the sonnets of Shakespeare do not all copy one another. Regardless of the specific words which are to be found in these 154 poems or the different ideas and conceits, the ebb and flow, the music of them all, vary and one would have to have a pretty deaf ear not to hear their individual differences. Is this of no interest? Is it of no importance for aesthetic theory? Even if an aesthetician argues that the artist's purpose is to show variety-in-unity, the variety cannot be explained away as epiphenomenal, illusory, purely apparent. It is there and it is an integral part of the work of art.

But on the Neo-Platonic theory, the general is inherently better and more beautiful than the individual and this point cannot be debated. It is a basic assumption probably founded on the fusion of the three hierarchies. One may dispute the fusion of reality with value, for there have been plenty of men who have maintained the very opposite of this opinion. Reality, for all we know, may be evil and ugly. But it must be granted that the great tradition has not been guided to that course. We shall later examine the notion of the real but content ourselves for the time being with indicating its relation to a theory of value.[12] We

---

[12] See Chapter IX, p. 220.

have the following points of view in history: the real is the good; the real and the good are fundamentally different; the real is the bad; the real is both good and bad. The tradition stemming from Plato maintained the first of these theses; that stemming from Democritus, the second; that stemming from Schopenhauer, the third. I know of no theory which maintains the fourth. This is obviously over-simplification and in each of these traditions, as in all others, there were waverings. Thus in a materialistic hedonism, such as that attributed to Democritus, an argument might be raised about whether the pleasurable sensations which were the marks of value were real or not, but when a man says that only atoms and the void are real, he cannot logically maintain that something which is not atoms and the void is also real.

There is a second difficulty in this type of explanation which is more easily disposed of. That is the temporalizing of the Principle of Perfection. The difficulty here lies in the stability of the temporal pattern which is in conflict with the mobility of the events manifesting the pattern. The pattern itself, since it is found everywhere, is always the same, and thus when one reflects upon it, one sees no evidence of a before or after. It is like an algebraic formula which serves as a guide to the mathematician for performing a calculation. The calculation takes time but the formula is eternal. Similarly the Two Ways in the Plotinian universe will be manifested by temporal events, but the Ways themselves exist in both the temporal and the eternal worlds. For just as there is emanation this side of the Intelligibles, so there is emanation on the other side, "Yonder," as Plotinus says. But the latter kind of emanation is the relationship between premises and conclusions, and whatever priority and posteriority are there are logical. The former kind of emanation is the relationship between cause and effect, between the source of something and the thing itself, between the seed and the plant. And this obviously is chronological. Aspiration for the timeless is found down here on earth in the actual lives of human beings. It is dramatic, a struggle against evil, in which a soul may be the victim. But in the Intelligble World, since there is no temporality, the aspiration of souls towards union with the Soul of the World, the order which such aspiration exemplifies, cannot be a struggle in the same sense. Let me quote a passage from the *Enneads* (VI, vii, 20) to illustrate something of the problem.

> [After giving up the search for the good through desire] must we not turn to judgments and the contrarieties that objects manifest, such as order and disorder, symmetry and dissymmetry, health and sickness, form and formlessness, existence and destruction, in short, composition and decomposition? For would anyone doubt that of such things the first term of each couple is in the same class as the good? But, if this is so, then we must also place their source in the class of the good. And then virtue and intelligence and life and soul, at least the rational soul, are also in the class of the good. And furthermore whatever rational life seeks. Why not then stop, someone will say, at intelligence and set this down as the good? For soul and life bear traces of intelligence and soul longs for it. And moreover it judges and seeks intelligence, judging that justice is better than injustice and that each kind of virtue is better than that kind of evil; and the objects on which it places the highest value are the same as it chooses. But if it longs for intelligence only, perhaps one would have to discourse longer to show that intelligence is not the terminus and that all things [do not long for] intelligence but for the good. Of those things which do not have intelligence, not all seek to possess it, whereas those who do have it do not stop at it but seek further for the good, and they seek intelligence through reasoning, but the good even before they can reason. But if it longs for life and everlasting being and activity [rather than passivity], the object of its longing is such not as intelligence but as good and as proceeding from good and leading to good.

The search for the good is thus a search universally present and its termination is in the One. The set of contrarieties which opens this passage is itself evidence of how the good may be sought down here as well as up there. No commentator has ever disputed this. The clash in opinion occurs at the point at which it is realized that the search for the good down here has one particular characteristic which is not only different from but antithetical to the same search in the world up there. The leap from the world of time into the world of eternity does not seem so great as the reverse process. For when we contemplate the essences in our terrestrial life we do indeed seem to have escaped from time; we are not doing anything; we are simply looking. But if we start with the One, a moment comes when the leap into multiplicity and temporality becomes so great that it is both unpredictable and illogical. There is the same logical surd here as in the instance of essence and existence. Plotinus was in no worse a trap than anyone else who would deny the radical duality of ideas and their objects, essences and existents, classes and their members, universals and particulars, and so on. Though the ultimate design of change may be uniform, the distinction between temporal change and logical change, between processes, growth, development, what you will, and implication remains. Plotinus himself, like the rest of us, had to admit the existence of time, and, even if he found a way of evading it in the attainment of the good, nevertheless the fact that he had to evade it showed that it existed.

Like the causalist and the teleologist, Plotinus thought that he had discovered the basic structure or pattern of the universe. Like them, too, he maintained that when one asks why something happens, the answer is that it exemplifies in its occurrence the general pattern. But since the formulas of explanation seem to express something beyond the way we think, explanation seems to depend upon metaphysics. In denotation the statement that something is seeking the good is no different from the statement that something is moving in a predeterminable direction. Thus such a theory as Spencer's evolutionism would be a species of the same kind of explanatory technique as Plotinus's. For Spencer, too, believed that the cyclical process of natural change was both a movement towards greater integration and a counter-movement towards disintegration. Again, an historian who sees the course of human events as progress towards the better unconsciously pursued by the race as a whole or by separate nations or cultures or civilizations duplicates the anabasis of the Neo-Platonists without committing himself to the theory of the two worlds. When he introduces a counter-movement of inevitable decline and fall, the duplication of the katabasis also is introduced. And since the Intelligible World was in effect the eternal pattern of the Sen-

sible World, a pattern in which change was frozen, as it had to
be if any pattern was to be discovered, the outstanding difference
between such theories and that of Plotinus was in the connotation
of the words in which they were expressed. This type of explanation appears then in various disguises. Sometimes it appears as a
theory of cosmic cycles, a theory adumbrated in what is left of
Empedocles, in Stoicism, in Nietzsche's notion of eternal recurrence
—based, however, on quite different assumptions—and in the
historical speculations of Spengler. There is a suggestion of the
same sort of thinking in Bergsonian evolutionism, where the
swing between mechanism and vitality, habit and adventure, intellect and instinct, matter and life, is analogous to but not identical with the Plotinian Two Ways.[13] The main difference between
such theories and that of the Neo-Platonists lies in their being
usually restricted to one range of changes, biological, cultural,
political, religious, instead of being established as a cosmic rule.
But the fundamental tenet is always two ultimate goals for all
changes, goals which are given a positive and a negative value,
which values need not be present to the minds of the individuals
undergoing the changes. Thus integration and disintegration were
respectively good and bad in the eyes of Spencer, just as the words
chosen by Spengler to name the first and last periods of historical
cycles connote goodness and evil. It is clear that to be born is
not in itself a good, nor is to die necessarily an evil. Surely no
argument is needed to prove this particular point. But there is
always an atmosphere of gloom in accounts of declines and falls
as of euphoria in accounts of births and growths. Even so tough
a mind as Stalin, when he wrote about history, urged his readers
not to "base [their] orientation on the strata of society which are
no longer developing, even though they at present constitute the
predominant force, but on those strata which are developing and
have a future before them, even though they at present do not
constitute the predominant force."[14] If one asks why that which is

---

[13] For undulatory theories of history in antiquity, see Lovejoy and Boas; *Primitivism in Antiquity,* Baltimore, 1935, pp. 2, 6, 173.

[14] Joseph Stalin; *Dialectical and Historical Materialism,* N.Y., 1940 (Little Lenin
Library, Vol. 25), p. 13.

coming to birth is any better than that which is "no longer developing," the only answer is faith in the future. The dialectical process was in itself an assurance of the triumph of the good, as defined by the dialectician. In Stalin's case the good was the dictatorship of the proletariat and the ultimate achievement of the classless society. As a practical politician, he seems to have been somewhat reluctant to cast his burdens on the dialectical process, but such a conflict between what a man believes and what he does is not so unusual as to cause surprise.

Explanation by the Principle of Perfection is not then confined to Plotinus, if one is willing to extract its fundamental assumptions from it and to recognize them when not used for religious purposes. The value of using Plotinus as the model of this type of thinking is the clarity with which the Principle is expressed. In his works we need have no doubts why he believed it to be a universal law; its universality lay in his fusion of the three hierarchies as we have tried to make clear. Later thinkers sometimes dropped one or another of these hierarchies, but no one who sees change as a change in the direction of some value, set up as a goal towards which all things are moving, can deny that he has incorporated into his system a fusion of fact and value. There is, however, another type of explanation in which general laws are established which do not seem to involve values. That type was called legalism by Emile Meyerson. We shall now turn to it.

Chapter VIII

EXPLANATION — BY GENERAL LAWS

By "general laws" I mean generalizations about the behavior of things which may extend from small classes to the universe as a whole, if it is a whole. Since it is my conviction, based upon reading the history of philosophy, that all types of explanation are such laws, however they may be phrased, I am in effect denying the popular distinction between the "why" and the "how." This naturally does not entail the impossibility of making such a distinction, for it is obvious that if one insists that only teleological explanations are valid, then legalistic explanations will not be, unless the laws are teleological. For the sake of brevity, I shall call explanation by general laws "legalism."

The classic example of legalism is found in Newton's *Principia*. It will be recalled that out of the three Laws of Motion, corroborated by what the seventeenth century called experimentation, much of which was purely intellectual, Newton deduced the Law of Gravitation. This law defined in mathematical language the relationship of two or more gravitating bodies as a function of mass and distance. He made two cardinal assumptions, the well-known assumptions of absolute space and absolute time, which appeared in a scholium to Definition VIII, the definition of "the motive quantity of a centripetal force."[1] We are not here interested in discussing these two assumptions. But it should be pointed out that there was a procedural assumption also which

---

[1] All quotations from Newton and Cotes in this chapter are from *Sir Isaac Newton's Mathematical Principles* . . . , Motte's translation edited by Florian Cajori, Berkeley, 1946. This edition has been put into modern English. In view of Cajori's great erudition in the field of mathematical history, it seemed wiser to rely on him than to make new translations of my own, which would be more likely to be wrong.

requires some study. That appears frequently both in Newton's own comments and in the famous preface to the second edition of the *Principia* by Cotes. That assumption elucidates the subject-matter of the laws.

In Cotes's preface we find a distinction being made between three sets of physicists: the Peripatetics, the Cartesians, and the Newtonians. The Peripatetics, he says (p. xx), attribute "to the several species of things, specific and occult qualities, according to which the phenomena of particular bodies are supposed to proceed in some unknown manner . . . They affirm that the several effects of bodies arise from the particular natures of these bodies. But whence it is that these bodies derive these natures they don't tell us; and therefore they tell us nothing."[2] As far as dynamics is concerned, Cotes is referring ultimately to the Aristotelian theory of natural positions according to which there was a theoretical correlation between what we should call the chemical composition of a moving body and its natural motion. The adjective "natural" has to be inserted here, since it was possible and indeed usual for a body to be in a position which was not natural, as is seen when water bubbles up from beneath the earth or falls from the clouds or when earth is carried up and then dropped. There is, moreover, room for believing that if Nature had been allowed to take her course unhindered by unnatural events, all the four elements would have been always in their natural positions and local motion would not have occurred.[3] Cotes therefore is objecting to a theory which cannot reach a set of uniform laws covering all motions of all bodies, regardless of their "natures." He is assuming that variety is itself a problem and that it must be explained as having what he calls a source or cause. Why he calls the qualities in question occult is probably his reliance on Renaissance physicists rather than on Aristotle himself, for Aristotle actually defined the four elements as com-

---

[2] One might reasonably ask Cotes why he thought these natures had to be derived from anything.

[3] For those interested in what Aristotle took for granted, it may be worth while to refer to my article, "Presuppositions of Aristotle's Physics," *American Journal of Philology*, Vol. LVII, No. 1 (January 1936).

binations of two primary qualities, heat and moisture, and their absence, coldness and dryness. Hotness, coldness, dryness, and moistness were far from being occult. They were just as phenomenal as anything measured by Newton. But it is true that they could not be measured quantitatively or at any rate were not by Aristotle.[4] Moreover, as I have suggested above, the possible motions of the four elements were observable and more harmonious with common-sense observation than the motions which occur in accordance with the Law of Gravitation. No one as yet has ever been able to keep a quantity of air beneath a layer of water without interposing an impenetrable screen between the two, and candle flames still mount upwards as rain continues to fall downwards. But that need not occupy us here at length. Cotes was not really writing a commentary on Aristotle.

His objections to the Cartesians were based on their hypothesis of vortices. He accepts their doctrine that all matter is homogeneous and their procedure of "going on from simple things to those which are more compounded . . . if they attribute to those primary relations [i.e., the relations involved in the compounds] no other relations than those which Nature has given." But the theory of vortices, he maintains, involves the assumption of "unknown figures and magnitudes," "uncertain situations and motions of the parts," "occult motions," and from these nothing can be deduced but an "ingenious romance." By "simple things," Cotes seems to mean scientific laws based on observation, such as the First Law of Motion, from which consequences can be deduced without introducing new explanatory hypotheses. In this he is in agreement with Descartes himself who in the *Discourse on Method* had posited as one of his rules the organizing of ideas from simple to complex, which clearly in the context meant from

---

4 Insofar as hotness, for instance, is a felt quality, it could be found in various degrees of intensity, and similar things could be said about the other three basic qualities. But intensities can be measured in only two ways: (1) by asking observers to arrange their qualitative experiences in a scale or (2) by correlating the felt qualities with physical "stimuli" which can themselves be measured quantitatively. The former procedure is faulty for obvious reasons. The latter is the procedure adopted by Renaissance physicists and their modern successors. But it denies the primacy of the qualities as factors of the non-human world.

the logically prior to the logically posterior. Moreover, that is precisely what Newton himself did in the section following his definitions, the section giving his Axioms or Laws of Motions. Now no one would maintain that the First Law of Motion was a straightforward description of observed events, for no one could observe any body in "uniform motion in a right line," unless he were first to remove all friction and the resistance of the medium through which the motion is taking place. In fact Newton is so aware of this that he himself explains why we do not observe this, citing the example of projectiles and tops. I am not presumptuous enough to object to Newton's procedure, for its elegance and utility are beyond question. But it is just as well to know what is happening in contrast to what is claimed. The three laws were to be sure based upon sound procedures, nor is my testimony required to prove this. But the procedure itself was devised to prove the laws which themselves were required to make the deductions of the *Principia* valid.

The third group of physicists, the Newtonians, "possess experimental philosophy." Like the Cartesians, they "derive the causes of all things from the most simple principles possible; but then they assume nothing as a principle, that is not proved by phenomena." But the phenomena in question are not the sensory data of a Mach, to say nothing of a Comte. They are the observations which occur in highly controlled and highly purified circumstances, controlled so as to give maximum generality and purified so as to construct—or enable one to imagine—a situation in which only the factors under investigation are present. This is necessary if one is to reason in what Newton in the *System of the World* called "a mathematical way" (p. 550). Thus in his Scholium to Book I, Proposition LXIX, Theorem xxix (p. 192), when he is discussing his use of the word "attraction," he says, "I use the word *attraction* in general for any endeavor whatever, made by bodies to approach each other, whether that endeavor arise from the action of the bodies themselves, as tending to each other or agitating each other by spirits emitted; or whether it arises from the action of the ether or of the air, or of any medium whatever, whether corporeal or incorporeal, in any manner impelling bodies placed therein towards each other. In the same general sense I use the word *impulse,* not defining in this treatise the species or physical qualities of forces, but investigating the quantities and mathematical proportions of them . . . In mathematics we are to investigate the quantities of forces with their proportions consequent upon any conditions supposed; then, when we enter upon physics, we compare those proportions with the phenomena of Nature, that we may know what conditions of those forces answer to the several kinds of attractive bodies. And this preparation being made, we argue more safely concerning the physical species, causes, and proportions of the forces." Attraction then is something which is a phenomenon only in the sense that it appears in spatio-temporal changes of relation: the bodies are nearer to or farther from each other at different times, and the space and time are given. Similar comments may be made about impulse. We can see and measure the distances and correlate them with the masses, which latter may not be observable but can be calculated. But though they may be either phenomena or inferred from phenomena, they are far from being the neutral entities of the radical empiricists or the Bertrand Russell of the *Analysis of Matter.* There is no "pure experience" in Newton— nor for that matter in anyone else of that period—and indeed if experience is pure enough, it would furnish us no rules whatsoever for organizing it, since it would be momentary and irrelevant to anything else. Newton is simply rejecting the idea popular in his age of inner natures, but rejecting them merely as fit subjects for scientific study. He wishes to "avoid all questions about the nature or quality of this force [i.e., the force which moves the heavenly bodies] which we would not be understood to determine by any hypothesis" (p. 550).

Even Cotes realized that the phenomena in question were not the sensory data of common sense. To begin with, he relies on the consensus of scientists. "It is now agreed by all philosophers that all circumterrestrial bodies gravitate towards the earth" (p. xxi). Observations must not be confined to the experience of one man but must be corroborated by that of others. This necessity is not given in any experience, as is obvious, but is assumed prior to announcing an experience as valid. Moreover, when he comes to the matter of the Third Law, he feels the obligation of proving it; he does not simply ask his readers to look and see for themselves. But what could be more self-evident than a phenomenon in the sense in which that term might be used by a positivist or radical empiricist? He is also aware of the need of some rule upon which generalization can be justified. That rule was later to be called the Uniformity of Nature. "Effects of the same kind," he says (p. xxvi), "whose known properties are the same, take their rise from the same causes and have the same unknown properties also. For if gravity be the cause of the descent of a stone in *Europe,* who doubts that it is also the cause of the same descent in *America?* . . . All philosophy is founded on this rule; for if that be taken away, we can affirm nothing as a general truth. The constitution of particular things is known by observations and experiments; and when that is done, no general conclusion of the nature of things can thence be drawn, except by this rule." Whether one like the principle of the Uniformity of Nature or not, or approve of its formulation in these words, it is used by Cotes as a method of going beyond observation which, he quite correctly says, is always of particulars. Our own contemporaries would properly invite Cotes's attention to the words, "effects of the same kind," for the qualifying phrase already extends the observation beyond what is before one. Moreover, if what one sees is known to be an effect, then phenomena must be of such a nature that they have already been organized intellectually in a matrix of relations which includes their causes. The total complex in that case is the known-cause-plus-the-known-effect and the phrase "of the same kind" presupposes a knowledge of either things which have preceded the occurrence of whatever is before one or of the anterior phases of it. But surely one of the great questions which the natural scientist had to face was whether all effects were of the same kind, and that question could be answered only by accepting the conclusions of one's predecessors or by fiat, if one was to begin as Newton began.

Most modern theories of knowledge, whether positivistic or not, acknowledge the duality of rules and of descriptive statements. The rules tell us how to make the statements and therefore are said to be neither true nor false. But if they are not, then the question arises of in what sense the statements which they dictate can ever be true or false. If we elaborate a rule according to which we can predict that water will flow uphill—a rule that everything seeks the higher levels of reality—we can undoubtedly make certain deductions by its help. But it is questionable whether anyone other than its inventor would ever use it. If then we say that we must frame only those rules which will enable us to make predictions which can be verified in particular instances—which is a second rule—then we must solve the problem of how much deviation we shall accept as normal. That water always flows uphill can be disproved by one instance, but that water always flows downhill cannot be proved by any finite number of instances. That may well be one of the reasons why the history of the sciences proceeds by the rejection of disproved theories rather than by the complete verification of proposed theories.[5]

In spite of their abandonment of occult properties, the Newtonians did not deny the difference between the inner nature of things and their overt behavior. What things did was attributable to their inner natures, but the inner natures could not be known. When Newton in the *System of the World* (p. 550) says that he is not trying to frame an hypothesis about the nature or quality of the force which moves the heavenly bodies, he does not deny that there is such a nature or force and he is not using these terms simply as a sop to his opponents. In a letter to Bentley, quoted by Cajori (p. 634), he says, "It is inconceivable that inanimate brute matter, should, without the mediation of something else, which is not material, operate upon and affect other matter without mutual contact, as it must be, if gravitation, in the sense of Epicurus,

---

[5] Cf. K. R. Popper's interesting article, "Three Views concerning Human Knowledge," in *Contemporary British Philosophy*, London, 1956.

be essential and inherent in it. And this is one reason why I desired you would not ascribe innate gravity to me. That gravity should be innate, inherent, and essential to matter, so that one body may act upon another at a distance through a vacuum, without the mediation of anything else, by and through which their action and force may be conveyed from one to another, is to me so great an absurdity, that I believe no man, who has in philosophical matters a competent faculty of thinking, can ever fall into it. Gravity must be caused by an agent acting constantly according to certain laws; but whether this agent be material or immaterial, I have left to the consideration of my readers." This is not simply a denial of action at a distance; it is also an insistence that the spatio-temporal dislocations of material bodies must be caused by something which is not the bodies themselves. That something, he maintains *(ibid.)*, must be a single being, for though bodies can be seen to move in a great variety of directions, describing all sorts of paths as they move, yet their paths can be calculated according to one law, the Law of Gravitation. He himself is merely trying to prove that law and is making no hypotheses about why it should prevail, what its agent or executive is. He is here assuming that a variety of phenomena of the same kind must be describable in a single generalization, which is almost tautological, and that matter itself is ineffectual, an assumption which was common in his time. When one reaches the laws of which one is in search, one will attain in Cotes's words to a knowledge of those laws "on which the Great Creator actually chose to found this most beautiful Frame of the World, not those by which he might have done the same, had he so pleased" (p. xxvii). And again, "All sound and true philosophy is founded on the appearance of things; and if these phenomena inevitably draw us, against our wills, to such principles as most clearly manifest to us the most excellent counsel and supreme dominion of the All-wise and Almighty Being, they are not therefore to be laid aside because some men may perhaps dislike them" (p. xxxii). The agent or cause of gravitation then is God. In other words, when we reach a universal law, we can go no further and must simply rest from our labors. The law acquires the status of a fact, something with which one is confronted and which must be accepted as it is without further question. Thus the law which is the goal of inquiry can never itself become the source of further inquiry. Since God actually plays no part in whatever demonstrations are elaborated to prove the law, one can disregard His presence and be satisfied with legalism.

It is strange that Newton who is usually cited as the most perfect example of the legalistic scientist, should not have been thus satisfied. Quite the contrary, he felt that he had to proceed still further. In his famous *General Scholium* he pointed to the direction of his further progress. After indicating the orbits of the planets, comets, and satellites, he says (p. 544), "This most beautiful system . . . could only proceed from the counsel and dominion of an intelligent and powerful Being." But such a conclusion was not deduced from his scientific data and inferences, as given in the body of the *Principia*. A new premise seems to be introduced, namely the premise that physical law must be laid down by a legislator as required in the cosmological argument for God's existence. But the meaning of "law" then appears to be ambiguous, meaning both a generalized statement of the way things are—in this case, the way bodies gravitate—and an order directing them to be so. But if one introduces this ambiguity and utilizes it in argument, there seems to be no compelling reason to postpone its introduction until the end of the book. He continues, "And if the fixed stars are the centres of other like systems, these, being formed by the wise counsel, must be all subject to the dominion of One; especially since the light of the fixed stars is of the same nature with the light of the sun, and from every system light passes into all the other systems: and lest the systems of the fixed stars should, by their gravity, fall on each other, he hath placed those systems at immense distances from one another." The first inference need raise no new questions on our part, but the second inserts teleological explanation in its appropriate theological form. Newton had taken note of the immense distances between the various stellar systems and, lest someone should ask why they are not closer together, gives a purpose: the distances prevent collisions. But once more there is nothing in the body of the *Principia* from which one could deduce the desirability, the value, the goodness of the gravitational order which has been mathematically described. But once the Law had been given imperative as well as descriptive meaning, then one is led on to ask what good is accomplished by it. Would it not be as reasonable and more self-consistent simply to state the immense distances, if that is of interest, and let it go at that? There is surely nothing mathematical in the Newtonian sense of that adjective in such teleological speculations and much that runs counter to the mathematical spirit.

Now Newton, we must insist, since we are living in a time when it is customary to doubt the sincerity of authors, was deeply in earnest in his *General Scholium*. He proceeds to discuss why "this being" who "governs all things," is called "Lord God, *pantocrator*, or Universal Ruler." He insists upon God as a ruler, as having dominion over creation; he is not the God of Descartes who, as Pascal remarked, stepped back after giving the initial push to the moving universe. He has "true dominion," "and from his true dominion it follows that the true God is a living, intelligent, and powerful Being; and, from his other perfections, that he is supreme, or most perfect. He is eternal and infinite, omnipotent and omniscient; that is, his duration reaches from eternity to eternity; his presence from infinity to infinity; he governs all things, and knows all things that are or can be done" (p. 545). But he does all this, Newton is careful to say, not as the Soul of the World but as Lord over all. In other words he has existence separate from that of the cosmos. Moreover, "He is not eternity and infinity, but eternal and infinite; he is not duration or space, but he endures and is present." He is a subject which has attributes. Newton is emphatic about this: "He is omnipresent not *virtually* only, but also *substantially;* for virtue cannot exist without substance." Yet though he has so many characteristics of other subjects, there is one which he does not have: he is utterly unaffected by the things which are contained and moved in him. The transitive relations which he sustains to Creation are asymmetrical and indeed seem to be without converses. "He is all similar, all eye, all ear, all brain, all arm, all power to perceive, to understand, and to act; but in a manner not at all human, in a manner not at all corporeal, in a manner utterly unknown to us . . . We have no idea of the manner by which the all-wise God perceives and understands us . . . We have ideas of his attributes, but what the real substance of anything is we know not. In bodies, we see only their outward surfaces, we smell only the smells, and taste the savors; but their inward substances are not known either by our senses, or by any reflex act of our minds: much less, then, do we have any idea of the substance of God." The distinction between substance and attribute, between the inner and the outer natures, is thus intensified, and our ignorance of both substances and inner natures is said to be universal. But so far Newton gives no reason to make the distinctions involved, and one is driven to assign them to tradition alone. As far as God is concerned, he says (p. 546), "We know him only by his most wise and excellent contrivances of things, and final causes; we admire him for his perfections; but we reverence and adore him on account of his dominion: for we adore him as his servants; and a god without dominion, providence, and final causes, is nothing else but Fate and Nature." As far as other things are concerned, we know them by their sensory qualities and their behavior. On what grounds does he separate God from His wisdom, power, dominion? Even if we assume that it makes sense to speak of the wisdom shown by a single law of gravitation, rather than by several laws, it does not follow that there is a personal center of this wisdom, a mind which is wise. But Newton cannot rid himself of the idea that adjectives must modify nouns and that if no noun is forthcoming from his data, he must invent one. This appears even more clearly in the lines which he writes on the "cause of gravity."

"Hitherto," he says (*ibid.*), "we have explained the phenomena of the heavens and of our sea by the power of gravity, but have not yet assigned the cause of this power. This is certain, that it must proceed from a cause that penetrates to the very centres of the sun and planets, without suffering the least diminution of its force; that operates not according to the quantity of the surfaces of the particles upon which it acts (as mechanical causes used to do), but according to the quantity of solid matter which they contain, and propagates its virtue on all sides to immense distances, decreasing always as the inverse square of the distance . . . But hitherto I have not been able to discover the cause of those properties of gravity from phenomena, and I frame no hypotheses; and hypotheses, whether metaphysical or physical, whether of occult qualities or mechanical, have no place in experimental philosophy. In this philosophy particular propositions are inferred from the phenomena, and afterwards rendered general by induction. Thus it was that the impenetrability, the mobility, and the impulsive force of bodies, and the laws of motion and of gravitation, were discovered. And to us it is enough that gravity does really exist, and act according to the laws which we have explained, and abundantly serves to account for all the motions of the celestial bodies, and of our sea." What he has accomplished is the formulation of a general law from which motions can be predicted, given masses and distances. All motions fell under this law, whether sublunary or superlunary, regardless of the chemical constitution of the moving bodies. But he is still uneasy about the cause of these motions. In the language of common sense, he wonders why the law is as it is rather than otherwise. And to this there was naturally no answer. For (1) if his law is universal, which means, if there are no exceptions to it, there is no problem of why it is as it is; for it is an answer, not a question. And (2) if the universe is a single and all-inclusive system, there is no explaining anything about it as a whole. In regard to the first remark, cause can be introduced only to explain deviations from the rule, and there are no deviations. In regard to the second, the whole cannot be described in terms other than those which refer to things contained within it. If the universe of moving bodies is as self-contained as Newton thought it was, then being unique and *sui generis,* it can be referred to no anterior or external beings, since there are none.

It is, however, well known that Newton was not satisfied to leave things at this point. The last paragraph of the *Principia* contains the famous hints of "a certain most subtle spirit which pervades and lies hid in all gross bodies, by the force and action of which spirit the particles of bodies attract one another at near distances, and cohere, if contiguous; and electric bodies operate to greater distances, as well repelling as attracting the neighboring corpuscles; and light is emitted, reflected, refracted, inflected, and heats bodies; and all sensation is excited, and the members of animal bodies move at the command of the will, namely by the vibrations of this spirit, mutually propagated along the solid filaments of the nerves, from the outward organs of sense to the brain, and from the brain to the muscles" (p. 547). This subtle and elastic spirit was a descendant of the *pneumata* of the Ancients and a remote ancestor perhaps of Kant's *Dinge-an-sich.* Its appearance justifies Meyerson's conclusion that Newton himself was not satisfied with legalism, even though Newton admitted that he was not "furnished with that sufficiency of experiments which is required to an accurate determination and demonstration of the laws by which this electric and elastic spirit operates" *(ibid.).* But even if he had been so furnished, would he not have raised another question: why does it operate in accordance with these rather than other laws? Or would he have stopped and said simply that it was operating according to the will of God? "Experimental philosophy" would have given him the laws and then he would have been faced with the problem of the inner nature of that which the laws governed. This was inevitable if an existential distinction was to be made between natures and behavior. And Newton to the end clung to that distinction.

In what way does it clarify our minds or settle our doubts? Does it actually give us any more information than we had before we put the question and made the distinction? The kind of question which Newton raised in such passages emerges out of the following presuppositions: first, that all action demands an agent; second, the existential and qualitative duality of subject or substance and its attributes; third, the causal inefficacy of matter; fourth, the necessity of an ultimate purpose which the subjects of ultimate law achieve. All of these assumptions were commonplaces and it is unlikely that anyone in the seventeenth century would have thought of questioning them. Locke indeed questioned the objective existence of the secondary qualities but never the distinct existence of spiritual and material substances; Berkeley later did away with material substances but not with spiritual; Descartes kept them both, and though Spinoza called them attributes of a single substance, *Deus sive Natura,* the general principle that attributes must be attributes *of* something was not doubted by him. Even Gassendi, Neo-Epicurean though he claimed to be, never questioned the existence of substances which had inner natures, and as late as Hume we find scepticism simply about their natures, not their attributes. Condillac himself, who tried to be a thorough-going "sensationalist," nevertheless retained a spiritual substance to be the subject of sensations. The distinction between a thing's nature and its properties was not seriously questioned until the time of Fichte who, as is well known, ruled the unknowable *noumena* out of existence, but he ruled them out because of their unknowability, not because they were substances. His Ego is as much a substance as Locke's perceiving mind is; in fact, it is both a substance and an agent. In Descartes, the great doubter, the existence of an agent for all acts is never doubted. One knew it in the act of doubting. For an act required an agent, and, though he insisted that the *ergo* in his *cogito* was not the *ergo* of an argument, all he could possibly have apprehended in the act of doubting was the act itself. That matter was passive, something to be acted upon and never acting, was as old an assumption as Plato and was frequently used by philosophers to prove the existence of a spiritual agent to act upon it. It was essential to Plotinus's hierarchy and was inherent in Aristotle's *Metaphysics,* if not in his *Physics,* for the matter which contained the potentiality of forms, could not develop until an efficient cause had acted upon it. Even a superficial knowledge of the English Platonists will uncover the same motif running through their works, and I suspect that the reason why Newton found his subtle and elastic spirit activating matter will be discovered in the same quarter of the intellectual world. As for the ultimate teleology which was usually asserted, any kind of general order was in itself utilized as evidence of an orderer.

Unless I misread intellectual history badly, the assumption that all action demands an agent rests upon the preliminary analysis of all events into beginning, middle, and end. The termini isolate the events from one another, and though we do not usually ask why they stop, we seem compelled to ask why they begin. There are, to be sure, in many events dramatic breaks which are easily apprehended, breaks with the environing circumstances. In the life-cycle, for instance, we have no difficulty in distinguishing between the pre-natal and the post-natal periods, infancy, childhood, youth, maturity, old age, and death. But we also know that the dividing line between these periods is very indefinite and that the end of one merges into the beginning of the next continuously. We can atomize the living being into cells which compose his body, but the cells themselves are further reducible to chemical substances which in turn become physical particles which the atomic physicist studies. These substances may be immortal, and the only changes which they undergo are changes in position, changes in electrical charge, changes in velocity, and changes nowadays in mass. But such changes reveal no agent of a special nature to bring them about, unless the physicist operating his machines and measuring instruments can be called such. The periods of a cycle such as the life-cycle are determined on the level of gross perception. This does not mean that they do not occur or that they are unreal or illusory or "merely subjective." It simply means that by using instruments of cognition other than our unsupplemented sensory organs we shall not be able to find the same periods. Moreover, on the level of gross perception we find conditions under which the changes take place and without which they will not take place. But these conditions are far from being spiritual. The right temperature, the right food, and such things are perceptible and controllable. All that one gains by introducing them into the discussion is an extension of the context in which the cycle occurs and which plus the cycle make a large universe. In vulgar language, which a scientist might deplore, when a child eats food, the food both acts upon the child and is acted upon by him. It makes little difference to the metaphysician, though it makes a great deal of difference to the biologist, which is considered the agent and which the patient. It is, I imagine, granted that all animals need oxygen in order to live and that plants need carbon dioxide. We can say either that animals exist in order to provide carbon dioxide for plants or that plants exist in order to provide oxygen for animals. Similarly when one considers the nitrogen cycle. The roots of leguminous plants and atmospheric electricity fix some of the nitrogen in the environment; inorganic nitrogen compounds in the soil are absorbed through the roots of plants and form proteins; the proteins furnish food for animals which is eliminated and broken down into the nitrogen compounds which are again taken up by the plants; and some of the nitrogen in these compounds is also released into the air. Shall we say that the leguminosae exist in order to fix the nitrogen, that the plants exist in order to form proteins for the animals to eat; that animals exist in order to release nitrogen for the plants? Any of these statements would be possible, but would add nothing to our knowledge of botany and zoology. If there were no available nitrogen in the soil, then certain plants could not live. But there is no evidence here for anything other than the simple proposition that certain plants require nitrogen and find some available. Some of these also do not find any and die. We, having discovered the nitrogen cycle, can use it for our own purposes, and there is scarcely a farmer nowadays who does not supply the necessary fertilizer or does not plant a field of clover every so often and plow it under to help out. But if God were specially interested in keeping the cycle going, it would be easy enough for the Omnipotent to do so. The usual answer to this sort of observation is that God's purpose is to make us discover things for ourselves. Be that as it may, a cycle of this sort is rather proof of the intimate interrelations of things which seem external to one another, rather than of the presence of a spiritual cause operating through the cycle.

It is, moreover, just as difficult to understand the action of a spiritual agent on a material body as that of one material body on another. The unintelligibility of the latter was emphasized by Malebranche and Leibniz and later utilized by Hume in his celebrated critique of the ideas of causality. The difficulty of the former was noted by Descartes but nevertheless was swept away in his assertion of psychophysical interaction. It apparently seemed easier for him to believe that the mind, absolutely immaterial and non-spatial, could act upon the animal spirits than to believe that it could act directly upon the efferent nerves and the muscles. This may have been because the animal spirits seemed less material than nerves and muscles did; there is no way of knowing now. The difficulty, which led to Spinoza's parallelism, arose from the causal postulate which we have already examined, the postulate of the identity of substance between cause and effect. Only similars could sustain the causal relation. But there were greater difficulties too. If we so dematerialize the spiritual agent that it is not in space, then it obviously cannot act upon anything whatsoever which is in space, for it is neither here nor there, but is nowhere. It neither acts at a distance nor in contiguity with that upon which it acts. Therefore one cannot tell directly whether it is acting or not. Its presence can be detected only by the supposedly resultant act so that the assertions, "X takes place," and "X takes place because of the spiritual agent S," are equivalent, and the latter adds nothing to the former except a poetical aroma. I do not maintain that the meaning of the two sentences is the same, for it clearly is not. But I do mean that the latter sentence adds nothing more to the former than would be added if it read, "X takes place in space-time," or "X takes place as far as I know," or "X takes place according to the evidence at hand." For these additions are all in the nature of generally admitted conditions of investigation.

If spiritual agents can be differentiated from one another, so that one such has dominion over terrestrial events and the other over those events which occur in the planets, or such that some have dominion over mineral, others over vegetable, and still others over animal events, and if one can differentiate them not merely by what they do but also by what they are as distinguished from what they do, then the spiritual agents might serve to explain why certain events occur here and others there. But we have no evidence that will permit us to distinguish mineral spirits from vegetable and animal except the evidence of what the inhabitants of each kingdom do. Newton himself was inveighing against such occult qualities, and the clearest account of them that we have been able to find is that given in Aristotle. For there the vegetative soul is simply the power of nutrition and reproduction, as the animal is that of sensitivity and, though he did indeed speak of these souls as if they were separate entities lodged in various bodies, he spoke in this way seriously only in the case of the active reason. His souls were final causes and the final causes were what the things did when acting in accordance with Nature. The soul is the actuality of a body;[6] it is the function of the body. Actualities are found in final causes and exist only potentially before the final cause is realized. But if spiritual agents are interpreted in this way and are generalized to be spread into the inorganic world, then they are identical with natural law. For natural law is what things do on the whole. One can then identify the spiritual agents after the event but not beforehand, and what one discovers is a descriptive statement of a class of events. The spiritual agent in Newton's cosmos would be described in the Law of Gravitation and there would be no other agent discoverable. Aristotle, extended as I have suggested, would then assert precisely what Newton denies, namely that God acts as the Soul of the World and the Soul of the World would be the universal order which the events in the world ex-

---

[6] De anima, 412 b, 5.

hibit. That order would require no further explanation for there could be no further explanation. One would have legalism under another name.

The distinction between subject and attribute also goes back at least to Aristotle and is, as we all know, sanctified by language. The subject is both the grammatical and the metaphysical subject and the attributes are in the predicate. Theoretically any verb could be turned into an adjective and joined to the subject by the copula, though a sentence which asserts a relation between two things named by nouns resists such translation. If we say, "Chicago is west of New York," it is questionable whether "west of" is adjectival, but that need not concern us here. Most grammatical subjects are observable things with observable attributes. They are people, animals, plants, artefacts, and usually present no mystery since their "nature," or at least that part of it of interest to the person who says the sentence, is expressed more or less clearly in the predicate. But if the attributes are all reducible to sensory qualities and if the sensible qualities by hypothesis do not form an essential part of the subject's nature, then we have to have some criterion by means of which we can distinguish between those attributes which are an integral part of the subject and those which are not. In Locke the primary qualities belonged to the nature of the subject when the subject was material and the secondary did not. The primary qualities, as we have said, were those which were sufficient and for the most part necessary for the construction of Galilean physics. I say "for the most part," since configuration for example was not needed by Galileo, though no moving thing could be without some configuration. In some of the authors of the Middle Ages the primary qualities were those which were apprehended by touch.[7] But when we come to men like Hobbes and Locke, to say nothing of Galileo, the primary qualities are those which are constant and susceptible of mathematical treatment. They are,

---

[7] See for instance St. Bonaventura's *Itinerarium Mentis ad Deum*, II, 3. The qualities of number, magnitude, figure, rest, and motion were called *sensibilia communia*.

moreover, the qualities of that which causes the secondary qualities to arise. By the application of the causal postulate, discussed
above in Chapter V, unless the secondary qualities could be
transformed into modes of motion, they would be inexplicable.
For it soon became clear that colors, sounds, odors, feelings of
heat and cold, pain, tastes, and so on were more intimately associated with human beings than with the world of mechanics.
Unfortunately they were left stranded in the mind as somehow
or other unreal and, as Leibniz saw, their occurrence was not ac-
counted for by belts and cogs. What Leibniz wanted was a
causal explanation which would equate cause and effect. What
the mechanists wanted was a material ground for the secondary
qualities, and if they could conduct the motions of the material
and extra-somatic world into the human body—as they did
through the nerves—they were satisfied. The powerful word
"subjective" or one of its equivalents, when applied to the secondary qualities, seemed to dispose of them in a satisfactory
manner. It is strange that they did not correct their notion of
causality and flatly declare that there need be no such equality
between cause and effect as they had imagined. But the influence
of Galileo and Newton was such that the causal world had to be
the mechanical world, even though every moment saw men moving their own bodies about under the influence of secondary
qualities.

Unhappily substance, as Galilean matter, lacked, as Newton saw,
the power to do anything. The tradition of material inefficacy
was so strong that when matter seemed to be doing something,
its activity had to be attributed to some occult power within it, as
we have seen. If, as in Berkeley, only spirits could act, then we did
know and know intimately the nature of substance, for we ourselves were spirits. And by making the ideas in the mind of
God a vast and eternal system of causes which would preserve the
causal postulate and also account for the rise of all ideas in men's
minds, Berkeley was able to construct a world which would
replace the world of Nature and create none of the older problems. But it did create new problems, for if everything is ideal,

the adjective loses all discriminatory meaning, and Berkeley had to distinguish between God's ideas and our own, and to provide some way by which we might err. Since he was unwilling for a variety of reasons to accept Malebranche's theory of vision in God, the inner nature of things became almost as unknowable as it had been in his predecessors. Almost, since after all he did know that it was ideal.

Now the notion of an attribute can easily be extended to cover both the functions of a thing and its various relations. It is true that historically, beginning to all intents and purposes with Aristotle, there were sensory qualities which, like the elemental qualities of hot, cold, moist, and dry, floated from one bit of matter to another. But history does not compel us to accept all its confusions and we can retain the useful distinction between subject and attribute without being driven to unknowable noumena. A flower which smells sweet is a subject whether its color, texture, weight, and all other properties are primary, secondary, or tertiary. If you ask what is the nature of a rose, its nature is in part to smell like a rose. Its nature is also to have a certain number of petals, leaves of a certain configuration. Anything that can be truly said about a rose is part of its nature. Any book on botany will give the essential characteristics of the family *rosaceae,* and they are the nature of that family. But someone will say that these are not the characteristics of the matter which forms roses. That is certainly true, but we are talking about roses, not about chemistry. But similar things can be said about any nature. A popular description of *oxygen* runs, "An element with the atomic weight of 16.000. An odorless, invisible gas; the most abundant of all the elements; forms approximately one fifth of the atmosphere; chemically very active; etc. etc. Used for welding and metalcutting."[8] All of this and more are its nature. A nuclear physicist could undoubtedly add more to the description, and what he would say about the element would differ from, but not contradict, what the chemist says about it. But again someone might object, these

---

[8] Abridged from Uvarov and Chapman; *A Dictionary of Science,* Penguin Reference Books, *s.v.*

are all variable characteristics. As the perceptible rose fades and disappears, though its material substance remains in some form or other, so the perceptible forms of oxygen also may change. Now it appears as iron oxide, now as carbon dioxide, now as free oxygen in the atmosphere. We are, such an objector would insist, in search of the permanent substratum which can move about and take on these different aspects without itself changing. That permanent substratum nowadays may be identified with the various entities that are discovered within the atom, the electrons, protons, neutrons, and so on. But, alas, some of them change too under certain circumstances and change in a fashion which seems lawful to the physicist. But is it not their nature to behave as they do? Would it not be more reasonable to accept the mutability of substance as one of its permanent traits and to wake up to the fact that what does not change is the law in accordance with which the changes take place? Finally it should not be forgotten that when one says that oxygen is *really* a sub-atomic congeries of entities studied by the nuclear physicist, he is saying no more than that his methods of study are limited to certain phases of the gas. We do not breathe protons and electrons; we breathe oxygen. And similarly the carbon compounds which are *really* the rose are not what we smell and grow in our gardens.

One of the more amusing aspects of the history of this idea is the sight of substantial traits turning into adjectives and adjectives turning into subjects. If we say, "The rose is red," *red* is an attribute; but if we say, "Red is a color," then it becomes a subject. Linguistically we find that all common nouns have adjectival forms, just as verbs do. Even the verb *to be* has been substantialized into *being,* and in mediaeval Latin we find, *esse, essentia, ens, essentialis,* and *essentialiter.*[9] These metamorphoses ought to suggest that such distinctions are grammatical and are made for purposes of discourse. If we can talk about something, it becomes a subject and its duration is irrelevant to its substantiality.

---

9 Most of these do not occur in classical Latin, though Seneca attributes *essentia* to Cicero in *Epistle* 58, 6 and *essentialiter* is found as early as St. Augustine, *De Trinitate,* vii, 2. See Harper's Latin Dictionary, rev. by Lewis and Short, *s.v.*

But as long as we cling to the assumption that substance must be immutable and everlasting, we shall indeed find that it is unknowable. It would seem more intelligent to classify the scientific and philosophic constants as the permanent beings, substitute them for the Galilean substances, in which case we shall be able to have knowable substances and put them to some use. What we need is reliable knowledge, not a permanent material world. If our procedures are unvarying, we shall be bound to find two things: a world which they are suitable to examine and a world which eludes their examination. The latter will probably be also broken up into several other worlds. And the one over-all constant will be whatever logical rules we adopt.

We have already spoken of the third of Newton's assumptions, the causal inefficacy of matter, and shall not dwell upon it in this place. It is enough to say that if matter is simply that out of which things are made, Aristotle's material cause, then it would indeed be impossible for it to turn into an efficient cause. Aristotle himself was willing to accept the efficacy of some kinds of matter, organic matter, for in the *De generatione animalium* he makes the semen the efficient cause acting upon the catamenia which are the material cause. But in general the Ancients wished to make a sharp division between the active and the passive, corresponding to the grammatical division in verbs, and they had to have something which was always active and something which was always passive. It is likely, but not certain, that the metaphor of the craftsman was behind this and that the efficient cause was in origin someone who made or did something. Even as recently as Whitehead, we find a philosopher seeking some experience which would enlighten us about the nature of causality and discovering it in our feeling of effort, of exerting power. Such anthropomorphism seems deplorable but may very well be what philosophers have meant when they have spoken of causes *producing* their effects. But Whitehead did not relegate productivity to a special realm and that which is produced to another. There may be, for all I know, some things which are absolutely incapable of entering into causal relations, totally inefficacious, though I confess to having no idea of what they are. But anyone who has ever engaged in even the most elementary chemical experiments will not believe that matter is one of them. It is more intelligible to say that oxygen combines with iron to form rust than to ask what there is in oxygen to cause it to oxydize certain metals. The oxygen is sufficient cause, granted the necessary conditions, one of which is spatial contiguity. But the doctrine of material inefficacy has not died out, and the Thomistic argument for the existence of God based on motion is a good example of its survival.

The fourth assumption, the necessity of an ultimate purpose, is a residue of Newton's theological beliefs. There is no reason to deduce any ulterior purpose whatsoever from astronomy and that the order of the universe is its own purpose could be accepted by us as it was by the Stoics and Spinoza. Not even the most pious of us would ask what was the purpose of things this side of the ultimate, the purpose of the seven spectral colors, of the inaudible sound waves, of the variation in atomic weights, of the liquidity of mercury, of linear perspective, or even of the distribution of the prime numbers. We may utilize these things for our own purposes and we may admire them all. But when we come to the "first and last things," we begin to look for purposes. If there is an anthropomorphic God, then it is probable that the present order of the universe accomplishes some purpose of His, for one of the essential characteristics of a man is to be purposive. But a purposive being ought to have choice, ought to be able to change the order of things as he sees fit, and if he has created something which always exemplifies eternal laws, then he has created a machine. His purpose in creating this particular machine will never be discoverable since we have no knowledge of other machines which he has created and thus have no means of comparison. If, in accordance with most theologies, he has neither past nor future, he has nothing to accomplish by creating this machine of ours. It exists as a work of art, admirable in the simplicity of its design and the complexity of its detail. And like many works of art, its purpose is to be what-

ever it is. But such an assumption is gratuitous, since it is not
needed for any scientific purpose and the passage from the last
words of the body of the *Principia* to the *General Scholium* remains a logical gap.

But even if we leap over that gap and think we have discovered
the ultimate purpose of the universe, we shall have to phrase it in
terms of a general order of things. We shall not be able to ask
the further question of why that order and not another has been
imposed upon the world for the simple reason that we have no
evidence (a) that there was ever a possibility of another order's
being available, (b) that there was a time when this order was
first imposed, (c) that the order is a means to a further end.
Hence willy-nilly we fall back into some form of legalism. We
may of course dream and imagine all sorts of things, but we are
talking here of rational discourse not of fantasy. If the facts are
that which we have reason to believe, and if they are the answer
to our questions, then the inquiring mind will have to be satisfied
with them and not seek for super-facts. A set of purposes may
be a fact, but if it is, then it will have to be discovered in the
same way as we discover any other facts. A clear difference must
be defined between goals as termini of events and goals as intended purposes. The latter may of course when repeatedly pursued become habitual and compulsive and consequently drop
below the level of consciousness. But if this distinction is not
made, then death itself becomes one of our purposes since all
life, except possibly in some of the unicellular organisms, terminates in death. Moreover, if all regularly achieved termini of
events are to be identified with purposes, then we revert to
Aristotle's physics in which moving bodies seek their natural positions. Finally one of the differentiae of human purposes is
overlooked: the persistent overcoming of obstacles in order to
reach a goal, which frequently eventuates in variations within the
sequence of details leading to the goal.

It goes without question that if we mean by the word "why,"
"what purpose is achieved by the change," that no statement of a
non-teleological law will ever explain anything. The scientist in

that case will have to take one of the following positions: (1) that there are some explicable events (purposive) and some which are not explicable; (2) that all events are explicable (purposive); (3) that no events are explicable. Our own position is that purposiveness is a recognizable feature of some events and that non-purposiveness is a recognizable feature of others. The correct explanation of a purposive event is teleological; of a non-purposive event is non-teleological. But even when we are discussing purposive events, no explanation is possible unless such events can be classified and a general rule framed. Thus if two men starting from the same point reach the same goal, that in itself is not enough to warrant our explaining both events as purposive. For we must allow for the possibility of an event's reaching a certain terminus accidentally without any purpose whatsoever. Thus two men may be found to fall off a high building and hit the ground and be killed. But one man may have jumped with the purpose of committing suicide; the other may have lost his balance and fallen or have been pushed off or have been blown off by the wind. If this difference is not admitted, then, for instance, all attempts at framing laws which include intentions in their statement are futile, and there is no such thing as desertion distinguished from absence without leave or first degree murder as distinguished from accidental homicide. Deliberate and intentional acts may be hard to identify, but the difficulty does not entail their impossibility. Thus to argue that because one event looks like another in its initiation, sequence, and termination, does not permit us to infer an entire identity between them. But of course no one who refuses to believe that there is anything which might be called a human mind would accept this point of view.

CHAPTER IX

EXPLANATION — GENERAL SUMMARY

We have now looked into four types of explanation: explanation by causality, by teleology, by the principle of perfection, and by general laws. These are not to be taken as the only types possible, but simply as the four which seem to an historian of philosophy to have had the most influence in the past. They have not been discussed in order of importance or plausibility, nor have I assumed that any one thinker or any one period was consistent in utilizing any one of the methods. It is likely that teleological explanation was earlier than causal, but the likelihood may be simply a residue in my mind of Comte's influence. If so, then I should lose no time in pointing out that I see no evidence that there is such a thing as a group-mind or *Geist* which develops in time. All the evidence goes to show that at any given period people's ways of thinking are diverse. Socrates, Democritus, and Protagoras were all contemporaries and so were Kant and the French Idéologues. Hence there is no point in asserting that Mankind starts by explaining things as fulfilling the purposes of gods, goes on to depersonalize the gods, continues by framing one general law which covers everything which happens in a metaphysical manner, and ends up with positivism. The fragments of the Pre-Socratics illustrate how in one man, to say nothing of one period, several modes of explanation may be used. The Love and Strife of Empedocles are causes, and yet the whole cosmos obeys a cyclical law. The *Nous* of Anaxagoras occupies the same logical or systematic position as God in Christian theology—though not, as far as we know, the same religious position—but it functions in accordance with the principles of separation and combination.

Many things in the *Timaeus* are created by the Demiurge, but he works both as a geometer and as an artisan who strives for the best. In Aristotle's *Metaphysics* there is a frank admission of four causes, and no explanation is complete unless all four are given. He speaks sometimes as if he were describing vital growth and sometimes as if he were painting a pictorial map of the cosmos, and it is clear that in his writings the word "why" switches its meaning as problems change. Sometimes, as in Newton's *General Scholium,* there is a clear break between two types of explanation, one of which is used for explaining phenomena and another for explaining "ultimates." This break is necessitated by his belief in the Biblical account of Creation, the break between the creature and the Creator.

Yet in all types of explanation certain characteristics are to be found.

(1) There will always be a point at which the philosopher stops and is satisfied. That point is an irrational. It is the point at which he says, "These are the facts," or "Such is the will of God," or, "This is the general rule," or, "Beyond this we cannot go," or, "These are the frontiers of the Unknowable." If he is seeking causes, he will obviously stop when he has found them and will not raise the question of why a cause always produces the same effect or what purpose is achieved by the effects in question. His explanatory method rules such questions out. If he is a teleologist, he will not stop until he has organized all purposes into a larger purpose which is usually some supposed good, or, more rarely, some aesthetic value. He could to be sure flatly maintain that there is no single purpose but that on the contrary the teleological laws are in conflict with one another. Such a technique was that of the Manicheans, but there is no *a priori* way of limiting the purposes to two. If he is a Neo-Platonist, he will utilize his threefold hierarchy to substitute one type of perfection for another or one type of degradation for another until he has reached either the One or brute Matter. He will not thereupon ask why the principles of degradation and rehabilitation govern the world; he will accept them as final. And if he

is a legalist, he will stop when he has reduced all laws to one or to a very simple set which he will probably hope to be able to reduce to one at some future date. None will ask why the facts or the will of God or the general pattern of the universe is as it is or, if he does, it will be after shifting his point of view. Explanation is the organizing of knowledge, and each man is the best judge of when his organization is completed.

(2) Each of the types of explanation arises out of the extension of a basic metaphor. Though I have dealt only with four types of explanation, I did not intend to identify them with Pepper's four root-metaphors; I am, however, in hearty agreement with his theory that all philosophy—and I should add on my own account all judgment—is metaphorical. The distinction between metaphor and simile is purely rhetorical, the difference being that a metaphor is not so often an acknowledgement of analogical reasoning as a simile is. The simplest assertions of identification, "This is an X," contain an analogy, for it cannot be said unless the "this" is compared to other things which are then discovered to be similar in some respect. A more complete statement of identification would be of the form, "This has certain resemblances to other things which are X's." If, however, we are able to apprehend universals through immediate intuitions, this would not be true. But if we are confronted with individuals, then no complete identifications are possible. Teleological explanation, when it is extended beyond human behavior, is admittedly metaphorical. No one, for instance, would any longer deny that when we say that a stone seeks its natural position, the stone's search is a figure of speech and when Aristotle says over and over again that Nature does nothing in vain, he is personifying Nature and treating her as if she were a goddess and had purposes of her own. In his writings, oddly enough, these purposes were invariable, so that from the operational point of view he might just as well have said, "The universe is regular and orderly." Theological explanations are obviously analogical, though the analogies have only one term, for no sophisticated theological philosopher ever says that God is enough like his description of

Him to make the analogy more than plausible. As early at least as Philo, the analogy broke down, for the second term was confessed to be so unlike the first that in most respects His characteristics were polar opposites of the characteristics of the first. Generalized causation is metaphorical in that, as it is usually applied, there is no possibility of identification between cause and effect. And when causation breaks down, as it does between the objective and the subjective, the legalist steps in and says that a statement of the necessary and sufficient conditions under which an event will take place are enough to answer the question, "Why?" But the very notion of sufficient and necessary conditions is a figure of speech, for necessity is a projection either of our feelings of compulsion and restraint or of logical entailment or implication, and it would be absurd to maintain that because we have a feeling of effort in doing certain things, so does a billiard ball which hits another and sends it rolling across a table. As Hume saw, the sight of constant and similar occurrences will undoubtedly arouse in us feelings of necessity, but we have no evidence that anything corresponding to such feelings inheres also in the events. As for entailment or implication, they belong to sentences, not to events, to the inter-relations between judgments and propositions, not to the inter-relations between things.

(3) All types of explanation will be based upon a metaphysical theory either overtly acknowledged or concealed. By a metaphysical theory I mean a collection of assertions supposedly holding good of the universe as a whole. Such theories are not committed to the proposition that the universe is susceptible of one single type of assertion such as, "The universe is a system of material bodies colliding and rebounding," or, "The universe is the fulfillment of a divine plan." They may be assertions of pluralism or even beliefs that the universe is fundamentally irrational or in fact may deny the possibility of valid metaphysical systems. For such statements can be rephrased affirmatively, if they contain any intelligible meaning. A thoroughly causalistic theory would have to assert that all events are causally related to one another, so that even if events could be classified into types,

such as mechanical, vital, mathematical, or what not, the types themselves should be so related that one could be seen to be the cause of some of the others. Such a system has never been worked out to the best of my knowledge, but an approach to one has been made by those people who say that all mental events are caused by physiological events which in turn are caused by bio-chemical events and so on. But it is also metaphysical to assert, as Santayana does, that there are several "realms of being," and that there is no causal connection between them.[1]

(4) Historically an explanation has consisted in integrating all events into whatever metaphysical system the philosopher believes in. This usually has demanded a distinction between at least two worlds, the intelligible and the sensible, reality and appearance, noumena and phenomena, the rational and the perceptual, the objective and the subjective, and so on. The real world in that case becomes those events which lend themselves to such integration without change, and appearance becomes all the rest. Now most philosophers follow a rational technique, rather than guess-work, revelation, intuition, or myth. When a philosopher believes that certain things can be known only by some non-rational instrument, he bases his belief on evidence. But most philosophers also have a tendency to project the rules of reasoning into its subject-matter. Thus, to take a stock example, if reasoning demands universals, it is asserted that there must be something which the universals name, and that such beings must have the timelessness, the immutability, the unity, and the logical inter-relations of universals themselves. The next step is to abstract these general traits and then use them to define the real world, relegating everything which is temporal, which is mutable, which is multiple, and which has no logical relations to other things—for what logical relations do particulars have until they are envisioned as examples of universals?—to appearance. The notion that the instruments of knowledge must resemble their objects has been elaborated to such an extent that we find Bergson,

---

[1] That at least is what he seems to say in his later works, though in *The Life of Reason* the gaps are not so pronounced.

for instance, maintaining that the intellect cannot know the vital because the vital is not timeless and static as the intellect is. But that cognitive instruments must resemble their objects is an assumption which can be questioned. If cognition is made up of judgments which we pronounce for our own ends, then I fail to see why there should be any similarity between them and the structure or substance of their subject-matter. If one judges that the sky is blue, that does not entail the belief that the judgment is also blue, any more than a mathematician would insist that the square of a number must be a plane figure bounded by four equal straight lines. Yet that was precisely what some mediaeval philosophers did believe. But I am arguing that judgments are not icons, like maps or portraits.

Since all judgments are an intellectual simplification of what we believe, the facts, the question is bound to arise of how far such simplification can go. Since it is admitted by logicians, unless I misread them, that all predicates attributing something to two or more subjects succeed by neglecting some of the attributes which are there but which are considered to be irrelevant, it will be impossible to find any universal predicate. This gives rise to the suspicion that there is no reason to maintain that all types of structure and substance can or must be necessarily reduced to one. Even if one say, "Everything is a possible subject of conversation," we have presupposed a distinction between the possible and the impossible, the possible and the actual subjects of conversation. Hence it would look as if the best one could do would be to stop at some form of dualism. Traditionally there has always been a dualism between appearance and reality. Now this distinction is also one which arises out of experience. An illusion appears to be something that it is not. We discover this by first knowing what are the traits of that which it appears to be and by then discovering that they are absent. If they are not absent, there is no illusion. This holds good of the time-honored bent stick, as well as of the more recondite appearances. A particular, for instance, is not an apparent universal unless it looks like a universal. But everyone agrees that it does not look like a universal at all. It looks like what it is, a particular. If it did not, the problem of its relationship to appropriate universals would not arise. Hence, to call one of these classes of beings real and the other apparent, is using the two terms in a new sense. The ordinary sense of the apparent is used when one mistakes one thing for another and to do so is no rare occurrence. It is at least frequent enough for us to know what it means without further clarification. But to mistake A for B demands at a minimum some knowledge of B. One cannot mistake A for something which one has never experienced, either directly or through hearsay or literary description. Usually the mistake occurs through the resemblance of one thing to another, sometimes because of psychological factors, such as expectation or genuine hallucination or hypnotic suggestion. But if A in no way resembles B, it does not appear to be B. When then we say that a table top appears to be solid but is really empty space with sub-atomic particles whirling about in it, we are certainly not mistaking the solid table top for the empty space plus the sub-atomic particles, nor saying that one looks like the other, nor that the solid table-top is an hallucination. We are saying that it has no holes in it which are perceptible to the naked eye, but that when described in terms of physical equations it is sub-atomic particles whirling about in empty space. Since in both cases instruments of observation and rational procedures intervene between whatever it is that we are talking about and the judgments we make about it, there is no more reason to call one real than the other. We do not say, I believe, that the way something looks under a microscope is any more real than the way it looks to the naked eye. We simply say that it looks that way under the microscope. If we leave out of consideration the conditions under which an observation is made, we are left with an incomplete statement. The scientific table is constructed first by eliminating some of the table's features which are of no interest to the scientist. It then becomes a table which is no longer a table at all; it is transformed into a field studded with atoms which in turn are analysed, and the elements are then found to be distributed throughout its space in a certain manner.

It is not even a wooden table top; it is a conglomeration of carbon and oxygen atoms plus whatever other atoms happen to be in it. If we mean by "appearance" the way things appear to the human mind, then one table top is no more or less apparent than any other. If we mean by "apparent" that which appears to the naked sense-organs, then obviously the scientific table top is not apparent. But to call it real, as if any other table top had a kind of second-class existence, is unwarranted.

If, to take another example, we say that the table top is really a rectangular parallelogram but appears to be rhomboidal, we mean that if we measure the sides with a yard-stick, we shall find that the opposite sides are equal and that the front side and the rear side are not unequal as they appear to be when one is standing in front of it. We are also able to lay down the rules in accordance with which such visual deformations will occur. But here again two different systems of observation are used. No one ever mistook the visual table top for the geometrical table top for the simple reason that no one is purely visual. It may well be true that the geometrical table top is called the real one because the visual ones are so numerous and changing, and custom confers the adjective "real" on that which is permanent. That usage could be accepted by everyone, if desired, but then a new verbal distinction would be required to differentiate between normal sensory experience and illusions, dreams, and hallucinations. This distinction cannot be based upon the subjectivity of the one set and the objectivity of the other, even if the visual data are subjective. For the geometrical table top is no more nor less subjective. Our sense-organs are as much instruments of observation as yard-sticks are, and the yard-stick simply adds one more instrument to those with which we are endowed by nature. Moreover, when we seek more precise measurements, we note the variations in several measurements and accept the average one as right. Each reading will deviate somewhat from that average, and the easiest way to get a set of stable and permanent measurements is to measure in large units and drop out all fractions. Are we then to conclude with Eddington that reality is mind-stuff? This does not follow, for although people with minds are making the measurements and choosing which system of measurement one will use and how minute one wants one's measurements to be, there is no reason to suppose that the instruments themselves are made up of mind-stuff. To suppose that would be analogous to identifying a symbol with what it symbolizes, a word with its meaning. We can use a steel hammer to drive a wooden peg.

There are no absolutely neutral methods of observation which flash reality before us. We can lay down certain criteria of reality if we wish—and we do so wish—but they themselves will help determine what reality is. For purposes of simplicity it is desirable to choose those criteria which will select the most stable features of our subject-matter and those in terms of which we can deduce sets of appearances. If we can deduce the characters of the macroscopic world from those of the microscopic, that would be a marvelous and beautiful achievement. If we can proceed and deduce the characters of molecules from those of their component atoms, and the characters of the larger masses from those of the molecules, no one would deny the importance of the venture. But none of that would imply any greater illusoriness in the deductions than in the premises. The axioms, definitions, and postulates of a system of Euclidean geometry are fewer in number than the theorems and yet are the source of the theorems. Are the theorems therefore apparent and not real? Finally, whatever one calls the realm of the real, one does not get rid of the realm of appearance by giving it a bad name. It will be also necessary in the interests of metaphysics to explain it causally, teleologically, legalistically, or in some other way. Even if the cosmos is really mind-stuff, the question is bound to arise of why it does not seem to be so. And if it is really bits of matter, an analogous question arises.

Any substantial monism will be confronted with the same type of problem, whether the realm to which the laws of the basic substances do not apply is called appearance or not. The very drive to seek an underlying substance is initiated by the experience of multiplicity. Similar remarks can be made about structural monisms. For if we turn away from substance and investigate the kinds of law which govern the course of events, we shall seek one kind because there appear to be several. As we said in discussing Plotinus, the differentiation of the One has to be expected and accepted, and one could translate the metaphysical question into, "In what sense is the diversity of law unifiable?" The diversity is given, the unity is sought. Hence even if one should come upon a single law or very general laws which would accurately describe the so-called underlying nature of everything, we should still be faced with the problem of why the underlying nature does not emerge into the light of day. Such questions, I am maintaining, are the metaphysical questions which every epistemologist will have to face, and his answers are the metaphysics which will determine his special brand of explanation.

On the traditional interpretation of causality—the reduction of qualitative difference to substantial unity—no one has ever yet succeeded in explaining the rise of sensations as psychic events. For if one defines physical objects as Lovejoy does in *The Revolt against Dualism*,[2] then the duality of psychical events and ideas on the one hand and physical events and objects on the other is inevitable. For psychical events are seen not to have and to be unable to have the defining characteristics of physical events, and the same holds good of ideas and objects. Yet we can determine the conditions under which certain psychic events will arise, and some of them are somatic and some extra-somatic. This has not been done satisfactorily even for all sensory data, but the procedure is clear and is carried out daily in psychological laboratories. And it shows well enough that a sound as heard is not identical with an air-wave nor a color as seen with a beam of light. And this will be true even if they are both the ends of a single event, for they are not the same end. If we insist on finding an identity of substance between the two, we shall fail. The course of wisdom then is to redefine our concept of causality. As a matter of cold fact, few people do look for identity of substance in this situation,

---

[2] See especially pages 17 and 27.

and common-sense for once has been ahead of philosophy in accepting psychophysical dualism and interaction. It should not be forgotten that the primary source of all problems is common-sense, of which science and philosophy are refinements. But if we redefine causation as the necessary and sufficient conditions for the occurrence of an event, then the problem of substantial identity disappears. For some of the conditions are not substantial at all but consist in a network of relations including date and location.

If we are to follow the teleological course, then we must find a purpose for the discrepancies such as that between reality and appearance. One of the more obvious purposes might be to make philosophy possible, for if man is a rational animal, and if his purpose in life is to actualize his rationality, then he would have to have obstacles to rationality to overcome. It would be vain then for Nature to be too clear. Or, if that purpose is not satisfactory, one can turn to a traditional thesis of Catholic philosophers, that since the Fall man's reason has become weakened and he does not apprehend reality directly. The difference between the two realms is both a punishment for our inherited guilt and a possibility of rehabilitation. Or one might take a Neo-Fichtean point of view and maintain that the Ego creates the world of appearance in order to have something to understand. I confess never to have found such explanations proposed in detail. Teleologists are seldom as thoroughgoing as one would wish. Usually they are satisfied with bewailing the presence of the Veil of Maya, attributing it to the senses, and developing a set of mystical exercises for penetrating to the other side. This, if we may digress for a moment, is standard practice of some metaphysicians. They want to use their ontologies for moral education, and what begins as description turns out to be valuation.

If one follows the practice of the Neo-Platonists and can make the steps in the cosmic hierarchy intelligible, so that one can actually define their progress up and down, then the doctrine of degrees of reality might be made acceptable. Plotinus himself, as we have said, simply laid it down as a dogma that the One

poured out its being in descending levels of reality and gave no
reason why it should do so except that everything did so, with
the exception of Matter. The universal purpose of all things was
to create something lower than itself and to ascend to higher
levels of being. If from Matter there emanate sensa and from
them ideas, the purpose would be exemplified in the cosmic anabasis and if on the contrary, as in Lord Herbert of Cherbury, the
ideas give rise ultimately to sensations, it is exemplified in the
katabasis. This seems reasonable enough, granted the primary
dogma. But one is still confronted by the problem of how the
degrees of reality are to be defined. And we have already seen—
in Chapter VII—what difficulties this problem entailed. It is
easy enough to understand what it means to be a real man, a
real hero, a real coward, or even a real physical object. But to
be a real nothing in particular seems impossible. In Plotinus the
degrees of reality were first indicated by the abstractness of the
terms concerned since the logical hierarchy was always present
to his mind. And, as we have tried to show above, degrees of
abstractness were correlated with degrees of value. Appearances
then might be less abstract, less beautiful, and worse than realities,
and if we could tell when something was less beautiful and less
good and if we could always identify the objects of knowledge
with logical essences, then the Principle of Perfection could be
profitably utilized. But such conditions are too much for most
philosophers to meet.

Legalism does not run into these difficulties unless its practitioners insist that one law can be found to cover all types of
event. For it has only to formulate a set of laws in accordance
with which events, whether illusory, apparent, real, material,
psychical, or what you will, occur. The problem of appearance
is no problem as long as one can explain its occurrence, and the
explanation will again consist in stating as far as possible the
conditions under which appearances arise. It must be granted
that few philosophers have ever been willing to accept legalism
as ultimate, for we are given to seeking causes and purposes
which are not open to scientific scrutiny. But to ask why we see

two objects when we press upon an eyeball and expect to get a teleological or causalistic answer is like asking what purpose is served by the constant acceleration of falling bodies or the inverse proportionality of the pressure and volume of a gas at a constant temperature, or to seek the substantial identity between a blow on the head and the pain which follows. Legalism, as I understand its consequences, eliminates the distinction between appearance and reality except in the ordinary sense of those terms, the sense in which it occurs when an illusion or error of judgment arises. The hierarchy of reality vanishes, for there is no proof that anything is higher or lower than anything else. But this does not prevent scientists and philosophers from seeking those laws which are most general. If there are two or more sets of things or events, then there will always be an attempt made to see whether in some respect they do not obey a single set of laws. And it may well turn out to be true that certain very general statements will hold good of everything knowable. Nevertheless judgment must also be suspended until such laws have been discovered, and even if they are discovered, their existence would not demonstrate the unreality of difference. Things are reduced to unity by eliminating difference from consideration, as when chemical properties are eliminated from the consideration of physicists or biological properties from the consideration of chemists. But not to consider something is far from annihilating it, and though it may be possible to state the conditions under which a substance of which we know the atomic structure will manifest certain chemical properties, that does not prove that the chemical properties are not real. The study of anthropometry does not consider the mental traits of the people measured, but it does not have the pretension of saying that these people do not have mental traits. If some of the recent studies in the correlation between bodily types and mental traits such as emotional behavior, aesthetic preferences, professional aptitudes, develop greater precision, it may well be shown that predictions can be made about the latter group from the presence of the former. But that in itself would not be proof that the latter are less real

than the former or that they can be identified with them. One of
the greatest abuses of logic is to identify the most general characters of the members of a class with their real characters. I am
not saying that we have no right to define "reality," the word,
in any way we please. But when a special value is attached to
reality, the thing and not the word, then the practice can become
maleficent.

The maleficence appears perhaps more distinctly when certain
metaphysical adjectives are used as terms of praise and blame in
value-theory. Such terms as "universal" and "eternal,"—in the
sense not of "timeless" but of "everlasting"—have been used to
designate those values which are the highest or most worthy of
pursuit. Here the differentiae of the ontological real are transformed into the differentiae of the greatest good. Regardless of
whether there are any such values, it does not follow that because a mode of living or a kind of art is everywhere the same,
it is better than one which is uniquely located in some one part
of the world. Most people are agreed that warfare, obscenity,
and superstition are amongst the greatest of evils. They may be
wrong. But they would not be wrong if universality were any
mark of goodness. For though the way in which people make
war, the things which they call obscene, and the kinds of superstition vary—as everything else does—the differences are far from
being as great as those to be found in the education of children,
sanitation, and the pursuit of knowledge, which most of us think
to be good. If universality is any test of value, then truth is the
least valuable of our aspirations. Similar remarks may be made
about eternality.[3] For though the retention of obsolete practices
is traditional and confers value on what is retained, nevertheless
what is retained is obviously something which may well be irrelevant to our needs. We have only to see what has been retained from our primitive background and compare it with what
we have invented for ourselves to realize how poor a differentia
of value is the immutable. The longitudinal cross-section of his-

---

[3] Cf. Aristotle; *Nichomachean Ethics,* 1096 b, 3.

tory, like the lateral cross-section, demonstrates to be sure certain enduring traits. But once again many of them will not withstand the criticism of reason. Illiteracy is certainly older than literacy, and few people, despite the authority of Rousseau, consider it as nobler. Anti-intellectualism has also had it proponents in occidental civilization since very early days: are philosophers convinced that to be an animal is better than to be human, assuming that one is a man? Eternalism in value-theory should start from the values which appeared in any given civilization at its earliest date and trace its survival. Little is ever lost, though sometimes what is retained changes its name, and we can find vestiges of savagery in the most modern communities. Frequently they are to be found in religious ritual. Thus theophagy, for instance, survives where cannibalism has died out. Inherited guilt and vicarious atonement will be discarded by the courts while retained by the church. Nothing will be gained by listing such examples in detail, for the mere mention of them will stimulate emotional outbursts of denunciation, so powerful is their hold over the human soul.[4]

If beauty and goodness are qualities, then they are neither increased nor diminished by their spread in space and time. A thousand beautiful pictures are not more beautiful than one and a thousand good deeds are not better than one. No one would maintain that a thousand triangles were more triangular than one nor that a thousand red patches were redder than one. Such arguments would be obviously absurd if anyone were to assert them. But they are usually concealed in a different form. It may well be desirable to have as many beautiful pictures as can be produced and to give as many people the possibility of seeing them as is feasible. Similarly it would be better for a thousand people to be good than for one to be good and 999 bad. But neither of

---

[4] May I add that some religious enthusiasts will maintain that theophagy in at least some Protestant sects is only symbolic. If its symbolical status differentiates it from the primitive practice of eating one's totem, then it is not a practice which is unchanging. In fact, the transformation of acts into symbols is simply eating one's cake and having it too. I do not deny the value of this. The Queen of England is an example which would refute any argument against it. If the Throne had the ancient powers of rule, the English would rise up and crush it.

these sentences implies that what is common to the behavior of a thousand people is better than what any single one of them does. Nor does the previous sentence imply that what is common to a thousand paintings is more beautiful than what is peculiar to one of them. Are we to say that what makes Mozart's *Requiem* beautiful is its similarity to the Verdi and the Brahms *Requiems,* to say nothing of the scores of other requiems in the musical literature? Are we first to compare *Mme Bovary* with all the other French novels from *La Princesse de Clèves* down to *A la Recherche du Temps Perdu* and then declare that its greatness lies in its similarity to them? These are purely rhetorical questions, for everyone knows that he can feel the deeply moving quality of Mozart's *Requiem* without ever having heard another. And there must be thousands of French novels which the readers of *Mme Bovary* have never looked into, and yet they pronounce it a great book. All novels, all musical masses, all portraits, all works of art, have something in common. But one does not have to know what it is before seeing the beauty of what is before one. If that were not true, then no one could see the beauty of anything, for no one could possibly be so learned as would be required if it were not true.

The position of these lectures is individualistic. We have assumed in our opening chapter that things and events are complex structures located in space-time and that classes are intellectual devices which shift in accordance with our rational needs. We can talk about certain aspects or parts or phases of things without regard for the others, just as we can look at things without tasting or feeling them. The values of things, we maintain, are to be determined in a context of which the human being is an integral item, though we can talk about the values without bringing ourselves into the conversation. So we can talk about the seven colors of the rainbow as if they were all the chromatic sensa possible, though we now know that the eyes of bees are sensitive to the ultra-violet rays also and are insensitive to red.[5]

---

[5] See Karl von Frisch; *The Dancing Bees,* tr. by Dora Ilse, N.Y., 1955, p. 67.

I fail to understand why the apprehension of values is in any different situation. To locate values in the human context would not be to deny their reality, their power over our acts, their binding force, when they have any, any more than the fact of the invisibility of red to bees denies its visibility to human beings. A relativistic statement of fact is simply a careful statement; it attempts to set down all the conditions under which alone a sentence is true. There are some sentences which are true under fewer conditions than others. Thus it is true that all human beings are born of ova fertilized by spermatozoa. But it is not true that all human beings are reared by their biological parents, that they are all reared in the same way for the same ends, or even that all fertilized ova are born. It is also true that all human beings communicate with one another. But it is not true that even within a given society they all use the same language, communicate in any way they wish, or communicate with anyone they wish. It is true that all human beings eat, unless they are on a hunger strike or are being punished or are sick. But it is not true that they all eat the same things, eat them whenever and with whomever they please in any amounts they please. There are several fundamental biological needs which being biological are universal, as well as universally and eternally satisfied. But none of them are always satisfied in the same way under the same conditions. Eating, procreation, communication, education, production, consumption, and distribution of economic goods, as well as scores of other necessary activities, are all regulated and they are regulated in various ways by various peoples. Is there then one way which is right? And if so, how is it selected? The most popular method of selection is that of setting up the dominant way of our own culture as a standard and appraising others by their approach to it. And since our way is based upon Revelation, *de moribus nostris non disputandum.*

The argument from Revelation is efficacious in persuading people of a culture which accepts Revelation to follow its precepts. I do not say that all people of the Christian Occident act as if they accepted the Decalogue and the precepts of the Beatitudes. If they did, the results would be clear. But I do mean to say that if they wish to be good and accept Revelation, they can then be persuaded that the good and right are what Revelation says they are. For strangely enough, human beings can both break the law and feel guilty about breaking it. The only possible law which could be framed about human nature, if human nature were actually uniform, would be descriptive, a simple scientific generalization. As things stand in modern society, people fall into groups the interests of whose members, possibly even their physiological constitutions, determine what their values will be. Within a group there need be little if any variation in wants, and in that case people would be as submissive to the rule as sticks and stones are. The rule then would be as compelling as Revelation, and no justification would be sought for its dictates beyond its existence. But the problem of conduct arises when someone breaks the law, not when he obeys it. And in a complex society the impulses to break the law are numerous. For aside from personal traits which might lead to recalcitrancy, few individuals lead lives entirely circumscribed by the frontiers of the social group into which they have been born and within which they spend their early childhood. Most of us do not have to live very long before we become aware of the clash in standards between our family and our group and other families and groups. To be bad then is defined as breaking one or the other set of laws, and a person who is in such a situation has to choose which of two evils he prefers. If now he believes in Revelation, for no matter what reason, he will choose the evil which does not violate the commands of Revelation. He may then be good within, let us say, his family and bad within some other group. The parting of the ways is the Choice of Heracles, a choice which has been known to mankind since the fall of Adam.

In other words, when a person is asked why he considers something good, he will always appeal to a general principle, even if the principle is simple, "The good is what I desire at a given moment." But this must not be taken to imply that he thinks of the general principle before choosing. On the contrary, he first chooses and then judges his choice. For no critical principle can be applied before there is something to judge. It is of course possible that in certain circumstances a man may actually have time to reflect, apply his general principles to the various possible choices, and then choose. But it should be remembered that the choices are made not between things now present but between courses of action to be taken at a future date. The easiest situation would be one in which the choice lies between two acts whose consequences are of no importance, or between two motives whose significance is clear and distinct. I confess to being unable to exemplify such situations. Anyone can tell the difference between sweet and sour, straight and curved. And if one could be confronted with choices which are clearly virtuous and vicious, one would be in an analogous situation. One then could act from habit, compulsion, or conscience. But no lengthy proof is needed to show that the virtues and vices are not so clearly defined as all that. We have no "laboratory conditions," no sea-level or sunlight by which we can measure the heights of wickedness. And the names of our virtues, prudence, fortitude, temperance, and justice, are easier to represent in emblems than to find exemplifications of in conduct. For each example proposed is infected with impurities of motive, of consequence, or manner, and the like. It is here that Aristotle's famous sentence on the passions to which we referred in our second lecture, hits the target when he says, "to be afraid, courageous, to desire and to be angry, to pity and in general to feel pleasure and pain are matters which admit of excess and of defect and both are bad, but [to feel these passions] when one should and how one should and towards whom one should and for what end one should and as is right is both the mean and the best, and this is the course of virtue." [6] As he says himself, ethics is not a mathematical science but operates within fluid margins, and for that, if for no other reason, general laws become inapplicable.

When this is grasped, the philosopher has to decide whether

---

[6] *Nichomachean Ethics*, II, 5; 1106 b, 18.

each act is an individual historical event without eternal relevance or whether the variations amongst acts of the same general nature are important. The scientist may expect deviation from his standards and may, as we have repeatedly said, set up conditions in which they are reduced to a minimum. The things which are his subject-matters neither suffer nor rejoice over what he says about them and continue to behave as if he were not present. But the human condition is such that (1) we think that we must obey laws just as everything else does, and (2) feel guilty when we do not obey them, and (3) are punished when we are found guilty. The ethicist might be asked to consider whether there is any justification for expecting human beings to act uniformly or whether the conflict between the eternal, that is, the scientific, man and the historical man is not inevitable. I should not wish to argue that human beings could not be educated up to a point of greater uniformity. Quite the contrary, monasteries, the armed services, indeed some factories have succeeded admirably in attaining such a result. We can discard the infractions of the law in religious orders as trivial—though even there they do exist—but it should be remembered that in the other two cases no individual lives his entire life under the laws in question. Even the soldier in times of peace has a family life, a social life, a religious life, and occasionally can get off by himself for peace and quiet. The laws which he obeys when on the post are often quite different from those which he is expected to obey elsewhere. Consequently the uniformity is only temporary, but nevertheless it is true that from reveille to retreat the soldier has been trained to live in accordance with a set of rules which are invariable. He can also be brought to feel guilty when he violates them. But such examples are far from typical of modern urban society.[7] Ordinarily the human being has to act without appealing to a general rule, though after he has acted, he will, if called upon, explain why he has acted as he did by referring to a general rule.

---

[7] In fact, as any ex-soldier knows, I have over-simplified the situation.

This in most cases is likely to be rationalization, as psychiatrists use that term. I shall not pretend that I can cite the psychological or psychophysical laws which describe the behavior of human beings, even in our society, under all conditions. Every such generalization which I have examined turns out to be erroneous. We have all seen that recourse to innate temperaments, endocrine glands, racial traits, economic motivations, the moral sense, intuition, all break down sooner or later. They would have to break down unless the following conditions obtained: (1) complete psychophysical uniformity of the people examined; (2) clearly definable purposes which these people might be expected to seek; (3) a limited number of social conditions in which the purposes would arise; (4) uniform sets of standards, few in number and intelligible, pervasive of the education—or "background"—of the people in question; (5) the possibility of transferring from one social situation to another of the standards which are to be applied. But such conditions can be laid down only in the most abstract form.

(1) People would not be called people if they were not alike in some respect. But they are alike in their dissimilarity to animals and vegetables. They differ in so many ways that it is well nigh impossible to list them. They differ in what used to be called temperament, in metabolic rate, in sensory acuity, in emotional sensitivity, in heredity, and of course in their education, using that word in a wide sense. But any of these traits — and these are only a few which ought to be studied—may be decisive in a matter of behavior.[8] It will always be possible, when the subject-matter is amenable to measurement, to calculate a mean, but the very fact that one has to calculate one is evidence of the original heterogeneity.

---

[8] See Thomas, Bateman, Lindberg, and Bornhold on "The Individual Effects of Smoking on the Blood Pressure, Heart Rate, Stroke Volume and Cardiac Output of Healthy Young Adults," in *Annals of Internal Medicine,* Vol. 44, No. 5, May 1956, pp. 874-892, where it is shown that even when a group of people who might have been expected to be highly homogeneous (113 medical students, 103 men, 10 women, between 21 and 35 years of age, with a mean age of 25) was studied, and when a very simple problem was under investigation, as shown in the title referred to, the results were significantly various.

(2) Are the purposes which we are expected to pursue clear
and definite? One has simply to meditate upon the theological
virtues of Faith, Hope, and Charity, to see how the distinction
between Us and Them arises even in such sacred matters. One
is not supposed to have faith in everything preached by everyone, hope for the same ends as all people strive for, charity to
those who are heretics. These virtues, like all human purposes,
are selective and seem universal only when they are kept vague.
We are told also to be always truthful. It would be unnecessary
to do more than hint at the casuistry of veracity. May we have
mental reservations when talking? Must we be truthful to people
dying of an incurable disease who ask what chances they have of
survival? Are we to be truthful to everyone, under all circumstances, regardless of the effect of truth on their well-being? Is
there such a thing as a white lie? In how many cases do we
actually know the truth? The very fact that we live in a variety
of social groups, each of which has its own purposes, throws us
into a state of conflict when we attempt to organize our purposes,
even when we know what they are.[9]

(3) Can the virtues and vices be defined without reference to
the people concerned? Are not the virtues and vices other-re-
garding? Do they not always involve acts towards other people?
Or towards God? Or towards the dead? Or towards our future
reputation? Can one be brave or prudent or wise in a vacuum,
in isolation?

(4) Is it the case that the name for our standards of behavior
mean the same thing in all the social groups which compose
Society? Was Hector a coward when he fled from Achilles? Was
Achilles right in refusing to yield the body of Hector to Priam?
Should Jason have remained loyal to Medea? Was Antigone a
criminal when she insisted on burying her brother? Or, to take
modern examples, to whom was Klaus Fuchs disloyal? To the
United Kingdom or to his brothers throughout the world? Was
Benedict Arnold a traitor or a loyal servant of his King repenting

---

[9] Cf. Chapter II, above, p. 47 f.

of his rebellion against him? Was Talleyrand a scoundrel or a patriot? And how about Robert E. Lee? The names which will be given to the men in question and their acts will depend upon what we are likely to call the point of view. But if it is possible or necessary to take a point of view, then a general and absolute, non-relative description is out of the question. Such considerations are commonplaces and are introduced here because they are commonplaces. But if such commonplaces did not exist, there would be no books on moral casuistry.

(5) It is acknowledged by all that the soldier not only does but is ordered to do things in war which would be punished if he did them in times of peace. Homicide in civil life, except when accidental or in proved self-defense or committed when insane, is always punishable. But there is no need to point out that it is of the essence of warfare. The civilian once in uniform is expected not to transfer his feelings about homicide to the enemy. Again, euthanasia is condemned on the ground that life is sacred. But no government ever held that life was sacred, and none has any compunction against taking the lives of some felons. Yet felons are alive. Not even the Church, which condemns birth-control on the ground that life is sacred, considered the lives of heretics sacred.

But such arguments are vain. They point to conflicts which we all know about and which we all accept either submissively or in resignation. But we accept them. And in spite of the inner troubles which they may cause, we continue to demand explanations for everything and explanations will always be based ultimately on general laws. At most the general laws which are invoked as standards of human behavior are expressions of someone's hopes, not of his observations. They have not as yet been scientifically sound for the simple reason that we have not as yet devised a technique for reducing the variables. As Maine de Biran said in his *Journal*,[10] we are asked to do things and no one knows whether we can do them or not.

As things stand, the scientific law is used as a model for pre-

---

[10] *Journal Intime de Maine de Biran*, ed. by A. de Lavalette Monbrun, [1927?], Vol. I, p. 41.

scriptive law. But whereas the scientist is willing to follow the dictates of his subject-matter, the ethicists and other value-theorists expect their subject-matter to follow the laws. It will be replied that there is a radical difference between the "ought" of a scientific law and the "ought" of an axiological law. Yet both kinds of law are supposed to hold good of classes of beings and consequently to have reduced the individual differences amongst the members of the classes to triviality. This brings up once more the question of realms of being, and it may turn out that values and facts are so different that there is no bridge between them. We shall now turn to that question and examine the whole matter of "realms," in the hope that by throwing some light on the way in which they are established, we may also illuminate some of the philosophic problems which they initiate.

CHAPTER X

REALMS OF BEING

Let us say at the outset that if a single technique of explanation is employed by a philosopher, then when he comes upon a group of events which he cannot handle by that technique, he will locate it in a separate realm of being. If he is a causalist and finds that, for instance, his conception of causality will not apply to the interaction of mind and body, he will construct two realms, one of mind and the other of body. If he is a teleologist and finds that some events have no discoverable purpose, he will construct two realms again, the purposive and, let us say in order to give it a name, the mechanical. If he is a legalist and comes upon events which are chaotic and recalcitrant to generalization, he will differentiate between the realm of the lawful or regular or rational, and the realm of the heterogeneous and irregular. It is also possible that any such philosopher will state his ignorance of the similarity between the supposed two or more realms and maintain that his ignorance is merely temporary and that in time the link between them will be discovered. And sometimes the link actually is discovered, as it was by Newton when it was a question of those laws which would describe the dynamics of both the sublunary and the superlunary worlds. But it is more usual for a philosopher to say that the recalcitrant realm is merely subjective or illusory or apparent or a special form of the other. But I know of no philosopher who has ever maintained that any realm could be discovered about which no true statements whatsoever could be made except Cratylus; that within any realm no consistent propositions could be made; and that there is neither specificity nor multiplicity of members. There are some mystics who maintain that multiplicity is only apparent and not real, and that specificity fuses into unity in the Beatific Vision. Yet even they admit that in the realm of appearance there is multiplicity, just as pantheists are usually willing to grant that though all things are in God and God in all things, nevertheless the unity of God's being does not appear on the plane of perception.

This probably arises from the necessity of applying the Law of Contradiction to the realm of existence. Within any formal system the use of this law is easy enough to understand since it determines the system. Our truth-tables eliminate certain possible assertions automatically and what is left over is assimilable within the system. The two phrases which appear in the Law as it is commonly stated, "at the same time" and "in the same respect," become metaphorical when they appear in purely formal discourse. For there is no time in a formal science, and the only "respects" one has to consider are the relations between the theorems and the premises, though one might wish to qualify this by pointing out that the imagination of the scientist contributes something to what he is going to infer. But such a qualification would be ruled out, if I am not mistaken, as psychologism. In a set of assertions which are supposed to hold good, to be true of the facts, to describe existence and not merely to show the logical relationship between essences, dates and respects, as we all know, have to be brought into the conversation. However we define experience, we run headlong into this difficulty and the only way we have found to avoid it, is to imagine situations in which the things we talk about are lifted out of the temporal series, lose their qualifying relations to other things, and are handled as if they were essences. Thus we turn biography into psychology, history into sociology, and freeze the course of events. This gives us a set of propositions which are consistent but are not usually true of anything in particular. It causes little trouble since they are not supposed to be true of particulars. But the margin of difference between what is and what ought to be is always there, and it is that margin which makes the difference between the rational and the sensible, the logical and the temporal, the essences and the existents, and so on. If we seek refuge in the technique of statistics, we seek a shaky refuge, for the rules by which we make our calculations are just as non-temporal as the rules of formal logic.

The Neo-Platonists are in a happier situation. By the Principle of Perfection there are no gaps between the levels of the cosmic hierarchy. As Plotinus said, Everything is everywhere. Moreover, all the lower realms contain within themselves the potencies of the higher, and the higher are the sources from which emanate the lower. Multiplicity seems to increase as one goes down the ladder of reality and to decrease as one goes up. Yet even his Trinity, even his supreme One, gives rise to diversity by an inevitable law of the universe. His three hypostases are distinct and on separate levels, but nevertheless they have their actuality in the One. Plotinus never explains how separation takes place, though there seems to be a hint of what is bound to happen after the initial diversification of being. For it is at least possible, though by no means certain, that the logical hierarchy is somehow or other more intimately associated with the *Nous* than with either the *Anima Mundi* or the One; the hierarchy of values with the *Anima Mundi,* and the hierarchy of reality with the One. Yet this is far from being clear, and indeed clarity is not the most common character of this type of philosophy. Plotinus's Intelligible World is distinct from the Sensible World, but he does insist that the passage from one to the other is continuous, on the analogy of the passage from individuals to varieties to species to genera, and so on. This of course does not account for the difference between the more distant realms, and in fact it is likely that Plotinus was willing to take over from the Ancients bodily whatever he believed them to assert. Thus he applied the categories of Aristotle to the Sensible World and those of Plato to the Intelligible. Yet it is doubtful whether the former could be understood as an emanation of the latter. When he comes in the first three books of the sixth *Ennead* to discuss the kinds of being, he eliminates the Aristotelian categories from the Intelligible World by pointing out that each of them presupposes dialectically the Platonic categories. There can be no quantity in that world, no quality, no action nor passion, nor any of the other general predicates. But each of these presupposes identity and difference. One can follow his reasoning, granted his technique, but when one comes to derive quantity and quality, to say nothing of the other categories, from the Same and the Other, one is forced to find exemplars of these possibilities in the Sensible World and then to argue that since they exist, they must have emanated from more abstract concepts.

I should now like to list some of the realms of being which have figured in the history of occidental philosophy and discuss the principles upon which they have been differentiated.

1. The most clear-cut case of two realms of being is found in Descartes. By using his two primitive concepts, thinking and extension, he was able to differentiate between two kinds of being of which one had none of the properties of the other, except insofar as things which we talk about all have to have something in common. By what he thought of as purely logical means he was able to deduce, he believed, the modes of thinking and of extension, and he never needed to use any of the modes of one attribute to define those of the other. The resultant substantial dualism is too well known to require exposition here, but it will be recalled that, though its inventor himself believed that causal interaction was possible between the two realms, his immediate successors, beginning with Cordemoy, were quick to point out that this was an impossibility, granted the definition of causality then common. Since everyone did grant it, it was only reasonable that the three theories of Occasionalism, Psychophysical Parallelism, and Pre-established Harmony should have been elaborated to eliminate an interaction which seemed to occur in both sensation and volition. There was of course another way out of the difficulty, that of denying the postulate which gave rise to it. It might be quite possible to state the necessary and sufficient material conditions under which sensations would arise and the analogous conditions under which volition would be effective. But as long as one maintained that there must be a community of

substance in cause and effect, one could scarcely also maintain that the mind could cause material effects and the body cause mental effects.[1] It is interesting to observe that when Descartes came to proving the existence of God through the characteristics of the idea of God, he again resorted to this postulate, but failed to notice that if intellection was one of the modes of thinking, and if his finite intellect was entertaining an idea which he was incapable of framing, because of the incongruity between its characteristics and his, then the occurrence of the idea to his intellect was just as mysterious as the interaction between mind and body. He had recourse, as everyone knows, to the theory of innate ideas. But the fact that an idea is innate does not solve the problem of how it could occur to a mind incapable of framing it. If he had maintained that all ideas were innate, in the sense that like some of our instincts they would arise automatically when we reached the proper age, then the situation would have been entirely different. He would have been in the position of Lord Herbert of Cherbury and his Platonistic colleagues, who believed that all ideas which might be argued about—that is, expressed in judgments—emanated from innate ideas on the model of Plotinian emanation. But that was not his point of view. In short he could easily prove the existence of God as the only adequate cause of the idea of God, but that did not explain causally how the idea arose in the mind of man.[2]

If we waive any logical defects in Descartes's technique, we can grant that his two realms were distinguished by characters such that they were peculiar to each realm, though both realms when established could be explored *more geometrico*. But we now come upon a set of realms

---

[1] In the nineteenth century the objection to interaction often was based on the Law of the Conservation of Energy. If the body affected the mind, as in sensation, it was argued that energy would be lost; in volition energy would be created. This argument was presented vigorously by C. A. Strong in his book, *Why the Mind has a Body*. W. P. Montague tried to avoid the difficulty by identifying the mind with potential energy.

[2] This paragraph does not deny that Descartes added a third realm to the two discussed, namely the realm of God and the angels. That realm was not, however, reached by the same argument which established the ultimate differentiation between mind and matter.

which are differentiated by the intellectual techniques themselves.

2. In Auguste Comte the very methods of thinking have a history, as they have in a member of his school, Lévy-Bruhl. If one think in terms of divine wills, metaphysical essences and powers, or the observations of the naked eye, one will see that one can make no transfers from one realm to the others. For the inhabitants of each realm are peculiar to it, just as the methods of manipulating them or operating upon them will differ. That is, there are no gods in the realms of metaphysics or sensory observation, no essences in the realms of gods and observation, and whatever observations there may be in the other two realms are accidental, not essential. In fact, one takes no account of them; one need not even know that they exist. They are irrelevant to discourse. But here Comte did not assert the existence at any one time of all three realms, as Descartes did of his two, though he was intelligent enough to admit that there were residues of obsolete thinking in all periods, just as an adult may retain vestiges of his childhood and youth in his maturity. By turning his account into a history of the human mind and maintaining that only the mature mind was right—at least as of 1825—he was able to say that neither gods nor essences existed. This was not a distinction between appearance and reality, but that between falsity and truth, or non-being and being. A savage could not be blamed for thinking theologically, but a civilized man could be. If one is to be theological, one is quite right to engage in magic, for only magic can influence the divine wills, the magic of placation and punishment. Similarly in Lévy-Bruhl, if one is prelogical, one is forced to argue in terms of the Law of Participation, not in terms of the Law of Contradiction, for the latter has no place in prelogicality. But again Lévy-Bruhl, though he recognized vestiges of prelogical thought in modern man, did not retain a prelogical world alongside of the logical world. It was something which we had outgrown, a kind of thinking utterly foreign to the kind of thinking which civilization requires.

3. If I accentuate this, it is because there have been other thinkers who establish different realms on the basis of the cogni-

tive instrument which permits us to enter them and who also maintain that all these instruments are equally valuable. We have various means of knowing, but these means are not to be appraised by their dates in the history of the mind. For instance, we have had and still have philosophers who maintain that the instrument of faith opens the door to one realm of being and that of reason opens it to another. Here two propositions may be equally true, and yet in the case of one realm the Law of Contradiction does not apply whereas in the other it does.[3] In the one realm we have ideas which may be internally inconsistent, such as those represented by the mysteries, which are true though—or perhaps because—they are logically absurd. Their proponents know that they are true, but they are not true in the same sense that rationally founded ideas are true. What they are true of is so different from what reason is true of that we can speak of it only analogically or symbolically. The analogies are based upon rational discovery: common nouns, adjectives, verbs are used to express them as if they were being applied to the things of the rational world. And yet it is usually admitted—though not always[4]—that the analogies are imperfect. An imperfect analogy is still a statement of similarity, and if there is similarity, the gap between the two beings which are compared is bridged. If God's wisdom is perfect wisdom, it is still wisdom, and presumably a person who believes that God is wise knows what imperfect wisdom is. When one gets to the point where the similarity breaks down,

---

[3] Personally I should be inclined to believe that if two propositions are contradictory and yet both true, it is because the verbal symbols used in framing them do not mean the same thing, i.e., they are really puns. I am assuming obviously that they appear to be about the same subject-matter. If then we say that something is true by faith and false by reason, the something in question is probably two different things. In short "true" and "false" become ambiguous. The difficulty is compounded by the necessity of putting one's beliefs into words which immediately subjects them to logical criticism. But a belief which cannot be put into words is scarcely a belief. For one may doubt the truth of something because it does not seem convincing or right, without being able to state definitely wherein its weakness lies. Thus a belief held on faith may be simply a doubt about a rational statement, a doubt which is expressed as the contradictory of the rational statement. Such doubts, however, are not the basis historically of theories which establish a realm of faith. See below, p. 241.

[4] Witness not only Tertullian on the Incarnation, but the attitude of the Church regarding the dogma of the Trinity.

then the bridge collapses and the use of the word "analogy" is of
no help, except emotionally. If we say, for instance, that God is
so wise that He knows not only all actuality but also all possibility,
then possibility is a word which has changed its meaning. For at
least one of its common uses is to name that which has not yet occurred, but may or may not occur in the future, or may or may not
have occurred in the past or may or may not be occurring somewhere now. If it is known whether it is or is not occurring, then it
is clearly misleading to call it a possibility. And so with the past
and future. If now we change our sentence to read, "God is so wise
that all possibilities are actualities to Him," we have not simply
said that He is wiser than we, but that "wisdom" has taken on a
new meaning, and hence it is dubious practice to call Him "wise"
at all.

4. The distinction between the realms of faith and reason leads
to that between the supernatural and the natural. Faith seems to
vary as knowledge does, for faith usually asserts the truth of those
ideas which the traditional religion of the tribe has sanctified.
One has found Indians and Chinese having faith in Christian
dogma only since missionaries have brought the records of Revelation to them. And few Westerners have ever had faith in non-
Christian dogmas before reading the non-Christian sacred texts.
Finally amongst Christians themselves some men have had faith
in ideas which turned out to be so wrong that they were burned
for having faith in them. There are, to be sure, some people, sur-
vivors of Deism, who maintain that all these dogmas say the
same thing in different symbols, and though Deists did not resort
to faith to prove their points, yet one might modify their point
of view and then say that Catholics, Protestants, Jews, Buddhists,
Moslems, Shintoists, and all who resort to faith are really having
faith in the same ideas. Let us speak this way, however displeas-
ing it will be to the adherents to these various religions, for what
is important here is that faith is taken as evidence of a separate
realm of being in which reason is impotent. If there is such a
cognitive instrument as faith, then it ought to be able to assert
the truth of almost any proposition, rational or not, for rational

criticism cannot touch it. The man of faith is in the situation of the mystic or for that matter of the man who is reporting on his aches and pains. He alone can tell what he has knowledge of. If he has faith in an inconsistent set of assertions, reason may point out their inconsistency, but he can always reply that reason is inadequate to the realm of faith. Rationally such ideas will be called mysteries, but that is of small moment.

The difficulty with such a position arises, as we all know, when the man of faith—or the mystic—speaks. Whatever he says is by its very nature insusceptible to reason's demands. Many mystics have maintained an attitude of stubborn silence or, what amounts to the same thing, of speaking in paradoxes. They recognize the hopelessness of expressing the non-rational in rational terms. In that they resemble the man who attempts to describe, not merely name, a color or a taste. The Beatific Vision is an experience, not discourse, and its nature as an experience prevents its being adequately described. But the man of faith is not necessarily a mystic. He is asserting propositions which are held to be true of existent beings, God, the soul's future life, the angels, the Blessed Trinity, transsubstantiation, vicarious atonement, the incarnation, the inevitable triumph of the good, to cite only a few Christian illustrations. These statements are believed to be true, absolutely and incontrovertibly true. But what does "true" mean in this context? In Catholic circles it means exactly what it means in any context. "Faith," as Gilson says, "teaches truths which seem contrary to reason; let us not say that it teaches propositions contrary to reason." [5] In 1840 the Abbé Bautain subscribed to the principle that faith was no substitute for reason if one meant that the dogmas were irrational. And at the Vatican Council the same principle was reasserted. Presumably what is now asserted by faith could have been proved by reason if man had not weakened his reasoning powers through the Fall. And no one is ignorant of the efforts of such Catholic writers as St. Thomas and the other scholastics to push the frontiers of the rational as far back as

---

[5] In the introduction to his *The Christian Philosophy of St. Thomas Aquinas,* p. 18.

possible. Reason properly used could never contradict the truths of faith—though there might be some ground for discussing the meaning of "properly"—so that strictly speaking there is no irreducible difference between the two realms in Catholic tradition. Practically there is, and the supernatural remains at least in the form of the mysteries. The mysteries are mysteries because they cannot be phrased in rational language. But clearly if man's resemblance to God lies in his reason, then God is a rational being and the reason is the link between the natural and the supernatural. One ought to be able to rise out of nature into super-nature by argument, as for instance in St. Thomas's five proofs of the existence of God. But where one cannot do this and must return to faith, then the split between the two realms is reasserted on the basis of the source or instrument of knowledge.

In Kant the whole thing is reversed. For though he showed the impotency of the reason in matters of morals, the moral needs of the individual were sufficient to permit him to assert the existence of God, freedom of the will, and immortality. As Rousseau had made his Savoyard Vicar declare that reason would lead to atheism but that *le sentiment* had every right to assert what reason denied, so Kant asserted (1) that the Practical Reason had authority over the Pure Reason and (2) that the universe must be so constructed that man could be moral—as he, Kant, defined morality—in it. Shaftesbury, Bayle, Spinoza, and others had pointed out that some people were moral who were also atheists, pagans, and otherwise non-Christian. Kant might have taken their data into consideration. But he did not on this point and preferred to bolster up traditional ethics by a metaphysics for which no reason could be given. In him the realm of faith—or of the Practical Reason— was quite different from the realm of reason. But again he held that certain statements could be made about it which were true and at the same time based on non-rational premises. They were shown by him to be non-rational in the first *Critique*. How did he know where to stop?

5.   Similarly there have been attempts made in recent years to show that there are different kinds of truth, not that the word

"truth" is ambiguous, but presumably that it is a genus of which there are several species. The genus has never to the best of my knowledge been defined. And the species are not so much differentiated by cognitive methods as by our symbolic modes of expression. Thus there is said to be poetic truth, aesthetic truth, scientific truth, symbolic truth. A poem does not mean what it says; but it means itself. To quote Archibald MacLeish, "A poem should not mean but be." May I say that I personally am in hearty agreement with him, if what he means by that verse is that he disapproves of didactic poetry? But if he means that a thing when it is composed of words and sentences can simply be and mean nothing, then he is seriously oversimplifying. For anything whatsoever can turn into a symbol and acquire meaning, however innocent it may be of such intentions and however detached from a human origin. For the meaning of words and phrases is given to them by human beings and not by Nature. It is true that we speak of "natural signs," which are usually either causes of known effects or effects of known causes. But the meaning which such signs have is far from being the kind of meaning which symbols have. Smoke "means" fire in any language and clouds often "mean" rain. But it does not require the discriminative sense of a Duns Scotus to realize the difference between that kind of meaning and the meaning of a word or sentence. Poems and other works of art have still another kind of meaning, in that they may stir our emotions deeply and suggest vague thoughts whose origin in our past experiences is forgotten. That kind of meaning used to be associated with the word "connotation"; it was the fringe of pleasurable and painful feelings which we were supposed to eliminate before discussion. That fringe was a great source of *argumenta ad hominem* and was therefore just the sort of instrument which might be employed in hymns of praise, invectives, college songs, prayers, and other ejaculatory devices. It could be said to convey no ideas which could be reasonably called true or false; it varied greatly from person to person; and yet was one of the most valued aspects of a work of art. There was no need to erect a theory of truth and falsity upon it; one had simply to discriminate between what was said in a poem and what feelings the poem aroused. To call the feelings true was playing upon words. Even if there were certain poems—or for that matter pictures, musical compositions, statues—which aroused the same deep feelings on the part of great numbers of people who had enjoyed the same education or upon an élite, that fact did not reduce the ambiguity in the word "truth." It simply pointed to a psychological phenomenon of interest to aestheticians and possibly moralists like Tolstoi. The sound of a bugle at Retreat or Taps may have the same emotional effect as a poem, but no one to the best of my knowledge ever spoke of the sound as true, except in the sense that it was not out of tune.

One should not have the arrogance to tell others how to use words and any author has the right to call this kind of feeling true or false if he wishes. But in that event he had best use another term for the kind of truth possessed by declarative sentences. Ambiguities in words cannot establish diverse realms of being. Nor is there any reason to believe that they always arise from an exfoliation of a single original meaning. Barley sugar is not made out of barley. No special realm of being is required to house works of art if the one argument for its establishment is the special kind of truth which they possess. When we say that a portrait is true to life, we may mean nothing more than that it resembles its sitter as we think of him. When its painter emphasizes certain traits of the sitter so that his character appears as we think of it, we may translate his interpretation of that character into words and announce that they are true. But the truth of representative art is the truth of icons, and that is not in question when special realms of truth are set up. The truth which works of art are supposed to have by those who suppose them to have it is a higher or more spiritual or even an ineffable kind of truth. Again, why call it truth?

6. It is obvious that one could not deduce by logical means alone the connotation of a set of symbols. Because of the vagueness of the word "connotation," we shall call it from now on "significance." Only a psychologist could predict the significance

of any given symbol in any given social group. Some terms are decent, others indecent; some are decent when expressed in Greek and Latin derivatives and indecent when left in Anglo-Saxon derivatives. Some terms are eulogistic in one group and pejorative in others. There is nothing mysterious about it unless one presupposes so great a uniformity of human nature that variation becomes a problem. But regardless of that, there would be no way by purely deductive procedures of deriving the significance of a word or sentence from the symbols themselves. When one already knows the prejudices and verbal taboos of a social group, one can indeed predict the significance of certain symbols. But to do so demands that we go far beyond the symbols themselves.

Similarly it has often been pointed out that one cannot deduce from fact any value whatsoever. One cannot argue that because A exists, therefore A is good, bad, or indifferent, unless, like Alexander Pope, one has already inserted an axiom into one's discourse to the effect that whatever is, is right. This seems to be the basis of the theory that the realm of fact is quite different from the realm of value and that the two realms must be acknowledged to occupy different "levels" in the cosmic hierarchy. One then proceeds to enumerate the essential differences between the good and the existent, or the beautiful and the existent, and concludes that the differences are so great that one cannot be grounded in the other.[6] But the possibility remains open that one may originate in the other and arise out of it and nevertheless have characteristics vastly different from those of its source. Living beings have characteristics which are not found in the biochemical substances which compose them; and even groups of people have characteristics

---

[6] For the sake of simplicity we shall omit any consideration of those men who accepted the Natural—in one of its many senses—as the norm. Courbet, for instance, insisted that if one copied Nature, one's pictures would be bound to be beautiful, in spite of the violent reaction of his critics to his own copies of Nature. But the tradition was at least as old as the Greek Cynics. The main trouble with the idea was that no one was quite sure what was natural and what unnatural and as far as Courbet was concerned, it was soon seen that Nature had to be viewed by a human eye and that the contribution of what Zola called temperament was never going to be eliminated. Anyone tempted to resort to the Natural as a norm of value, had better first study A. O. Lovejoy's analysis of the various meanings of the term in his appendix to *Primitivism in Antiquity*.

which their members do not have individually. This has been used to differentiate realms to be sure. But since one can presumably tell what are the conditions under which these peculiarities will arise, though they are to be sure logical surds, they do not appear to be unnatural, supernatural, or otherwise mysterious. Consequently, if one can predict when and how values will arise, either within the soul of an individual or within a group, one may admit a break in the logical series from fact to value, and yet not assume the existence of a special realm with an ontological gap between it and the other realms.

But nothing is more common than the rise of values out of compulsory behavior patterns. In fact, one of the peculiarities of habitual behavior is the compulsive coefficient which it acquires. The good within the life of a single individual could be identified with that which he wants and has usually wanted on specifiable occasions: food, sexual satisfaction, intellectual satisfaction, companionship, health, and the like. But no individual is ever so isolated that he is entirely dominated by his peculiar desires, and he awakens to the sense that there are values other than those which satisfy his own desires or interests, when the social group to which he belongs criticizes his behavior. We are brought to a sense of the good, as distinguished from the satisfaction of our desires, by such criticism. It is administered by one's parents, one's brothers and sisters, one's schoolmates and teachers, one's reading, and later by one's colleagues. When a man also desires conformity to what is approved by his group, he will seek to follow its values, and it is doubtful whether anyone was ever so ego-centric that he did not want the approval of some group. The interplay between what one wants oneself and what others want one to want is so great that it is futile to build up a theory of values on the basis of a supposititious isolated individual, such as the natural man, the economic man, the child, or Robinson Crusoe. For what one wants may very well be induced from babyhood by the comments of others, by training, by one's desire to emulate or not to emulate one's associates. To look for the natural good, in the sense of that thing which all would desire if they were isolated beings moving about in free space, is about as intelligent as looking for the natural language. For no one is isolated nor could he remain alive for long if he were.

Here again it is clear that unless one admits that our judgments have a history, values, like knowledge itself, will have eternal and spaceless being. For when we begin to reflect upon them, we find them already there, and as we have said elsewhere in these lectures, disconnected from their historical roots. But if we follow that course, the whole universe turns into a set of disconnected beings which may fall into certain classes, to be sure, but into classes between which there is no conceivable passage. It seems either reasonable or unreasonable to consider man as eternal or temporal and which it will seem cannot be determined by rule. The soul of man, works of art, social minds, fictitious beings, mathematical concepts, indeed everything which cannot be deduced from whatever premises one starts with, form separate realms and it is a question only of what A. O. Lovejoy has called metaphysical pathos how one will arrange them.

7. The difficulty of passing by logical steps from realm to realm seems to have been recognized by Santayana in his *Realms of Being* as it was in his *Dialogues in Limbo*. For there the systematic premises chosen determined each realm: the realm of matter being determined by what one would find if one selected out of the universe those beings which were describable in terms of natural science; the realm of essence by perceptual inspection; the realm of truth by logic; the realm of spirit by our sense of values. Santayana himself probably had his own preferences among the realms. At times he liked to pose as a materialist, since he was convinced that the material world was the necessary, if not sufficient, condition for all the other realms. He enjoyed playing upon the non-existence of the essences which in spite of their timelessness entered into and departed from human experience as they would. He apparently believed that it was a matter of ontological indifference whether one spoke like Democritus or Avicenna or Socrates, though it was of great importance that one be able to speak like them all. He was of course a "friend of the Ideas,"

and saw no reason to give them any genesis in history. He took his beings as they occurred to him and explored their inter-relations within their own realms. One may question the inner structure of each realm in his writings, and indeed some of the inhabitants which he found in them severally might be expelled by other administrators. It is surely questionable whether one comes upon fictions and illusions in quite the same way as one comes upon colors and sounds. But if one is using the instrument of perceptual inspection, one will without question stumble into hippogriffs and mermaids, to say nothing of men whose heads do grow beneath their shoulders. And when one questions this technique, one has to ask oneself just what is wrong with it. The best answer is that it conflicts with common sense. But what has common sense to do with the question? Is not philosophy a corrective of common-sense? We are brought back here to the initial premise of the system, the premise which determines the technique of investigation.

The gaps which Santayana found have had their analogues in the works of other philosophers. If, for instance, one is to define matter as Locke defined it, then the characteristics of the material world are so different from those of the mental world that there will be no way of getting from one to the other. There simply is no identity between the perceived color *red* and the light rays which when reflected give us that color. One need only list their traits and assign dates and location to them to see this. Arthur Collier argued in similar fashion in his *Clavis Universalis* when he asked his readers to compare the size, the color, the shape of the perceived moon with the material moon as described by astronomers. He fortified his argument by asking them also to press upon an eyeball and see the perceived moon break in two while the astronomical moon remained whole. In the *Revolt against Dualism* the date at which the visual stimulus originated and the date at which the perception was experienced were also introduced, on the ground that one of the differentiae of material objects was to be in one place at one time. Material objects, Lovejoy said (p. 27), are spatial as well as temporal; some or all of their parts continue to exist during the interperceptual intervals of any or all percipients and no part belongs to them solely by virtue of the occurrence of a perception; the extended things existing in space go through causal interaction; the causal sequences continue even when not perceived; and this order is a common factor in or behind the experience of all percipients. If one defines a material object in this way, then the perceptual object cannot be identical with it and an epistemological dualism results. One may of course quarrel with the definition and ask that material objects be defined as they are in Whitehead, in which case "simple location" may be eliminated. But it should be noted that even if the perceptual object is one terminus of an event of which the other is a star which was extinguished centuries ago, the two termini are not existentially the same.

8. Sometimes the realms are distinguished by a comparison of the laws which describe the behavior of their occupants. Thus dreaming and waking introduce us into realms which may be perceived by the same mental apparatus—though no one to date has been found wearing his spectacles in bed in order to see his dreams more clearly—but the way in which the dream-objects behave is not the same as the way the waking-objects behave. If we begin by simple inspection, we shall not be able to distinguish between the two realms since qualitatively they look so much alike that while dreaming we seldom know that we are not awake. It is only upon reflection that we discover the profound differences between them. We do not therefore use simple inspection to distinguish the two realms, any more than we do in the case of veridical and illusory experience. When we suffer from an illusion we are misled by the illusion and the date of our recognition of its illusory character is always later than that of the illusion itself. But reflection upon an experience is not inspection of the experience, and if we decide to accept the criteria of subsequent reflection as decisive, we have shifted our ground. If it is true that savages believe in two entirely different realms of waking and dreaming, in the latter of which the soul of the sleeper may leave his body and its location and wander about the cosmos, visiting distant places and even

the past, then the savage is refusing to assign a status to dreams on any basis other than *reine Erfahrung*. He is in fact the one philosopher who may be called a consistent radical empiricist. That there is any soul to wander about might be questioned and the picturesque terms of his account of what has happened might seem unwarranted to people who consider themselves to be more sophisticated than he is. But if what-is-there is what exists, then the characters of the object must be accepted at their face value and no attempt must be made to explain them on the basis of causes existing in some other realm. No one dreaming is aware while he is dreaming of the somatic or unconscious causes of his dreams. If he were, the efficacy of the dream in pleasing or terrifying him or conveying an important message to him—its symbolic meaning either in the sense of such old dream-books as that of Artemidorus or in the sense of Freudian and post-Freudian psychology—such efficacy, we repeat, would wither away. If Milton knew *while he saw* his late espoused saint why he saw her in terms of what he had eaten for dinner that afternoon or in terms of his repressions, the impression which the dream made upon him would scarcely have eventuated in a sonnet.

There have been philosophers, as we said in our first lecture, who have clung to the method of inspection to such a degree that they have admitted the subsistence, if not the existence, of a realm of illusion, negative facts, impossibilities, fictions and the like. This was a courageous gesture on their part and should not be deprecated by empiricists. For the objection to the theory was mainly its incapacity to explain the similarities and differences between the two realms. The subsistent objects resembled too closely the existent ones, and since no one had ever been able to deny that our imaginations were limited by our perceptions, there seemed to be some sort of genetic relation running from the latter to the former. But this would not have appeared from inspection alone. The discovery that centaurs and Cyclopes are not so real as ivory, apes, and peacocks comes from biology, not from perception. It again is discovered by reflection and by the determination to go beyond perception in granting reality to things. No one seeing a centaur would believe in what he saw, no matter how cleverly the benevolent monster was constructed. But the reason would not be because of the perceptual form of what he saw. It would be because he had learned not to believe in what he saw. There would be no great difficulty in a zoologist's explaining why centaurs were not viable forms. The answer is a simple physiological one. It is not logical in the sense that there is some inner contradiction in the torsoes of men and horses. We have plenty of pictures of centaurs and we know what they look like. We can close our eyes, if we enjoy strong visual imaginations, and see one. We cannot see a round square or a white rat which is at the same time and in the same respect black, but we can see centaurs. If then we prefer the world of science to that of the visual imagination, it is not because the latter is not vividly present to us under certain conditions. It is rather that we cannot accommodate the descriptions of the one to the laws of the other. If, however, there are two sets of laws—though I am far from certain of what they are—we can simply assert that the two realms of existence and subsistence are distinct realms and that there is nothing that we can do about it but swallow hard and accept them. And this is what such philosophers as the early E. B. Holt and Montague and, I gather, Meinong did. To look for the roots of subsistence in existence is an attempt at simplification and is, most of us would agree, an exemplary kind of behavior. But it is also a passage beyond the radical experience of which many philosophers have prided themselves.

9. There is another technique of setting up realms which rests upon an ultimate and irreducible difference of kind discovered by reflection upon the methods of reasoning itself. I refer to the difference between the realm of contingency and that of necessity, which is related to that between the realms of possibility, actuality, and, one supposes, impossibility. Here the method of handling the realms is different. It is no longer a distinction between inspection and reflection, knowledge-of and knowledge-about, appreciation and description, *kennen* and *wissen,* but between discovery on the one hand and the art of logical consistency on the other. We are

all familiar with the break between existence and essence, induction and deduction, and similar terms, and we learn early in our careers that purely logical reasoning gives one a series of necessary truths whereas the scientific method—or methods—can at best give us contingent truths. In Descartes and his school one began with clear and distinct ideas which were apprehended by intuition and which by their very nature could not be doubted. These truths when handled by the deductive procedures in use in mathematics were supposed to generate other truths by what was known as the sheer force of logic. Spinoza's *Ethics* was a typical example of this type of thinking, and the rationalistic treatises of Wolff and his disciples exemplified its extension into fields not covered by earlier philosophers. Thus in Wolff there was always the possibility of having two sorts of investigation into any subject-matter, in his words the empirical and the rational. Empirical psychology, for instance, was a collection of psychological data from which generalizations were made; rational psychology was the organization of such generalizations into a logical system with all the apparatus of theorems, corollaries, and scholia such as might be found in a book on plane geometry.

If there were self-evident propositions which could serve as premises to such a system and if these premises were true to fact and not simply capable of generating—with the help of logical procedural rules—a consistent system of theorems, then it could be seen that necessity was a characteristic of ideas which were descriptive of the real or physical or empirical world. But it was known as early as Plato, if not earlier, that the material world was recalcitrant to the demands of logic. In Aristotle the order of observation was impregnated with Chance, and whether because of matter or something else, one must not expect it to manifest the purity of the world of Necessity. The two worlds in Aristotle gave rise to a fundamental conflict within his philosophy,[7] for though mathematically Necessity might rule and Chance have no place, almost anything might happen in the world of matter. Thus

---

[7] See "A Basic Conflict in Aristotle's Philosophy," *American Journal of Philology,* Vol. LXIV (1943), pp. 172-193.

monsters and accidents could prevent the actualization of natural forms and often did. If the incorporated Ideas of Plato were not prevented by Chance from fulfilling their natural development, the Sensible World would have been a perfect model of the Intelligible World. But both Plato and Aristotle noticed that they were so prevented. And this was one—but only one—of the reasons why Plato had to posit a world of ideas which would legitimatize reasoning.

In our own time, that is, since the fourteenth century, men have looked for some rule which would enable us to discourse rationally about the world of contingency. Bacon and in the nineteenth century Mill attempted to formulate such a method. But both men ended with concepts which were transformed into general ideas when they came to the problem of reasoning itself. Mill knew that the existence of mathematics was a stumbling block to any purely inductive system, and his attempt to derive numbers and by extension other mathematical concepts from observation was a failure. It was a failure for the simple reason that the subject-matter of mathematics had to be timeless, and the only contingency permitted is the dependence of one's findings on a rigorous clinging to logical procedures. The Law of Identity demanded that no term change its meaning throughout an argument, and the Law of Excluded Middle demanded that only two possibilities be open. When things and events were substituted for logical terms, as is inevitable if one is talking about facts and not ideas, it was of course found that things did change their natures and that furthermore elaborate procedures were needed before one could purify experience to the point where logical terms would be applicable. Such purification went on in laboratories and so long as the scientist stuck to macroscopic matter in absolute space, the correlation between the two worlds was fairly successful. "Fairly," because even in the early days of Galilean physics it was known that accidents might happen. Nevertheless by the use of such concepts as measurable mass, velocity, distance, which could be set up without regard for other properties resident in the things which had the masses, moved, and were at specifiable distances from one another, mathematical systems could be and were devised which were true enough to facts to cause no trouble. We know what the subsequent history of such systems has been and how the subject-matter has been acknowledged to be intellectual constructs.

When scientists tried to do the same sort of thing for more complicated subjects, the procedure was far less fruitful. A living being, for instance, the simplest vegetable, is more than mass and motion, though it too has mass and moves. But the things it does require explanation in terms of something more than dynamics. The plant or animal is to be sure chemical. The introduction of life-forces and entelechies was of no explanatory value and it did not take long for people to realize this. But the chemistry of living organisms might inform us of the conditions under which certain vital behavior might occur, conditions without which it would not occur, but only superficial minds were willing to say that a dead cat was precisely the same as a living cat or a dead cabbage the same as a living one. The very relations between the organism and the environment might make a difference, and where sometimes the organism would go in search of an environment proper to its success in life, in other cases it would perish for lack of one. Moreover the difference between members of the same species began to be noticed in the seventeenth century, and as early as Lamarck it was seen that the very word "species" named a collection of individuals which might be quite different in some ways, however similar they might be in those upon which the classification depended. To handle such things *more geometrico* was possible only at the price of so modifying the phenomena which were being discussed that the results were well-nigh inapplicable. Thus a moving body could be described exclusively in terms of mass and distance from other bodies, but the life of an organism was a function not only of what Aristotle called its matter and form, but also of the possibility of getting sufficient appropriate food and of competing successfully with other organisms demanding the same food. By the time of Malthus, as is well known, a formula was devised for calculating the relation between the amount of food needed for a series of generations increasing at a normal rate and the number of individuals who would presumably want the food. This is all an old story and need not be dwelt upon at length; its moral is that the number of variables which had to be taken into account was very great and, what was worse, they did not vary independently. There were, for instance, the chances that some individuals would fight with others to get the food and would kill others in the struggle. Some individuals might be more successful in getting mates than others and the dead would have no descendants. Some organisms would artificially increase the food-supply, as human beings do. Some clearly were born defective in a variety of ways. And some might themselves prove appetizing to other animals and be eaten by them. Now the fact that a situation is complex does not entail the conclusion that it cannot be handled rationally. But here was a case where what occurred simply could not be interpreted exclusively in terms of physico-chemical theorems. The fact that horses eat grass and are not carnivorous or that men are polygamous may be correlated as far as I know with the biochemistry of their organisms. And the fact that men can be educated into being monogamous may also be correlated with similar factors. But who knows whether horses are herbivorous because of the chemistry of their digestive systems or their digestive systems have become what they are because the horses eat grass? And what determines the variations in human biochemistry which makes one man stubbornly polygamous and another educable into monogamy? By starting out with simple and univocal concepts such as "life," "the environment," "good," "the horse," "man," and deducing what will happen to individual living beings in specific environments, we might be able to reach conclusions which would be consistent, but would they be true?

Happily a method originating as "political arithmetic" and becoming in modern times statistics was developed. Joining together with the calculus of probabilities in the eighteenth century, it provided a tool for handling groups of individuals which might vary within certain limits, measuring the probable error, and predicting the future of the collection, if not of the individuals making it up. This retained both the factor of chance and the regularity of mathematics. But the statistical method was not a substitute for logic. No one would argue that the sum of the angles of a triangle was more or less than 180 degrees, though it is possible that were one to measure a triangle drawn on a piece of paper, that would be the result. The geometrical method might tell us what ought to be, what would be if there were only universals and no particulars; statistics would tell us what to expect since there are particulars. One could imagine that, assuming the Gaussian curve of distribution to be normal, it would shrivel to a point in any mathematical class. But that of course is only fantasy. The statistical method is based on the existence of individuals more or less alike, in space-time, and attempts to discover among other things just how much regularity there is in fact. The geometrical method is based upon universals, each of which is self-identical, eternal, and can never be contradicted by observation. The distinction which has been made by physicists between pure and applied geometry illustrates our point. Pure geometry is self-contained and as long as it is without inner contradiction is beyond criticism from experience. Applied geometry must find physical equivalents for its concepts and it must be true to the facts. Without the statistical method, collections of individuals cannot be handled intellectually. A statistical group gives us a range of variation and all generalizations must be qualified by some such phrase as "on the whole," which corresponds to the phrase "under ideal conditions."

Professor Quine in an interesting article, *Two Dogmas of Empiricism*,[8] has shown the interdependence of analytic and synthetic propositions. It would seem just to extend the argument to rational and empirical judgments as a whole. The calculus of probabilities itself is a rule for reasoning; it is not an empirical observation. But similarly the premises of any deductive system are purifications or simplifications of experience. The historians of mathematics have shown how the crude statements of Euclid have had to be continually refined until there need be no equivalence

---

[8] Now available in his book, *From a Logical Point of View*, Cambridge, 1953.

between them and the small areas of space in which we live. It may not be too audacious to suggest that even such concepts as *equivalence*, or proofs by substitution, are not without empirical origin, whatever their destiny may have been. How does one know, for instance, that such relations as "and" and "or" may be used with profit? It is all very well to toss off the adjective "arbitrary," and to insist that all rational systematizing is a game. But it is a game which strangely enough sometimes applies to real inference. It was not unusual in the early days of symbolic logic to point out that such a theorem as, "A false proposition implies any other proposition," was duplicated by such a sentence as, "If that is true, then anything is true." But this should have been of no interest if the system was only a game. The insistence on the part of C. I. Lewis that material implication should yield to strict implication was an expression of his desire to provide a logic which could be used in inference about real things, a kind of inference which would not be simply a game.[9] Whether one use a little *v* or the word *or* is a matter of choice; the symbol originated in the word, and it was because of the known existence of alternatives that it arose. If one were to invent a set of symbols which had absolutely no verbal correlates, no one would know what to do with them. But for that matter, how does one know that two straight lines cannot enclose a plane figure? A mathematically straight line has never been defined to the satisfaction of mathematicians, and when we use the concept we are certainly relying on intuition or its vestiges. The Laws of Thought may not be properly described as having anything to do with thinking, but originally they were descriptions of the way people thought when they were thinking consistently. They determined consistency. What is more, they determined a world in which alone they could be applied, a world in which terms did not change their meaning, in which there were only two alternatives—if I may be forgiven the redundancy—X and Not-X, and in which both X and Not-X

---

[9] Though this has been a constant preoccupation of Lewis dating back to his *Survey of Symbolic Logic*, it can also be found emphatically stated in his recent work, *An Analysis of Knowledge and Valuation*, La Salle, Illinois, 1946, pp. 212 ff.

could not be entertained at the same time, though what time had to do with it is doubtful.

The founder of classical logic had no illusions about the relation of his rules to either thinking or reality. A good part of the fourth book of his *Metaphysics* is given over to discussing the ontological reference of the Law of Contradiction. He declares flatly in the third chapter of that book (1005 b, 19) that it states not what we might call a relation between propositions, but a truth about objective fact. And as he continues his discussion in later passages, he uses the evidence of thinking and believing as fortification of his position. To him it is a question of a subject and its attributes, and if he introduces the qualifications, "at the same time," and "in the same respect," it is because he is thinking of ontology. Nowadays such a position would horrify the pure logicians. And again, if they are willing to overlook the origin of their concepts, they are right. They are undoubtedly dealing with what might be called an eternal realm into which space and time have no entrance. Logical necessity would be immediately sullied if any of their objects turned out to be material. Material things have a way of individualizing themselves in various degrees, some being more, some less amenable to purification. When our intellectual procedures are incapable of dealing with certain objects, they may be relegated to a special realm of trivialities, illusions, appearances, or what you will. But when a new method is elaborated which is capable of dealing with them, then a special realm is set up for them. Before the calculus of probabilities was developed, chance could be attributed to our ignorance. Now we know how to calculate chances and ignorance has lost its hold. When we are really ignorant, we had best not introduce chance or anything else. Reasoning of any type has to deal with statements, ideas, propositions, judgments, assertions, sets of words which say something. It does not deal with things and events but with the symbols which take their place. The distinction between judgments which we make about things and the things about which we make them has to be preserved if we want to permit the possibility of being mistaken. And mistakes would seem to be one of those events whose occurrence must be provided for at any cost.

When chance events are said to be those events of whose causes we are ignorant, either a new interpretation of causality has been introduced or the traditional interpretation has been overlooked. No individual event can be caused unless it is an ideal example of a class of events, for causality is a relation between classes of things. There is no contingency in the Law of Falling Bodies or Boyle's Law or the Second Law of Thermodynamics as laws; the contingency appears when historical incidents are described in their terms. Anything can happen to a real falling body or to a real gas or even to a kettle of hot water. But no one would be so misled as to say because a falling object might strike a ledge as it falls or the vessel in which the gas is contained should be broken or someone should light a flame under the kettle as it was cooling off, that for those reasons the laws were violated. These are historical accidents in the same way as the birth of a child or the death of a man is an accident. We know how children are born and how men die, but we do not know why this particular child was born or why this particular man died. The intersection of too many historical strands are involved in both cases—which would in itself only make the task harder to perform but not impossible—and the child is not simply a specimen of childhood but an individual boy or girl. Insofar as he is a child, of course the laws of genesis hold; no one would deny that. But insofar as he is John Doe, they may well fail to hold. We can, I suppose, know what the chances are of any fertilized ovum's developing into a viable organism, but that is quite a different story from knowing what the future of any particular fertilized ovum will be. It is the margin between the individual and the class into which a scientist for his own purposes wishes to integrate him which measures the distance between contingency and necessity and as long as that distance exists, the two realms will also exist.

10. There is, however, an historically important distinction between two realms based on the notion of complete unknowability.

This is the distinction between the world which we know and the world of Inner Natures, Noumena, the Unknowable. Even Hume believed in inner natures and believed also that they were unknowable, though he also believed that all knowledge was composed of impressions and their faint copies, ideas. The Unknowable in this usage is not merely that which is practically unknowable, things which we suspect of existence but which are too far away either in distant space or in the past or future. We can not know what was the name of the men who painted the animals on the walls of the cave at Lascaux or whether there is life on some remote planet or for that matter whether there will be a war between China and the Soviet Union in 1976. But such things, like the song the Sirens sang and the name Achilles assumed when he hid among the women, are not unknowable by their very nature. We simply lack the means of discovering the answers to such questions, much as we lack the means of discovering the real motives of Alcibiades or why Caesar was bald. The Unknowable is theoretically unknowable. There are no means and never will be means of discovering it, if the words of those who speak about it are to be taken seriously. Things have both an inner and an outer nature, they say, and we can know only the outer.

The use of "inner" and "outer" is metaphorical and the reasons for making the distinction is only a matter of conjecture. But one can surmise that it was based (1) upon human nature itself with all the obscurities of motivation and the possibility of a man's concealing his thoughts and (2) on the notion that all knowledge is derived from sensory impressions which are by definition representations of something concealed. An epistemological dualist might be tempted to maintain that the ideas of the secondary qualities, to use Locke's language, were the outer shell of hidden things, and it is possible, though far from certain, that Locke's *powers* were that which was hidden. The mere fact that an idea of a secondary quality is an effect of air waves or light rays is no proof that behind or beyond the secondary quality there is something concealed which we cannot know. For both the causes and the effects are present to observation, though not to simple perceptual observation. The light rays may be inferred from the colors and from the way the colors behave, but they are not for that reason occult. Their speed, their lengths, their position in the spectrum, their effects upon the eye can all be discovered, and though there are to be sure many unsolved problems connected with their existence, they in themselves are not unknowable. Analogous assertions can be made about air waves and the other material causes of sensations. It is plausible that all acquaintance with the external world is first made by means of sensory perception and the variations in perceptual data may indeed be the source of the many questions which have arisen about them. But why anyone should conclude from their occurrence that they conceal inner natures which cannot be known is obscure.

In reality no one has ever been satisfied with leaving the Unknowable alone. Kant, as is common knowledge, attributed to the Unknowables the power of causing knowledge. As he said in the preface to the second edition of the *Critique of Pure Reason,* it would be an "absurd conclusion" to infer "that there is phenomenal appearance without something that appears."[10] But the absurdity is nothing more than the connotation of the verb "to appear," as used in ordinary language. For what appears is not something behind the phenomena but the phenomena themselves. Is Kant simply arguing that "to appear" must have a subject which is "behind" the appearance? It would seem so. But such prepositions as "behind" are nothing more than figures of speech which in this case may well turn out to be misleading. If he is projecting the demands of language into ontology, he has simply to change his terminology and thus to get rid of the problem. He could have called his appearance perceptual data and gone on from there. The problem of inner natures then does not necessarily arise because we see, hear, taste, smell, and touch things; it arises because we name such sensory data by a term which in itself "implies" something which they conceal. That something is not their cause, for their causes are discoverable and have to a large

---

[10] Max Mueller's translation, London, 1949, p. 698.

extent been discovered. The causes too when they are discovered have to have inner natures. But one could also argue that the inner natures of material things must differ from the inner natures of mental things, and since the two classes contain within their frontiers varieties of behavior, one could then divide up the inner natures of each grand class into smaller classes. For if the inner natures of all material things were homogeneous, it would be impossible to explain why some material things appear in one way and others in another. If the inner nature of air-waves is all of a piece and if it has any effect on their outer natures, why do the waves themselves differ in velocity and length and why do we hear so many sounds which themselves have various pitches, intensities, and timbres? Or again, if the inner nature of matter is all of a piece, why are there so many different chemical elements? What in the inner nature is the source of the outer heterogeneity? But such questions are by hypothesis unanswerable, and one must conclude that natures are whatever they appear to be, that a thing is what it does.

This in no way allows us to infer that there is no legitimate distinction to be made between what a thing appears to be and what it really is. But the distinction, which is both reasonable and necessary, unless the world is to be a chaos, must be made on the basis of what can be theoretically knowable. We happen to be living in a world in which knowledge arises on what have—unfortunately—been called "levels of experience." But regardless of that unhappy figure of speech, it is true that we can describe any object from the point of view of uncorrected perceptual experience, the-way-it-looks-to-me; from the point of view of corrected perceptual experience, the-way-it-looks-under-standard-conditions; from the point of view of classical physics, the primary qualities of Galileo; from the point of view of chemistry, if it is a physico-chemical object; and obviously from the point of view of economics, aesthetics, religion, sociology, or any other field of human inquiry. It is undeniable that some things look one way to one person and another to another, depending on all the details mentioned in the tropes of Aenesidemus and a score of other things. But the fact that Aenesidemus and others could list the variables of which the look is a function, shows without further demonstration that such looks are individual historical events and when isolated from all other events, are useless for science. The standardized object, the "it" which appears in all these guises is probably a residue of the common-sense physical object. The standardized object, let us say the visual object, is quite another sort of thing, for it is seen, we can assume, in sunlight, at a determinate distance, from a specified position, by normal observers. The normal observer is himself one whose observations are modal and hence useful for further calculation and prediction. The determinate distance, illumination, position, are also introduced as that from which deviations can be measured. It seldom need appear; but if utilized in discourse, it will give us a permanent—or almost—thing of which we can predict individual appearances. To say that a visual object appears small at a given distance and large at another, is not to attribute to the object an unobservable size which is its real size. Visual objects have to be seen, and the observer's reports cannot be eliminated by fiat. The truth is that we never are content with visual objects, for we can harmonize and simplify perceptual experience by using an object with standard properties determined by means other than uncorrected vision. That object is "more real" than the visual object only in the sense that its existence can be used to explain the occurrence of the visual object. But this standard object will, as we have said, take on other traits as soon as we integrate it into the totality of our experiences. Objects are liked and disliked, are bought and sold, are produced and destroyed, are judged beautiful and ugly, are manipulated in a hundred different ways according to human interests. And nothing is gained by asserting flatly that the real object is one of these of which the others are appearances, for the preposition "of" is itself of doubtful usage. When one proceeds to assert that behind the real object is an unknowable inner nature, then obviously one has done nothing more than to wrap up an appearance in a vestment of mystery.

We have sketched in this lecture then theories which set up

different realms of being. Sometimes the differentiation of the realms is made on the basis of the kind of knowledge which understands them, sometimes on the kinds of beings which are in them. But difference is found in primary sensory observation as well as in more abstract spheres, and there will always be a question of where difference is so great that a special realm must be allotted to the things which possess it. Red does not resemble blue, but we are willing to put them both into the class of colors, though there is no observable similarity between any two colors. Here the instrument of observation, roughly the eye, is enough to serve as the ground of the classification. Colors do not resemble sounds, tastes, odors, textures, pains, thermal sensations; and yet we are willing to group them all together as sensations or sensory data. On the other hand, dreams do resemble waking experiences, and yet we set up two separate realms to house them. Universals are sometimes met in the world of particulars, though particulars are never met in the world of universals. But here the timelessness of the former is never found in the latter, and the logical properties of each set are antithetical. I do not know whether the idea of blue is itself blue—though in Santayana it was—but there are some universals, such as justice, which presumably can be found incorporated in human beings and recognized when met. But regardless of that—and we have no intention of reproducing Plato's *Parmenides* or *The Sophist*— it is the logical functions of each class which are irreconcilable, not their empirical traits. We are thus confronted once again by the problem of ultimate differentiations and shall give over our next lecture to that.

APPENDIX TO CHAPTER X
Faith and Reason in Catholicism

In order to remove any doubts about my interpretation of the relations between faith and reason in official Catholic doctrine, the following is taken exclusively from Denzinger's *Enchiridion Symbolorum et Definitionum* and no use has been made of com-

mentaries whether by Catholic writers or others. I have left the
material in Latin to avoid charges that I have mistranslated.

In the *Index Systematicus rerum quae cum Dogmate cohaerent*
(1 b) we find the following summary.

> Praeter veritates etiam rationi pervias revelatio christiana continet
> Mysteria tum *late dicta* ut aeterna Dei decreta, tum *stricte dicta,* quae
> rationi omnino impervia sunt, immo etiam angelicam intelligentiam
> transcendunt, quae cum progressu scientiae intelligi aut demonstrari
> non possunt; tamen rationi non contradicunt, sed eam superant, et
> semper obscura manent; non sunt inventa hominum communi bono
> adversantia.

For our purposes it suffices to point out that this says (1) that
besides the truths which are open to rational investigation there
are mysteries, expressed in both figurative and literal language,
which can in no way be so investigated, (2) that these can never
be scientifically understood or demonstrated, and yet (3) they
are not in contradiction with reason, that (4) they are supra-
rational, i.e., "above" the reason, and (5) always remain obscure.
The last clause is irrelevant to our discussion. The authority for
the first point is given as the second chapter of the *Constitutio
dogmatica de fide catholica* issued by the Vatican Council in 1870,
which states that though God can be known certainly by the
natural light of reason and from creation, nevertheless He has
retained some truth to be known otherwise.

> Eadem sancta mater Ecclesia tenet et docet, Deum, rerum omnium
> principium et finem, naturali humanae rationis lumine e rebus creatis
> certo cognosci posse; . . . attamen placuisse eius sapientiae et bonitati,
> alia eaque supernaturali via se ipsum ac aeterna voluntatis suae decreta
> humano generi revelare . . .

The authority for the second clause, namely the impervious-
ness of some truths to human reason, is given in the Encyclical
Mirari vos arbitramur of Gregory XVI, 1832, which was issued
in condemnation of Lamennais.

> Superbi seu potius insipientis hominis est, fidei mysteria, quae
> exsuperant omnem sensum, humanis examinare ponderibus nostraeque
> mentis rationi confidere, quae naturae humanae conditione debilis
> est et infirma.

There are, however, frequent repetitions of this pronouncement which can be found in the Index by anyone interested in checking them.

We can skip the matter of whether the angelic intelligence can understand these matters and proceed to their relation to scientific progress. The authority for this is the Allocution of Pius IX, *Singulari quadam* of 1854, which assigns the weakness of our reason to the Fall.

> Atque huiusmodi humanae rationis sectatores seu cultores potius, qui eam sibi certam veluti magistram proponunt eiusque ductu fausta sibi omnia pollicentur, obliti certe sunt, quam grave et acerbum ex culpa primi parentis inflictum sit vulnus humanae naturae, quippe quod et obfusae tenebrae menti et prona effecta ad malum voluntas . . . Nunc quando ex originis labe in universos Adami posteros propagata extenuatum esse constet rationis lumen, et ex pristino iustitiae atque innocentiae statu miserrime dedicerit humanum genus, ecquis satis esse rationem ducat ad assequendam veritatem?

And in the Epistle *Gravissimas inter* of the same Pope of 1862, we find after a condemnation of the opinion that the Mysteries can be rationally explained, the sentences,

> Quocirca ex eiusdem auctoris sententia concludi omnino possit ac debeat, rationem in abditissimis etiam divinae sapientiae ac bonitatis, immo etiam et liberae eius voluntatis mysteriis, licet posito revelationis obiecto, posse ex se ipsa, non iam ex divinae auctoritatis principio, sed ex naturalibus suis principiis et viribus ad scientiam seu certitudinem pervenire. Quae auctoris doctrina quam falsa sit et erronea, nemo est, qui christianae doctrinae rudimentis *vel leviter imbutus non illico videat planeque sentiat.*

Inasmuch as the Epistle was written to an archbishop about the teachings of a professor of the University of Munich, the last sentence may seem a bit strong. But it may well be that the professor, Jakob Frohschammer, was not even *leviter imbutus* with the rudiments of Christian doctrine.

Though there are many statements that faith is not contrary to reason, for God *qui nec falli nec fallere potest*[1] could not ask us to believe in falsities, perhaps the most succinct statement of the

---

[1] Pius IX in the Encyclical *Qui pluribus,* 1846, Enchir. 1638.

principle is in the Syllabus of errors, where we find *Christi fides humanae refragatur rationi* listed almost immediately after the error that *Humana ratio, nullo prorsus Dei respectu habito, unicus est veri et falsi . . . arbiter.* The truths of faith then must rest on Revelation and if they are contrary to human reason, it is because human reason is too weak to grasp them. That they are above the reason was demonstrated by the Pope also in *Gravissimas inter* when he said, *Et sane cum haec dogmata sint supra naturam, idcirco naturali ratione ac naturalibus principiis attingi non possunt.*

I trust that these quotations will dispel any doubts about the accuracy of my interpretation of the doctrine in the body of this lecture. The question still remains of how one knows what a doctrine held by faith, i.e., supra-rational, asserts if it cannot be subjected to rational discourse. The sentences in which such a doctrine is expressed will of course "make sense," will have subjects and predicates, be affirmative and negative, and as sentences will be handed down by tradition. But the moment one asks what they mean, one will hope to have another set of words more easily understood, and if those words contradict rational principles, one will be at a loss to know even what one is believing. I doubt, for instance, whether anyone believes in the real existence of mermaids. The reason is not that none of us has ever seen a mermaid; for none of us has ever seen the other side of the moon, and yet we all believe on good grounds that it has another side. On the contrary, we have reason to believe in the unviability of organisms described as mermaids are described. If now someone advanced the propositions that one should believe in the real existence of mermaids on faith, while admitting that they are unviable organisms, he would surely be told that either he had described mermaids inaccurately or that he was talking nonsense. It is likely that if then he announced that belief in mermaids was not contradictory to reason but transcended reason, he would then be asked to rephrase the belief in question so that it would not appear to contradict reason. For if I am told that an apple is both red and not-red at the same time and in the same respect, I shall reply that such a statement is contrary to reason and that its rational inconsistency appears in its phrasing. It is not sufficient to call such assertions "mysteries," for one does not even know what they mean. And one might imagine that even faith demands information about that in which one is asked to have faith.

CHAPTER XI

DIFFERENTIATION

The problem which confronts us is that of how much difference is necessary to establish separate realms of being.

To begin with, it should be pointed out that existential multiplicity has never been questioned. For even the most obdurate monists have been willing to admit that there is a plurality of beings, if not of kinds of being. No one has ever denied that some general ideas or class-characters are exemplified in several individuals, though many have wondered about the principle of individuation. Individuation or the existence of individuals then may be said to be taken for granted. Socrates is not a realm of being separated from Plato, though he may have a life of his own and a private domain of consciousness. There would be nothing to prevent a philosopher from thinking of each man's inner life as a distinct realm and in the works of Leibniz as well as those of the Personalists, this has been done. That the procedure has not been more widely followed is probably due to the difficulty of explaining the interrelations between the monads or persons.

In the second place, qualitative differences, such as appear in perceptual inspection have usually been granted. Since no one is completely anaesthetic, it may be assumed that everyone perceives some such differences as that between two colors, colors and sounds, round and square things, and soft and hard, even when these qualities belong to a scale along which they occupy different positions. The technique for absorbing these differences is, as we have suggested previously, by means of their physical causes.

In the third place, quantitative differences which are measurable are usually taken for granted. No one disputes that some things are longer than others, some swifter than others, some heavier than others. This is interesting, for the measurements have to be made by people using instruments which they have devised for the specific purpose of making the measurements. Usually the investigator has to make a series of measurements rather than one, and accept the average as the correct one.

In the fourth place, as a derivative from existential individuality, some but not all philosophers have differentiated between the terms of a relational complex and the relation or system of relations in which they occur. Some have maintained that all terms are external to their relations. But others have insisted on the internality of all relations. Of the latter Hegel and his school are the most representative, and Hegel is well known for his belief that only the whole is real. Strictly speaking, an Hegelian should not admit existential individuality, and in both Bosanquet and Royce a good bit was made of the interconnectedness of things. If their arguments hold, then we cannot even assume existential difference as real. And since quantities, as we have said, are always determined relatively to the instruments and procedures of measurement, it may also be necessary to discard quantitative difference as ultimate.

This would leave us with qualitative difference as residual. What qualitative differences will be observed will always be dependent on what the observer is looking for, and that will be determined by the questions he has in mind and the interests which guide him, all of which may be habitual. But nevertheless he will assume the possibility of finding such differences, for if everything is like everything else to the point that their possible differences are unrecognizable, then nothing whatsoever can be said about anything. The fact that the qualities whose differences will be observed can theoretically be predicted does not permit us to deny the occurrences of such differences. They may turn out to be subjective, illusory, momentary, or what you will, but if they are observed, that is sufficient for our present purposes.

Qualitative difference at a minimum allows us only to assert that A is different from or other than B. And we can equate this with the assertion that A is not-B. No principle of negation is needed for this, no negative facts, no non-being. For, as is well known, to assert that A is not-B, is not to say what it is. I am assuming obviously that A and B stand for single perceptual experiences, not for sets of experiences.

This works out well enough if one confines one's reflections to subject-attribute propositions. But in a relational statement it cannot be applied so easily. Though I am not denying that relations can be perceived, that is, that one sees a book upon a table or to the right of another book, when one says that the book is not on top of the table, is one observing qualitative difference? It seems dubious. We may, if we please, assert that the book is elsewhere; but it may be nowhere. Sartre in *l'Etre et le Néant* maintains that in such a situation one actually perceives non-being.[1] This is playing upon metaphysical terms in an unnecessary fashion. For what happens is that one's expectations fail to be fulfilled. And though logically the sentence has nothing to do with expectation or non-expectation, psychologically it does. As I write this, I have a table before me, the top of which is empty of contents. I can truly say, "No book is on the table," "No orange is on the table," "My book is not on the table," "Perrault's façade of the Louvre is not on the table," and any number of things of that sort. If I were looking for any of these and expected them to be on the table, or thought that they might be on the table, then it would be reasonable to say that they are not there. But which of these assertions I actually make will depend on what I was looking for. It will not depend on any prior logical considerations, for the realm of non-being is immensely capacious. Negation in this case is the failure to verify a proposition or judgment which I thought would be true. What is there is the empty table top and that is other than the anticipated observation. But this is a pragmatic test, like James's test of the right way home. To make such an assertion, I must, as so often, have had a

---

[1] "Non-being does not occur in things through the judgment of negation; on the contrary, that judgment is conditioned and supported by non-being." *Op. cit.*, p. 46.

question in mind, and some past experience in terms of which I could answer it. If I did not know what a book looked like, I should never be sure whether it was on the table or not. And if I were not in search of something definite, there would be no more point in saying that the book was not on the table than in saying that the Declaration of Independence was not on the table. If finally one says, "Nothing is on the table," a sophist could immediately ask one what one meant by nothing; how nothing could be anywhere rather than somewhere else, and the like. But the word "nothing" in this sort of case is simply used as a shorthand expression for the fact—not the proposition—that the expectation of finding any specifiable object on the table will be frustrated.

We return then to our initial assumption that the world may be thought of as that which answers or fails to answer our questions. And what questions will be asked will depend naturally upon our interests. Among these interests is that of integrating into an accepted system of ideas new experiences. This involves formulating judgments—and I persist in calling them judgments—anticipating one's expectations. It is these judgments which are either verified or not verified in such circumstances as we have been illustrating. After the judgments are verified and become propositions of fact, they can obviously be arranged in logical order, and then the consistency of the total collection of propositions will be sufficient test of their truth. But at that moment the question of the identity or difference of the verifying experiences or things or events, for it matters little what one calls them, will arise. That is, if I wonder whether my book is on the table, and I find that a book is there, I must either assume that it is my book or that it is not. For if I am simply relying on sensory data to verify my conclusions, I can only conclude that what is before me resembles my book. I may be said to utilize the Principle of the Identity of Indiscernibles, if one will, but I do not have two data to compare and of course rely upon my memory.

No one actually goes through such a process of reasoning, but spots the book as his and judges it to be his. For he will take for granted a continuity in time which will alone preserve the continuing identity of physical objects. This identity cannot be reasonably attributed to the sensory data, for they come and go and we all know why. But the minute a distinction is made between the sensory data and the physical objects, it will be seen that a cut has been made through the world of things, between their appearances and what can only be called their substance. If the appearances are observed to be very different from what they were expected to be, I shall wonder whether the book is really the one I was looking for. If the differences are very slight or the kind which I have become accustomed to, I shall accept them as "normal." In short, for there is no need to complicate the issue, I assume a certain order in the universe, an order in this case which permits different rates of change in things, but also an order which I have accepted as the structure of the world in space-time. I may distinguish between those traits of objects which can change rapidly and those which change so slowly as to be almost permanent, that is, to be unnoticed under ordinary conditions. I may not be able to give any rule for making this distinction, but I can recognize the distinction nevertheless. For instance, I shall be willing to admit that the color of my book's binding may fade, that the hinges may break, that some of the pages may get torn, and still assert that the book is the one I was looking for. But if my book had 400 pages and the book before me has only 200, or if my book was labeled *Aristotle's Criticism of the Pre-Socratics* and the book before me is labeled *Black Beauty,* or if my book had my name on the inside of the cover and the book before me has someone else's name, I surrender and admit that the book before me is not the book which I was looking for. I will not admit that a 400 page book could lose half its pages automatically, however desirable that might be, nor that it could turn into a story about a horse though it had originally been a detailed account of an event in intellectual history, or that my name might evaporate and another take its place. If such things could happen, I will say, anything could happen. And one of our cardinal principles in answering questions is precisely that anything cannot happen.

When I say that anything cannot happen, I must not be interpreted as saying that great quantities of various things do not happen, but that within a set of limiting conditions, certain events are ruled out. These conditions may have a wide or narrow range, but they all originate in the past experience of individuals. I am not the only person in the world, I am happy to say, who owns a copy of *Aristotle's Criticism of the Pre-Socratics*. And it is always possible that one of my friends may have left his copy on my table by inadvertence. But unless someone has played me a practical joke, it hardly is likely that my signature should have disappeared and that of my friend should have taken its place. The likelihood is close to zero not because I have never seen other people's signatures in books, nor that ink has not been known by me to fade out, but because I have never heard of a signature turning into another signature except when someone has deliberately made the change. Things can happen that I have never heard of; that is indubitable. But I use that sort of expression as a substitute for the order which I expect to be exemplified. In other words I have learned that events proceed in a regular manner, *other things being equal.* In this case I can state with more or less precision what are the things which have to be equal. My ability to do this is fortified by experience, even when my personal experience is irrelevant to the order in question.

Thus the Heraclitean flux is no stumbling block to the acquisition of knowledge, unless one refuses to accept its orderliness in time. But to accept that kind of order is a methodological rule; it cannot be accommodated to an epistemology which is constructed out of sensory data, for the data are by their very nature momentary or close to it. The amount of difference which will be observed will vary greatly, depending on what one is looking for. What one looks for does not create what one finds, but it does determine what differences one will find. Unless one grant that one's experiences move from the past into the present and that the human mind has an accumulation of experiences, which the sensory empiricist cannot grant, the whole affair becomes an insoluble mystery, or what is worse, lands one in the solipsism of the present moment. No empiricist of the type mentioned has ever been hospitable to that idea, however logically it may follow from his premises. And his very reluctance to accept his conclusion is significant. There is no sound evidence, as we all know, in the presence of any datum or complex of data for anything else whatsoever. To confine oneself to the flux of impressions and ideas, as Hume saw so clearly, is to close any entrance into a world of causation or for that matter into any world with a temporal order. There might well be order in the flux, but we should have no evidence of it, unless we were allowed also to remember the past. But why should there be any order? Why are we not satisfied with a sputtering flux? The answer which these lectures have proposed is that our experience itself has a temporal dimension and that we assume that the world which we experience has one too. If this is castigated as a "mere" assumption, it should be noted that the denial of it is also a mere assumption. One has to have rules to guide one's reflections, however lenient such rules may be.

If John Locke laid down the five primary qualities as the differentiae of material substance, it was in part because they were less mutable than the secondary qualities. There were other arguments as well, such as that motion, configuration, and the other three could be perceived by a variety of senses, whereas each secondary quality was perceived by a special sense. The differences discovered between them came out of physics, not out of sensory data, for, as Berkeley soon pointed out, as sensory data solidity, extension, motion, number, and figure, were just as momentary and subjective as color, sound, taste, and odor. Looking at a physical object, one can differentiate between the quality of color and the qualities of extension and solidity, for such distinctions are self-evident. But just looking could never tell one that the order into which motion can be absorbed is any different from the order into which color can be absorbed. The color of a billiard ball has no influence upon its velocity, its solidity, or its weight, though the latter group may and often do influence color. But such "influences" again are discovered after long experience. We can easily affirm that everyone knows this and indeed everyone does. But unfortunately philosophy often avoids what everyone knows in order to achieve what its practitioners think of as a simplified account of things. Certainly the simplest account is one which will omit time and shrivel experience to the present moment. But a philosopher having committed himself to a position, might be expected to accept its consequences. If solipsism were true, it would be strange that anyone would want to reject it after taking as his premises assertions which entail it. What is even stranger is that philosophers who begin with these premises—witness Santayana in *Scepticism and Animal Faith*—when they proceed to emerge from their solipsism, somehow or other know in advance just what sort of world they want to reconstruct. And that world is the world of common-sense, corrected by the sciences, the world in space-time, with material objects, other people, falsity as well as truth, and in fact the whole paraphernalia of the "plain man's" philosophy. Animal faith may of course guide us in many of our travels, but when it operates in the field of epistemology, it seems itself to be under control of some higher power.

We now have the following principles of differentiation: (1) perceived qualitative differences; (2) differences in rates of change. To these we add a third which I shall call differences in causal range. By causal range I mean the domain of efficacy, the kinds of events which a given set of causes can cause. Thus the causal range of perceived colors is different from the causal range of material masses. A perceived bit of red, as on a flag, may cause us to tear it down in outrage at the sight of it, but it cannot cause the flag to fall down. But the weight of the flag or the chemical constitution of the red dye or the force of the wind or the thickness and height of the flagstaff, may cause it to fall down. We cannot integrate our sense of outrage into the system of propositions which describe the possible causes of the flag's fall; that is, if the flag falls simply because the dye has caused it to disintegrate, or because the staff is too thin for its height, or the flag is too heavy for its staff, or the wind is too strong, then we need not bring into the conversation also our feelings on seeing it on the staff. We shall say that these feelings are irrelevant in the sense defined in our opening lecture. This is so elementary that one is ashamed to mention it.

But what is meant by the phrase, "We *need* not bring it into the conversation?" Simply that another of our methodological rules will be to keep the explanation as simple as possible. We are using the Principle of Parsimony, a principle which will be discussed below. Now, as we have said earlier in these lectures, the simplest possible explanation of any event is the will of God. But it also appears to have been the will of God to endow men with reason, and reason has its own procedures which are independent of religion. It makes good sense to say in a teleological type of explanation that the reason for the flag's fall was God's indignation at seeing the ensign of a group which denies His existence. But it is not good sense to say that if one is talking of causes. The sight of a red flag may cause a sense of outrage and the sense of outrage may cause a man to pull the flag down. But it is also to be noticed that the sense of outrage, if it is to cause the flag to come down, must eventuate in a physical object—the man's body—moving through space and getting into contact with the flag. There may be such a thing as extra-sensory perception, but there is no case on record, as far as I know, of extra-motor action. Here the restrictions of a causal range are empirically defined. And the extent of another causal range is involved in the definition. The principle then upon which one may differentiate between two types of things can be seen to reside in the spread of their causal efficacy.

There is no need of a special theory of causation to demonstrate this. Any theory will do. We can state the sufficient and necessary conditions of a material object's falling after it has been tied to something high and we can state the sufficient and necessary conditions of the same object's arousing a sense of outrage in an observer. Our statements may be incorrect and the spread of error may be greater in one case than in the other. Red flags on flagstaffs are not a common subject of physical discussion, and should a physicist be asked to explain why the flag in question fell, he would translate the question into terms of mass, distance, velocities, and the like. It would no longer be a red flag; it would be so much matter at such and such a height from the ground. The possibility of such translations rests on the existence of certain generalizations which themselves are possible only because scientists have learned that certain properties of objects can be eliminated from their discussions. To be able to talk about mass without bringing color, for instance, into the conversation is no evidence for the belief that masses can exist without color, that masses are objective rather than subjective, that mass is real whereas color is unreal—except by fiat—or that mass has some special status in the ontological world. It at most means that variations in mass, if any, can be calculated without regard to color, and though this is a great discovery, it is not in itself the discovery of an ontological fissure. The establishment of the very concept of matter, as distinguished from this and that kind of matter, demanded the assumption that dynamics could be formalized without any consideration of *kinds*. People are not just confronted with matter; they are confronted with all sorts and conditions of material objects, some light, some heavy, some solid, some fluid, some stable, some evanescent, some swift, some slow. To have been able to neglect such differences, which all are found on the plane of simple qualitative inspection, though not in such large groupings, was the great triumph of the scientific imagination. But it will be observed that it could not have been achieved without a long preliminary preparation. In the first place, men grouped the tremendous variety of what we call material substances into four kinds, the four elements, and no one will maintain that this was an obvious grouping. Then the elimination of the four ultimately different elements was not performed by noticing that earth, water, air, and fire had observably identical characters. They actually do what Aristotle demanded of them, and as long as no more was demanded, their irreducible differences would never have been reduced. For matter in Aristotle is the four elements only in his physical writings; in his others it may be the human body in relation to the soul, the vegetative soul in relation to the animal, even the passive reason in relation to the active. In the *Metaphysics* it is all these and more and operates as a device for receiving the potencies which are constantly being realized, wherever and whatever they may be. In a man like Galileo different questions were put to Nature, and he, to be sure, had the ground prepared by his fourteenth- and fifteenth-century predecessors. But it is interesting to see that, though the anecdote of his dropping different weights off the Leaning Tower of Pisa is inauthentic, nevertheless he did argue to the falsity of the Peripatetic theories of dynamics before putting the questions which he did put. As Popper has pointed out,[2] science often progresses by refuting theories already held and not merely by advancing new hypotheses and testing them. At the risk of misinterpreting his thoughts, one might say that truth is furthered by the discovery of error. As long as no one sees the falsity of a theory, it will be retained. But though no one can prove a theory by citing confirmative instances, one can always disprove a theory by citing negative instances.

But instances, whether positive or negative, have to be instances *of* something and, it goes without saying, they are instances of the beliefs which real flesh and blood people hold. That Nature is a collection of instances is only roughly true. That is, if one makes the right guess, one will find instances to corroborate the guess. But the way is always open, if history tells us anything, to the discovery of events which do not corroborate the guess. In such a situation two things may happen: either the investigator says that these events are a special case demanding special treatment or that they and the old cases must be put into a larger class which includes them both.[3] His imagination is then called into play to find some such class, and the operation of his imagination will be directed toward putting to the data a single question

---

[2] K. R. Popper; "Three Views concerning Human Knowledge," in *Contemporary British Philosophy*.

[3] He may, as we have repeatedly pointed out, also say that they are merely subjective, accidental, monstrous, or trivial.

which both classes can answer satisfactorily. After all, no one had any way of knowing in advance that sublunary and super-lunary dynamics were not two separate kinds of dynamics. No one ever had a revelation that they were not. But the drive toward simplification, the success of which depended upon sacrificing the observed differences, was in the long run responsible for finding a set of laws which would cover both classes of data. It was all very well for Osiander or Copernicus to declare that Nature al-ways followed the simplest course. It would have been more accurate to say that Science always follows the simplest course.

Now one would be foolhardy to maintain that such simplicity as is framed in the laws is in any literal sense of the word im-posed upon the natural order. It is to be sure imposed upon our thinking about the natural order, but when the simplicity is too great, we sooner or later find that out, if not by our own re-searches, by those of our critics. One cannot verify any assertion whatsoever at will. Some sentences are downright wrong. But the point is that their falsity is not contained in the symbols in which they are expressed nor in momentary experiences. We first have to have some idea of what experiences are relevant to the ideas under examination, are cases of the law in question, are instances of something, and a single experience, as we have repeated *ad nauseam,* may be an instance of a great variety of general classes. This is nonsensical if knowledge does not arise out of judgments, but is simply impressed upon us by an external world. We cannot, then, discover any type of order in Nature which happens to please us at the moment, and yet the right type of order does not leap out of the conglomeration of things and arrange itself before our eyes automatically. The reason why there have been so few theories about pretty nearly everything, aside from tradition, is that the human imagination is admittedly limited by experience—in the extended sense of that word—and that most people's experience contains only a few kinds of order. Differences are spotted very early in life, and as we grow older, we begin to learn that some of the orders may be eliminated as the effects or as sub-classes of wider kinds of order. To have classified all the kinds of material objects in the world into the four elements must have required great insight. But it would not have worked unless Nature itself manifested the kinds of motion which Aristotle read into the local motions which he observed. For to see a candle flame pointing to heaven is no proof that all fire moves towards the periphery of the cosmos, and there must have been thousands of Greeks who saw flames pointing upwards without making generalizations about them or wondering why they did not point down to earth. Before Aristotle had finished with his physical writings, the elements had become simply names for the way in which certain objects moved, actualizations of the potencies of the hot-dry, cold-dry, hot-moist, and cold-moist. Things did not have to look like air to be chemically air, nor look like fire to be chemically fire. He was able to pass through the appearances to those aspects of his substances which obeyed his fundamental laws. The selection of the primary qualities, heat and moisture, and their privations depended upon still another principle.[4]

The difference here between appearance and reality is surely not that between the unreal and the real. Here something is judged not to be what it really is; it is not judged to be non-existent. So as children we are amazed to learn that diamonds and lumps of coal are both really carbon, however different they may seem. But the reality, or their identity, is their both reacting to certain laboratory tests in the same way. These tests do not annihilate the differences between the two objects; on the contrary, anyone can see the differences. It is the identity which is not seen. No one would be willing to say that diamonds are not hard transparent crystals or that graphite is not black and oily. The chemist who identifies them both as carbon is only accidentally interested in their differences, unless he is studying the allotropic forms of carbon or allotropic forms of the elements in general. We must therefore repeat that looking with the naked eye is as much testing as is applying laboratory tests, and the

---

[4] Cf. Israel Drabkin; "Notes on the Laws of Motion in Aristotle," *American Journal of Philology,* 1938.

differences which result from the two types of testing may be very great. I confess to an inability to see in this any reason for setting up separate realms of being. For if there is, then where does one stop? If we are to have a realm of beings composed of things as they appear to the unaided sense-organs, then we must have another which will include the differences in our sensory perceptions. Diamonds, to revert to them, vary very greatly, we are told on good authority, some being "purer" than others, some being bigger, some whiter, some yellower, some almost blue. The eye which can spot these differences is in great demand, and I suppose—though this is far from being a field with which I have any acquaintance—that the diamond merchants actually do differentiate by means of these tests and do so not for scientific but for economic reasons. By pursuing the road to diversity we land in a world in which there are no general laws except those which establish the procedural rules which we apply to our work. And we want general laws as far as they are obtainable.

We must assume in that case that knowledge may be common to groups of investigators using the same exploratory technique. We have learned how to discount the personal equation, if not the human equation, and we do it on the ground that a true description will be true for anyone. There is no need to do more than mention that an observation which includes the personal equation is just as true as one which has eliminated it. But a collection of such observations will have to submit to other manipulations before they can be of any use to a scientist. For since any personal observation is an historical, not a logical, event, nothing can be inferred from it alone. If ten people report that they see the same thing, the blue sky, it would of course be foolish to deny that we would accept their observation. But until the observation is translated into more general terms, it is only of historical interest. Nothing is more common than to find groups of people who report that they have seen incredible things: the angels at Mons, the Loch Ness monster, flying saucers, ghosts, a witches's Sabbath, and so on. For years psychologists have re-

ported on the unreliability of such reports.[5] It would be folly to
say just what such people did see and furthermore irrelevant.
The reason why their joint reports are not acceptable is not that
they did not see what they say they saw, but that their interpretations of what they saw are in conflict with accepted opinion. One
could, if one wished, give up the accepted opinions, but they are
themselves so intimately related to a whole system of other beliefs that to give them up would be to abandon the very foundations of several sciences. If I have a vision of Great Caesar's
Ghost, I do not report simply that I saw a shape of such and
such dimensions resembling a man wrapped in a toga with a
crown of laurel concealing his bald spot; I call what I have seen
a ghost. The word "ghost" gets its meaning from a theory of
human survival, of the return of the dead to this earth, of their
visual appearance, usually clothed, if I am not mistaken, in
white or pale gray. Psychologists could at least theoretically explain why I have seen what I am reporting as having seen, so
that no one need accept my report at its face-value. The fact that
they will want to explain it is that they do not accept all the
propositions which are behind my use of the word "ghost." If
no one had heard of mass-hysteria or mass-hallucination, no
scientist would be stubborn enough to refuse to investigate the
truth of reports about the angels at Mons or the other reported
visions. If he has to set up a class of phenomena in which ma-
terialized angels figure, he will do so, but the report on the
angels is just the starting point of his research. He will insist
that the objects be described in general terms: namely, that the
word "angel" be defined so that anyone can tell whether he has
or has not seen an angel; that the distinction between a mate-
rialized angel and an incorporeal angel be also framed in intelligible language; that some test be devised by means of which
one can distinguish between an hallucinatory angel and a real
angel. That this is not merely optimism on my part is shown by
the interest which scientists have shown in telepathy, survival

---

[5] For a standard and still interesting book on the subject, see Hugo Muenster-
berg's *On the Witness Stand.*

after death, communication with the dead, and other phenomena which are sometimes called parapsychological. The arguments pro and con may be equally bad, and often prejudice against novelty makes itself felt to the obfuscation of science. But nevertheless the position taken by the scientist is the only one possible, unless random reports are to be collected in a sort of gigantic scrap-book and take the place of science. The scepticism of scientists, when faced with novelty, may be discouraging, but it arises from a definite intellectual demand that all knowledge be susceptive of systematic statement. And that demand arises ultimately from the conviction that Nature itself can be ordered.

This conviction can be justified only by its results. It is what leads up to and fortifies expectation. That we expect certain things to happen is simply a psychological truth—there is nothing logical about it, for in logic nothing happens. Our personal development proceeds in the same way and we take it for granted that on the whole the world will come up to our expectations. And on the whole it does. If it always did, there would be no novelty in our worlds and it is probably true that in some regions tomorrow always repeats today. One can imagine a world, if that is the right word, in which climate never varies, in which the sun always rises and sets at the same moment, in which the food-supply is always regular, in which everyone obeys the law and knows what it is, and in which babies appear at stated and regular intervals. In such a world there could never be any questions about anything, assuming that I have listed a fair sample of the possibilities of variation. But it is next to impossible to work out the fantasy to its limits, for the inhabitants would have to be sedentary, like oysters, and absorb their food from the ambient atmosphere to make the fable more plausible and even the sun would have to be fixed in one spot in the heavens—in fact, it would be better if there were no sun at all but simply an all-enveloping light. The more one forces his imagination to picture such a world, the more one sees the difficulty. For differences and alterity arise in spite of all we do and if there were more than one inhabitant, they would see one another and be aware of personal plurality, and even the one inhabitant would do better not to grow. This is so contrary to fact and to fact of which we cannot help but be conscious, that it is wiser to admit change and to posit expectation as essential to inquiry and validation.

One may be resigned to novelty but clearly one cannot expect it. One can and usually does admit that tomorrow will not exactly repeat today, but one cannot foresee in detail just what novelties will occur.[6] To be ready to meet anything is a fine moral slogan, but it is an impossibility. One can be prepared only to meet what one has already experienced or that of which an intelligible description can be given one. The New England states could not be prepared to meet hurricanes in 1938 for the simple reason that no one had ever thought a hurricane would pass through them. Hurricanes, like death, happen to other people. The number of things which can happen is very great, though of course finite, and we cannot be prepared even for half of them. Hence we pick out by habit the things most likely to happen, and they are the things which have occurred regularly or very frequently in the community's past. This is the order of life which establishes our ideas and in terms of which we plan our futures. If the future were entirely novel, obviously there would be no understanding it, for where all is deviation, there is no rule. The situation is a mixture of novelty and sameness, and we have to accommodate the novelty to the laws we have already accepted as the order of history or to frame new laws to account for it. This is such a commonplace that we have forgotten its significance. For both in the history of science and of general culture there have always been men to close their eyes to the problems as they have arisen and, by extending their tolerance for exceptions farther and farther, to adjust to a changing world. And here by "world" I also include the world of ideas. As far as I know, there are always exceptions, very small sometimes, to any generalization about events, and the tolerance with which

---

[6] I trust that no one will think that I am denying the validity of astronomical predictions or others based on recurrent cycles.

they are accepted varies widely. If that were not so, then the history of science would have been vastly different. When Count Rumford showed that a body of water could be heated in a sealed container by being rotated rapidly and that no caloric could get into the container, the believers in caloric were far from defeated. They simply replied that caloric could squeeze between the pores of the densest material. When it was pointed out that a hot object ought to weigh more than the object when cooled, it was answered that caloric was imponderable. To be faced with an imponderable substance might have floored some minds, but the caloricists were never convinced. They simply died out. Scientists like philosophers seldom convince their adversaries; they make disciples.[7]

If negation arises out of otherness, and if otherness, both existential and qualitative, is ineradicable, then any hopes for a substantial and structural monism disappear. A substantial monism first could be built only on the discovery of substance and substance is that which remains the same when difference is eliminated. Sometimes this is found, as in eighteenth-century materialism, by identifying it with the most general cause of all events, or by attributing general laws to a single substance as if the laws stated their attributes. But sometimes, as in Berkeleyan idealism, by

---

[7] Rumford's two sets of experiments were read before the Royal Society on January 25, 1798 and May 2, 1799 respectively. They were reported as "An Inquiry concerning the Source of Heat which is excited by Friction," and "An Inquiry concerning the Weight ascribed to Heat." But as late as 1835 Poisson in his *Théorie Mathématique de la Chaleur* (p. 7) in the *Notions préliminaires*, says that he adopts the theory that the phenomena of heat should be attributed to *une matiere impondérable, contenue dans les parties de tous les corps aussi petites que l'on voudra, et pouvant s'en détacher et passer d'une partie a une autre, ce qui fait varier avec le temps la quantité de cette substance renfermée dans chaque partie.* And he adds that this matter is called *calorique* or *matiere de la chaleur* or simply *chaleur*. Though I am going too far afield in commenting on Rumford's experiments, it is interesting to observe that when he first tried to prove that frozen water was no heavier than the same water when thawed, in opposition to Fordyce, his experiment failed. One might think that this would have convinced him that Fordyce was right. But so strong was his conviction that the temperature of matter was irrelevant to weight, that he refined his methods until the difference in weight was no longer found.

For those interested in such matters, it may be worth while to point out that the name "caloric" was invented by no less a scientist than Lavoisier and his associates to name *la cause de la chaleur, le fluide éminemment élastique qui la produit.* See Lavoisier's *Traité élémentaire de Chimie*, Pt. I, ch. 1, p. 19, in the edition of 1864, Vol. I.

pointing to a universal cognitive instrument or set of instruments. But since effects are as real as causes, they need be of no substance other than their causes, and unless one first assume an identity of substance between cause and effect—as is traditional—they may be of different substances. A poem, for instance, cannot be written or spoken except through words whose meaning is conveyed by ink on paper or by air-waves. But the poem itself whose permanence is thus insured, is neither ink on paper nor air-waves. As for structural monism (the theory that a single set of laws, ideally deducible from one primary law, rules the cosmos), one is forced to conclude that every realm of being not covered by those laws is an anomaly, is appearance and not reality, and furthermore that such a realm is chaotic. For the reason why it is called by some such name as "appearance" is that its behavior cannot be deduced from the fundamental laws. No one has ever denied the existence of both substances which are inefficacious effects or of substances which cannot be known by the instruments of cognition at our disposal, though many have refused to use the word "existence" in speaking of them. To speak of mere appearance is simply an excuse for not attempting to meet its challenge. Appearance may well be explained, but it is not therefore reduced to Non-Being. If we end with both order and chaos on our hands, we still have both, and by the very presence of chaos our structural monism is defeated. One need not deny the great conquests of physical science in the field of the unknown to see that sub-atomic physics, for instance, does not assert the non-being of works of art, of ideas, of moral values, of sensations, to list only a few of the things it is sometimes accused of annihilating. It may describe the *sine quibus non* of all such things—though I know of no instance of its doing so. It does not say that the laws of quantum mechanics are also the laws of psychology or of jurisprudence or of aesthetics, even when it seems to say that the microscopic world is the real world. When philosophers talk that way, they overlook the fact that psychologists, jurists, and artists exist, and that they do their work usually without the slightest regard for quantum mechanics. Even if the laws of dreams could ultimately be deduced from the laws of quantum mechanics, the differences between the two realms would still exist, and a dream might still reveal a man's repressions or ugly aspirations. Descartes's elaboration of analytical geometry did not eliminate the difference between algebra and geometry, though it enabled us to define curves by means of algebraic equations. And the fact that all living beings feed themselves and reproduce their kind does not reduce them to reproductive and nutritive souls and nothing else. Plants feed and reproduce themselves and so do animals, but nevertheless the animals breathe in oxygen and the plants breathe in carbon dioxide. This difference is not wiped out by their similarities.

If difference is an ineradicable character of the universe, then the amount of difference needed to establish different realms of being will be settled by the intellectual needs of the philosopher. He can stop on the road to unity anywhere he pleases, though it is his duty to tell himself what stops him. He can stop at the existential plurality of things and qualities and even refuse to name them, lest he be betrayed into asserting the real existence of classes and Platonic ideas. He can stop with the classes of perceptual qualities. He can go on to the material sources of these qualities, or to whatever matter turns out to be according to physics. He can proceed to the mathematical laws in accordance with which physics and eventually all the sciences are organized. Or he can begin with sociology with Auguste Comte and go on to mathematics through biology, chemistry, physics, and astronomy. If he is inclined to teleology, he will discover either from Revelation or Authority what are the natural purposes and may even be able to find a single purpose in everything he investigates. If he has Neo-Platonic ambitions, he may arrange his classes of structures into a hierarchy from the most inclusive laws to the least—or the other way round—and will stop when the hierarchy is described. And if he is a legalist, he will arrange his laws in logical order from priority to posteriority. Such feats have never been successfully accomplished, but that is of no moment here. Even if they were accomplished, diversity would still exist, diversity among the "levels," and diversity within each "level." Though the whole cosmos and not merely the Heavens declare the glory of God, each part of it seems to do so in its own way. And no being can be annihilated by explaining its existence.

None of this is intended to cast doubts upon the processes of simplification and generalization. For understanding rests upon them, and I am assuming that the inquiring mind desires understanding. If, for instance, the theory of organic evolution is true, then no historian would deny the value of those preliminary classifications of plants and animals which were made by such men as Linnaeus. But even when the classification is complete—a hope, not a fact—it does not wipe out the differences which exist among the various species of the genera, but on the contrary is made because of those differences. When the theory of evolution was completed by Darwin, no explanation of the diversification of forms was attempted. All that Darwin tried to do was to explain the retention of certain diversities of structure and function and the extinction of others. He accepted diversity as accidental, except in those cases where the individual through use and disuse might perfect some organ or allow it to atrophy. His main problem was to explain the retention or loss of organs and functions in the history of species themselves. And the idea that species might have a history was in itself a novelty, anticipated to be sure by his predecessors. It would seem nonsensical to a zoologist to say that the differences between the domestic cat and lions or tigers were less real than their similarities, or that domestic cats, lions, tigers, leopards, pumas, ocelots, and so on existed in one realm of being, whereas felinity—without felines—existed in another. Nor, as far as I know, would he argue that chronologically there first appeared felinity and then the various felines. But by pointing to the similarities in structure of the various felines, he would nevertheless be able to illustrate a possible, indeed probable, historical affiliation and that would in turn raise the question of how the affiliation had taken place in time. He is thus confronted with both unity in the form of similarities and diversity in the form of the existent animals. That there was an *Urkatze* I am not arrogant enough either to affirm or deny; for that is the affair of the biologists. If there was such a creature, it must also have had a mate, one imagines, and their children must have manifested some of that accidental diversity upon which Darwin relied in order to fix certain traits in their descendants. But the multiplication of cats was not a logical division of a family into orders and genera and species, except when people began to talk about them. Historically it was procreation.

If I use the example of the theory of organic evolution, it is because it illustrates how a scientist accepts diversity and also explains it. The diversity within a generation, such as the off-spring of two parents, is accepted as normal; the inheritance of some of the diversifications and the loss of others is explained on the basis of their value or lack of value in the struggle for food and mates. But in metaphysics, where the procedure is as purely logical as reflection can well be, there is no explaining why genera should break up into species any more than there was any explanation of why the *Ens Realissimum* should give birth to the *Entia Realia*. In Plotinus, whose system is a paradigm for this sort of reasoning, a law of emanation is laid down presumably on the basis of "the facts." The One gives rise to the *Nous* and the *Anima Mundi* as the Monad gives rise to the numbers: it happens. The paradoxes which the system induced need not concern us, though they concerned all philosophers and theologians who believed in the system. It was easier for Plotinus than for Christians to argue in this fashion since to his way of thinking there was no moment in time before which there had been no emanation and after which emanation began. But the theistic philosophers were faced with the extraordinary dogma that an eternal being at a moment began to create the temporal things which constitute our world. The question of why God should have created the world puzzled many of them, and one of the favorite answers was that which they derived from the Principle of Plenitude. If all possibilities must be realized, and if this world was a possibility, then it too had to be realized. The question of course then arose of whether there were not also other possible worlds. If there were, then they too would have to be realized and, as all historians know, the question of the multiplicity of worlds was not neglected. This problem was answered by Leibniz with his usual ingenuity by combining the power of creation with the limitation of goodness—if it is a limitation—and since God could not create anything bad, the world which He did create had to be good. Consequently this world was not simply an outpouring of God's creative power, but the creation of that world which alone was the best possible. But the Principle of Plenitude, which had been flatly denied by Aristotle,[8] was an assumption which was senseless without the possibility of diversity.

To ask whether diversity or unity is prior is futile. For there can be no diversity without unity nor unity without diversity. The very meaning of the terms demands a complement. No one would say that things were simply many without specifying just what essence was multiplied. Existentially there are many things, many colors, many cats, many books, many causes, many purposes, and so on *ad indefinitum*. A dialectician can therefore push a pluralist into a corner by asking him what he is diversifying and then waving that essence before him as a unity. But in reply the pluralist can always ask the monist what has been unified. Is it material substances, qualities, categories, existences, dates, places, or what? To be one without being one anything is as much nonsense as to be many without being many anything. These correlatives have to be defined in terms of each other. There is no question of logical priority, though it is easier to derive unity from multiplicity than to derive multiplicity from unity. So it is easier to derive affirmation from negation than negation from affirmation. Classification aims at unity; observation finds diversity. The danger always faces us of substituting logical discourse for genetic processes, for though the confusion has frequently been noticed, the notice has been often neglected. It was for instance seriously

---

[8] See especially *Metaphysics*, 1050 b, 10.

neglected when Hegel's beautiful dialectical structure was applied to history. In the *Logic* as in the *Phenomenology* the element of growth is a metaphor. Hegel certainly did not mean to say in the *Phenomenology* that babies or savages had bare consciousness or just the idea of *Being*. But when he wrote his historical treatises, he did mean something like that. For in such works, which parallel in their organization the *Logic* and the *Phenomenology,* the dialectical process is temporalized. In fact most philosophers who have been affected by Judaism or Christianity go through the same sort of procedure, for by assuming that the world has an origin in time, and accepting the diversity of periods or ages or epochs, they seek some order which will furnish an abstract or logical pattern for them, the details of which are susceptible of deduction. The temptation to posit a unity temporally prior to diversity seems too great to be resisted, and even those of us who do not try to base our metaphysics on the first chapter of the Gospel according to Saint John, still insist that in the beginning was the Word. The Word may be in the logical beginning without being in the chronological beginning, and this should have been obvious. If Milesian philosophy was as it is described as having been by Aristotle,[9] then the Milesians too argued as if that which was the universal substance must also have been the primordial substance. But historically there is no more reason why unities must predate diversities than that diversities predate unities. Languages, as we have had occasion to point out, manifest an increasing simplicity of case and conjugation. Some animals, such as the marine mammals, may be thought of as anatomically simpler than their phylogenetic ancestors. Technologically instruments and measures have become increasingly standardized. Laws have moved in the direction of uniformity.[10] In general one could make out a good case for the thesis that the pattern of change is from the many to the one.

---

[9] This just for the sake of argument. No one who has read Cherniss's *Aristotle's Criticism of the Pre-Socratics* will swallow Aristotle's historical chapters without a liberal sprinkling of salt.

[10] Cf. Thomas Morgan's *Critique of The Theory of Evolution*, Princeton, 1916, for an illustration of how mutations in the fruit-fly actually appear in time.

The case would be just as good as its contradictory, but certainly no better. I may of course have committed some egregious errors in my reasoning. But if I have not, there could be no moment when either unity or multiplicity would alone exist. For even if one is simply staring at the wide blue heavens, he is either seeing nothing whatsoever or he is seeing blue. If the former is the case, then silence is the course of wisdom. If the latter, then as soon as he speaks, it will be to differentiate blue from non-blue. If he is looking at a random collection of qualities, he may again stare in silent wonder. But once more, if he speaks, he will name what he sees and thus unify. The duality of logic and knowledge, of essence and existence, will always dance before him, and as his experience grows, he will move from one to the other. And that in accordance with his intellectual requirements.

The Principle of Parsimony has often been invoked to justify some sort of monism. But the Principle includes the words "beyond necessity."[11] No one has ever given us a measure of the necessity beyond which we should not multiply entities, but I think that a measure of too great unity could be given. For each classification may be supposed to be made in order to permit the scholar to project into what he suspects to be a new member of a class all the characters of the class as a whole. Thus if all cats have the characters, A, B, C . . . N, and if the animal before me looks like a cat in that it has the characters, A, B, C, I want to be able to attribute all the other characters to it up to and including N. Some of these characters are its relations to other animals—let us say, its loathing of dogs, its fondness for mice and birds, its tolerance of human beings—its behavior as well as its color, size, and shape, its entire economy. If then I have unified a class in such a way that the domestic cat is not differentiated from the wild felines, I have over-unified. For there is presumably nothing in the differentiae of felinity which would allow me to deduce

---

[11] I have used the term, the Principle of Parsimony, rather than Occam's razor, because it was not invented or discovered by Occam. It occurs throughout Aristotle and even in the Middle Ages it was known before Occam's time. See W. M. Thorburn, "The Myth of Occam's Razor," *Mind*, Vol. XXVII, p. 345. Cf. P. E. B. Jourdain's "The Logical Significance of Ockham's Razor," *Monist*, Vol. XXVI, p. 504.

that there are some little felines which can be domesticated, will eat birds, mice, and fish, lap up milk, and so on. That the general class of felines is actually so divided as to be represented by all the various kinds and specimens of kinds of cats is something which I must discover by myself, assuming that "I" means zoologists. There is moreover no inherent necessity of a logical or historical sort which will allow me to infer that the *Urkatze* was or was not a generalized cat. The unity reached is of course abstracted from the actual cats either now extant or from those plus the extinct cats. It is and must be a logical construct useful for purposes of classification but of no use for determining what flesh and blood cats do exist or have existed. This lesson is not needed by zoologists, for they no longer try to dictate to Nature. They know that the divisions which can be made in larger genera by logical instruments are not necessarily those which will appear in experience. For if one did not know beforehand that felines were not distinguished, for instance, by their musical talents or by the number of legs which hung from their bodies, there would be no reason why one should not first break up felinity into musical and non-musical felinity or feline bipeds, tripeds, quadrupeds, and polypods. But having learned that all cats are quadrupeds, the zoologist does not attempt to deduce from any higher class-concept the number of legs that a cat must have. The word "cat," or better the word "felinity," becomes a synonym for a large number of traits which some animals have in common; it is no longer an idea attained by analysis of the meaning of a more inclusive idea.

But when such devices are used by philosophers, this lesson is forgotten. There is no more inherent evidence in the word "Being" of its possible division into material and immaterial being than there is in felinity of its possible division into wild and domestic felinity. One could with as much justice divide it into sonorous and silent being or sweet and non-sweet being. The dichotomies would be indisputably correct but useless. For obviously the possession of the negative traits, non-sonorousness and non-sweetness, are important only when we have reason to ask why certain things are not sweet when we might expect them to be sweet or non-sonorous when we might expect them to be sonorous. If we have discovered the correlation between air waves and sounds, then we can ask why some air waves are not heard by us, but the non-sonorous things extend well beyond the air waves. But similarly the immaterial beings, though they will include all things which are not material, are simply those things who do not possess the traits which material beings possess, and, as far as we know *a priori,* these may be legion. Amongst them may be found a great variety of classes of beings, and all the negative prefix does for us is to warn us not to attribute to them any of the differentiae of a certain class. If we find that effective causality is one of the differentiae of the material, we can indeed assert with confidence that the immaterial beings cannot be causally effective. From this two questions would arise: (1) what relations do they sustain to the material beings, and (2) how would we discover them? I doubt that anyone would deny the impossibility of answering these questions without putting his fingers on the beings first, that is, by first finding out the denotation of the word "immaterial." If we have attained an idea which is such that we cannot find out what it denotes, then we may not have a nonsensical idea, but we do have a useless one.

Unity then is too great when it prevents our discovering difference. But when this is said, one falls into a circular argument. For we are back again at our starting point. We are at the point at which we must decide whether unity is given or achieved. If it is given, then difference is clearly the problem; if it is achieved, then it is the problem. Neither problem can be solved by dialectical means alone, since a unity can be only the unity of a group of ostensibly different things; difference can be only the differences amongst ostensibly similar things. One could play upon the changes inherent in this dialectical problem, but it would be fruitless. For if philosophy is to be in some sense of the word applicable to the world of experience, then the contributions of experience can no more be rejected by it than they can be by a special science. The entities which the Principle of Parsimony is to shave off our universe are those which are sterile, and their sterility is to be determined by their usefulness to the inquiring mind. If meaning is given to words and phrases by us and is not discoverable by the contemplation of the symbols themselves, then the Principle is a directive to human beings and not descriptive of the universe. But this reintroduces a duality again between our ideas or ways of thinking and the subject-matters of which we think.

There is one more question which we should not neglect. In what sense do we talk about the world as a whole? It is obviously not a whole in the sense that physical objects are seen to be cut off from their surroundings. And yet one suspects that the images of chunks of matter moving about in the air lie behind the notion that the cosmos—all things together—form some sort of single *thing*. But surely one will not deny that if we are serious in talking about the universe, we must include its past and future, as well as its present, and the problem will confront us as it did Parmenides of how we are to delimit it. To delimit something which is all-inclusive is a logical impossibility for reasons which no metaphysician will question. The word "whole" is a misnomer, not merely because we are limited in our knowledge to bits of whatever it is that we are talking about, but because every term which we use or can use must by its very nature exclude certain possibilities from the subject to which it is applied. We can of course say what the universe is not as a whole, but the possibilities, though probably not infinite, are very great and furthermore, since what it is not is definable only in terms of what some things are, we shall only be playing with words no matter how long our list of impossibilities grows. We do not know whether even the words "the whole of science" mean anything, for we have no evidence that all the sciences can be made consistent. In any science there must be prescriptions about the instruments of observation and measurement, the conditions under which the observations and measurements are to be made, the technique of verification, to state only the most obvious requirements. If there were only one set of requirements for all subject-matters, one way to answer all problems, then the laws of quantum mechanics, or biology, or linguistics, or any other discipline at choice, would cover all other phenomena, and we know that such is not the case. Each set of laws selects a definite field of which it is true. As Quine says tellingly, "The totality of our so-called knowledge or beliefs, from the most casual matters of geography and history to the profoundest laws of atomic physics or even of pure mathematics and logic, is a man-made fabric which impinges on experience only along the edges."[12] The fact that a given set of propositions can be true, regardless of its logical relations with other sets, is evidence enough that we have misunderstood the nature of both knowledge and that which is known. The one kind of truth which is certain within the normal limits of error is truth about individual matters of experience. I am certain that I am now writing these words. But such certainty is irrelevant to scientific theory which, whatever else it may do, deals with classes of events.

---

[12] See *From a Logical Point of View*, p. 42. The whole passage is worth close study. I am informed by Mr. Quine that he does not take the phrase "the totality . . . of knowledge" seriously; he means simply the sum total of what we know.

CHAPTER XII

INDIVIDUATION

The attempt to see the structure of logic in the world of experience has introduced into philosophy a number of problems which might have been avoided had philosophers been less frightened at the prospect of multiplicities. Among these problems is that of individuation. A monist, whether substantial or structural, is faced with this problem. For if he says that all being is material or mental or logical or some *quartum quid,* he must explain not only the diversities which his fundamental substance manifests but also how it happens to be broken up into individual examples. Thus Aristotle, when he is thinking of Nature as a system of matter and form, and of the forms as the final causes of matter, introduces the forms to individuate the matter, for he is not unaware of the implication of his doctrine that every bit of matter, each substance, has a career of its own. Thus in the case of human beings, rational animality is the form of the body and as an entelechy individuates the body. For undifferentiated matter and the matter of the four elements obey or are describable in terms of general laws which hold good of every bit of matter, whereas any specimen of matter or any one kind of animal acts differently from another. But the problem also arises when he comes to consider individual men, Callias, Socrates, Antisthenes. As men they all act as men and move towards the actualization of their rational animality. But again he sees that Callias does not behave as Socrates does, except in this very general fashion, and the problem of why he does not must be met. The answer here is not unallied to that which responded to the former question. It is the souls of these men which individuate them. But what individuates their souls? The essence of the human soul is to be the final cause of the body. But the individual as the *infima species* can have no essence. For only that which can be defined can have an essence[1] and individuals cannot be defined. Could he conclude, as Plotinus was to conclude, that there are ideas of individuals? The soul for him was not an idea; at least it was not one in the Platonic sense of that term. Even a casual reading of Aristotle will show that he simply assumed the individuality of these souls and left the problem unsolved.[2]

The most celebrated attempt to solve the problem of individuation is that of Saint Thomas Aquinas, to whose way of thinking *materia signata* is the principle of individuation. In his *De Ente et Essentia* it is clear that *materia signata* is not merely matter, but material position in space. Matter in itself can no more differentiate than it can do anything whatsoever. It is the universal patient. It is differentiated by its designation, its being here and there. But if one set up co-ordinates which will define positions, then a point at *xa* and *yb* will be already individuated before it can individuate anything which happens to be there. A rigid set of points in a matrix is already established, and the technique of naming the points is simply a recognition of what has already been presupposed. In the case of human beings, Saint Thomas had to have some explanation of individuation since his theological and ethical views did not permit him to believe that all human beings were alike. They were all human, to be sure, and insofar as they were human, their humanity might be individuated by matter. But Peter had certain problems to solve which Paul did not have, and these were not grounded either in the matter which composed their bodies nor in the various positions in space which they occupied at various times in their lives. They were individually responsible for solving these problems and furthermore they were free to solve them as they chose. Consequently when Saint Thomas comes to questions which in-

---

[1] See among other places Metaphysics, 1030 a, 6.

[2] Cf. Harold Cherniss; *Aristotle's Criticism of Plato and the Academy*, Baltimore, 1944, pp. 174-5, 470-478.

volve the human soul, he switches his point of view and at times[3] relies on Aristotle's statement in *Metaphysics,* 1018 b, 33, where it is said that as universals are prior in definition, individuals are prior in perception. At such times matter individuates the human being only as he represents or is an example of human nature, but his soul which is immortal in no way depends upon the body, can be liberated from the body after death, and therefore is an individual regardless of the matter in which it has been incorporated. It is not perception which individualizes this part of the soul, for it cannot be perceived; it is an individual presumably individuated by God, so that the problem is simply pushed back a step.

It is inevitable that if we begin with general ideas, there will be no way to individuate them non-empirically. Each idea or universal is different from every other, but in itself it has no power to be exemplified. For we know that we can erect an indefinite variety of ideas which are not exemplified and which need not be exemplified. For we know of no compulsion which God or Nature exercises over them to force them into actualization. One need not go back to the Ancients for authoritative texts to prove this. One can see the possibility of defining all sorts of numbers which will never be realized; a number greater than the number of all existing things can be defined arithmetically; the concept is not meaningless. In fact, if we symbolize the number of all existent things by N, there obviously is an infinite range of numbers which are greater than N. I do not say that such *jeux d'esprit* are of any great interest to mathematicians; but they do at least illustrate our thesis. Their occurrence is a striking illustration of how little experience limits the human imagination. But no demonstration should be needed of that, for we know that inventors exist, that we hope for things which we have never had and some of which we may never have. We can have, for instance, a concept of world-peace and define what we mean by it in precise language. But no one would be so naive as to think

---

[3] See for instance his commentary on William of Moerbeke's version of the *De Anima;* in the translation of Fathers Foster and Humphries, London, 1951, par. 377.

that the possibility of our conceiving it is proof of its existence
either now or in the future, though if we did not conceive of it,
it would probably never exist.[4] But even in such cases, the ideas
themselves are thought of as individuals. The individuation may
come about in two ways, either as *my* idea of world peace contrasted with someone else's, or as an imaginary state of affairs
determined by specific relations between nations. But this technique is also misleading, since if I am an individual whose ideas
are individuated by their being mine, I have already assumed
individuation, and if the ideas themselves are imagined to be real
events, individuation is again assumed.

It would be more fruitful to follow the nominalistic tradition,
to begin with the individuals and attempt to explain the universals. But if this is done, then it will have to be granted that
individuality is indefinable though its occurrence may be demonstrated. It will be that in terms of which general symbols will
be defined. The individual is obviously that for which only a
proper name can be given, a label, and this is a recognition that
individuals are logical surds. The human being is such an individual, beginning at a certain time and in a certain place, and
this is so even though the materials out of which he is made may
have existed before his birth, as indeed they did, and will continue to exist after his death in his descendants, if he has any.
Though what Weismann and others called his germ-plasm is inherited, nevertheless the peculiar combination of genes which is
to be found in his chromosomes is unique, unless he is one of two
identical twins. Like a Leibnizian monad, he is shut off from all
other individuals and is aware of his individuality in the feeling
that others are shut off from him, are different from him, oppose
him or for that matter agree with him. All his gestures of dem-

---

[4] It might of course just happen against everyone's desire, though that seems unlikely. The reciprocal pressures of two very powerful nations might be so great
that stability would result. But that would both presuppose the impotence of all
other nations and the literality of what is after all nothing but a poor figure of
speech. At the time of writing these words, November 1956, it is not so much the
"pressure" of large and powerful nations which is disturbing the peace, but that of
small and weak nations.

onstration, of simple pointing, individuate. He sees this particular thing, not simply anything in general. He drinks this particular cup of coffee, not simply coffee. He loves this particular woman, not simply womanhood. He is usually aware of separate moments of time, whether he differentiates merely the past, present, and future, or this morning, or a moment or two ago, just now, and this afternoon, or in a few minutes, or immediately. It is only in his thinking that he is able to universalize, to utilize abstractions, and when he wishes to express his thoughts, he is forced to introduce general unindividuated terms. There is nothing novel in this; it is fundamental in Aristotle and Plato. The curious interplay between history and eternity is one of the sources of the puzzle which we have introduced in this lecture. If then I am forced to think in terms of universals which I do not create myself, what is their position in the cosmos? There is no need to expound the problem here, for everyone knows how it is phrased.

But it has not always been seen that the simplest kind of declarative sentence illustrates the interplay. Someone sees something and is asked what it is. He replies, "This is a cat." Should anyone attempt to define the meaning of "this" except by saying that it is one of the words which we use when we designate things, he would find that he has reintroduced the idea of demonstration occultly if not overtly. Pointing is a specific, dated and localized act. One cannot just point in general. If one tries to avoid this trouble by saying that "this" is what one sees now or here, or is what a given individual sees at some moment or in some position, the matrix itself is shown to have individualized times and places, or the person who sees is already individualized. Any ostensive act will be described in terms of the here and now, the there and then, and the like. It is only in mathematics and logic that we can say, "Let ABC be *any* triangle," "Let *p* be *any* true proposition." We do have the power of letting individuals stand for universals, and it would be folly to deny this. But this power cannot be identified with the act of pointing or seeing at a given moment. It is one of the peculiar characteristics of what is usually called experience, as distinguished from reflection, thinking, reasoning, and it was recognized as such by Aristotle in the passage cited above when he said that the individual was prior in perception, the universal in definition.

Even in the works of those epistemologists who insist that the object of perception is a universal,[5] it is a peculiar sort of universal. For it is a timeless being which somehow or other can descend into time and space without changing in any way. None of these writers, to the best of my knowledge, denies that universals are timeless, and one of them, Santayana, plays upon their non-existence when perceived, presumably to emphasize their timelessness. One may see two patches of red which are so much alike to the instrument of observation that they cannot be told apart. Thus we may be persuaded that they are universals within the field of perception. For one red patch, it will be said, cannot be in two places at the same time, and the only being which can perform this feat is a universal. But if one follows this course, there is no reason to stop with patches of color. One can maintain that every property which is perceptible is universal, for as soon as one names it, the name will be an adjective or a common noun. Even the thing itself can be universalized and, if it is not called a cat, can be called felinity. But even if that miracle is performed, the positions in space cannot be identified, and the philosopher has not avoided the problem of individuation. In a higher sense, all places may be in one place; in fact it might be said that since they are all places, they participate in "placehood." Analogous remarks could be made about dates. This is the annihilation of experience itself, its elevation to the realm of eternity. It may also be true that Peter is no different from Paul and that his nature flows into that of his fellowman and becomes indistinguishable

---

[5] Such thinkers now seem to have little influence. But twenty or thirty years ago they flourished in both England and the United States. They included Santayana, C. A. Strong, Durant Drake, Dawes Hicks among others. If anyone is still interested in a criticism of the theory, he might look into the following articles, notes to which give bibliographical references: "Beyond the Essence," *Journal of Philosophy*, Vol. XXII, 1925; "The Datum as Essence," *Ibid.*, Vol. XXIV, 1927; "Mr. Dawes Hicks's Theory of Perception," *Ibid.*; "Mr. Drake on Essences and Data," *Ibid.*

from it. But the stubborn fact which gives rise to the problem is still there, and as we have repeatedly insisted, one does not annihilate anything by relating it to other things. Thus if we say that Peter is like Paul, we may phrase the resemblance in such a way as to make it seem as if there were a reified quality which is present in both of them. But to resemble something is a relation, and there is no evidential value in the words which we use to translate the meaning of the relation. If we say that San Francisco is west of Chicago, we surely need not argue that *westhood* is present in San Francisco and *easthood* in Chicago.[6] To take another example, larger wholes may absorb smaller, as men are absorbed into their families, their clubs, their political organizations, their churches, all the social groups in which they satisfy their interests and with which they identify themselves. But however Hegelian one may become, one does not deny that on some level, assuming that we know what a level is, they exist as individuals. Otherwise there would be nothing for the group to absorb. As a matter of fact in Hegel himself, the relationships worked both ways. The individual was determined by the group, the group by the individual. No one, for instance, is quite the same in an ecclesiastical group as he is in an economic group. If he were, many of our ethical problems would be avoided.

The "is" in our sentence has at least three meanings. It may simply signify classification: This is a member of the collection known as cats. It may attribute a quality to a subject: This object has the quality of felinity. It may signify the exemplification of a universal: This is an example of felinity. The common meanings of "existence" and "equality" need not be considered in this context, for the "this" presumably points to an existent being, and no one any longer would say that it was equal to or identical with felinity. In fact, many a child has expressed the thought contained

---

[6] This is about the way some of the English Platonists argued—Henry More for instance—when they tried to demolish the notion of the objectivity of relations. If 4 is half of 8 and twice of 2, then, he maintained, one was involved in a paradox. For how could two contradictory properties be asserted of one subject? He might have gone on to ask how London could be west of Paris and at the same time east of Plymouth.

in the sentence without having the vaguest idea of what felinity is. He spots the thing as a cat perhaps because he has been told to so spot it. Now to be an example of something, to have a certain quality, to belong to a class, will be all symbolized by the names of relations which are universals. But we are not saying in such a sentence that there are cats, nor that felinity is sometimes and somewhere exemplified. We are not even defining the meaning of "felinity." We are stubbornly pointing to an object, isolated from its surroundings, and saying that it is a cat. That the use of "is" may be said to presuppose the possibility of classification, qualification, or exemplification, need not be denied. Any articulable experience will be expressed in terms which follow from some presuppositions. I am merely saying that the use of this general verb, "to be," does not in any way nullify individuation. It might even be plausibly argued that the "is" should not be separated from the rest of the sentence and that it is an integral part of the total meaning which is analysed verbally but by an analysis which is quite unnecessary. Such philosophers could maintain that the "is" by itself is meaningless; it acquires meaning when it is followed by a predicate. Hence one should symbolize subject-predicate propositions not as, "This is a cat," but as, "This is-a-cat." For who has not heard people mutter with a shrug of the shoulder, "H-m, a lot of nonsense," or seen a child point and say, "Kitty," or himself have looked at his watch and said to himself, "Ten o'clock." If such events have not been noticeable in the experience of anyone who comes upon these words, let him look in the margins of books in a library and read the pencilled comments. They may convince him that the copula is not only tiresome to write but that if written, it must be joined to a predicate. The union of copula and predicate might be thought of as indissoluble in which case the interpretation of sentences containing one would have to be revised radically.

The use of the indefinite article, "a," is however the best example of the kind of individuation which we all make ourselves. We are not talking about felinity at all, we shall say; we are talking about *a* cat. We have in our minds this distinction before we open our mouths to talk. We know the difference between felinity and pointing to a cat. The two operations are so different that, if we should be asked after saying, "This is a cat," what we mean by calling the object by that name, the demand would not be unreasonable. In the case of cats, the problem seldom if ever arises, but it does arise in so many other cases that one has simply to mention it for anyone to see its relevance. Ostensive definition and logical definition—whether by genus and differentia or otherwise—are two quite different things, and one is forced into the former only when the latter is unintelligible. It is bound to be unintelligible in the case of individuals, and one of the reasons why we identify things by pointing is that we know the impossibility of defining the individual. There are of course occasions on which our sentence might be classificatory in the scientific sense, as when a zoologist may speak of the wild felines as cats, but even then there would be presumably an individual animal before him and not merely an incorporated universal.

As for the word, "cat," that like all common nouns symbolizes something which is not an individual. It names that which is supposed to be individuated. Whether it is interpreted as an attribute, a class-concept, or a Platonic idea, it is different from the "this." If it is interpreted in extension, it will not have to be individuated, for in that case a class is just a collection of individuals who are more or less alike in some respect.

All this pedantry is written out to suggest that which might have been obvious—if anything can be obvious in philosophy—namely, that demonstrative sentences express the fact of individuation. This need not be so, for one might say, "This is Tabby," which does not mean, "This has the quality of Tabbyhood." In fact, one can easily imagine a situation in which a youngster would say, "This is *not* a cat; it is Tabby." But for that matter, when one is looking at pictures or reading poems, one often does just that. If you call Keats's *Ode to a Nightingale* just a poem or an ode, you are certainly missing the larger part of what it is without misrepresenting anything. It is both a poem and an ode and, what seems most important of all, it is Keats's *Ode to a Nightingale*.

Again, to take another example, Millet's painting of a child beginning to walk was copied by Van Gogh. The copy is enough
like the original for anyone seeing them both and knowing their
dates to realize which is the copy of which. But that does not
mean that the copy is interchangeable with the original. There
are thousands of paintings of the Annunciation in art galleries.
They are very much alike, as they would have to be, given the
subject. But if someone should be looking at a photograph of Fra
Angelico's *Annunciation* in the Convent of San Marco, and was
asked what it was, he would not simply say that it was an Annunciation, nor even "a" Fra Angelico. He would probably say
that it was Fra Angelico's *Annunciation*. The use then of symbols
of universal import in demonstrative sentences does not necessarily
mean that we are classifying; we may be simply identifying as
best we can. Any predicate which we may use other than the
proper name of what is before us will select out of the very large
number of possible predicates one or two or three. That may be
why some people have maintained that an individual can be described by a coincidence of universals. It is A and B and C and . . .
N. It is doubtful whether such a process could ever exhaust the
catalog of properties, not that the number is infinite or that life
is too short, but that the one thing which will not be included in
such an enumeration is something corresponding to the "this."
We may on faith decide that there are not two such identical collections in existence, but it would be only faith which made the
decision. Nor is the difficulty avoided by introducing Duns Scotus's
haecceity. For that too is no more than a name for the very thing
which we are trying to describe.

If our class-names really stated the essences of things, if classification were made by Nature rather than by human beings, the
problem might be more pressing. For then, as in Aristotle, definitions would be real and not nominal and could be criticized on
the basis of their truth or falsity. But if what we perceive is in
part determined by what we are looking for, and if we never perceive a thing or event in its entirety, then how would it be possible
for us to abstract its natural essence from perception except by

accident? Perception is always selective even when limited to one quality, such as the dark in a dark room or a space filling odor. In such cases we do not select one quality out of what is present to us, for only one quality is present. But we perceive the dark or the odor against the recollection of what has gone before. If we lived in the dark, we should not perceive it. But if perception is selective, any statements made on the basis of perception will also be selective, however accurately they may express what is or has been perceived. We can always round out our perceptual experiences and indeed have to if we are ever to move beyond them. But the rounding out is done by adding other properties to those with which we have come in contact. A definition to our way of thinking is always of a word, a concept, an idea, an essence, a class of things. But each of these beings is general and for that reason, if for no other, transcends history and also impoverishes it. A common noun limits our interest to one feature of that which it names and that is why common nouns are so useful.

Euler in his *Letters to a German Princess*[7] points out for reasons different from ours that it is impossible to know what he calls "the essence" of an individual. His argument is based on the complexity of the parts of any physical object which he seems to think are infinite in number. But regardless of that, his point of view has as much interest today as it had in 1761 and I quote a part of it.

> The more general a notion is, the less it comprises of the characters which constitute the essence [of the individual] and consequently the easier it is to recognize this essence. We understand more easily what a tree is in general than a cherry tree, a pear tree, or an apple tree, and yet these are species. And when I say, "That which I am looking at in the garden is a tree," I am not mistaken; but I could well be mistaken should I say that it is a cherry tree. It must then follow that I know better the essence of a tree in general than I do the species. I shall not confuse so easily a tree with a stone as a cherry tree with a plum tree (p. 17).

Whether or not we accept the theory which lies behind this, which is probably that of the inverse ratio of connotation and

---

[7] *Lettres à une Princesse d'Allemagne,* ed. Emile Saisset, Paris, 1866, Pt. II, Letter 53, in Volume II.

denotation, what he is describing is undoubtedly true. We have the faculty of grouping things into larger and larger classes, and when we engage in rational discourse about them, we have to use the class-names. But this does not mean that what things have in common is somehow or other more real or more indicative of their natural essence than what they do not have in common, in spite of the long tradition which attributes greater value to the universal than to the individual. There is probably a great variety of class-concepts under which one might group an individual depending on the problems which confront one. If I am a physician trying to diagnose a sickness, what good would it do me to know that man is a rational animal? He is before me as a physiological specimen in which something has gone wrong. Again, if I am planting vegetable seeds, what good does it do me to know that material objects—since we have mentioned Euler—all have impenetrability, extension, and inertia? The essence of what I am handling will shift with the problems they stimulate. And those problems in turn will arise from observed deviations from the norm. But the norms in question are themselves plotted in view of certain prior considerations. In the case of human beings, we have norms of height, weight, intelligence, income, debt, and scores of other things, and many of the data have been intermingled so as to get results which will be truer to the complex facts. But in every investigation we recognize that some things are irrelevant. Few if any *a priori* rules can be laid down to establish relevance, for any day something may turn up which will indicate an unsuspected relation between phenomena. Thus one might say that height and weight could be profitably plotted against each other, but it would take little reflection to see that age and sex had also better be brought in. But should the classes of human beings about whom data are being plotted be also analysed into economic groups? Are the poor as tall and fat as the rich? Are intelligent people as tall and fat as stupid people? And how about national origins? Are descendants of northern Europeans any taller than descendants of southern Europeans? Any such questions might be relevant to the main problem confronting the anthropometrist.

But he should never overlook the hard fact that the more qualifications he introduces, the closer he is going to approach the individual, and if he is not careful, he will come out with the result that John Smith living in Bangor, Maine, at 3500 Jones Street, 25 years of age, is five feet eight and weighs 145 pounds.

This ludicrous result might have been an initial datum. But even if it had been, it would have been acquired to satisfy some intellectual purpose. No general definition of mankind would have been needed either to make the original measurements or to infer from them anything about the relation of height to weight to sex to intelligence to anything else one pleases. Yet how easy it is to be snared by the logical puzzle which immediately arises! One says, "I measure the heights of so many men of such and such an age, etc. etc. . ." He is at once asked how he knows that they are men, the problem of the *Meno*. The answer is that he is not deducing *more geometrico* from the essence of mankind anything whatsoever, but on the contrary proceeding on the road to finding out something about men. He does not have to know the essence of mankind to do this; he has to be able to distinguish between men and non-men. When he impatiently shrugs off the philosopher's question by saying that everyone knows what a man is, he is right if he means that anyone can recognize a man. But he is wrong if he means that everyone can formulate a definition of mankind which will be acceptable to everyone else. Nothing is more common than the experience of recognizing that which you cannot define. The reason why this can happen is that the kind of recognition about which we are talking is based on habit and requires simply the recognition of certain perceptual characters. One may recognize another person by his face, his walk, his clothes, his voice, and one seldom has to check one's decision. We are more accustomed to recognizing human beings as human for social purposes than for anthropological. And the social amenities do not usually require anthropological prefaces. Thus one starts with individuals, more or less clearly described, and proceeds towards sharper and finer delineations. But none of this makes any sense if one refuses to accept the temporal dimension of experience.

This technique of recognition by bits and scraps, rather than by extensive investigation, may sometimes lead us astray. But it is characteristic of perception nevertheless. The dairyman who knows his cows, the horse-breeder who knows his horses, the sailor who knows his ships, like the airplane spotter who knows his planes, all operate by seizing upon some detail of the individual before him and using that detail as if it were a set of finger-prints. This is indeed the way we read after we have learned to read; we do not spell out the words but grasp them by some salient features. If challenged, we can then examine the data more closely and we shall find that only certain combinations of more precisely defined characters are trustworthy. The child who is learning to read has more difficulty in recognizing his words, especially if he is being taught to read by the analytical method. But once he has learned, he spots his words rapidly enough. As the Gestalt-psychologists have shown, sometimes large groups of data are grasped as a whole, but the data are individual data only after analysis. This would seem to me, if not to others, to be critical in the appraisal of sensory empiricism. For there is no reason to suppose that given a single physical object, two people will apprehend it by means of the same sensory data.

The problem of individuation would not arise unless one presupposed that there was something to be individuated as a baker might individuate dough in little molds. If we think of the universals not as extensive materials out of which the individuals must be cut, but as intellectual devices useful for classification and deduction, then it does not arise at all. They may indeed be statistical groupings, and the universal term may be an expression for a whole range of individuals. In the empirical order we can say without too much error—we shall qualify this below—that we begin in the Aristotelian fashion with individual experiences and erect generalizations upon them. In the eternal or logical order we begin with universals and sometimes hope to find exemplifications of them. The qualification to which I refer must

be made, since unless experience is to be inarticulate, it will begin
to be organized at a very early age in terms of overindividual
categories. The various studies of Piaget show how this is done,
and though some of his details may be disputed—on the ground
of the number of children whom he studied and perhaps even
their cultural background—yet he has shown definitely that the
categories change as people mature. This does not lead to epistemological individualism since there are always enough people
who speak the same or related languages to socialize their basic
concepts. In short, children go through a course of education
which is more than teaching them how to eat, to dispose of their
excrements, to bathe, to dress, and other such economic matters.
They are taught how to think and how to express their thoughts.
Surely this primary fact ought not to be forgotten for the sake of a
truncated empiricism. The folly of building all science out of
universals which in turn have not been erected on a foundation
of experience was well demonstrated in the early Renaissance.
As we have insisted, the margin between logic and experience
can be as wide as the individual scientist is willing to tolerate.
He will never completely eliminate it for obvious reasons, and if
he dislikes it, he can always stick to pure mathematics. But if he
prefers truth to consistency, he will have to put up with it. It is a
function of his instruments of observation, his rational technique,
and the amount of accuracy he needs.

This is far from being a novelty of my own invention. I quote
the following from Milhaud's classic study of the limits of logical
certainty.

> As the process of observation and experimentation is carried on
> and refined, the mind tries to disentangle from it ideas, laws, formu-
> las, theories, which make it possible to constitute science, that is, to
> interpret facts in a comprehensible manner, substituting unity for
> multiplicity and order for disorder, connections and relations for
> ruthless diversity, and constancy for perpetual change. This interpre-
> tation by means of a language created by the mind while in contact
> with things and inspired and suggested by them, allows it further-
> more not only to understand by inter-relating those phenomena whose
> complexity is the form of reality, but even to predict them and finally
> to make better and better use of them. Because of a natural selection

determined precisely by the progress accomplished in his dual development of theoretical understanding and practical application running parallel to the observation of facts, ideas, laws, and concepts succeed one another, at times only for a short appearance, and at others, due to their usefulness, giving the impression of becoming permanent. Thus in parallel channels of experience and thought, a double but indefinite progress is achieved. And so science begins and will continue to grow. The absence of logical certainty is here equal to the necessity that science be never finished at any point and that it continue to move forward as long as humanity itself exists.[8]

There may be some doubts about the last sentence of this paragraph, for humanity may well fall into total imbecility or into collective indifference. But the general drift seems well established.

We have been talking of the individual as if we all knew just what an individual was. But without going into the excesses of Neo-Heracliteanism, we can see that the frontiers of the individual are not any too easy to draw. We set up the idea of individuality, it would seem, on the analogy of perceptual *things,* agglomerations of solids clustered about small areas of space with different kinds of matter separating them from one another. Thus trees, stones, books, tables, people, lie about the universe in air or water or some other fluid medium, and we appear to be able to handle these things and forget the medium. It is very convenient to be able to pick up a book and lay it down and be unconcerned about what is going on in it as a system of molecules, atoms, and whatever is inside the atom, to say nothing of its inter-relations with surrounding objects. A librarian may feel differently about this, especially if he is worried with the problem of preserving the books. A tree is, however, in a somewhat different situation. It may quite properly be thought of as an integral part of the nitrogen-cycle, and even on a less recondite plane, its relation to

---

[8] G. Milhaud; *Essai sur les Conditions et les Limites de la Certitude Logique,* 2d ed. rev., Paris, 1898, p. 201. Cf. p. 103. This might well be compared with a paragraph of Hermann Weyl's *Symmetry,* Princeton, 1952, p. 27. "The laws of nature do not determine uniquely the one world that actually exists, not even if one concedes that two worlds arising from each other by an automorphic transformation, i.e., by a transformation which preserves the universal laws of nature, are to be considered the same world."

water supply is much more important than its silhouette against
the sky. As something withdrawing nitrogen and other chemicals
from the soil and carbon dioxide from the air, its individuality is
going to be very different from what it is, for instance, when it
is thought of as simply a source of wood-pulp for manufacturers
of paper. Its individuality as a thing is precipitated out of a large
mixture of human interests, and it is of course several things at
once. And one of these things contains its past history and its
future, if it has any. In this context it is impossible to imagine
it as a mass of carbon compounds and nothing more, isolated
from other material masses by spatial intervals. When does it
begin and when end? Where are its lateral boundaries? I doubt
whether in this respect it differs from anything else in the universe, but its differentiae as an historical event are harder to
neglect since they keep intruding themselves upon one's meditations. No forester would deny this, one thinks, however much
he may follow the common—and indeed unavoidable—practice
of talking about it simply as a maple, oak, or pine.

But similar remarks may be made about human beings who
also spread out beyond their ostensible bodies. Does it seem
reasonable to speak of Plato without relating him to Socrates, to
Speusippus, to Aristotle, and to the hosts of people before him
who influenced his thoughts and those after him whom he has
influenced? It is doubtless of little importance to us now whether
he had mumps and measles as a child, whether his voice was
tenor or barytone, whether he liked his broth hot or cool. But it
would be of importance to know whether he really went to Syracuse or not, was really sold into slavery, and wrote the nonsensical letters which have been attributed to him. When we
think of him, we are not likely to think of his corporeal boundaries, though his admirers probably would like to know every
detail of his person. We are much more likely to think of him
as the source of a great intellectual tradition. But this is so fluid
a conception that it is next to impossible to pin him down, and
when we try to do so, we accomplish the feat by arbitrary methods.
Where is the inner Plato and where the outer? Spatial delimitation

seems absurd, and it is only the demands of language which force us into speaking of him as a *thing*. He was of course a person; he was an individual; in that he was different from all other people and things. But even the most foolish of the legends told about him—his divine parentage, the story of the bees, his life of eighty-one years, the square of the magic nine—picture him as part of a network of relations from which he cannot be extricated. As a package of carbon compounds, he can of course be isolated, as we all can, from other packages of chemicals, and it may well turn out that the biochemical story points to those conditions without which we should not have had the Dialogues. But if one pursues that trail, one will not stop this side of the subatomic world which was the condition of the biochemical. He, like every other individual, will be identified in accordance with what one is trying to find out about him. And we still shall not have discovered a single antecedent for the pronoun "him."

Individuation is even more difficult to grasp when one comes to the sciences as separate fields of investigation. The reduction of mathematics to logic seems to be ultimately responsible for the notion that all science is one and that in spite of its unity, one can by logical devices alone erect a system of separate sciences which are the natural divisions of Science. It may be true that a single method for answering all questions could be devised. This method could be pure deduction, the geometrical method of Descartes; it might be the statistical method; it might be that vague practice known as the experimental method. It would seem absurd to tackle mathematical problems statistically and to plot the deviations from a mean which would be found when a pound of coffee is added to another pound, a quart of milk to another, to see whether 1 plus 1 is "really" 2. If the coffee is material coffee and the scales a material scales, there is little doubt that no two experiments would give one exactly the same results. There would always be some tiny fraction of an ounce lacking or in excess. And the result would be that 1 plus 1 gives plus or minus 2. But it would be equally absurd, or so it seems to us, to study the relations between production and consumption *more geometrico.* How could the phenomenon of diminishing return be anticipated logically? Or Gresham's Law? Would it not be more logical to conclude that if the desire of a man for food determines the value of a basic amount of food as x, then $100x$ is 100 times as good as x, and that a man will desire it with 100 times the intensity that he desires x? If good money is in circulation, why on purely logical grounds should bad money drive it out of circulation? But for that matter, why on such grounds should a human being ever reach a maximum height, once his rate of growth in childhood has been discovered? Finally, it seems absurd that either mathematical or economic questions should be answered by the experimental method. To experiment in order to discover the square root of a number would be wasted time and to experiment in social questions would be barbarous, even if tolerated. For such reasons—if they will be accepted as reasons—we have doubts about the unity of science.

In Aristotle, to whom one has always to return, a science is delimited by the set of primitive contraries which it studies.[9] In each pair of contraries, one term is always privative of the other. Such contraries are, it is perhaps needless to point out, the hot and the cold, the heavy and the light, the moving and the not-moving, and so on. These primitive contraries were "opposites" and each pair established a genuine "universe of discourse" which could be explored logically. One might have expected that in his opinion the whole body of knowledge would be a logical pattern into which every special science fitted, but on the contrary he differentiated between theoretical and practical sciences, the theoretical being physics, mathematics, and theology.[10] The practical sciences, such as ethics and politics, studied subject-matters in which chance played a part and hence they could not give the exact results which the theoretical gave. Because of his reification of chance, Aristotle never saw that there might be a genetic relation between theory and practice, though he did see that when

---

[9] *Metaphysics,* K 3, 1061 a, 18.
[10] *Ibid.,* 7, 1064 b, 1.

theory was applied to the material world, it was contaminated. Moreover, his notion that knowledge was contemplation and that there was a strict mirroring of ontology in logic, prevented his examining the kinds of questions which men put to experience and the kinds of answers which those questions demanded. His syncretism of the four causes into a single mode of investigation made it impossible for him to think of each cause as a legitimate orientation of inquiry, and he was more inclined to think of his predecessors as rudimentary Aristotles than as scientists with special problems. The result was that in the *Metaphysics,* which was the science of being as being, he wavers between the empirical and the logical techniques, now deducing what must be true and now looking to see if some conclusion or other—of his predecessors—actually is true. One of his troubles arose from the theory that the contraries must subsist in some underlying substance, a theory entailed by the meaning of the terms, not by observation, so that he finally reached a universal substance which he thought he could talk about though it had no attributes whatsoever beyond those given it by experience. When it is thought of as "existing apart," it serves no function other than that of providing a possible subject of which attributes can be predicated. Since these lectures are not primarily engaged in either criticism or exegesis of Aristotle, we suggest a study of *Metaphysics Lambda* to those who may think this account unfair.

That methods of studying Nature have varied and that some have become obsolete is shown by history. No one any longer practises divination before putting his plans into operation, consults oracles, or casts horoscopes, except in backward areas. We no longer look for divine purposes in the appearance of comets, earthquakes, or floods. The theory of signatures is as dead as the theory of animal spirits. Anatomy is no longer based on the similarity between the microcosm and the macrocosm. Yet I find it hard to believe that the men who engaged in such practices and theories were inherently stupider than we are, though if they were living now, it would be a bit of a strain to call them intelligent. These methods were simply various techniques of answering questions and they were utilized, just as modern experimentation is utilized, within a larger context of ideas which made them seem reasonable. Sometimes where vestiges of such methods persist, it may well be due either to the inadequacy of other methods to answer the specific questions which arise, a failure to analyse the questions properly, or to simple ignorance that there are other and more fruitful methods. In psychological reports it does not seem inaccurate to speak of a man's purposes as determining his behavior, though when the teleological method is used in physiology, it is with apologies. It would be inaccurate, however, to think of all scientists of a given date asking the same type of question to which the same type of answer would have to be given. The uniformity of method has always been greatly exaggerated.

It may, moreover, be true that, since the selection of a problem is itself oriented by what the scientist himself as an individual investigator observes, a given scientist may ask a sheaf of related questions which when answered will set up a new science. Thus, to take but one example, biophysics has arisen since men asked physical questions about living organisms. The questions could not be answered unless the organisms were amenable to physical laws, but to ask whether biophysics is really biology or physics is nonsense. It is really biophysics. Such a situation would be inexplicable if each science had its own subject-matter which was entirely mapped out by Nature. For in that case the frontiers between physics and biology would be sealed. The failure of pure behaviorism, as Watson used that term, is a good illustration of how fluid these frontiers actually are. If all mental phenomena were describable in purely physiological terms, then indeed the brain would secrete thought as the liver secretes bile, to use the famous apothegm of Cabanis. But it was soon discovered that although introspection was considered *infra dig,* nevertheless verbal reports were still necessary if the psychologists were to answer their questions satisfactorily. They could to be sure and sometimes did avoid asking questions which necessitated verbal reports. But there was an element of bigotry in that procedure which alienated a certain number of psychologists. A verbal report was conveyed in air-waves in response to other air-waves, but no one was willing to say that it was the mechanical impact of the air-waves which gave significance to the reports. In the first place there were too many homonyms to make that conclusion valid. In the second place they could be phrased in any language, and thus a single meaning could be conveyed in a great variety of sounds. It could therefore not be the sounds alone which stimulated the responses, and of course it had to be granted that it was the meaning of the sounds. If it was argued that the responses were simply conditioned reflexes, the difficulty still was not avoided, for a single type of reflex could be conditioned again by a variety of sounds. There is very little sonorous identity between the following two sets of sounds: "When you see the red light, press the button;" and, "Lorsque vous verrez la lumière rouge, appuyez sur le bouton." Yet they convey the same command. And what is more, a bilingual individual could obey them both in the same way.

All this would lead one to conclude that the unity of science is more of a program than an accomplished fact. What we call a science is a collection of answers to questions which have been accepted as true, plus a uniform technique for getting the answers. Furthermore, sometimes a scientist may become interested in differences rather than in similarities.[11] He may wish to discover to what extent an individual or a group differs from others which might be expected to resemble it. Here the presumption of uniformity is wrecked on the evidence of observation. This sort of thing occurs in unanticipated ways. When aviation was in its infancy, it was assumed that aerodynamics would exhibit the same laws as hydrodynamics. The assumption turned out to be wrong. The science of aerodynamics has had to be built up step

[11] Cf. Ancel Keys; "The Physiology of the Individual as an Approach to a more Quantitative Biology of Man," *Federation Proceedings*, VIII, no. 2, June 1949, p. 523.

by step in an empirical way.[12] This might seem astonishing when one recalls that both air and water are fluids. But what makes it astonishing is that when we have a general term, *fluids,* all things named by it, we think, ought to be alike in all their properties. But there is no more reason to believe this than its contradictory. No one imagines that fishes ought to breathe with lungs like mammals simply because both require oxygen to live. And scientists have had to swallow facts contrary to the most sacred traditions when they met them. Mammals may be viviparous, but the platypus is both a mammal and oviparous. Who would have thought when the Periodic Table was elaborated by Mendeleev that isotopes would be a possibility? The history of the sciences exhibits both differentiation and integration, both diversity and unity, and it would be folly to insist that one was more essentially scientific than the other. Once again experience gives us diversity, logic unity, and the interplay between them is natural science. This seems unfortunate only if one presupposes that one or the other ought to triumph. Human beings learn by experience, and when something is learned, it becomes hardened into a fact and is used as if it were eternal. It would be better for us to substitute the word, *belief,* for *fact,* since what we acquire by experience is beliefs. A belief will be held until it is contradicted. But the kind of contradiction involved here is not the internal contradiction which may be discovered in a set of logical statements. It is rather a kind of conflict such as what occurs when a person acts upon a belief and finds that his action is frustrated. There are many kinds of frustration, of which the most common is the failure of an expectation to be fulfilled. But clearly if knowledge were simply the absorption of facts from an external world, no expectation ought ever to fail of fulfillment.

The problem of individuation, we have said, arises because one assumes the priority of universals. It is the name of a process, of something that happens or is done to something else. To in-

---

[12] See Jerome C. Hunsaker; "A Half-Century of Aeronautical Development," *Proceedings of the American Philosophical Society,* Vol. XCVIII, no. 2, 1954, esp. p. 122.

dividuate is not simply to differentiate. It is to establish beings which are unique in some respect, however much they may resemble other beings in other respects. Thus the integers are individuals in spite of their resemblances to one another. And presumably the points in a set of Cartesian co-ordinates are individuals as are the dates in a calendar. The process of individuation in such cases is carried on by human beings and clearly is not the historical or existential exemplification of eternal universals. For no one would say that 2 is to be understood simply as the exemplification of "numerality," or a given point simply the exemplification of "punctuality," or 1956 an exemplification of "annuality." The probability is that it is always we, as individual and unique human beings, who do the individuating, as centers of experience. The abscissas and ordinates intersect in us, whether we are perceiving or imagining or thinking. But in a sense it is unwise to call ourselves individuals, for such a term seems to mean that we are individuated out of a universal humanity. On the contrary, one of the most stubborn and ineradicable elements of experience is our struggle to find those common traits which will give the world some order, some pattern, in terms of which we can understand it. This struggle is constantly going on, for both in the history of thought and in the biography of any one mind, we find steady revision of the knowledge which seems to have been acquired for good and all. This struggle might be taken as the starting point of an epistemology. Questioning and learning, rather than looking and seeing, might be thought of as characteristic of human experience and in that case such concepts as fact, truth, and judgment, might become less obscure.

We have used the word "experience" throughout these lectures and used it loosely. Let us now see whether we can make it more precise.

Chapter XIII

EXPERIENCE

If I have called these lectures *The Inquiring Mind,* it is because I have thought of knowledge as the terminus of investigation or inquiry. In this I could well be wrong. But I have failed to see how by thinking of experience as contemplation one could arrive anywhere but at a point of complete nihilism. For surely one of the features of cognition which ought never to be overlooked is intellectual dissatisfaction. Why are not all solutions to philosophical problems equally satisfactory? Why should such a standpoint as that of the solipsism of the present moment be evaded?

If philosophy were a purely deductive process, this would be absurd. For whatever else logic may be, it is supposed to exercise some control over our thinking and to oblige us to accept the conclusions it dictates. It is no answer to reply that such a solipsism denies common sense, unless one has already accepted common sense as the criterion of truth. The fact that "everyone" believes in the reality of the past and future, or remote portions of space, or of other people's minds, or of the insides of things, is not in itself a compelling reason for also believing in them. In the first place, everyone does not believe in all these things and in the second, even if he did, one of the jobs of philosophy is to clarify the bases of common sense and to see whether any of them are rational. But it is bad technique, I feel, to take as one's premises assertions which lead one into an uncomfortable position —that is, a position which violates common sense or tradition or language or the theorems of some science—and then to get out of trouble by introducing new problems which should never have arisen if one's conclusions were true. If solipsism or phenomenalism were true, the question of other people's minds would not merely be insoluble but ought never to arise. If the mind is an asker of questions and not simply an observer of passing phenomena, provision must be made for the rise of questions as well as for the possibility of answering them. If a question blocks assertion, frustrates one's generalizations, conflicts with one's conclusions, then it would seem reasonable to infer that there is a difference between knowledge and contemplation. That difference could be clarified if one were willing to assume, and I grant that it would have to be an assumption, that the mind of the individual has a history, belongs to the world of time and not to that of eternity. And if one says that there are several legitimate forms of inquiry, then some suggestion should be given of why one has to shift his method here and there.

This conflict between history and logic, genetics and the pattern of things, can be explained away in two fashions. One can either deny the importance of history or that of logic. I have preferred to accept them both and to interpret the latter as the crystallization of the former. It is of course true that if one looks at a man, one does not have any evidence in his looks to prove that he has ever been a child, to say nothing of having been a foetus. If one looks at a poem, one has no evidence of its ever having existed in a first draft or in that original flash of insight which may have been no more than a jingle or a simile in the poet's mind. If one looks at a modern version of plane geometry, one would never know that it grew out of practical methods of measuring land, if it did so grow. It is only faith in the irreducible reality of time that makes the acceptance of history reasonable. But on the other hand, if one accepts only temporality and refuses to think about eternity, as I use that term, then the control which logic legitimately exercises over our thinking becomes vain playing. Again I have preferred, and it is only a preference, to investigate action or growth or history, and to see whether the fixation of symbols, of patterns, of forms, is not the result of action. And it has seemed to me that one of the features

of all change in living beings has been precisely the development
of fixed ways of doing things. This seems to apply not only to
the habitual ways of gross behavior, but also thinking itself, to
the concepts in terms of which we organize experience as well as
to the kinds of things which we like and dislike, the values which
we put upon things, and the goals of all our pathetic striving.
Minds vary in their acceptance of rules. Some people are more,
some less, recalcitrant. Even in those societies in which authority
is paramount, there is rebellion, and in those in which rebellion
is admitted, rebellion itself becomes organized. Amongst the
outstanding lessons of the history of philosophy is this tendency
both to differentiate and to unify, to accept and to reject. No one
seems to have been an incorrigible Romantic, if that highly ambiguous word can be once more abused, nor an incorrigible Tradi-
tionalist. Moreover, it is disturbingly true that a given individual
will rebel against some rules and docilely submit to others.
Antigone and the early Christian martyrs rebelled against the
state and submitted to God. Our contemporary Communists rebel
against the bourgeois capitalist state and resign themselves to all
the shifts in doctrine which emanate from Moscow. The reason
for all this is plain enough. Programmatic rebellion against
everything is impossible, since the rebel has to know what he is
rebelling against, what he is rebelling for, and how he is to make
his rebellion effective. But again programmatic submission to
tradition is impossible, since new situations arise, and sooner or
later one has to meet the challenge of novelty. One cannot continue indefinitely populating the realms of appearance with new
inhabitants, though I should be far from denying that reality has
suffered a serious decline in the birth-rate. But if one is willing
to accept human beings as one accepts the natural world of sticks
and stones, then one will find that their variety alone explains
the conflicts in opinion which have arisen in the history of our
subject. Fichte was not inherently more intelligent than Kant,
nor Kant than Fichte; but what seemed acceptable to Kant seemed
unreasonable to his disciple.

The failure to see a problem may be due to ignorance of pos-

sible trouble. Hasty generalizations obviously do not seem hasty
to the people who make them. It seems to me, for instance, that
when Descartes used his *cogito* he was arguing from Indo-European grammar which demanded a subject for every verb, either
stated or "understood." To have thinking without a thinker,
action without an agent, seemed impossible to him; to me it
seems quite comprehensible. But surely I ought not to be so
arrogant as to appraise my intelligence above that of the founder
of analytical geometry. The reason why I can imagine action
without agents, and change which is not in a substance, is that
I live in a period when the integration of time into the structure
of the universe has been accomplished. The acceptance of time
is a modern achievement, but the struggle to reach it began, or
so it looks, in Heraclitus. As far as the fragments are evidence
of the way he thought, the river into which we step and do not
step was inacceptable as the basic structure of the world. In
general, western philosophy has agreed and time was reinterpreted
as simply a dimension of appearance, the moving image of
eternity. But the dome of many colored glass is our natural
covering; our problems arise beneath it; and the bright radiance
of eternity is at best a dream. This will horrify many philosophers
who still can find no reality except where experience is denied.
But if knowledge is the settlement of our disputes with experience, it cannot be denied.

Now I shall not be so audacious as to say that the mystics do
not know what they are talking about. On the contrary, they
seem to me to be peculiarly gifted in that they know it so well
that they accept its ineffability. One can know what one is talking about without being able to translate it into words. In fact,
the mystic should stand as the greatest and most consistent of
empiricists. For if experience is a momentary being, a glimpse
of fleeting qualities, flashes of insight, as Mach might have said,
then surely the Beatific Vision cannot be thrown aside as trivial.
But if experience is something which grows, corrects itself,
codifies and recodifies, guesses, experiments, then the mystic could
reasonably be asked to examine his special experience as he does

his other experiences. A new experience usually invites doubt, not assertion. We can be expected to ask, "What is it?" as well as to declare, "It is A, B, or C." For how can one identify anything without having previously acquired a knowledge of possible classifications? When we come upon something which our acquired classifications and categories do not fit, we have either to relegate it to a special realm of being or to invent a new class in which to locate it. Our reluctance to do this is probably attributable to our stubborn love of simplicity. But it is sometimes forgotten that a sentence or a judgment cannot affect the ontological status of its subject-matter. We cannot on the basis of sentence-structure or syntactical rules modify the universe. But such a declaration itself accepts an irreducible duality between knowledge and being. Nevertheless the acceptance seems justified by all our experience. We are all men, rational animals, featherless bipeds, apes who stand erect, whatever you will, but we are still individual men who are as likely to combat one another as to agree. The fact that philosophers can abstract from our complexities and differences a set of common characters does not eliminate our differences, except for purposes of conversation.

So much is assumption. But now let us examine the traditional notions of experience and see what is bound up in them. The most extreme form of empiricism is that which insists that only those perceptual data which are immediately given are true. Such data are qualities and sometimes relations. As we pointed out in the first lecture of this series, such data are inarticulate and say nothing.[1] To pronounce the word "blue" is neither a sentence nor a judgment, unless one is occultly saying, "The sky is blue,"

---

[1] See my "Truth of Immediate Knowledge," *Journal of Philosophy*, Vol. XXIII, no. 1, 1926. Cf. "Learning from Experience," *Ibid.*, Vol. XLIII, no. 17, 1946, and "The Perceptual Element in Cognition," *Philosophy and Phenomenological Research*, Vol. XII, no. 4, 1952. My conjectures in those papers have been confirmed by the experimental work of Bruner and Postman; see especially, "Symbolic Value as an Organizing Factor in Perception," *Journal of Social Psychology*, Vol. XXVII, 1948, and the most interesting reports in *Human Behavior from the Transactional Point of View*, ed. by Franklin P. Kilpatrick, Institute for Associated Research, Hanover, N.H., (1952). See also Oliver Martin; "The Given and the Interpretative Elements in Perception," *Journal of Philosophy*, Vol. XXXV, 1938. This note must not be taken as asserting that all these authors agree on all points.

or "Her eyes are blue," or something of that sort. But even such immediately announced judgments may be false, if we are serious. For one may not be seeing the sky at all. I realize that most adults know the meaning of the word "blue," and if they are not blue-yellow color blind, will not mistake the quality which they are seeing for another quality. But that is irrelevant. Blue in itself may be the answer to a question, but it is not a sentence and therefore cannot be either true or false. Second, any single quality or group of qualities may terminate a variety of investigations. There are scores of questions which can be answered by the perception of blue, for there are thousands of things which are blue, and the perception of blue does not selectively answer one question or group of questions at all, unless we are classifying all things on the basis of their color. Third, why should anyone ever judge that he is seeing blue, unless he was asked or had asked himself what color he was seeing, or knew beforehand that he was looking for something blue which would distinguish the thing before him from other things—as in flame tests in elementary chemistry or in spectroscopic analysis? But the blue cannot give him the previous question, since the question is by hypothesis previous to the perception of the blue. Fourth, every perceptual datum is dated as of the present and hence can be no evidence of anything past or future, unless one has preliminary evidence which does not arise out of the quality itself that there is a temporal matrix into which data can be inserted. Nor can it, fifth, be evidence of any of its causes or other possible relata, for blueness is not in itself evidence of anything other than blueness, unless one previously has learned that it may be. We need not accept Kant's theory of the categories of the understanding or the forms of sensory perception to realize this. But the Kantian factor of cognition is nevertheless present in the sense that a relevant set of relations is not to be found in the perception of qualities themselves. Sixth, a qualitative datum could not in isolation from previously accepted knowledge even raise a question, let alone answer one. If I ask what the weather is and see that the sky is blue, this blueness answers my question.

But blueness is not in itself fair weather. If someone wants to know whether a certain woman is blonde or brunette, the blue eyes may be partial evidence—we shall assume that the woman is otherwise veiled. But blueness is not even evidence of there being any women in the world, to say nothing of their being of various complexions.

But even if one add to this simple type of empiricism the assumption that there are objective, physical, stimuli—light rays, air-waves, and so on—we still do not find a one-to-one correspondence between a given stimulus and a specific judgment or bit of knowledge. F. P. Kilpatrick in his statement of the theory of transactionalism commits himself to the following: "In visual perception one is faced with the fact that any given visual stimulus-pattern can be produced by an infinity of different external conditions, and this holds true for both monocular and binocular vision. But we never see an infinity of configurations; we see just one. This means, of course, that perception cannot be 'due to' the physiological stimulus-pattern; some physiological stimulus probably is necessary, but it is not sufficient. There must be, in addition, some basis for the organism's 'choosing' one from among the infinity of external conditions to which the pattern might be related. Thus, any notion concerning a unique correspondence between percept and object must be abandoned, and a discovery of the factors involved in the 'choosing' activity of the organism becomes the key problem in perceptual theory."[2] George Horsley Smith has found when studying the relation between a person's liking or dislike for a human face, that pleasant faces, or those which were liked, were judged to be larger than those which were unpleasant or disliked, and added that "it is impossible to spell out even a major fraction of the cues involved in a simple act of perception."[3] Philip K. Hastings found that "the perceptual act as it occurs in the 'now' is meaningless unless we consider as part of it the prior experiences and expectancies for

---

[2] "Statement of Theory," in *Human Behavior from the Transactional Point of View*, p. 88. I doubt that the author means the word "infinity" to be taken seriously.

[3] In "Size-Distance Judgments of Human Faces (Projected Images)," *Ibid.*, p. 138.

the future of the observer," and that "individuals who give evidence of being relatively insecure tend, when placed in an ambiguous perceptual situation, to see objects closer to them."[4] If knowledge is something to which the terms "true" and "false" can be significantly applied, that is, if it is analysable into judgments, then the immediate data are only a small part of the story, and whether one calls the cues which turn the observer in one way rather than another habit or transactions or assumptions or the apperceptive mass or the total personality of the observer is of no importance for the epistemologist. What is of importance is that one must admit that the truth is not absorbed by a neutral mind from a completely objectively determined set of possible objects of knowledge. And by "objectively" we mean extrasomatic.

But even if we did not have the findings of experimental psychologists to corroborate our views, the momentariness, the qualitative isolation, the inarticulateness of the perceptual data ought to be sufficient to show that they cannot be the constituents of knowledge, however relevant they may be to knowledge. I am simply maintaining that there is a difference between judging that an identifiable object is blue and having a blue datum before one. The point is especially telling when one reads so lucid a writer as Hume. In Hume the connections between perceptions —impressions and ideas—are made automatically as described by the laws of the association of ideas. But are these laws themselves impressions or ideas? Is the possibility of an impression's being repeated found in any impression? If this seems like an unfair question, one has only to turn to Hume's own critique of the ideas of causality and of personal identity. That critique is based on the impossibility of the ideas' being copies of any impressions, for they have properties which cannot be found in any impression. In the case of personal identity, this argument is fortified by Hume's own introspection which, he admits, may be peculiar to him. But introspection is brought in only as additional and

---

4 "An Investigation into the Relationship between Visual Perception and Level of Personal Security," *Ibid.*, pp. 141, 150.

unneeded evidence. If one can disprove the validity of an idea
by its failure to copy an impression, then the laws by which ideas
are associated ought to copy some impression, but in their shifting
and gliding, their passing into view and out of it, they could not
be evidence of any fixed impressions. This does not disprove the
validity of the so-called laws. But it does, I think, show that
they could not be valid if Hume's theory of truth were valid.
But for that matter, how does he know that ideas are faint copies
of impressions?

The Viennese Circle was more generous than Hume. They
were at least willing to assert a duality between the syntactical
rules and that which they governed. They also recognized that
rules can be justified only pragmatically and they were frank
enough to admit ahead of time what results they wanted. Much
as I sympathize with their aims, for if they had been attained, we
would have had a great system of highly organized knowledge,
they were too willing to assert the unity of cognitive procedures,
that is, they asserted the possibility of organizing all knowledge
in accordance with a few rules. As we know, different languages
had to be set up before long which included languages about
languages. Moreover, the rules eliminated the discussion of a
great number of questions as meaningless and prevented any inquiry into what their framers actually meant by them. Assertions
were thus isolated from judgments, and it seemed to be maintained
that one could tell by simple inspection whether or not a sentence
had meaning. It seems preferable to ask a man what he means
before telling him that he is talking nonsense. But according to
the rules of the game, he could have no share in establishing the
meaning of the symbols which he was using. This seemed fantastic to some of us, however appealing the general practice was.
The temptation seemed too great to reply to a theologian, for instance, that he was talking nonsense when he talked of God, freedom of the will, and the immortality of the soul. He may indeed
have been talking nonsense, but that could not appear from the
mere presence of certain forbidden words in a sentence, except by
fiat. Comte thought it was nonsense to use microscopes rather than

the naked eye, and it was nonsense if one were to decree prior to investigation that only the observations of the naked eye were valid. For that matter, why are we allowed to use microscopes anyway? Only because we have presupposed the legitimacy of a higher degree of simplification of data than the naked eye permits.

Once a distinction is made between the rules of knowledge or of verification or of scientific investigation and that which they rule, we have on our hands an analogue to the ancient Aristotelian distinction between form and matter. In Aristotle one never finds the two existentially separated except in the case of the active reason and possibly that of the Unmoved Mover considered as the Form of the World. A given form could not be imposed on any bit of matter indifferently; certain forms were found only in living matter, others in art, others in dynamics; and the matters in such instances were differentiated from one another. It is true that sooner or later one arrived at primordial matter but one never found it as such in experience. Hence it made good sense to say that the forms themselves were discovered by scientific investigation and were not imposed upon Nature. We have perhaps a tendency to think of experience as formless until we come along and give it form. But the rules by which we think, though subject of course to correction, may themselves emerge out of the thinking process and, as Kant saw, even if they are purely human contributions to knowledge, so long as they are in universal use, there will be no way of coming upon formless experience. But we need not revert to Kant whose epistemology has too many inherent difficulties in it to be any longer acceptable. We can see for ourselves that some structure will always be found in experience and its discovery is not dependent upon its being either objective or subjective, whatever those terms may mean. Thus if certain perceptions repeatedly occur under certain ascertainable conditions, we can discover the order of their appearance, and if our emotional attitude towards certain symbols makes us see them smaller or larger than they would appear when measured with material instruments, that too can be discovered. Otherwise it could not have been discovered. Furthermore, an order can be repeated without the repetition of that which manifests the order, in spite of the fact that nothing completely formless or unordered could ever be discovered. The formless is simply that whose order has not yet been given a name.

There are three types of judgment on which we are all dependent which demand repeatable experiences. (1) They are identifications: *This is an A.* To say that something is an A requires previous knowledge of what A is, of how one can identify A's, as well as perceptual apprehension of some traits of a supposed A or of something which leads one to assert that what is before one is an A. If I say, "This is John Doe," I have to know ahead of time what John Doe looks like, sounds like, acts like. I cannot perceive all of John Doe for obvious reasons and must use some short and simple test of his presence to identify him. If he is, for instance, in the next room, I may merely use his voice as the perceptual mark of identification. But this does not entail John Doe's nature as a composite of vocal sounds, facial pattern, bodily gestures, which the antennae of my mind pick up out of the welter of possible percepts. For not only may my percepts be wrong, but they are in part, if not as a whole, *my* percepts. The perceptual marks of identification are what I use to form my judgment that the sound I hear is the sound of John Doe's voice. Similarly when I identify the presence of strontium by a flame test, the color of the flame is not the color of strontium until a bit of it or of some compound of it is put in the flame. (2) They are also hypothetical statements: *If this is an A, then I ought to perceive B.* But surely one cannot make this assertion seriously unless one has gained for oneself or taken on the authority of others, information which will make the conditional sound. C. I. Lewis has used this type of judgment as a paradigm for all valid judgments of existence.[5] Whatever the logical weakness of proving the antecedent of a hypothetical syllogism by asserting the consequent—and Mr. Lewis needs no instruction in such matters—it works very well within limits and is the basis

---

[5] He has not said that it is a paradigm for all valid judgments in general.

of much experimentation. Medical diagnosis for instance usually proceeds in this fashion and it is at least a tentative technique of corroboration. But again it rests upon our faith that there is an order in experience, an order of repetition such that under ascertainable conditions which have been learned, certain perceptual experiences will be enjoyed. But no one would be so rash as to say that the consequent of such conditionals is invariably associated with the antecedents. *If this is an A, then B,C,D . . .* may be used to prove that it is an A. The number of consequents is far from being indefinite, for if it were, then strict implication, as distinguished from material, would be impossible. Each of us uses by preference a few such consequents upon which we have learned to rely. But insofar as they are perceptual data, their reliability is derived not merely from seeing them appear but from the large mass of previous acquaintance which one has had with that whose existence they are to prove. We have to know before we begin to verify an existential judgment of the conditional type what consequents will be valuable as evidence. This knowledge is not acquired by any single experience nor in the nature of the case could it be. Let us suppose for instance that I am trying to unlock a door and have been given a large bunch of keys to open it with. I have to find the right key. There are several ways I can do this. I can begin with the first key that comes to hand and try it; if it fails to open the door, I can then try the next key, then the next, until I come upon a key which fits the lock and opens the door. Or, and this would be more sensible, I look at the lock and conclude from the shape of the keyhole that only a certain kind of key will fit it. I therefore exclude from the trial all keys which do not have the right shape. Or in the third place, after having differentiated the keys in this way, I look at the lock to see how the key should be inserted, for some keys, I have learned from experience, will unlock a door if inserted in one way but not in another, some having one straight edge which must be either beneath the serrated edge or above it. But this sort of thing cannot be done unless I have already learned something about locks and keys, and though my hypothesis that such and such a key will open the door is verified if it does open the door, and though this is a complex perceptual experience, the relation between antecedent and consequent is not in that perceptual experience. (3) They are also predictions: *If A occurs, then B will follow.* This is the sort of assertion which occurs in weather predictions, in moral exhortations, in planning battles, or in cooking. Behind them is an accumulation of information about natural rhythms and cycles, causal laws, and rough and ready generalizations about human beings and natural events. The same events obviously cannot recur, but the same kind of event does recur. The great question here is how alike do two kinds of events have to be to be the same kind of event. This may sound empty and pedantic, but predictions of this sort often go astray because the kinds of events are too loose and the particulars put into the pigeon-holes rattle about too freely. The measure of excess freedom is the failure of the prophecy. This is poignantly felt when we make prophecies about political and economic sequences. Yet, however weak they may be, we have to make them when we go to bed and when we arise in the morning, and all I want to insist upon here is their ground in repeated experiences.

But only memory can tell us whether an experience is a repetition of the past. But memory is as selective as perception, if not more so, and as soon as it gets its head under the tent, it outdoes the Arab's camel and sooner or later drags into the tent not only its own past but that of the whole herd. Thus when one admits that a little bit of memory will be acceptable but not much, the test of how much memory can be admitted can be made only by repeatedly relying on various amounts and then seeing where its reliability fails. We know of course that some things which we remember from our childhood are more reliable than some which we remember as having happened yesterday. The reliability of a memory is not to be found in its vividness, its recentness, or its simplicity. It is found in corroboration by other people or documents or both. But again, the need for such corroboration is not felt in any immediate perception even when accompanied by a recent memory; it is found only when one has relied on one's own memory and found it misleading. If the isolated knower were the starting point of a sound epistemology, the question of corroboration through other people's experiences would never arise. In fact, it does not arise in some cases, as when I recall a dream which I had before waking this morning or the somatic sensations which I am experiencing now.

Whatever else pure experience, neutral entities, essences, sense-data may be, by themselves they could not be evidence of any orderly structure into which they might be integrated. Even if it is possible for a group of people to apprehend exactly the same sensory datum, the datum occurs now and here and is evidence of nothing there and then, or there and in the future, until we have learned that it may be an item in a regular sequence of events, such as the effect of a known cause, or the cause of a future effect, the symptom of a known state of mind, the stimulus to a kind of action. The order of empirical sequences is, as Kant and before him the English Platonists realized, prior to experience in the sense that without it nothing can be said whatsoever. Rather than erect an *a priori* set of forms guaranteed only by the transcendental unity of apperception, it is simpler to read order into experience itself. A man living in isolation would never need to question his memories; for if they misled him, he could always say that the world had changed. He could say it only to himself of course, but we do say such things to ourselves if we are unwilling to admit that we have changed. But no one is so isolated, and since the categories of our thoughts are for the most part absorbed from others, the dead as well as the living, we must attribute to experience not only existence in time but also existence in a community of other people. For knowledge may grow as much from the opposition of others as from the docile absorption of their ideas. Thus the order of things is in part observed by us and in part conveyed to us by conversation and reading. It may sometimes be reached by eliminating from discussion everything that is recognized as not being common to a set of experiences belonging to various people. For inquiry is a social enterprise.

In a book published almost thirty years ago, Professor John F. Markey reported a group of experiments made by himself and others which tended to show the social basis of our cognitive symbols.[6] His conclusions run:

> The facts brought out in the last chapters should have made it clear that symbols are developed in action and are stimuli for action. The converse of this is that symbols mean no more nor carry no more content than the social experience of the individuals of the group can bring into them. This may seem like a hard statement, and certainly, in the eyes of some, will detract from the glamor of symbols, ideas, and knowledge. It means that, after all, the control of the individual and the group rests upon action and experience in the final analysis. Apparently, about the best we can do is to make the accumulation of experience less and less expensive. A main problem is how to short-cut and eliminate futile experimentation. The mobility of experience is very significant in this respect. The increased mobility made possible by symbolic behavior (thinking and reasoning), and the utilization of experience in symbolic situations may make a small amount of experience function in many different ways, until new additional experience becomes necessary with new and changing conditions . . . From the standpoint of the content of the symbolic process the question turns directly to those phases of group life which are most active and most decisive in action as being outside of understanding and controlling significance in symbolic behavior.

If I understand this paragraph, it is harmonious with the theory of knowledge suggested in these lectures, as it was with that of the late George Mead. I am not sure what Professor Markey meant by "action," but surely he could not have restricted it to the movements of the body through space. In any event I myself am not referring to the twitchings of the striped muscles or the transportation of our skeletons when I talk about conformity or rebellion. For we have the power of concealing our thoughts and purposes, as well as revealing them, whatever psychiatrists may be able to discover by their own investigations. If this were not so, psychiatrists would have little if anything to do. Men do

---

[6] John F. Markey; *The Symbolic Process and its Integration in Children,* New York, 1928. The passage quoted begins on page 163.

have a private life and they also have to struggle at times to make themselves understood by others. But the irony of it is plain: even in concealing our thoughts we must use a social symbolism to do so. And if we invent our own symbolism, we are impelled to define it in socially acceptable terms. Even Descartes in his warm room was conversing, soliloquizing, and such meditations would seem to me to be as much action as what goes on in laboratories or counting houses. For when one thinks, one tries out ideas, investigates their implications, accepts and rejects, compares and contrasts, exemplifies, corroborates, and though the body may engage in no more local motion than is involved in the incipient motions of the vocal chords, yet the inquiring mind is busy.

One can see how the genesis of even very abstract ideas may be modified by experience when one stops to consider the Law of Contradiction. This is a law which applies only to propositions, statements, assertions, declarative sentences. In its most abstract form it will run, *P or not-P*. But by the time it has reached this level of abstraction, the two propositions are to be found in a single logical system. Yet traditionally it will read something like this: an object, O, cannot both have the property, M, and not-M at the same time and in the same respect.[7] There have even been philosophers who see in the Law of Contradiction an ontological law. But there is no contradiction between M and not-M as properties. What contradiction is there between red and green, good and bad, beautiful and ugly in themselves? Such symbols name properties or attributes or qualities—the term is irrelevant— and until they are inserted in a judgment and the qualification of respect and date is put in, they assert nothing whatsoever. This is so trite an observation that one is ashamed to make it. We do of course find that nothing is both red and green at the same time and in the same respect, and we think that we know how to define respects and dates. But empirically the problem, which seems so easy of solution when we ascend from history to eternity, constantly confronts us. For in the first place most

---

[7] Cf. Aristotle's *Metaphysics*, 1005 b, 19 and 1061 b, 35.

of our dialectical troubles arise from different people's seeing the different aspects of things and in the second place from the things themselves changing as time goes on. We eliminate the different people and we petrify the things as of a given moment and thus imagine the monolithic world of logic. Society demands that we converse, communicate our thoughts. We can do so only in a language which is generally understood. That language uses terms which are supposed to be univocal, and so we impose upon experience a stability of quiddities which is not there. Thus we arrest the flux. If one asks for the justification of the Law of Contradiction, the answer may be (1) that beneath or above or behind the flux is a system of unchanging things or substances; (2) that to deny the Law is to reassert it, which was Aristotle's justification of it in *Metaphysics*, IV, 4; (3) that it is necessary if logical thinking is to go on; (4) that it is simply a rule for discourse. If the first of these statements is true, then there is an eternal realm to which the Law would apply in the sense that the realm could be described in sentences which would never be in conflict with one another. Such a realm is reached through the intellectual devices of the sciences which erect concepts such as matter, mind, ideas, as well as perfect specimens of each which are uniform in their behavior. The other three justifications make a sharp distinction between thinking and existence, a distinction which itself is justified by our difficulties in bringing one into harmony with the other. For the Law suppresses time by the very fact of its being forced to qualify what it says by the inclusion of dates. And yet we have no evidence that anywhere, except in logic, is there a realm in which time does not manifest itself.[8]

Empirically neither the Law of Contradiction nor those of Identity and Excluded Middle could ever be justified. What makes experience so radically different from logic is its irreducible diversities, its rates of change, and its "points of view." The simplest and most innocent judgment is forced to be symbolized in terms which eliminate these three features. For symbols are and have

---

[8] But see chapter XIV, p. 374 below.

to be inter-personal if they are to be intelligible, and by making them inter-personal we have to use one symbol for that which is multiple. This need not drive one into the position of Gorgias or Cratylus. One has only to accept the fact that logic is not ontology but a purification and hence a simplification of existence. The terms themselves, being universal in import, attempt to name that which is common to groups of things and the relations, even when merely that of attribution, are elevated beyond space-time. The Laws of Thought can neither be verified nor disproved by our experience of things for the simple reason that they are not about experience, even when it is maintained that they are about a nobler and occult kind of experience.[9] For our vital problems, as distinguished from our logical problems, do not arise within this nobler realm. Yet it is possible that their formulation in ancient times reflected the conflicts which we find, the relative stability of certain things, and the necessity of choice between one alternative and another. There is no need to indulge in speculation about this, tempting though it be, for if we did, we should find no answer. But the very fact that logical rules are interpreted as descriptive laws is to some extent evidence that they have been thought of as such in their origin. We find an analogue to this in mathematics. People have always existed who saw in arithmetic a refinement of counting and in geometry a refinement of surveying. And no one would deny that there is always a range of experience within which mathematics applies without much margin of error. Logic probably did emerge out of experience, but once emerged it developed traits of its own. And there is no point in trying to read back into logic as it exists at present those primitive characters which it had at its birth. That would be a commission of the genetic fallacy at its worst. But at the same time we have no evidence to disprove the empirical origin of any law, however abstract, for we know how experiences congeal into stability and processes turn into things.

There are certain postulates of all systematic thought which,

---

[9] I realize that it is no longer fashionable to call them Laws of Thought, but the same situation would obtain no matter what one calls them.

as far as I know, are anti-empirical. By anti-empirical I mean
something which could not be asserted of experience. One such
is the postulate of the independence or atomicity of attributes.
Thus, to take a homely and well-worn example, one can discuss
figure without mentioning motion, though the velocity of a material object affects its perceived shape and the resistance of a
material object to the air or a surface on which it is moving is
partly determined by its shape. We can discuss weight without
mentioning volume, though no material thing lacks some volume;
color without mentioning texture, sound without mentioning
color, taste without mentioning sound, and so on. If we could
not do this, the structure of formal science would have to be
radically changed. This is, as I say, a commonplace. But although
the conjunction of several attributes in one object or substance
has been known for centuries, and Aristotle provided us with a
special sense to apprehend this conjunction, the disunion of the
attributes in thought and the fruitfulness of the disunion has not
been given the attention it deserves. For though necessary for
formal thought, its justification lies not merely within the domain
of formal thought. The theorems of Galilean dynamics actually
work within experience under laboratory conditions, as if the attributes which the physicist is talking about did exist in separation
from one another and were not influenced by their neighbors.
The same is true of timelessness. The attributes once abstracted
must not change their nature, and the terms which symbolize them
must remain identical in meaning throughout an argument. But
as we all know, within experience all attributes change, and the
terms which name them have a way of shifting their meaning
in different contexts. Yet again, reasoning, which insists on the
retention of univocal meanings, the elimination of ambiguity,
also works when it is applied to experience. Similarly with the
postulate of generality, by means of which all sorts of non-
empirical concepts are elaborated by, let us say, mathematicians.
No one is worried by the non-empirical character of negative and
imaginary numbers, transfinite cardinals, or non-Euclidean geom-
etries. For though many such beings have been found useful in

interpreting experience, that is certainly not the reason why they
are discussed in mathematics. Negative numbers were not invented to permit a man who has overdrawn his bank account to
say that he has minus-X dollars in the bank. He could say just
as well, and more clearly, that he owes the bank X dollars.
Transfinite cardinals were not invented to express the perfections
of God. But regardless of that, the history of mathematics demonstrates that almost any logical structure may turn out to be a
satisfactory interpretation of some empirical situation, or, if one
prefer, to provide the answer to some empirical problem. If this
is so, then again one can only speculate on why it should be so,
and the most reasonable answer seems to be that our imaginations are restricted to setting up orders which can be made manifest in the empirical world. For even when thought contradicts
empirical judgments, one can usually find their empirical analogues. Thus Lewis Carroll, by combining the structure of a
looking-glass world and that of a chess-game, was able to lay out
a pattern on which he could cut a story. If you have to run in
order to stay in the same place, eat dry biscuits to quench thirst,
you are in a world whose laws are the antitheses of the laws of
daily life. They consequently cannot be said to describe daily
life, and in that sense of the word they are not empirical. But
each is formulated as it is on the principle that it must contradict
the laws of daily life. If the latter were different, so would the
former be. One cannot contradict in a vacuum; one has to have
a sentence to contradict. Now the Laws of Thought may not be
about experience and yet they may have their origin in experience; they can be contradicted by nothing in experience and yet
be used to organize our reasoning about experience.

There is still another question which must be raised when one
is interested in the relation between logic and experience or
eternity and history. If one is given a set of premises from which
to deduce something, what will be deduced is not merely a matter
of logic, though if the deduction is valid, it must be controlled
by logical methods. The rules of logic are legislative or critical
in that they tell us what not to deduce. It would be only by ac-

cident that two students in a course in plane geometry, given the same premises, would deduce the same conclusions. One might be unable to see any implications in the premises whatsoever—in fact both might be frustrated. For usually such students are told by their instructors what they are to prove and they are also told that the *demonstrandum* can be proved by the theorems which they have already learned. This is exposition, not discovery.[10] But one can raise more fundamental problems than this. How does a man discover that the symbol for "or" is primitive in symbolic logic? How does he know that thinking must organize assertions and not terms? Whence does the notion of implication arise? Do these ideas emerge out of the purification of argument or are they given to us by God's revelation or by intuition? It has sometimes been said that logicians are simply moving little black marks about on sheets of paper. But they move them in an orderly fashion, substituting some marks for others, and orienting their substitutions according to rules which are, to be sure, the rules of the game and yet seem to be more than that. For once more it should be said that the rules themselves are not chosen at random even when they deny certain previously accepted rules. The empirical origin of the concepts and rules does not restrict them to experience, once they have originated. But experience does nevertheless restrict the kind of rules and concepts which will be elaborated. Riemann may have denied the parallel postulate, but what was put in its stead was a denial of that specific postulate. One might even plausibly maintain that the atomicity of concepts is grounded in the apparent independence of macroscopic physical objects on the level of uncorrected perception. Yet one of the greatest obstacles to the acceptance of physics by the popular mind is precisely its re-

---

10 I have tried the experiment in a Freshman course by dividing the class into two sections. To one section I gave the following two theorems: (1) The sum of the angles of a triangle is equal to 180 degrees: (2) All equilateral triangles are equiangular. I then asked them what they could prove by means of these two theorems. To the second section I said, "How would you prove that no right-angled triangle could be equilateral?" The results in the first section were *nil*, in the second they were almost perfect, though there may have been cheating.

moteness from such objects. No one any longer says that mechanical models alone will give one understanding, but just as Carnot spoke of heat as if it were a fluid, so we find Eddington when he was addressing a popular audience in the early days of quantum mechanics trying to make the concept of a quantum intelligible by using macroscopic figures of speech.[11] When he says that the nature of a quantum of energy is "paradoxical" because "although it is indivisible it does not hang together," it is clear that this might be paradoxical if it were asserted of a macroscopic object but that no paradox is necessarily entailed when it is asserted of a quantum, or better, neither divisibility nor coherence should be attributed to such a being.[12] Such paradoxes begin to fade away as soon as one gives up the search for correlates for their concepts on the level of ordinary experience. When Bridgman once suggested that we have no proof that light actually travels through space but is found only on screens placed here and there along its supposed route,[13] this dismayed his readers, since the fact that something could be found at two points along a line without traversing all the intermediate points was incomprehensible to them. They were thinking in terms of billiard balls and indeed Bridgman might have been scolded for suggesting the error to them.

One of the best examples of how an empirical concept may be purified and thus lose its experienced character is that of time. Time as a continuous series of moments along which all events may be plotted is of course in general use. But time as experienced is, as Bergson saw back in the '90's, not at all like that. We become aware of time as the measure of motion, to use Aristotle's formula. Its rate of flow may change for this reason if for no other. If we use the motion of the earth around the sun as our basic measure, then we have something which has not only the advantage of being traditional, but also that of being

---

[11] See *The Nature of the Physical World*, p. 184 f. and p. 200 f.

[12] It is only fair to Eddington to add that he recognized the difficulty when he said, (*Ibid.*, p. 200) "The extension of a quantum in space has no real meaning."

[13] *The Logic of Modern Physics*, pp. 150 ff.

applicable to all mundane experiences. But it also has empirical gaps, as anyone who has had the good fortune to fall into a sound sleep and then awake from it knows. Whether this is because we lose all memory of what transpired during our sleep or not is irrelevant. No one waking out of a sound sleep can tell without looking at a clock how long he has slept. Within his experience there is a gap in time. Moreover experienced time is individualized; it is my time. For such reasons the more lyrical philosophers have been able to speak of geological time, biological time, psychological time, and even of other times. Moreover, even the individualized time proceeds in spurts, marked by the succession of specious presents. The only use I wish to make of these remarks is to suggest the difference between the mathematical concept and the empirical concept. Whatever else mathematical time may be, it is an ordered sequence with a before and an after. And that detail, though it may be unique, is a residue of empirical time. Is it not also possible that the notion of moments of time is a residue of experience? There are dozens of experiences which might be the origin of the idea that time is a series of periods of longer and shorter duration from the feeling of pulse and heart-beat to the diurnal rotation of the earth. Observed changes might give us the image of time but not necessarily that of time as a continuous series of moments.

Eternity then is not simply frozen experience, but is what we have called a purification of experience. Like all distillations, there will always be some residues, and the business of the philosopher seems to me to be the examination of the residues as well as of the distillate. The history of thought in the Occident shows continuing and successive distillations and greater refinement of ideas until at any one moment the gap between experience and what is refined out of it seems very great. All such metaphors are likely to be misleading, and this one is too, to the extent that it may induce people to believe that there is uninterrupted progress in history from common sense to science. That of course is contrary to fact. But where men think, they refine and after they refine, they refine further, hoping apparently that some day they will reach a terminus. But lest one see this as a sort of inevitable procedure, a law of God, it should never be forgotten that every step forward is taken upon the discovery of an error. I trust that I shall not seem melodramatic if I suggest that error, rather than necessity, is the mother of invention. So evil is the mother of justice.

If logic were confined to the eternal world, to the relations between essences, then its application to the temporal world would always be suspect. We can argue that if Julius Caesar existed and if all men have mothers, then Caesar must have had a mother. But one cannot prove by logic alone that Caesar did exist or that all men have mothers. The former is proved by purely historical evidence and the latter is either assumed to be true or is an inductive empirical generalization. If we try to escape from this conclusion by the calculus of probability, we become ensnared in greater difficulties. For if the calculation is numerical and not simply guess-work, then the probability of two statements being conjointly true may be less than that of either of them being individually true. Thus if we assume that the probability of Caesar's having existed is $\frac{1}{2}$ and the probability of all men having mothers is 1, the probability of both is still only $\frac{1}{2}$. If the probability of his having existed is $\frac{1}{2}$ and that he was married is $\frac{1}{2}$, then the probability of his both having existed and being married is conjointly $\frac{1}{4}$. If the probability of his having had children is also $\frac{1}{2}$, then the probability of the three statements is $\frac{1}{8}$. As we seek further information about Caesar *on the basis of the calculation of probabilities and nothing else,* we find that the fraction becomes so small that it is a wonder that we accept any assertions about the occurrence of single historical events. My example is of course nonsensical, for it assumes that all the statements are causally independent, that one cannot deduce Caesar's existence from his having been married, or his having been married from his existence or his having had children from either one or the two together. The probability of a man's existence is far from $\frac{1}{2}$; it is much less than that. For one's existence results from the concurrence of a vast number of antecedent conditions whose joint probability is well nigh incalculable. The parents of Julius Caesar might easily enough have had a son, and if one knew enough about vital statistics in first-century Rome, one might be able to calculate the chances of that son's survival. But that the son in question would have been Julius Caesar, starting as that particular ovum fertilized by that particular spermatozoon with just those genes which made him Caesar—or were Caesar—is extremely improbable. And yet Caesar was born and did marry but seems to have had no legitimate children. The birth of a specified human being is no more nor less probable than the occurrence of any specific event. Probability, like deduction, is operative only in classes of events. When we say that if Caesar existed, he must have had a mother, we are basing our argument on empirical observation, not reasoning, and if this seems untrue, that is because we forget the origin of our generalizations. If we had reason to believe that Caesar existed and yet had no mother, we should probably conclude that he was not a human being.

Hence one cannot reach experience through the theory of probability any more easily than through deduction. Each specific event is either an accident or so improbable that it might as well be called one. In any case we are driven up against existence as if it were put there by the gods to frustrate our pride and humiliate us. It is further evidence for the great difference between existence and logic and leads one to conclude that just as there can be no purely logical science which will be true to experience, so there can be no strictly empirical science at all. All knowledge is a mixture of empirical and logical elements, the differences being due to the amounts of each which are present. One cannot escape this by analysing things into form and matter, as Kant did, for some of the forms are at least suggested by experience and experience does limit the kinds of forms which the imagination may project into experience. One can imagine a world in which solid objects may interpenetrate, but either the term "solid" will have to be redefined, or we shall discover that our world has no analogue in experience. Our perceptions and thoughts must be a function of our total personality, our sensory equipment, our habitual likes and dislikes, possibly even our somatic types. Habit is enough to give us the notion of permanent things by telling us what to expect. Our very repressions must be taken into account, for it may be they which focus our attention on some experiences and lead us to neglect others. Our moral, aesthetic, and religious ideals are surely not without influence over the theories we form and the structure of those theories. Elegance, economy, logical coherence are criteria of sound knowledge which certainly do not emerge from perceptual inspection. If we are going to have a theory of experience which will include all of experience and show the interrelations of the non-intellectual interests upon the intellectual, then there is no part of the total human being, with all his inner conflicts, hopes, aspirations, memories, habits, which can be neglected.[14]

---

[14] For the influence of bodily structure on thought, see Ernst Kretscher; Körperbau *und Charakter,* Berlin 1955. For a plea for greater consideration of man's total personality, see Iredell Jenkins; "Logical Positivism, Critical Idealism, and the Concept of Man," *Journal of Philosophy,* Vol. XLVII, no. 24, 1950, p. 684. Jenkins unfortunately for my purposes, makes a sharp distinction between kinds of knowledge, as if emotional, moral, aesthetic, and religious interests could be satisfied without cognition and cognitive interests were uninfluenced by the others. But a rereading of the article referred to is inconclusive, and I may agree with him more than I realize.

Chapter XIV

ORDER

It would be impossible for men to establish habits unless there were some regularity in the world, and habit itself establishes an order in experience. The simplest act is carried out because one can depend upon the repetition of certain series of events, and a man soon finds his way through the maze of possible experiences by what he has learned. One has only to think of all the phantasmagoria of sensations which are waiting to distract us as we wake up in the morning to realize how our habits have taught us to discard some and select others. A routine of action becomes our settled mode of life in infancy, gives us a feeling of security by eliminating problems of choice, and it is a matter of indifference whether we say that the world orders our knowledge or that our knowledge orders the world. For by the time we begin to order, and we project order. Series of events not only repeat themselves but are seen to repeat themselves. We begin to demand of the world a kind of order, and there is always a way of satisfying that demand. We can deliberately avoid all temptation to stray from the road to which we have become accustomed. There can never be complete success in this program, at least in modern urban society, and indeed even in simpler social structures there is always some degree of frustration, though people may for unknown reasons try to satisfy every wish which an individual may express.

It would be better then to analyse experience not into a collection of qualitative perceptions strung out in time but as a set of various forms of order. For it is the orders which transcend the multiple kinds of percepts. The series, not the qualia, repeat themselves, and though no one knows any longer which series first struck the imagination of man as a design which might be universalized, one can at least surmise that the life-cycle and the round of days and nights must have impressed themselves on people at a fairly early date. For the most ancient myths describe the world as something that was born or made, and the first chapter of *Genesis,* which must be fairly ancient, divides the process of creation into days. Such speculations do not belong here, and we have no evidence of how our feeling for order originated. But surely no one will doubt that expectation appears early in the child's life or that it would be folly to expect anything if there were no order to the cycle of days and seasons. If anything can happen, then all thought is futile. And it is not futile. But the fact that we are given to projecting the order of our own experience into the world in which we live does not entail the conclusion that all order is imaginary or subjective in some sense of that word. For even if the only discoverable order was that of our dreams, the order itself is not fabricated by the dreams themselves. We know now, thanks to the work of the psychoanalysts, that the world of fantasy, however chaotic it may seem, proceeds in a discoverable manner, that the repressions which are symbolically released are released in a regular way, a way which is the basis for the laws which psychoanalysis has been able to untangle.[1] If the dreamer were able while dreaming to see that order being made manifest, his dreams would be different from what they are. The order is not our invention but our discovery.

We know the world through and by means of our ideas about it, for if knowledge may be thought of as a set of judgments, these judgments may be either true or false. What we want is something reliable, something upon which we can count, and the devices of thought are so made that they will provide for a maximum of reliability. This is achieved by our capacity for neglecting certain features of the surrounding environment and

---

[1] I have used the general term "psychoanalysis" here since any special technique would give evidence of my thesis.

selecting others. We all know that no day ever repeats the experiences of its predecessors. It is not the things which even seem to reappear, but the order in which they reappear. The child is not a scientist, but he too soon learns that his mother or nurse may be different today from what she was yesterday. But he also soon learns that these differences are not important. So long as his bottle of milk appears, he is not interested in whether his mother is wearing the same clothes as she wore yesterday or not. That interest comes later. He can, if his life is normal, predict—that is, expect—that she will come at a certain time and feed him, but he cannot predict that she will wear blue rather than pink, or even be in good humor rather than bad. We too can affirm the minute of tomorrow's sunrise with accuracy, though the sun itself is a mass of flaming gases which may be shooting out streamers of flame tomorrow which were not evident today. We can predict that the sun will cross the equator on March 21st, that the days will begin growing shorter on June 22nd, that the sun will recross the equator on September 21st, and that the days will begin to grow longer after December 21st. But we cannot predict—at least at present—what the weather will be like on any of these dates, nor what else will be happening, nor even whether we shall be alive to see it happen. We know only too well that each spring is different from every other spring except in certain very vague respects, that some winters are colder than others, that some summers are hotter and drier, and some autumns colder and more rainy. None of this prevents our speaking of the four seasons as if they maintained a definite character as they appear each year. The fact that the summer of 1956 in the Middle Atlantic States was wetter than the summer of 1955 does not prevent our calling them both summer. But such natural rhythms and cycles are not unusual. There are so many of them that it would be next to impossible to list them. The migrations of birds and fishes, the fall of the leaves of the deciduous trees, the breeding seasons of some animals are just as orderly as the round of the planets. What is of interest to us is their existence, not their specific traits.

Language itself illustrates some of the principal orders, the order of action and passion, the order of cause and effect, the various spatial orders and the various temporal orders. Proverbial philosophy is full of such reflections, for proverbial philosophy is expressed in general terms, as if its subject-matter were laws. The fragments of the Pre-Socratic philosophers, elusive as they are in their brevity and lack of context, speak of the cycle of elemental transformations, the order in the flux, as if the earliest occidental scientists were first impressed by cosmic rule. This rejection of natural caprice was perhaps the primordial gesture of the inquiring mind. Even Hesiod, no systematic philosopher, gives us an order in history, with an inner inconsistency to be sure, but nevertheless in its general outline an order. Its clarification in Aratus is a fine and early example of how the imagination could take in a large collection of seemingly disordered events and organize them. The constant emphasis on the destructiveness of time which is found in popular poetry, as well as in the Psalms, show this same power, and it is fair to say that all people who meditate upon the course of history have at least a dim sense that the world is not chaotic. But what exactly is an order?

All temporal order demands repetition. A single life would have no order unless it could be compared with another life. Given any one event in isolation, anything could be predicted of it. It could have no cause or effects, no purpose, no regularity. For until one can compare it with other events which are like it, one has no evidence whatsoever of its nature or kind. One could presumably look at it but at most one could but wonder. For that which is *sui generis* is by hypothesis indescribable. We have spoken of this before, but it does no harm to repeat it, for if there is any sense in speaking of the world as a whole—which it is obvious that I doubt—there is no sense in trying to find a rule which it obeys or exemplifies. That may be the reason why when men began to wonder about it, they resorted to myths. It is also the probable reason why when men enter new fields of inquiry, they begin with a simile or metaphor, an analogy. Here we are again in the realm of pure speculation, but we do know that men at a very early date began to make things and that their earliest explanations of physical events are in terms of making and doing. In the Bible the making is done by command, as if God were a magician, but nevertheless it is done by a god acting like a man. Anthropomorphism has lost some of its power as time has gone on, but it still remains in fields for which no anthropomorphic fables were needed. Though no one, for instance, has any clear idea of how a cause could produce anything whatsoever if "to produce" is to mean what it does in human situations; yet the notion of causality as productive lingers on. But whether one says that the oxidation of hydrogen produces water, causes water, or is water, makes no difference to the facts. It does make a difference to the mind which feels impelled to make the judgment. When hydrogen is burned in oxygen, water appears in drops on the walls of the container. That happens regularly, and the words used to symbolize the event are used appropriately only because the series of occurrences is repeatable. If it had happened only once, it could have been called either an accident or a miracle. Or—and this is more likely —an illusion.

Now the interesting feature of repetition is that the structure is repeated and not the substance. This specimen of hydrogen is burned in this container of oxygen; that particular event cannot be repeated, as we all know, and the energy which is given off in the process of oxidation is dissipated.[2] But the event can be formulated in such a way that an order is untangled from it and it is that order, not that which is ordered, upon which we rely for our chemical formulas. By using such symbols as *Oxygen, Hydrogen,* and specifying the conditions with care, we can neglect the individuality of the specimens. To leap out of science into would-be science, we see the significance of this when historians talk of wars, revolutions, economic depressions, cultural move-

---

[2] See Emile Meyerson on reversible processes: *Identité et Réalité,* p. 239; *De l'Explication dans les Sciences,* vol. I, p. 199. But see the appendix to this lecture, p. 374 ff. below.

ments, and the like. They hope to find events whose similarity
is great enough to allow them to use general terms accurately.
In this they are usually frustrated. But when they think that they
know what they mean by a war, they think that they can also
discover its beginning and end, its lateral frontiers, and by comparison with other wars, see a pattern which all wars exhibit.
There is no *a priori* reason why this should not be possible, though
the difficulties in the way of its actuality are very great. Not
only do wars vary in length from a few weeks to a century, but
the succession of battles, of victories, of defeats, of truces and
armistices, varies also. In some wars there have been non-com-
batants, recognized as such and unmolested. In recent wars this
distinction has been well-nigh eliminated. In some wars only
military weapons were used, knives, bullets, and shells; in others,
lies, starvation, and treason have been among the weapons. Young,
an Englishman, could travel through France unmolested during
the French Revolution. Mme de Stael was able to travel to Russia
and then to England during the Napoleonic wars. But in 1941
United States citizens of Japanese ancestry were deported from
their homes in California and herded into concentration camps
elsewhere. How can one unify under one heading events so different in character? The one common characteristic of them all
is the mass destruction of life and property by human agents.
But if the historian wants to be scientific, he will be forced to
write as if there were a greater community of kind among all
the things which he calls by one name. He may know that nations are a modern invention; he will nevertheless write the
history of Mesopotamia, Greece, India, or Egypt as if these
geographical names denoted nations. And if he is bent on discovering laws, he will look for some pattern which is latent in
them all.

Now one can find only that order which one is looking for,
and one never knows in advance what order will be sought.
Though it may seem incredible to modern man, sometimes what
seems to us to be the most obvious sequences may be overlooked

in favor of some other sequence. We have already pointed out that according to anthropologists there are tribes which do not see the relation between sexual intercourse and procreation. There may be several reasons for this: intercourse before puberty may be one; a certain degree of promiscuity may be another; occasional sterility may be a third. At any rate in such tribes a woman will attribute the fatherhood of her child to whatever outstanding rock or tree she happens to pass at the moment she feels the embryo stir within her womb. Since the embryo does not move until a certain number of weeks has passed, there seems to be no inevitable connection between intercourse and the empirically justified presence of the child. If it rained on the first of the month and the ground was not wet until the twentieth, it is unlikely that we should attribute the wetness to the rain which fell twenty days earlier. The apparent discontinuity of events would be enough to make anyone judge that there was no causal connection between them. To modern man, as I say, this failure to understand the connection between intercourse and pregnancy seems incredible, and the true facts were discovered at a very early stage in human history. But again, one has only to think of the varieties of sexual satisfaction among all people, to say nothing of sterility, to make it more incredible that the truth should have been found out as early as it was found out. If these preliterate people were using Mill's canon of agreement and difference, they might nevertheless still refuse to believe that something so unlike a baby as semen could be the source of a child. Such people would look for a more plausible order of events. A child is alive, they might say, when one can get perceptual and empirical evidence of its presence and the first such evidence is its movements in the womb. Why not then argue that the most impressive feature of the landscape at the time such evidence occurs is the *fons et origo* of the evidence? I realize that no one ever argued in this fashion, for if one should, one would have in the back of his mind a matrix of correlations which would lead him to a degree of scientific explanation to which we have no testimony in the tribes concerned. This is in no way supposed to imply that such tribes cannot argue causally when other matters are involved—such as the necessity of planting seeds if they want crops, of rain if the crops are to grow, of using a firestick if the fires go out. For though we may think of these preliterates as if they were in some mysterious fashion the children whose maturity is embedded in us, they are just as shrewd and clever in matters of traditional interest to them as we are in technological matters of interest to us.

The orders which we shall seek are more likely to be determined by social tradition than by individual observation. There is a ritual of explanation as well as of everything else which human beings do. In our own society the order demanded or supposedly demanded by our theistic preoccupations dominated western science for centuries. The rationalistic explanations of Plato and Aristotle gave way to the crudest kind of teleology in the Christian period, crude because there was more caprice than order in the purposes of God. How often was the thought expressed that His ways were beyond understanding! They were indeed if His ways were manifested in an unpredictable series of events. Why should the sun, for instance, keep moving along the Eastern horizon from south to north and north to south? How did the sun which went down at night in the west find its way back to the east without being seen? Why did it sometimes veil its face and at other times flame? Why was it unable to warm one in winter and yet recover its warmth in the summer? It must have taken painful stretches of the imagination to think out regular arrangements which would cover such disorderly events. And when it was believed that the sun was created especially to provide warmth and light, would it not seem more reasonable to correlate its fluctuations with rewards and punishments? For sin may be concealed under a cloak of righteousness, and it would always be possible to maintain that even though a people might think itself innocent, it was secretly sinful, much as some psychologists would maintain today that a person's insistent benevolence might be an overt compensation for his repressed wickedness.

Social rituals have also been projected into science. For example, one might cite the persistent use of hierarchies in the Middle Ages. Hierarchies are in origin orders of control in which the levels are determined by the extent of power. It is worth pointing out that in neither Plato nor Aristotle does the hierarchical conception prevail, though a logical formula for a hierarchy was ready for use in the *Organon*. The world of the *Timaeus*, to be sure, was one in which mathematics was on one side and time on the other; yet there is no evidence in that dialogue that there were levels of reality from, let us say, pure matter to the Demiurge. It is indeed interesting that although the later philosophers found much in Aristotle to reinforce their hierarchical schemata, Aristotle did little or nothing with this. Thus in the *De generatione et corruptione* there is a constant interchange between the elements; in the biological treatises there are the zoophytes and the orders of animation from vegetables through animals to humans, from the vegetative soul through the sensitive to the rational, and a recapitulation of all souls in man; in his theory of the spheres there is an order from the Unmoved Mover through the Intelligences which guide the planets down to earth. But nowhere does Aristotle put these hints together and form a single system of power such as is found in Plotinus. But it should also be pointed out that it was not traditional in Athenian political life to set up a dominant power in the person of someone—a King or Emperor—under whom individuals of decreasing power were organized until one reached a social stratum—like that of the serfs in mediaeval Europe—in which there was no recognized power at all. The first remaining hint of this kind of thing in European philosophy is to be found in Philo, in such passages as that in which he interprets the meaning of Jacob's ladder with the angels moving up and down between Heaven and Earth. When he called the angels *dynameis*, he assigned them degrees of power and by the fifth century it was possible for Pseudo-Dionysius to organize the constitution of Heaven and the Church according to the same pattern. Though the details of his system were never completely exemplified in mediaeval lay society, the feudal system as it existed on paper, a system in which the Emperor was at the apex of the pyramid and the serfs at the base, was a fair image of how Heaven was organized from God to the guardian angels through the three groups of three kinds of angel. But the Church too exemplified the same type of order, with the Pope at the apex and the catechumens at the base. It would be obviously childish to think that there was a deliberate planning of such a society or a conscious transference of one type of order to another. One can only say that the controlling pattern was to be found in several embodiments and as the socio-political hierarchy existed long before the philosophical versions of the ideas, it was probably the image which was reflected in philosophy. A pyramidal order is a spatial pattern to be sure, but we know that it has long been customary for men to locate their most cherished goods on high.[3] If cultural history did not furnish us with scores of discussions of what art, what life, what occupation is the "highest," in the sense not only of which should be given the most honor, but also in the sense of which should dominate the others, one might take all this less seriously.

The Bridgewater Treatises, to which we have had occasion to refer before, are the last example which we have of detailed examination of another of these patterns. A society in which the idea of a God Who operated in accordance with the Principle of Sufficient Reason and in which sufficient reason is thought of as the determinant of choice, is one in which purposes are not capricious but intelligible. In other words, if God chooses in accordance with this principle, then we ought to be able to find types of situation which repeat themselves. And of course we do. Now since we cannot by hypothesis enter into God's mind, we have to discover some method of spotting His reasons. Where action is purposive and the mind which frames the purposes does not directly report them to us, we have the best indication of what they are in the relation of means to end. In the human sphere we have machines of one kind or another whose purpose

---

[3] They sometimes also located them deep down within something. And no one is unaware of the two meanings of *altus*.

determines their structure. These machines may have superfluous ornament and, as we know, may also have some residual characters of their ancestral machines, but one can presumably tell by an examination of their structure what they are good for. Whether someone who had never seen a needle could figure out that it was made for drawing thread through holes which it would make, seems doubtful to me. But regardless of whether he could or not, the person who would follow this technological schema would think that he could reason from the structure of something to its purpose. In the case of living animals and plants, the answers seemed clear. One could apparently tell that an animal was made to survive and to procreate his kind. In order to survive, he had to eat, though hibernating animals seem to spend a good bit of time not eating. One could then by observation—not by dialectical argument—discover what his species ate. From then on one could examine his anatomy and show how well it was adapted for eating the kind of food which it was observed to eat. Thus if it was a grazing animal, it would have one kind of teeth, and if an animal which preyed on other animals, another kind. The former would not need claws to grasp its prey; the latter would. The digestion of grasses and cereals would demand one kind of digestive system, the digestion of meat another. If it drew in its oxygen from the air, it would have to have an apparatus for getting the oxygen into its system and eventually into the blood-stream. If it took it out of water, it would need another system. If it were nocturnal, it would have one kind of eye; if diurnal, another. Elaborate studies were made on the adaptation of organs to needs, and in fact a man like Cuvier was able, he thought, to reconstruct from a few bones just what a whole extinct animal must have been. Such teleological studies are seldom made nowadays, especially since D'Arcy Thompson published his celebrated book on growth and form, in which good reasons were given for concluding that the forms of animals were better correlated with certain physical and mechanical laws. I see no evidence that the authors of the Bridgewater Treatises denied that living beings were also material beings. They knew that if they fell, they would obey the law of falling bodies. They could also have accepted the fact that digestion is a biochemical process, and if someone were to say to them with a sneer, "Digestion is simply the disintegration of food through the action of hydrochloric acid," they could easily have exclaimed, "How wonderful that the hydrochloric acid is there to disintegrate it!" Their method of explanation would have fallen to pieces if they had not previously assumed the existence of God and the Biblical account of creation. Behind it lay the question of whether one should attempt to integrate science into theology or keep the two subjects separate. So when Henderson wrote his book, *The Fitness of the Environment,* in which he showed that the environment provides just those things which are needed to sustain life, his argument was pointless unless in the back of his mind was the problem of showing how some purpose was being fulfilled in this world. For if he was just describing the state of affairs, he could have argued just as cogently that if the environment had not been fit, life would have been extinguished. That is, one could just as well assume that the environment existed before there was any life in it and that the only life which could survive in it was limited in structure and function by it. One usually finds no mystery in the fact that most piano compositions can be played by two hands.

Had the dominant conception of God been different, the technique of explanation would have been different. Minds living in terror of a malignant god would have projected his malignancy into the world, and the order which they would have sought would have been one in which, for instance, the frustration of human desires would have been the rule. Such men could have seized upon what others called fitness and seen in it the terrible limitations to satisfaction. The fish that might have wanted to fly could fly only for short distances, lest it suffocate in the air. The stag driven to water met his doom because he could not dive into the lake and live down there like an amphibian. The man separated from his goals by space and time was prevented by his very anatomy from transcending them. The plants rooted in one spot were prevented from searching for water and food. For the brute facts give us evidence of nothing until they are fitted into a pattern which is beyond them. One could ask, "Is there purpose in the world?" and answer it in both the affirmative and the negative; "Do all things come out well?" and answer it similarly; "Is everything the result of blind chance?" and again find facts on both sides. For obviously the questions in part determine the answers and a single fact may answer a variety of questions. For if a fact is that which we believe, our beliefs must be seen to be part and parcel of a set of judgments to which they are alone relevant. It has sometimes been argued that the conjunction of circumstances and materials which made this particular world possible is so improbable that it could not have come about by accident. But if an event is very improbable, it may well be an accident. Any reader of this book must be alive, and yet the probability of his being alive is so small, as we have pointed out before, that on that basis alone one finds it hard to believe in it. It is indeed wonderful that just those men, Franklin, Jefferson, Madison, Adams, Washington, the Founding Fathers, as I believe President Harding called them, should have existed in 1776. On the basis of our wonder we could perhaps argue that God must have been specially interested in starting a revolution in the Colonies and in providing the right men to carry it through. Aside from the fact that there seems to have been no special need to punish the British and their Hessian mercenaries, in spite of George III and Lord North and in view of Edmund Burke and Chatham, and aside from the auxiliary fact that He also provided Benedict Arnold and a certain lack of enthusiasm on the part of Washington's soldiers,[4] one might just as well have maintained that the malignant deity did all this just to start trouble, that his love of gore explains why the human race goes berserk periodically and that men who protest are imprisoned, shot, tortured, or all three. If one is going to argue that it is wonderful and evidence of divine

---

[4] See Brig. Gen. Emory Upton's *Military Policy of the United States,* Washington (Government Printing Office), 1905, a book which is strangely neglected.

purposes—either good or bad—to find the sufficient and necessary conditions of an event followed by the event which they condition, one might just as well grow lyrical over the fact that sulfur, hydrogen, and oxygen are here to form sulfuric acid or that heights are provided for falling bodies to fall from.

Since we have used an historical example, we might turn to the Great Man Theory of History which is now in eclipse. According to this theory, if one can generalize its structure, all great historical changes are brought about by the will of certain powerful individuals. Thus Pericles, Alexander, Julius Caesar, Gregory the Great, Charlemagne, Cesare Borgia, Louis XIV, Elizabeth I, Napoleon, various Popes, Emperors, Presidents, industrial leaders, reorient the course of events by the sheer imposition of their wills. In the United States we are accustomed to observe the growth of myths about certain of our leaders, men like Washington, Lincoln, and Jackson, not to mention the living or recently deceased. Just as a general is said to be responsible for the success and failure of his troops, and sometimes is held responsible, so these leaders are believed to be the prime movers of the outstanding events of their times. Thus Voltaire could write *Le Siècle de Louis XIV* as if the *Roi-Soleil* by the effulgence of his beams had the power to kindle the imagination of his subjects and bring their great works to life. In an absolute monarchy this makes a good bit of sense, for if one's success depends on pleasing a monarch, one will try to please him. It would be folly to do otherwise. But such an interpretation of history would be almost impossible if men saw the necessity of collaboration in all matters. When the artisan began to disappear and production became socialized, when even scholarship fed upon the work of others, when the fate of the individual was felt to be interwoven with the fate of social organizations, when parliamentary government began to take the place of personal government, then the popularity of the Great Man began also to decline. It can scarcely be denied that there have been times when the individual was less aware of the external forces which impinged upon his history. The small farmer on the isolated farm, who grew his own food, spun his own cloth, built his own house, reared his children as he would, was not likely to imagine that what he did was determined by "great economic forces." He would have no evidence of the existence of such forces. Similarly the Baron in his castle, switching his allegiance as he wished, the mercenary soldier, the Abbot of a powerful monastery, the *grand seigneur* on his land, such men were surely more conscious of their own power than of impersonal forces of which they were only the patients. For the universe itself was in the hands of a Person. And the vestiges of polytheism which are to be found in the saints, each with his special function and province, gave men reason to think that all changes which might occur were centered in personal wills. In fact, martyrdom was additional evidence that the person could not be overcome unless he wished to be and it was customary as early as the third century to write even the history of philosophy in terms of biography. One would never learn from Diogenes Laertius or Eunapius or Philostratus that the theories of the men whom they discuss formed rational systems each of which had a history, that their ideas were an intertwining of various strands of thought picked up in their reading of earlier writers, or that they had drawn out of such ideas new implications. Happily Mr. Edelstein has shown just what the situation was[5] and to what extent the individual philosopher was isolated from the community in general and to what extent he was allied with his intellectual predecessors. Historians of ancient literature know that Europe did not wait for the Renaissance in order to develop the cult of the individual. Hellenistic times already had this cult, as is shown by all those apocryphal letters and fictional biographies which were written in that period. The power of the individual was real, as far as anyone could see, and that was sufficient for using it as a model for interpretation.

No *Zeitgeist* is required to justify this. People do things, make things, create things, and destroy things. The supposed forces

---

[5] See his article, "Recent Trends in the Interpretation of Ancient Science," *Journal of the History of Ideas,* Vol. XIII, no. 4 (1952), pp. 573-604. See esp. p. 597.

behind them are not obvious perceptual facts, but are the products of methodological hypotheses in terms of which the perceptual facts are organized. Before the acts of human beings could be understood in terms of economic determinism—if that is in question—it had first to be agreed that all human beings acted in the same way on similar occasions. But such agreement could be reached only by suppressing individual differences. An approach to that end was provided in "political arithmetic," which might just as well have been used to prove the ultimate and stubborn differences amongst individuals. For even if the average number of deaths in a population is stable, the average is calculated from the different lengths of life. If everyone died at the age of 50, there would be no sense in looking for an average nor in calculating a death-rate per thousand inhabitants. However that may be, social statistics gave the early nineteenth century a feeling for social laws which could never be broken, and all students of the history of social philosophy know how it induced some of the otherwise kindly souls to argue that social reform was silly because impossible. Believers in the Wage-Fund Theory were not unique in this respect. Poverty and riches, business-cycles, the class-struggle, and all the rest of the baggage of the historical determinists, co-operated in persuading people that of all the beings in the cosmos, man alone was completely inefficacious. In fact within the lifetime of men living today, the sentiment has been voiced that if Mussolini or Hitler had died in infancy, another Mussolini or Hitler would have arisen to perform their sinister functions. If the nineteenth century did have a *Geist,* it was a spirit divided against itself.

In the Stoics there was also a theory of determinism, but it was a determinism which applied, or was applied, more to questions involving the freedom of the individual's will than to the course of empire. Were it strictly interpreted, each choice would have been predetermined, for the Stoic never hesitated to refer the order of events of Zeus, "most glorious of immortals . . . ever omnipotent, ruler of Nature, governing all by law." In the Hymn of Cleanthes the emphasis is upon the rule of law in the sense of commands: "No deed is done on earth against your will, O Lord, either in the high and divine heaven or on the sea." But there was one exception: "Save that which evil-mongers do in their madness." A stricter determinism would have included the maleficent as well as the beneficent. But Cleanthes apparently could not think of evil as any real part of law. "For there is no better prize for men or for gods than ever to celebrate the universal law in justice."[6] The very conflict between good and evil is spoken of in terms of law, law issued by a commander, and when the Stoics came to their cosmology, they were caught in their own metaphor. For if Cleanthes could think of evil as breaking the law, then law must have the character not only of descriptive generalizations, but also of statute. In the former sense, it must have no exceptions; in the second, it was bound to, since no one denied the existence of maleficence. In Aristotle on the other hand, the Unmoved Mover controlled the universe not by command but by attraction, in his famous phrase, as the beloved moves the lover. In spite of his relations with Philip and Alexander, his mind had not been seduced by the picture of the all-powerful commander. Thus his God was not only vastly different from the God of the Bible, but also from the God of Cleanthes. As a further contrast, the Demiurge of the *Timaeus* did indeed create the world, but he created it in accordance with strictly logical principles and Plato is careful to introduce "the Other" along with "the Same" as one of the primary ingredients. These various conceptions of God's power and the way in which it is exercised indicated to the philosophers in question how they should interpret natural law. We no longer have any way of discovering why they chose the conceptions which they did choose, but in them all human relations obviously played a part. We find God in the Pseudo-Aristotelian *De mundo* (398 a, 16) described as the Persian King who rules from within the palace, never being seen in public, and a similar description in Philo's

---

6 Cleanthes; *Hymn to Zeus,* in Stobaeus, *Ecl. phys.,* I, 2, 12.

De Decalogo (61 and 177-8).[7] Such considerations have to be
left vague from lack of evidence, but this is unfortunate, for if
we knew enough, we should also know what determines the
order which philosophers expand into the "world as a whole."

In our own times the matter is clearer. When Spengler or
Toynbee speak of the life-cycle of a nation or a civilization or a
culture, we know that they are projecting an order found in one
limited field, that of biology, into another. We can also affirm
with some justice that this is because of the popularity of biological studies in the nineteenth and twentieth centuries. Nations,
cultures, civilizations are not organisms, whatever similarities they
may have to organisms. Hence any biological order which is
imposed on them is an analogy. One cannot blame such men
for seeking some kind of order, for that is the only way we
have of understanding any array of data. But though Roman
civilization may be said to have died, Romans have continued to
live in Rome and to grapple with the problems of existence on
the Italian peninsula, more or less as they did in the days of
Romulus. When, moreover, the language in which a culture is
expressed, its literature, its architecture, its sculpture, its laws,
and many elements of its religion survive, what reason have we
to say that the culture has died? If any biological metaphor were
to be used, it had better be that of the unicellular organism which
divides and continues to divide, absorbs nutriment from the environment by throwing out pseudopods and engulfing it, modifies
that environment to its own needs, and so on. But that too is
misleading, for no unicellular organism, as far as we know, selects certain of its descendants as rulers, others as ruled, changes
its outward appearance so as to be unrecognizable, makes artefacts, including a language, and actually does what a society of
human beings does. One might even see in the fact that human

---

[7] Cf. Wolfson; *Philo*, Vol. I, pp. 220 ff., here he indicates possible Biblical
sources for this idea. In Plotinus, *Ennead*, V, v, 3, where he is speaking of the
two gods, possibly Kronos and Zeus, the language is somewhat similar. For the
reverse of this idea, namely that the Emperor is a terrestrial replica of God, see V.
Valdenberg; "Discours politiques de Thémistius dans leur rapport avec l'antiquité,"
Byzantion, Vol. I (1924), pp. 557-80.

societies have a history one of their distinguishing characters. If the philosopher of history were to impose permanent laws upon historical events, he would have to decide whether that which the historian described was in a real state of change or not. By a real state of change, I mean one which could not be explained away as simply superficial changes in language, in costume, in coinage, in short, in whatever the philosopher might think to be of no effect upon the nuclear substance of humanity which itself did not change. It was, to all intents and purposes, Vico who first saw in history change which affected the nucleus. His primitive men were fundamentally different from their children; they thought differently. And since Vico, like Herder and also Comte, believed that all action proceeded from thought, there was no accommodating the life of the Age of Heroes to that of modern man. Thus such philosophers were not able to use the formulas of Saint Augustine and see obedience and disobedience to God's commands as the sole explanation of historical change. And for that, if for no other reason, they turned to something which was alive, grew, matured, and died. That something was an invention of their own, either made in the image of the plant—as in Herder, or in the image of a single man—as in Toynbee.

Sometimes philosophers will select out of the many interests of their society one which might seem to have no relevance whatsoever with the facts which it is used to order, and nevertheless expand it to cover those facts. Number symbolism, for instance, is used by Philo as a clarification of the Biblical account of Creation. He was no doubt moved in this direction by the sacred text which he was trying to expound. Thus when he is discussing the texts which say that the Creation took six days, he has to explain why that particular number was chosen. "Order," he says,[8] "is a property of number, and of numbers, by the laws of nature, the most fertile is 6. For if we begin with the monad, it is the first perfect number, equal to its proper parts and the product of them; its half is 3, a third of it is 2, a sixth 1." He

---

[8] *De Opificio mundi*, 13.

goes on to say that it is both male and female, since it is a product
of 3, which is odd and male, and of 2, which is even and female.
"For it was necessary that the cosmos, being the most perfect
of things which have come into existence, should be in harmony
with 6, the perfect number." To get the full impact of this
procedure, one should also read the passages on 4 (*Ibid.,* 47)
and 7 (89 ff). This sort of thing did not stop with Philo. We
find the same type of thinking in Saint Augustine, in Boethius,
and throughout the Middle Ages and well into the Renaissance.
Masculine and feminine numbers, prime numbers, perfect numbers,
productive numbers, virgin numbers, square and cube numbers
out of which spatial squares and cubes could be formed, along
with a host of other peculiarities of integers were utilized over
and over again as examples of the kind of order which the
universe was said to reveal.[9] The mathematical interpretation of
natural science has gone far beyond these Neo-Pythagoreans, but
nevertheless, as we all know, the exploration of mathematical
orders as they appear exemplified in events, was one of the most
fertile ideas which scientists ever utilized. For simple arithmetic
revealed astonishing traits which apparently stirred the imagination of those to whom they suddenly appeared. Thus the elementary fact that the number 1, if multiplied or divided by itself
remains 1, struck them with wonder and seemed evidence that 1
was analogous to the immutable God. It was a perfect symbol
for the eternal. Such fiddling seems nonsense to the modern
mathematician, and it can easily turn into nonsense But who
would be rash enough to assert that it was not just that kind of
thing which made modern mathematics possible? For was it
not that free playing with mathematics which detached it from
material objects and practical action and established it as a
science in its own right? To divorce arithmetic from counting
and geometry from measurement purged them both of their

---

[9] This was so popular a technique, that even obscure figures used it. There is a
codex in the Johns Hopkins Library, the *De Macrocosmo* of Marco-Aurelio Trivis-
ano, left unfinished by its author in 1378 and so far unpublished, which is pretty good
evidence of the spread of this manner of thinking.

empirical connotations and that was essential if the science was to have a field of its own. The tetractys as a symbol of emanation may seem absurd to us, and those who so employed it never explained how the dyad could emanate from the monad. But to see the tetractys as a way of organizing one's ideas about something which ostensibly had no kinship with it, was eventually to stimulate men to take mathematical order as the one universal order.

This was not, to be sure, something which, as the French say, leaped to the eyes. And those whose eyes refused to see it continued to write essays against the infinite, velocity at a point, curved space, and pretty nearly everything else which appeared to be paradoxical when translated from mathematical symbols into words. Which tendency proved of greater value to the progress of science I leave to others. But the answer is easily predicted.

We have already referred in our third lecture[10] to another kind of order which was frequently used in the Middle Ages and Renaissance, the similarity between the macrocosm and the microcosm. One of the odd features of this method of organizing things was that it was devoted almost entirely to structure (anatomy) not to function. Since the macrocosm could not be seen as a whole, it was the human being whose structure was blown up into the structure of the universe. It could be asserted, and it was asserted, that the cosmos was born and would grow old and die, but other processes observable in human physiology were not usually attributed to the cosmos. The geometrical properties of the cosmos, its shape, the orbits of the planets, the spatial relations between the heavenly spheres and the earth, were apparently of more interest to the general run of scientists than its dynamic properties. Even in Aristotle there is the feeling that if Nature were left alone, it would be an immobile structure, something like a great piece of sculpture. So long as men were mainly interested in this type of order, the

---

[10] See p. 60 ff. above.

macrocosm-microcosm correspondence would work well enough. It failed when certain problems could not be solved by its means. Thus Plotinus argued that if the planets were the controlling factor in men's lives, twins ought to have exactly the same careers point for point, and this would be true even if they were not identical twins. (He might have noted that twins are not born simultaneously and thus do not have identical horoscopes.) Moreover, if the cosmos were a Great Animal, then man's free-will would disappear. And Christians wanted to retain free-will. But the greatest logical weakness in such theories arises from our inability to observe the manifestation of any order on a universal scale. We are clearly limited in what can be observed, and the rest is extrapolation. We can expect that certain things will occur, and when our expectations are based on reason, they usually do. But as Aristotle pointed out, sometimes things go wrong and Chance takes over. A man who puts a kettle of water on a stove will expect it to boil when the Centigrade thermometer reaches 100 degrees. But actually if one predicts that a specific kettle of water put on a specific stove will boil at the specified temperature, he overlooks the possibility of someone's turning off the gas, of his dropping the kettle before it gets to the stove, of the thermometer's breaking, or of any one of a variety of accidents that may happen before the predicted result is obtained. It is, as everyone knows, no disproof of the generalization about the boiling point of water that such things should happen. For the physicist is not talking about this particular kettle of water, this particular stove, this particular thermometer. He is talking in terms of purified concepts. Thus the transfer of scientific laws to historical events is irrelevant to their truth or falsity. For we must distinguish between inference and prediction. If inference is a matter of logic alone, the prediction is always dependent on chance. To make a prediction come out right, one must operate under laboratory conditions, and those conditions are set up specially to prevent the occurrence of chance events. It is customary to say that chance is simply a name for our ignorance, that if we knew enough we could predict the future with accuracy. If we knew enough, it is argued, we could predict just what would happen if two dice, shaken in a box, were to be spilled on a table top. But how much would be enough? When the question is examined, it turns out that if we knew how the dice would fall, we should be able to predict it. The shaking of dice and their falling and rolling can be broken up into several pseudo-atomic stages or periods for purposes of conversation, but these stages all flow into one another and cannot be distinguished in fact. Thus there is no way of determining what is cause and what effect, and chance is the best name we have for that kind of eventuality. Omitting all consideration of the metaphysics of causality, that is, the supposed identity of substance between cause and effect, the shaking and spilling of dice is not simply a very complicated event, for that is irrelevant, but it is an event in which there is no predicting just what will happen. In this respect it is not essentially different from the occurrence of any historical event. I have no doubt that one could invent a machine which would so shake the dice that they would always turn up in a chosen manner, showing 7 or 12 or what you will. But for that matter one need not shake them at all to get such a result; one need only place them on a table top with a 3 and a 4 showing or two 6's. The particular event which actually happens after one has shaken actual dice is no more subject to causal explanation than any other particular event. In a logical system the distinction between before and after is figurative, not literal. (It is obvious that I am not talking about the dates on which one states the premises and then the conclusion.) If I say that the chances of getting a 2 or a 12 are equal when a pair of normal dice are shaken, I am not making a prediction that either a 2 or a 12 will turn up; I am announcing odds for betting. Similarly when I say that there is a greater chance that when two dice are shaken and spilled, a 7 will turn up rather than any other number, I am again predicting nothing. One can calculate the probability of throwing dice ten times and not getting a 7 just as one can calculate the probability of tossing a penny ten times and getting straight heads and no tails. But this has nothing whatsoever to do with what we have called history. Anyone who has seen human faces knows what an enormous number of variations can result from the combination of a few features. One can of course predict that in general human beings will have two eyes, two ears, a nose, a mouth, and a chin. He can also predict that the eyes and ears will be disposed symmetrically along a vertical axis running through the nose. But why call this prediction? It is simply a generalized description of a human face. It is not in any sense of the word a description of any real face or a prediction—even if we leave monsters out of consideration—of what any unborn baby's face will look like. It is a hieroglyph. Instead of thinking of the causal series as that with which we start, it would be better to admit that we start with chance and hope to do away with it. Instead of saying that if we knew enough, chance would disappear; it would make more sense to say that if we knew enough everything would be a matter of chance. For chance can be eliminated only by assembling diversities into uniform classes and our empirical classes are never quite so uniform as we think they are.[11]

Does this confine us within a realm of "perspective truths"?[12]

If this phrase means that we always have to work from premises, within a system of order of our own choosing which is eventually abstracted from some part of experience and extended to all experience, then indeed all truth is perspectival. Beyond or above or behind all thinking, however, will be certain rules for inference, and these rules will not vary, at least within the system as a whole. For even if we simply name what is before us, we shall probably keep our names univalent and that is the result of a rule. And if we go on to more inclusive classifications, we shall disregard all features of the things being classified which might spot their purity. And that too is the result of a rule. I confess to seeing no way of constructing *a priori* any set of rules which

---

[11] Cf. Milhaud; *op. cit.*, p. 117. Cf. the section on *Abstractions par épuration* in Hélène Metzger's *Les Concepts scientifiques,* 1926, pp. 169 ff.

[12] For a discussion of perspectival truth, see A. P. Ushenko; "Truth in Science and in Philosophy," *Philosophy of Science,* Vol. XXI, no. 2 (1954).

will work in all situations. If one is to set up, for instance, a metaphysics such as Ushenko's "philosophy of power," which will be invariantly true, then one will have to find pure cases of power to begin with, externally related to whatever features of experience they may be associated with and which retain their purity through time. Ushenko himself, like many other metaphysicians, felt that there was an "objective control" exerted by the world "upon its representations by different philosophies."[13] This seems to me very dubious. For in the first place, that there is a whole world, in the sense of some describable entity, cannot be proved. If such a thing is to be described, it must belong to a class of things. And by definition it does not. That it can exercise any kind of control, objective or not, cannot be asserted of it. We are aware only of bits of the world, and we find something which may be intelligibly called control in these bits. The extension of the idea of control to an undefined "world" is neither warranted by the evidence nor necessary for philosophy. Moreover, we have no reason to believe that there is a single type of order which will be discoverable and applicable to all fields of interest.

This becomes the more plausible if all orders which we can imagine are derived from experienced order, it being understood that the derivation may be of a high level of abstraction. For in that case whatever order we decide upon, whether structural or serial, is admittedly relevant to only one kind of being. We have learned that there are discontinuities in Nature. They may be located in various ways, as we saw, I trust, in our lecture on realms of being. If there is no logical passage from one realm to another, what reason would we have to believe that all realms are describable in a single set of propositions? The fact that we may specify physical conditions under which we shall perceive certain colors or sounds or odors, does not identify the things perceived with the conditions of their appearance. Thus even if we could state a set of conditions which would have to prevail

---

[13] Op. cit., p. 116.

before anything whatsoever could occur, that would not be equivalent to the proposition that everything that could occur was identical with those conditions. Furthermore, though we could use the word "World" or "Universe" to denote all possibilities and actualities, the word would have no specific meaning and nothing could be deduced from it. Anything said about it would inevitably delimit it, and though we might say that we could deny certain propositions which someone might make about it as impossibilities, the best one could do would be to deny self-contradictory propositions. In short, any predicate which we might feel inclined to attribute to it would become a universal predicate and therefore meaningless.

There is one way to have your cake and eat it too, the way of Revelation. For since the source of Revelation is supernatural by definition, there is no making anything revealed intelligible. We may phrase Revelation as we will, and there is always some probability that the phrasing will be accurate. For accuracy would be consistency with the words of the prophet to whom the Revelation was granted. If Revelation tells us that there is a world, in the sense of some kind of whole, organic or material or otherwise one, a whole which can do this and that, we can of course make statements about it which are not ours, but those of the supernatural and divine source. Unfortunately Revelation comes to us in the ordinary language of mortals, full of metaphors and similes, and most exegetes have resorted to allegorical interpretation when they have seen the unavoidable ambiguities in the literal assertions. Hence Revelation as men understand it is as full of problems as experience is. Nevertheless, if we could be said to have a clear understanding of its message, and if that understanding could be expressed in intelligible human language, then we would be able to control our reasoning by something objective. Most philosophers prefer not to accept Revelation. But then they had best stop using terms which are unintelligible within the framework of human thought. We know what wholes are possible, but we do not know what The Whole is. We also are in the fortunate position of knowing why we cannot know what it is, because we can tell what it is supposed to be. If it names everything that was, is, and ever shall be *in saecula sae-culorum,* we are in a still worse posture than that of Parmenides, for we could not even say, "It is." The Universe, or the Whole World, becomes simply a proper name, and proper names tell us nothing.

APPENDIX TO CHAPTER XIV
The Temporal Order as Universal

My assertion that there is no discoverable order which might be universal might be contradicted by someone who would maintain the absolute prevalence of a temporal sequence. Since I have been so emphatic in the body of these lectures about the temporality of experience, it is only proper that I should discuss the larger question too.

It is clear that I have assumed the temporality of experience, that we have a past, present, and future, and that we cannot return to the past except metaphorically, that is, by memory. But there is nevertheless reason to say that if there were no change within a closed system, there would be no time in that system. This may have lain behind the thinking of such philosophers as Plato when they maintained that the Intelligible World was eternal or timeless. It is at any rate what lies behind mine when I have said that the realm of logic was timeless, congealed out of experience, and that the order of logical priority and posteriority was simply a figure of speech that should not be imposed upon the temporal order. If now one could have a closed physical system in which there was no change, it would look as if there were not time there either, though an observer would of course be able to observe it for some time. But the sequence of time in the observer's inspection of the system would not be inherent in the system.[1] If, however, within the system there was a libera-

---

[1] Cf. Niels Bohr; "Discussion with Einstein or Epistemological Problems in Atomic Physics," in *Albert Einstein: Philosopher-Scientist,* ed. by Paul Arthur Schilpp, N.Y., 2d ed., 1951, p. 222 f: "It must be realized that—besides in the account of the placing and timing of the instruments forming the experimental arrangement—all unambiguous use of space-time concepts in the description of atomic

tion of energy, then the Second Law of Thermodynamics would apply and this would provide a direction for the internal changes. But we have assumed that there are no such changes. Consequently there need be no assumption of temporal order.

If, as Reichenbach has said,[2] "The concept of causal chain can be shown to be the basic concept in terms of which the structure of space and time is built up," and if, as he continues, "Time order, the order of *earlier* and *later,* is reducible to causal order," then it would seem to follow that where the concept of causality is inapplicable, there is no temporal order. This is admittedly the case in eternal systems, that is, systems of formal logic or mathematics. No one would pretend that premises cause conclusions, and no one has pretended to see more than a figure of speech—and I should say a misleading one—in the logical before and after. If now we could find a physical system in which causality played no part, then it would be equally metaphorical to attribute a temporal sequence to whatever is found or observed within that system. But it would seem to be so in nuclear physics where, as Bohr suggests, there is an order of observation but not an order of events within the system. As a poor analogue to this, one may take a macroscopic object, such as a table, and observe certain of its properties in sequence, its color, its shape, its weight; but they do not occur in that order or in any other order. They are there all together. There is, moreover, no predeterminable way of deciding with which feature of the table we should begin, and this is true since all three properties are inseparable. Our attention may oscillate between shape and color, and though it takes time for the oscillation to occur, there is no oscillation between the shape and the color.

If such a physical system were found, then there would be no temporal order within it. I do not know whether Reichenbach was right in basing temporal sequence on causality or not, but

phenomena is confined to the recording of observations which refer to marks on a photographic plate or to similar practically irreversible amplification effects like the building of a water drop around an ion in a cloud-chamber."

[2] In "The Philosophical Significance of the Theory of Relativity," *ibid.,* p. 303.

one can at least grant that causation takes time and that the causal order is not reversible. One could also grant that if we have a situation in which the Second Law of Thermodynamics does not apply, there would be—or at least could be—reversibility. I am not presumptuous enough to say whether or not such situations exist. I am simply suggesting the conditions for their existence. And it must be granted that my argument falls to pieces if the temporal order is neither based on the causal order nor on the direction indicated by the Second Law of Thermodynamics.[3] For there may be other bases for our notion of the irreversibility of time which I have neglected.

Kurt Gödel in his contribution to the volume on Einstein already referred to, "A Remark about the Relationship between Relativity Theory and Idealistic Philosophy," points out with more authority than I can muster how shaky our ideas of a universal and single temporal series are. His argument is based on the requisite conditions for observing a lapse of time, and he concludes that "in whatever way one may assume time to be lapsing, there will always exist possible observers to whose experienced lapse of time no objective lapse corresponds (in particular also possible observers whose whole existence objectively would be simultaneous). But if the experience of the lapse of time can exist without an objective lapse of time, no reason can be given why an objective lapse of time should be assumed at all" (p. 561). I am using this quotation and the article from which it is taken simply as evidence that there is no reason to expand an order found in part of our experience to cover everything which exists. If we define temporal order in such a way as to make it irreversible, then obviously we cannot go backwards in time. But if we are thinking of it as a characteristic of certain actual physical processes, then we change its nature when we extend it beyond those processes. But what we must discover in them is what we discover in the primary experiences. And that in this case seems to be an impossibility.

---

[3] For a statistical treatment of the problem of reversible processes, see Richard C. Tolman; *The Principles of Statistical Mechanics,* Oxford, 1938, sec. 37, p. 102, and Chapter XI.

There is also a dialectical argument against making the temporal order universal in its range. Time, like every other concept, if it is to have any ascertainable meaning, must denote certain beings and not all. Like every other significant idea it must be selective. When it becomes a universal predicate, it loses all discriminative power, and though this type of argument is out of style, it should be taken seriously. If it is, then we are once more in a position of saying that we can talk reasonably about parts of the universe, what Quine has called bits of experience, and can talk only nonsense when we talk about the universe as a whole, whether "whole" be taken distributively or collectively.

Chapter XV

CONCLUSION

It may have seemed a bit cavalier of us to announce that all thinking is an attempt to solve problems, for it is clear that often we are forced to accept certain ideas as already demonstrated, that sometimes we wonder what would happen if certain ideas were true which are usually held to be false, that sometimes we wonder about the evidence for ideas which we have been taught in childhood and have never questioned, and that we sometimes puzzle over the meaning of assertions which we read or hear without asking whether or not they are true. But unless we are to include in the category of thought the whole process of daydreaming, every time we make a judgment, it is in answer to a question. The questions may not arise out of the business of daily living; they may be utterly detached, as philosophers above all others must realize, from any concern other than the satisfaction of curiosity. And when I have said that a problem arose when one observed a deviation from the rule, I have not intended to deny the possibility of imagining such a deviation. I am convinced, for instance, that Plato did not write the letters ascribed to him. But I can assume that he did write them and then ask myself how to reconcile their contents with those of the *Dialogues*. All arguments from style, from the implausibility of the incidents related in them, from the nonsense to be found in some of them, can be explained away and have been explained away by those historians who need the letters for purposes of their own. My ruminations are certainly to be called "thinking," though the problems are not taken seriously by me except for self-education or possibly masochism. I shall nevertheless act as if they were problems which I myself had discovered and which I felt impelled to solve. I can ask myself why if Plato went to Syracuse, there was no hint of it in the *Dialogues* or in Aristotle. I can also ask myself why he continually uses phrases from his other writings which are appropriate in them and inappropriate in the letters. I can again ask myself why one accepts these letters as genuine and not the letters of Anacharsis or Diogenes or Socrates? Or, to take another example, I can raise the question of what Gassendi and after him LaFontaine meant by speaking of the soul as "the flower of matter," or of what Kierkegaard meant by his interpretation of the story of Abraham, or of what Locke meant by "powers." Such questions are admittedly of no practical interest in the ordinary sense of "practical." But they are still questions, and I confess to being unable to understand them other than as what I have called a deviation from the rule. I must already have made up my mind—or have had it made up for me by others—about Plato's biography or his style or his intelligence or the authentic corpus, before I can consider the authenticity of the letters. I must have some idea of what "flower" usually means before I can question its meaning in the phrase "flower of matter." I shall wonder whether Gassendi is using the term in the botanical or the chemical sense or in some allegorical sense before I can wonder about the meaning of the phrase, and if I assume that he was using it in one of these senses, I have either settled the matter or detected some inconsistency between that sense and his use of the term.

But even if we grant that all thinking is the raising and answering of questions and that all questions arise out of observed deviations from the rule, we also know that human beings have a gift for overlooking deviations as unimportant, even when they see them. That we all neglect negative instances is an old story, but what is not so old is the question of why we do not accept all deviations as right and proper, requiring no explanation. Why do we not simply accept the world as a mass of heterogeneous and disordered things? One answer to this is that we could not do so even if we wished to. For our language, our perceptual habits, our need for action, all order the world of experience and are effective only if that world is amenable to ordering. We are suspended, as it were, between an alien environment which, as far as we know, does not share our own nature, and our judgments about that environment. As we have insisted throughout this book, we expect certain events to recur and rely on their recurrence. We are in a constant state of revising our judgments about our surroundings, sometimes only to a slight extent, sometimes very greatly. Theoretically we might ask why there are any deviations, but that would seem to presuppose that stability is what ought to be and change a defect in the natural order. There are, as far as I know, no *a priori* limits to inquiry and yet, if intellectual satisfaction were an animal need, like the satisfaction of hunger, there would soon be reached a point of diminishing returns. Historically at any rate a man is satisfied when fatigue sets in, when he has no further information at his disposal, when he has reached what he will call the facts. One can stop one's inquiries where one will and we know, if we know anything about the history of thought, that some of us stop almost at the point where others begin.

Now if the facts are simply what we believe, they may be simply the solidification of our beliefs. A comparative study of science or, for that matter, the history of a given science is eloquent testimony to our ability to find facts where we need them. Facts, in the sense of brute things cut off from human interests, are far from being univalent. It is their relevance to judgment which counts. If we believe that the earth is round, then the experience of seeing the tops of the masts of a ship coming over the horizon before the sails and the hull is relevant to that belief. But it requires no long series of meditations to realize that experience cut off from everything else might be relevant to a variety of beliefs. Even a solipsist could enjoy it, and I doubt whether one who believed in a flat earth would even notice it. Rainbows, I imagine, have been noticed for centuries, and yet their appearance was not evidence of the decomposition of white light before Newton. But we have twanged that string too frequently in these lectures to continue, and I think it may be granted that a given sensory perception may be relevant to a number of propositions. Consequently there is no one-to-one correspondence which can be set up between such experiences and statements. We also know that other people, both in the past and in the present, have got along in their vital concerns without much in the way of science and philosophy. This is true not only of other societies but of our own. An examination of contemporary urban society would undoubtedly show an intellectual stratification running from the most barbarous superstitions to the most refined rationalism. Our need for intellectual satisfaction seems to vary greatly, and the odd thing is that those who find it easily are none the worse off as far as their practical needs are concerned. Consequently a simple pragmatic epistemology will not work. For if truth is to be tested by its value in the struggle for life, then we need very little to survive. If this were not the case, the race would have died out before the dawn of civilization. I see no reason to believe that the great scientists and philosophers have met the challenge of the environment any better than the ignoramuses; they have been no healthier, no more successful economically, no longer-lived. Rough and ready lessons gleaned from our own and our parents' experience will guide us well enough if survival is all that is needed. And I am confident that even the early pragmatists would have admitted this, if pressed. For few men had the intellectual curiosity of James and Dewey and both went out of their way to raise problems which no biological needs could justify.

Moreover, if experience were both the source and the termination of knowledge, how could we explain the tremendous differences which exist in the knowledge of different people? Most men have similar sensory equipment, see the same colors, hear the same sounds, smell the same odors. The variations in sensory acuity are real, and they raise important problems. But they are not so great as to explain the difference between a Plato and a Diogenes of Sinope, a Plotinus and an Iamblichus, a Descartes and a Garasse, a Pasteur and a Bastian. The quantity of perceptual experience could not explain why Galileo or Newton knew more than their contemporaries, for surely they cannot be supposed to have amassed more percepts than their contemporaries. In fact, many of our most productive scholars have been less given to collecting percepts than their fellows.

Nor can we assume that knowledge is a precipitate from perceptual experience forming itself automatically according to laws like those of the association of ideas. For in that case, why do not these laws show up in all men's experience, rather than in that of a few? One of the reasons why the associationist theory was abandoned was because it showed that almost any two ideas could be associated, and it gave us minds which were simply a hodge-podge of elementary data. But any supposed law which stated the formation of propositions out of such elementary data would have been in the same position. It could not have explained either curiosity, questioning, judgment, or inference. For though we might say that curiosity was an effect of attention and attention varied with the intensity of an experience, as was common amongst Tichenerians, we know only too well that some knowledge, and not the least important, comes to us from paying attention to obscure details which have to be looked for and do not force themselves upon our notice. Again, to raise a question is the result of observing a deviation from the rule, as we have said, but everyone does not observe such deviations even when they are there before him. What is a prerequisite for any knowledge is a kind of wonder, an active curiosity, a willingness to see that all is not going according to rule, and though it is obvious that this could not occur without experience in the traditional sense of that word, it is also obvious that experience alone will not explain its occurrence.

Now one of the outstanding characteristics of experience, considered as a whole and not merely as sensory data, is conflict. The conflict is not between two percepts nor between two ideas, but between the ideas which we have already formed about our world and experiences which may or may not be perceptual.[1] In

---

[1] Cf. Einstein in the autobiographical notes to the Schilpp volume, p. 8. "Es ist mir nicht zweifelhaft, dass unser Denken zum groessten Teil ohne Verwendung

ordinary language this may be phrased simply as the failure of our expectations to be fulfilled. Such expectations need have nothing to do with the world of science. One is as often deceived by one's friends as by the material world. One is disappointed by works of art, pictures, poems, musical compositions, about which preliminary judgments have been made which are not justified. The logical rule that no amount of experience can prove a universal affirmative proposition, whereas one experience can disprove it, gives away the secret. Experience is the corrective of ideas.

Far from returning to experience for strength and support, the scientist and the philosopher flee from experience, escape from it into a world of order. When experience terminates a judgment, it does so by disproving it, for the conviction of error is the only conviction which is final. Confirmation may be comforting, but it is an endless process, and even when each new bit of experience fits into the pattern, there is always the likelihood that the next bit will not. Sooner or later the edifice collapses because sooner or later the order which one is seeking to universalize loses all meaning. This is logically inevitable and historically exemplified. The fact that no monistic philosopher, whether his monism was substantialistic or structuralistic, has ever succeeded, is simply corroboration of this point. But we can understand why his philosophy failed when we realize that whatever order he is trying to impose on the universe is found only in part of the universe and that when it is extended beyond its proper domain, the symbols in terms of which it is expressed become metaphors. Thus a materialism of any kind, whether it asserts that all things are made of matter or operate according to the laws of matter—two pretty vague assertions—is taking a concept which has literal meaning only, let us say, in physics and expanding it to cover

---

von Zeichen (Worte) vor sich geht und dazu noch weitgehend unbewusst. Denn wie sollten wir sonst manchmal dazu kommen, uns über ein Erlebnis ganz spontan zu "wundern"? Dies "sich wundern" scheint dann aufzutreten, wenn ein Erlebnis mit einer in uns hinreichend fixierten Begriffswelt in Konflikt kommt. Wenn solcher Konflikt hart und intensiv erlebt wird dann wirkt er in entscheidender Weise zurueck auf unsere Gedankenwelt. Die Entwicklung dieser Gedankenwelt ist in gewissem Sinn eine beständige Flucht aus dem "Wunder."

biology, psychology, sociology, history, aesthetics, ethics, and theology. Analogous remarks could be made about idealism.[2] My point then is not that no materialist or idealist has as yet succeeded in his program, but that by the very nature of the case he could not succeed. Literally "matter" means something special, something which, let us say, physicists and chemists study. Our ideas about its nature are of course extremely crude if we are not physicists or chemists. But crude or refined, they are judgments made about certain specific problems, not about the whole universe. The most expert physicist, if he speaks of matter, does so to differentiate it from other things he knows about or has heard about. What he has to say may be expressed in the form of equations or in the form of verbal sentences. That is of no importance here. But the only reason why he is able to write the equations or sentences is that they are true of some things and not of others. Regardless of the ultimate source of his judgments in experience, he has escaped from experience into a conceptual world. That world has given him the order which he wants. It is not an order unexemplified; quite the contrary. But it is never exemplified in its purity.

Put differently, my thesis is that man's primary cognitive experience is that of error. His infancy and babyhood have already stored up for him a set of habits which are, so to speak, his funded capital. Acting upon what he knows—or believes— he makes a mistake. This mistake need not be stumbling on a flight of steps or playing a false note on a piano keyboard, though both are good, if somewhat banal, instances of mistakes. It may be the failure of experience to verify an idea. The order of nature turns out to be different from what he had expected. But this order shows itself at times on paper, as when one discovers that his mathematical reasoning is wrong. It does not have to be a melodramatic incident in what is usually called "life."[3]

---

2 I have purposely kept these names as vague as possible.

3 The distinction between life and what goes on in a man's life seems to me to cause more trouble than it is worth. A man's life includes his thinking and in fact, most of his conscious life is given over to some form of thought. How absurd it would be to separate Einstein's life from his work, or Plato's or Descartes's or any-

Wherever there is a conflict between what one knows and what one finds, one is confronted by error. Experience is of error, not of truth. Truth is a property of ideas, judgments, propositions, not of experience. For how could an experience be either true or false? Experience either corroborates or disproves our judgments, but in itself it just is there. A pain, for instance, may be a symptom of a disease, but as a pain it says nothing. It is the physicians who know how to interpret the symptoms, not the patient. The same is true of any experience. Until it has been absorbed into a set of judgments, it is without meaning.

No experience therefore is in itself erroneous; it is we who are in error. Even illusions, as the New Realists liked to point out, existed as occurrences which obeyed the law. *We* then are mistaken and our cognitive mistakes usually take the form of trying to fit a particular into a pattern of universals. This is certainly the case when we make simple judgments of identification. The conflict here is between what the universal law says the particular exemplification ought to be and what the particular exemplification actually is. If all our experience confirmed all our ideas, we should settle down into a routine in which there would be no such thing as curiosity or wonder. As Justice Holmes once said when discussing experimentation in the law,

> One begins with a search for a general point of view. After a time he finds one, and then for a while he is absorbed in testing it, in trying to satisfy himself whether it is true. But after many experiments or investigations all have come out one way, and his theory is confirmed and settled in his mind, he knows in advance that the next case will be but another verification, and the stimulus of anxious curiosity is gone.[4]

Applied to the general run of mankind the lesson is quite as telling. When the stimulus of anxious curiosity is gone, one will

---

one's who has left us a record of his interests. It may be true, though far from credible, that a person could lead a life in which thought played no part, but it is likely that in such lives the thoughts of others have been the guiding force. Art and life, science and life, philosophy and life are about as reasonable a dichotomy as practice and theory. The fact that one's thinking may be absorbed into one's daily routine and drop below the level of consciousness should not mislead the philosopher into maintaining that it was never there.

[4] From *Collected Legal Papers*, p. 246.

accept whatever happens as the truth. For there is no compulsion within us forcing us to correct our routine. The technique of resignation may be learned early in life.

Just as error may be thought of as the particular seen against the background of the general, so evil may be thought of as the outcome of the individual's will against a background of a general will, the will of God, the will of society, or simply tradition. Our moral conflicts are always a conflict of desires and sometimes the conflict is that between the desire of the moment and the habitual desires of the past. The good is what we hope for; evil is what we are trying to escape from. And the judgment that something is good or evil may be either spontaneous inclination and aversion or the attitudes which are inculcated in us by others. It is no wonder that certain philosophers have insisted on the conflict between what ought to be and what is, for what is, though it may be by chance harmonious with what ought to be, usually is not. In fact, one might plausibly argue with Fichte and Vacherot that the two are never coincidental, since one cannot strive for that which one possesses.[5] Our moral education proceeds by denial, not by affirmation. We discover in various ways that our desires are far from being those of which the laws approve, and we turn away from our desires. It is in fact ironical that ethicists who emphasize most heavily the universal nature of all standards of goodness, also insist upon the fact that these standards are to be found in a world of ideals, not in the world of existence. For they are only too aware of the hard fight which is continually going on between desire and its fulfillment.

The analogy between moral and aesthetic values is striking. Ugliness like evil is the newly given which stubbornly resists integration into an aesthetic system. Whether the system in question is simply what we habitually like or an intellectual system of approbation, our problem is to find a place in it for what we encounter in experience. One does not have to deny that children are attracted to certain colors and shapes, to certain patterns of

---

[5] One could of course strive to retain it when threatened with its loss, or when one thinks it may be lost.

sounds, as if the attraction were inevitable, to see this point. On the contrary, if a child finds red pleasant and wants to be surrounded by red things, then when he comes upon green, he will find it unpleasant. The aesthetic problem, however, is seldom so simple. For it usually arises when an individual is confronted by a work of art, not a color or sound. The ugliness of a work of art will be found to be in direct proportion to its unfamiliarity. I do not mean that if one has never seen the *Winged Victory,* one will necessarily find it ugly. The *Winged Victory* is enough like other familiar pieces of sculpture to cause no shock of dismay. But if one has never seen sculpture like, for instance, that of Henry Moore, one will be at first repelled. One has nothing to compare it with; one automatically refers it back to previous experiences of sculpture for some analogue and finds none; it is a break with the personal tradition. Every student of the history of taste must have been impressed by the habit which people have of first expressing their associations when they encounter a novel work of art. "It looks like . . .;" "It makes me think of . . .;" "It sounds like . . .;" and the orientation of comparison naturally is something previously experienced which is unpleasant. Thus it may be said that we are looking for harmony and find discord. We want a continuity of affective experience, and we encounter gaps and shocks. That may be why so many writers on aesthetic subjects have spilled their ink to justify ideal beauty, the essence of beauty, the beauty which is eternal, which is beyond the sensible world. It is not merely that no particular beautiful object meets the demands of the ideal, but that the confrontation with the real, in the sense of the empirically given, is the experience of ugliness unless one can absorb it into the past. Have we not all noticed the struggle which aesthetic innovators have to wage to overcome the downright horror, the revulsion, which the majority feels on meeting their works of art? Do we not all know the pleasure which people experience when they meet the familiar? The break which the Impressionists made with pictorial tradition no longer seems drastic to most of us. Yet one has but to read the contemporary critics to appreciate how strongly they felt about that break.

What we believe then is the facts; what we desire is the good; what we are used to is the beautiful. And yet much of the energy of philosophers is spent on dissuading men from this primary dogma. For all knowledge is a systematization of experience by its very nature and for that reason alone an evasion of experience. This does not, let us repeat, in any way preclude coming upon a scene or a person or anything else and finding it beautiful, however that term may be defined. On the contrary, the whole tenor of these lectures has been to insist that the human being carries his past along with him, and that the past, as far as it is effective in influencing judgment, may be as powerful as the present, though one is not necessarily conscious of it. If the so-called aesthetic experience is immediate, that in no way proves that its aesthetic qualities are not the result of an interaction between whatever is "out there" and one's total experience. One does not have to explore the history of taste to see the variety of aesthetic experience; one has only to think of the women whom one's fellowmen have found beautiful. Unfortunately this sort of evidence has been avoided by writers on aesthetics, though it is surely much easier to interpret than the evidence embedded in works of art. Similarly in the sphere of morals; it is not impossible to come across an act which one is willing to judge good without further reflection. But that is only because it is an act which one can catalogue with other acts already known to be good. No human act is likely to be completely novel, for the number of gestures which a man can make is limited. Nor is any moral problem likely to be completely different from all others. But nevertheless every attempt to classify moral problems and acts by the categories of virtues and vices has turned out to be a failure, as the books on moral casuistry abundantly prove.

What the inquiring mind hopes for is an orderly world in which there is neither error nor evil nor ugliness. This can be only the world of ideas whether philosophic or scientific. What it acquires is at most a consistent set of theorems, distilled from our judgments, and though these theorems are by general consent never entirely exemplified, we have the extraordinary faculty of living within their frontiers as if they constituted a world by themselves. This may be called the Intelligible World, or the *Denkwelt* of Einstein, or just philosophy or science; whatever it is called, it is far from being the world of things, perceptions, or individuals. That world is chaotic and its role, as we have said, is to disprove our generalizations, not to prove them. In what sense either can be called a world is doubtful. For even if we could set up a universal system of theorems, which by definition would be internally consistent, we have every reason to believe that alternative systems could also be constituted.

Such a conclusion will seem defeatist, indeed nihilistic, to most of our contemporaries. But it is actually closer to the lessons of experience than more reassuring philosophies. For experience does teach us something, if only by corrective measures. It at least can teach us that we are wrong. We are then in a position of holding certain beliefs as tentative, or as hypothetical, if that term is preferable. Now, as we have insisted, no single person ever learns by himself. He is taught not only by his experience but also by other people. He begins his own discoveries after indoctrination, not before. The indoctrination proceeds by learning a language in which both vocabulary and syntax are given to him, not invented by him. It also proceeds from a pretty well ritualized set of conditions out of which he emerges, let us say, when he goes to school, and this set of conditions establishes an order upon which he thinks he can rely. The terror which he feels on being plunged into a new environment, for instance that of a school, arises from his inability to find his old expectations justified in the new environment. Some of us can recall vividly what this terror was like; its intensity probably varies with the novelty of the new environment. The boy becomes keenly aware that all children are not like him: they talk differently, wear different clothes, eat different things, and in short are not zealous in satisfying his desires. He also becomes keenly aware that all adults are not like his parents. The sharp differences between his teachers and his mother and father present him with another dramatic clash between his routine and his new problems. When he awakes to the fact that his parents are neither omniscient nor omnipotent, the blow is shattering. From then on he is brought face to face with a series of experiences for which he cannot be prepared, and it is through them that he learns whatever he is going to learn. He may retreat before them, refuse to acknowledge them, withdraw into himself or his home. Or he may of course do just the opposite and meet them head on and conquer them. These events would seem, at least to the author of these words, characteristic of a normal life, though things may have changed in the direction of smoothing over the transitions.

When philosophers talk about adjustment to the environment, they sometimes seem to be saying that one should accept the environment as it is, as if learning were resignation. We can of course reach a point of such complete submission that we shall wonder at nothing. This is a kind of intellectual quietism the result of which is peace combined with ignorance. No mind so submissive ever learned much of anything other than a *modus vivendi*. The scientists and the philosophers—and I should add the artists for my own part—have been the dissatisfied men, the curious men, the unadjusted men, the men who, however limited in their interests, within their limits refused to accept disorder. If the daily business of living were all that was at stake, there would be no need for the great critics, for after all the scientists and philosophers are critics. They are judges, trying to impose upon the world a set of standards which are rules establishing order. And their sets of standards are always what ought to be and never are. They are confronted with diversity; they seek homogeneity. They are confronted with multiplicity; they seek unity. They are confronted with change; they seek the immutable. They are confronted with probability; they seek certainty. But all these pursuits are by their very nature endless, and their continuation no more brings about a termination of inquiry than carrying out a repeating decimal will end in anything other than exhaustion. Intellectual satisfaction may be found in several ways: by asking questions whose answers are immediately given; by stopping one's inquiry sooner rather than later; or by not seeing the problem at all. All these ways have been tried. A man may suddenly see the Northern Lights on a winter evening. He may ask himself what they are. His answers may be a shrug of the shoulders, an assertion that the sky is streaked with pale green and yellow flashes, an assignment of the name *Aurora Borealis,* the effect of streams of electrified particles emanating from the sun, a sign of divine wrath, or any one of a number of other things. It is only the ritualization of inquiry and response which makes one or the other of such responses acceptable. If the Northern Lights are an effect of the streams of electric particles emanating from the sun, that answer can obviously be given only by people who have either found it out for themselves or who have read about it in a book or heard about it in school. If certain of these responses are not even mentioned in sophisticated circles, it is because the general context in which they arise has been rejected. Thus we no longer think of comets as portents of disaster. But a man who believed in certain traditional theological doctrines might well cling to such an interpretation and justly so. He might reasonably ask why God should upset the usual appearance of the heavens and send a comet blazing across them. To answer that comets appear and reappear in calculable cycles would be no satisfaction to such a person, for the kind of reason he would be looking for would be of an entirely different sort. His world would not be disorderly, but the order would be that of divine purposes in a world created for man. Even if he knew that comets had calculable orbits, he would still want to know why God assigned these orbits to them. When one engages in criticism of such a technique of satisfying curiosity, one should first ask why one type of order is better than another.

The kind of answer which will be given to this question will depend first on whether one thinks of intellectual satisfaction as a terminal or an instrumental value. If it is the former, then the investigator knows best whether he has reached his goal or not. If the latter, one must then ask what further end is to be served by knowledge. Various answers have been given to this question, running from knowledge as evidence for natural theology to knowledge as a means of survival in the struggle for existence. One of the most famous is incorporated in Bacon's, "Knowledge is power." By power, he may well have been thinking of power over the physical universe, power to control it and make it satisfy our wants. Another is the almost equally famous, "Knowledge exists for prediction and control." Another is the belief that knowledge is essentially a matter of aesthetic elegance, that a well-rounded theory satisfies our sense of beauty. Another might well be that since man is a rational animal, the satisfaction of his rational needs is one of his principal aims. It is likely that all such theories are overtly or occultly based upon a theory of truth.

As long as knowledge was thought of as an absorption of fact from the external world rather than as the integration of beliefs into a consistent system, Aristotle's conception of the truth would do as well as any other.[6] For to say simply, "The truth is a statement of that which is, the false of that which is not," seems clear and indeed indisputable. But as soon as one sees that it is statements—assertions—which are true and false, and that statements are made by human beings, and that human experiences are always articulated within a framework of categories, syntactical rules, methods of observation, and as a result of habit or learned procedures, the matter loses its simplicity. For now we observe that the most indubitable assertions are merely those which we do not doubt, for it goes without saying that we are talking here exclusively of judgments of fact. But such judgments are usually immediately made upon the presentation of a perceptual datum. This would be a good way out of our difficulty, if we did not know that perceptual data are themselves determined by psychical causes as well as by physical. If expectation, to

---

[6] Especially as given in *Metaphysics*, Theta 10.

mention only one of these causes, can influence what we perceive, then the truth of any perceptual judgment could not be a simple reflection of impersonal, objective, physical, or otherwise non-human factors. If one raises the question of why most people agree about what they see or hear, the answer will be that they are all trained to see or hear the same things, that is, to look for them. When one is asked, "What is that?" a dozen or more answers could be given, all of which could be accepted as true, even when a single perceptual datum is before one. That a dozen or more answers are not given can be explained only on the assumption that the observers know beforehand what kind of answer is expected. Hence there is supposed to be a kind of relevance to the question asked in the appropriate answer. But if we are right in defining relevance as a relation between two assertions—though we grant that some assertions may be made in abbreviated form[7]—then all truths are discovered in systems of ideas or judgments or assertions and not in single statements. And this makes truth a matter of consistency.

If there were but one possible system of assertions descriptive of the universe, and if the system had been elaborated, then we might expect to be in potential possession of all truth. But if we make judgments about bits of experience and at most ex-trapolate what we know into fields which we do not know, then there is no reason to expect that there is any such thing as all truth or consequently that we can be in even potential possession of it. Since knowledge is always a correction of experience, a correction made by simplification, purification, abstraction, anal-ogy, and so on, it is likely that the sciences will be found to be less and less true to perceptual fact as they develop. Each of us, whether we are aware of it or not has a protophilosophy con-sisting of basic metaphors, rules of organization, correct symbolic usage, methodological principles, and the like. The control which Nature or the world or whatever we want to call the subject-matter of knowledge exercises upon our judgments about it,

---

[7] As in, "What is that?"; answer: "A cat."

appears, we have said, when judgments fail to be corroborated, not when they are corroborated. This is borne out by what we have already tried to make clear in previous chapters of this book. If the relation of implication were symmetrical, this would not be the case; but it is not symmetrical.

I see then no hope for any kind of monism. Nor do I see any way of limiting the kinds of being which may be found to two or three. As long as logical gaps exist—and they do exist—they will be bridged only by neglecting them, in the sense of stating the conditions under which differences will be found. Thus we can state the conditions under which a single kind of cause—let us say light rays—will be seen as different colors. But the existence of chromatic differences is not eliminated by that technique. In fact it is the experience of seeing different colors which leads the physicist to seek for statable causes or conditions of those differences. The colors themselves are no more reduced to light rays than the light rays are diversified into colors. This is elementary. If we had some means of knowing the limitations of categorizing, we might then say that there were as many kinds of being as there are categories. Not only do we not know this, but we do know that all thinking to date has had to employ several categories. The mystic alone, by keeping silent or by uttering paradoxes, has escaped this. But if there is one thing which philosophy is not, it is silence.

Experience could not terminate inquiry unless it were capable of being broken up into atomic parts which could be put into one-to-one correspondence with a set of propositions, and if these propositions were uniquely expressive of the atomic experiences. This procedure has been tried and has admittedly failed. If a given perceptual datum can answer a variety of questions, and it looks as if it could, then experience, as the mosaic of percepts, is far from being univalent in "meaning." Anyone with normal eyesight can see what a physicist sees in a cloud chamber, but only certain persons can tell what it means. What is seen in a cloud chamber is either meaningless or a source of wonder to the uninitiate. But epistemologically the situation is no different from that in which the most ordinary perceptual experiences are enjoyed. In the one case we do not have the training to realize what is before us, in the other we do. The cloud chamber is of course an artefact, made to corroborate certain physical theories. And though our sense-organs are not artefacts, the controls by which we correct their reports are set up by us in order to help us arrive at a consistent set of propositions. Our ability to do away with time, to conceive of things rather than changing processes, to correlate percepts with their supposed material stimuli, to eradicate qualitative diversity by attributing it to sub-stantial unity, to classify, to identify, who can deny that these processes are a manipulation of raw experience? Why, moreover, should we imagine that such a manipulation is a superhuman photograph of the world, as if, since we are made in the image of God, our vision of the world is identical with God's?

Instead of thinking of funded knowledge after the model of an effect produced on a passive cause, or as a reaction to material stimuli, it might work out better to think of it as a kind of homeostasis, to use Cannon's term, in which the past experiences of the individual, including his experiences with other people, are kept in a state of equilibrium.[8] A homeostatic process is self-adjusting and nevertheless dependent on air and food for its continuance. Similarly the human mind, unless it is disturbed, will maintain a balance between the habitual and the problematic, will attend only to what it needs to observe, and yet will be sensitive to just those features of experience which may endanger that balance. Just as some bodies have less wisdom than others, so do some minds, but if one consider each individual by himself, one will be able to see his devices for maintaining an even keel. Such devices are most clearly manifested at the point at which he says that his problem is solved, his curiosity satisfied. This metaphor, like all metaphors, breaks down. It breaks down when one realizes that no body has to worry about what other bodies are up to; the sickness of my neighbor does not induce

---

[8] See W. B. Cannon; *The Wisdom of the Body*, N.Y., 1932. In the last chapter of that book Cannon himself extends the concept to fields beyond physiology.

sickness in me unless my sympathies are aroused to the point where I fall victim to a psychosomatic disturbance.[9] But no mind is cut off from neighboring minds, and the influence of communication, argument, dialogue, in some fields, such as philosophy, is almost paramount. It is doubtful whether anyone who had not been already introduced to philosophy through random reading or conversation, would ever ask a philosophical question. For such questions are so remote from the business of daily life that they present no obstacles to a man until they are raised by others. Once they are raised, they then become of the greatest seriousness, and no apology is needed for trying to answer them. Their remoteness is no more evidence of their unimportance than the remoteness of the atomic nucleus is evidence for the unimportance of nuclear physics. One did not have to know nuclear physics before 1946 in order to survive, as is proved by the fact that the race did survive up to that date in general ignorance of it. Now its applications have given us reason to think that all of us had better know at least the general principles of that subject. And it is interesting to see how rapidly popularizations of this and other scientific subjects have been provided to satisfy our curiosity. This is not attributable to our collective fear of being exterminated—at least I see no reason to believe that it need be—but simply to the fact that most social groups are talking about such things. The talk is random and usually ill informed, but that is of small importance. Hearing random and ill-informed speech, we feel impelled to clarify it and organize it.

If this makes sense, then we have to distinguish between the truth of acquired knowledge and the truth of knowledge which is in the process of being acquired. Our acquired knowledge, what we already believe, is funded and exists in a state of greater or less consistency. Ideally we should like to make it entirely consistent, but few of us are able to, even if it can be done. But knowledge in the process of being acquired is always tentatively held, and one proceeds step by step, not verifying each bit by

---

[9] Or, obviously, unless he has a contagious disease.

observation, but first determining what step to take by past experience and all the rituals of learning, and then verifying it. If there were such an activity as random curiosity, this would be absurd, and knowledge as the raising and answering of questions would be untenable. But since random curiosity is curiosity of whose orientation we are unaware, as we are unaware of most of our motives, all speculation may be seen as guided. In that case we shall call those answers true which maintain our intellectual homeostasis, and the traditional correspondence with fact need not be invoked at all. For since direct observation of sensory data is the least important part of acquired knowledge, and is pretty shaky evidence for any hypothesis, the correspondence sought will turn out to be consistency with the ideas in which we already believe.

For note what is required to formulate any bit of knowledge. First a basic metaphor in terms of which it will be expressed: the metaphor of a substance with attributes, the metaphor of satisfying a purpose, the metaphor of an artisan making something, of a cause effecting something, of an order of some persistent sort, rules for classification. Second, a knowledge of the categories in terms of which the information will be expressed. Third, a knowledge of what sort of evidence will be relevant to the inquiry. Fourth, a symbolism adequate to formulating the knowledge once acquired. No one could ever invent all these four sets of requirements, for after all he would have to do some thinking in order to invent them and that thinking itself would have to be formulated. Consequently, no matter how independent his spirit, he will have to rely on his past training for most of what he learns. Though the solution of a problem may flash into the mind of a person without his knowing how it arose, nevertheless he has always done a good bit of thinking, puzzling, wondering about it before the flash occurs. And after the flash occurs, the illumination must be expressed. He may invent a new vocabulary for its expression, but at some point he will have to explain to his interlocutors, real or imaginary, what the new vocabulary means and obviously can do that only in a vocabulary organized by a syntax which they will understand. Thus in spite of himself he will be utilizing old knowledge to illuminate new. Thus truth will be attested by consistency, but the consistency will be that of the newly acquired bit of information with that which is already acquired. It will not be that of an ideal system of theorems such as might be found in a completed formal science. The phrase, "a completed formal science," names nothing which actually can be found, as far as I know, but I suppose that one could imagine a set of theorems such that nothing more could be deduced from them. It would be valuable to discover whether any such system is logically possible, for if it is not, then inquiry is always also possible even in ideal situations. If it is possible, then one would have a model for a situation in which final, absolute, irrefragable truth would be found. The history of the sciences shows continual reworking of the basic concepts as well as new deductions. But it is granted that this process might be terminated at any time.[10]

Since we have frequently mentioned the influence of social groups on knowledge, it may be well to add a concluding note on that subject too. Besides the information which one acquires from one's fellows, we have to begin by absorbing their language, not only insofar as its vocabulary is concerned, but its syntax. What can be expressed and what cannot be expressed are in part determined by the fundamental categories of speech, and, what is more, there will always be a tendency to use the structure of a language as a mirror of the structure of existence. We have seen this in the insistence of philosophers on construing existence as a collection of things plus attributes externally related to one another. We have also seen that the active and passive voices of the verb provide another illustration, in the form of agents for all acts, which exist in separation from their acts. We cannot

---

10 This might not be true in "immediate inference" in Aristotelian logic, where beginning with a universal affirmative proposition and proceeding according to the rules, one returns to the original proposition. But needless to say, this is far from being typical of systematic reasoning and illustrates only one case of a very peculiar sort. It is more likely that by using Gödel's Theorem one could prove that no rule for completing a system could be framed.

prove that the thought is as it is because of the language or the language as it is because of the thinking, but a comparative study of syntax makes the former hypothesis the more plausible. But we also derive from social organizations some of our basic metaphors, such as the hierarchy, for here there is nothing in the non-living world which corresponds to it. The use of the hierarchy as the form of ontological systems has been common enough to make any further analysis of the idea unnecessary. One may say that such expressions as "God, the Invisible King," or even "Mary, Regina Coeli," are not to be taken literally, but when human beings behave as if God were really and not figuratively an absolute monarch, the thought expressed in the metaphors cannot be tossed aside as of only literary importance.[11] In fact, it seems probable, at least to me, that the notion of causality as production, creation, making, forcing something to become something else, is a concept whose origin lies in social organization. Our sense of values as transcending the confines of individual interest could not arise unless there were other people moving about whose criticism of our own desires could make itself felt. But similarly the notion of truth as something which is above the universe of individual experience and with which individual experience must make itself harmonious could hardly arise if the pressures of society were not compulsive. Then too since the increase in knowledge always comes about through dialogue, it is difficult to understand the history of ideas unless we take into account the contradictions to our own ideas which the ideas of others present. If we lived lives such that the people whom we met always agreed with us, it would be next to impossible for us ever to change our minds about anything, unless there were some law in accordance with which our knowledge grew. Finally we shall only mention the concept of minds as little societies in which there is conflict between the members and a program of reconciliation. The passions versus the reason, the senses versus the reason, the "lower" parts of the soul versus

---

[11] Literary importance is certainly important, but it is irrelevant to the subject which I am mentioning here.

the "higher," the tripartite division of the soul into senses, will, and reason, in fact, the whole faculty psychology, are examples of how the image of a social group is imposed upon the psychical side of our natures.

But over and beyond all this is the curious factor known as common sense, vague as that concept is. We have frequently mentioned in these lectures how extraordinary it is that even when philosophers do not know that they are right, they do seem to know when they are wrong, though their conclusions may appear to follow logically from their premises. The escape from solipsism is the standard example of this, an example the more telling since the people who land in solipsism begin with what look to them like indubitable premises. If their conclusions leave them so desperate that they have to resort to animal faith, common sense, or plain discomfort in order to untangle themselves, there is certainly a non-logical factor at work here, impelling them onward. They cannot justify their belief that there is something behind their backs, that there are other people who have minds, to say nothing of the other problems which they feel concerned to answer. Yet they raise such questions as if the questions themselves emerged from the conclusions at which they have been stopped. Why do these questions arise? Surely not from the conclusions. If a man begins with true premises and commits no formal fallacies, he ought to feel bound to accept his conclusions. But he does not so feel. It is no more absurd from the logical point of view to believe that oneself alone exists at the present moment than it is to believe that the sun is stationary and the earth in motion. Both ideas conflict equally with common sense and with straightforward observation. Yet we reject one and accept the other.

Unless knowledge is a social affair, I confess to seeing no exit from this type of maze. Common sense is not the sense which all people inherently possess in common; it is the sense which is instilled in one during infancy and babyhood, become habitual, and hence both immediately grasped and compulsive. Instilling ideas in other people is one of the primary enterprises of social groups, and unless we accept this as fundamental to any epistemology, we shall never understand the orientation of thinking, by which I mean here, the perception of a problematic situation. We have forced upon us from babyhood the consciousness of ourselves as different from others, and this consciousness is surely not just seeing or hearing other people. We see and hear ourselves too and yet make no distinction between our bodies, our voices, our looks and ourselves. What is more pathetic even in adults than their identification of themselves with their bodies? It is seen even in the care which we have in the Occident for the dead. But we do not identify ourselves with other people's bodies any more than we do with the material objects which furnish our houses. The other people by the commands which they give us, the frustrations of our desires which they erect before us, the occasional praise which they bestow upon us, their care for us as well as their neglect of us, in short, all the inter-relations between Us and Them rub into us at a very early age the feeling that They are there. Perceptually they are more complex and more ubiquitous than other things, but that is simply a complication which we would not be forced to consider seriously. Probably the most poignant evidence of the falsity of such a pseudo-doctrine as solipsism is the incredulity of others.

It is interesting to note, as we have remarked earlier in these lectures, that we cannot even state such a doctrine without dragging in the existence of others. For when we say, "I alone exist," the pronoun and the adjective which are necessary to state the case become meaningless unless We can be distinguished from Them. Now one can deduce nothing from our linguistic shortcomings, except possibly that language is incapable of expressing certain thoughts. But I have another point to make of it. And that is the paradox that living in social groups itself is needed if the denial of the existence of the others is to arise. This is not a logical but a psychological datum, or, if one prefer, it may be called a dialectical problem. We are caught in a position of not being able to assert our exclusive existence without also assuming the existence of others. But if we accept their existence, it is not on the evidence of the perceptions which we have of them. Would it not then be better to begin by putting perception in its proper place as that which we attempt to organize in harmony with the demands of society? That permits the others to put questions to us as we do to them and the whole enterprise of knowledge becomes a social affair. In that case there is the more reason to believe, I think, in the general thesis of these lectures, that is, in the human mind as an inquirer than in the human mind as a contemplative instrument. Certainty in that case is reduced to the level of social agreement, and we are back in the position of being confronted by error, evil, and ugliness, and all their progeny, and trying to eradicate them. This gives us a world in which frustration and tragedy are possible and there are no guarantees of terrestrial salvation.

SUPPLEMENTARY NOTES

1. *Metaphorical and Literal Statements*

I have referred to metaphorical statements so frequently in these lectures, that readers must have asked what a literal statement would be. My conclusion is that a literal statement is one whose figurative sense has been lost.

Metaphors are disguised comparisons in which the analogy involved has been suppressed. Instead of saying that S is like P, we say that S is P. This has been known since books on rhetoric were first written in Greece. That is, if an example is needed, one can either say that a woman's eyes are like twin stars or are twins stars. I have been maintaining that the simplest judgments are metaphorical in the sense that they all are based upon analogies or comparisons, though it goes without saying that the original analogy which is the basis of the sentence may be forgotten.

The simplest kind of judgments would appear to be judgments of identification. Such judgments can never be more than classifications, if the predicate is a common noun or adjective. But to situate two existentially different things in the same class cannot be accomplished unless they are alike in some respect. The likeness may arise from our inability to discriminate between them. Such inability in turn may arise from the instruments of observation which we are using. It is always possible that a given instrument may not discriminate between two things which other instruments would distinguish. For a scientific example of this sort of situation, one may take the case of isotopes and isomeres. For a non-scientific example, one may take the case (1) of the difference between the sound of a bell and the look of a bell, (2) the color of an object seen in peripheral and in frontal vision, (3) an object seen in waking life and in a dream. The third example is particularly striking in that one says that he saw such and such a person in a dream as if the person were actually there, whereas it is obvious that the dream-person was simply very similar to the person seen in waking life; during the dream the dreamer was not able to distinguish between the two persons. Identity through time cannot be asserted on the basis of our incapacities. But if evidence were demanded for the identity of two appearances or two experiences, or two things, the only evidence which could be given would be our inability to see any differences between them. In other words, Leibniz's principle of the Identity of Indiscernibles interpreted in humanistic terms. In all probability a variety of tests would be demanded of a person who asserted that two apparently different things were the same or even of the same kind, but though that would make the identification more complicated, the principle would be the same. To simplify matters, we can omit mention of any changes in the instruments of observation, in the conditions of observation, and in the observer, though there are always some.

Sooner or later, then, one comes down to the conclusion that to say, "This is a P," is translatable into the sentence, "This looks like O, which is known to be a P," when O is the symbol for an individual object or experience or appearance, and P is the common noun, the name of a class.

The etymology of some of our most ordinary words shows their metaphorical origin. I open a school-boy's dictionary and I find, "aardvark," from two words meaning together an "earth-pig"; "aardwolf," an earth-wolf; "abandon," to bring under jurisdiction; "abash," out of astonishment (bah!); "abate," from *à* and *battre;* "abbot," from the Aramaic for "father;" and so it goes. Now no one using such words as these thinks of their original meaning nor needs to in order to use them correctly. Even when the etymological meaning is clear, as in words like "accost," "depend," or "geometry," the metaphor is lost, and the word has become literal. This process of literalization, to coin a repulsive neologism, is so ordinary that it seems otiose to dwell upon it. Any philologist could trace most of our ordinary words farther back than I have, and I daresay if we knew enough—and we do not—all our common nouns would be shown to be generalizations in various grammatical forms of a few primitive roots. Thus the root *ga* and its dialectical forms has given rise to a series of words in Greek meaning, earth, giant, man, courageous, chief or king, queen, woman, marriage, to be born, to beget, race, class *(genus)*, father, and so on.[1] The root *or,* from which comes the Greek verb "to mount upwards," gives rise to words meaning to become excited, to push, a mountain, a mule, Orestes, the wind from the mountains, instinct or desire, straight (as in a straight line), the dawn, a bird, and distance. This must not be taken as an assertion on my part that the history of language shows a steady differentiation of block meanings. On the contrary what early languages we know show more complication and discrimination than modern languages do, discrimination both in the names of things for which we use one name and in cases and tenses. All I am interested in saying here is that it is possible to have a word which is figurative and which loses its figurative meaning as time goes on.

Sometimes a proper name turns into a common noun, as in the word *Kodak* which was composed to name a camera—itself a figure of speech—invented by Eastman but which at least in French became the common noun for any small camera. In fact, the Eastman Kodak Company was pushed into writing an advertising slogan to the effect that, "If it isn't an Eastman, it isn't a Kodak." In the second World War the name Quisling became a synonym for a special kind of traitor. Sometimes the reverse seems to occur, as when we use the common noun, "god," as a proper noun, God. It is even possible that all common nouns derive from proper names, though no one knows whether that is so or not. Yet one sees children generalizing proper names, such as

---

[1] See the *Table des Racines* in M. A. Bailly; *Dictionnaire Grec-Français,* 15th ed., 1933.

their special names for their parents,[2] and applying them to all men and women for a brief period. Whatever the case may be, one sees an interesting example of how a common noun is used for very different things in our categories. We have undoubtedly what might be called experience of space and time, of things, of subjects and attributes. But the space which is experienced is far from being the unbounded space of the metaphysician. It is a space which has both a center and an horizon. The individual is at the center and the horizon varies in a manner with which we are all familiar. But the perceiver moves more or less freely through the air or water, and as he moves, the center and the horizon also move. This may or may not be the origin of our idea of unbounded space. In any event the space of which metaphysicians talk has no center and has no horizon. To describe that kind of space is to use terms which apply to perceived space only in a restricted sense. That is, the perceived space has dimensions but the dimensions must be plotted from the perceiver if one insists on maintaining its strictly empirical character. If we were to be empirical in our general metaphysics, we should have to set up some center and also some boundary. The purgation of the empirical limitations is necessary, especially if all observers are to be in the same spatial matrix, and no one can object to the purgation. But the most we can say about the two kinds of space is that one of them is described in metaphorical language.

But the same is true of time. As Lovejoy once said,[3] time is "the most indubitable fact of our experience." But experienced time is the individual's time and the past, present, and future as experiences have to be calculated from and within the individual's point of view. As experienced, change moves at different rates of speed. But to determine a rate we have to have some standard,

---

2 Everyone knows that "father," and "mother," "sister" and "brother" are really what might be called dialectical forms of original Indo-European words and are about the same in all Indo-European languages. Though there used to be great dispute over the Sanskrit origin of "mother" and "father" in *ma* and *pa*, it is more likely that the words mean nothing more than "Mother" and "Father;" "mamma," and "papa," are proper names, terms of address, though they may be used as common nouns by adults talking to babies.

3 In *Contemporary American Philosophy,* New York, 1930, Vol. II, p. 87.

and empirically all we can do is to have recourse to the pulse and to respiration. Moreover, time as experienced has gaps and is not a continuum. The stock examples of loss of consciousness, deep sleep, being so immersed in a book or piece of music that we lose track of the passage of time, are good enough to show such gaps. If time is abstracted from our individual experiences, a learned act will seem almost instantaneous, whereas one which is being learned will seem prolonged, though the two acts may be of the same kind. Finally experienced time is irreversible. But such traits are far from being the traits of the kind of time which a physicist uses in his equations or an historian in his reports of the past. If there is one character of experienced time which is above all not projected into non-empirical time, it is its gaps, though the differences in rate might—at least for some purposes— be a close second. Hence if the experience of temporal order is primitive, anything said about non-empirical time becomes inevitably metaphorical. And if non-empirical time is primitive, then what we say about empirical time is metaphorical. I suspect, but of course cannot say with certainty, that empirical time is primary and that the projection of our experience of passage into the world about us accounts for setting up a general temporal order. For there are certain areas where something like a temporal order is discussed where there is no reason to believe in any temporal order at all.

For instance, the notions of logical priority and posteriority must be derived from our processes of inferring consequences. That takes time. What again does it mean concretely to say that numbers are arranged in series of before and after except as a figure of speech? Counting to be sure takes time but no one any longer is so naive as to believe that the number series is logically derived from the act of counting. In the third place we have a good deal on record about the beginning and the end of the world. But the only sorts of things which we experience as having beginnings and ends are living beings and works of art. And even there the stuff, the matter, out of which they are made has no beginning nor end; it is the organization of the matter which begins and ends. First and final causes, to cite one more example, can be taken seriously only if they mean beginnings and ends, and yet there is no more reason to assert dogmatically that the world must have had a beginning than that it must not have had one.

But, though I am not anxious to spin out this matter too thinly, I should like to suggest that the difference between wholes or units, alternatives (the *entweder-oder*), and finally of things experienced and of things not experienced is so great that what is said about the one cannot be literally asserted of the other. I mean by this that true assertions made about experienced wholes cannot be made about non-experienced wholes in the same sense; that is, one of the two assertions may be true and the other false, and therefore cannot mean the same thing. If, for instance, we say that the parts of a table are its top, legs, and possibly sides, and also say that the parts of the number 12 are 3 and 4, or 2 and 6, or 1 and 12, or any other combination which is arithmetically possible, we are not using "parts" in the same sense. I mean, to take the case of alternatives, that when we say that we must choose to go either to the right or left, we do not mean the same thing by "or" as we do when we say that a proposition must be true or false. And I mean in the third place, that to speak of a stone as a thing is not the same as to speak of an electron as a thing. Many of our familiar philosophical puzzles arise out of our taking our metaphors literally, that is, expecting to be able to assert of one of the two terms that which can be asserted of the other.

There are many examples of such puzzles. Think of all the problems which have arisen over universalizing the notion of matter and form, or from considering time as a series of moments, like beads on a string, or from looking for a first cause of the universe, or asking why this, that, or the other occurred, or why there is something rather than nothing, or finally from using universal predicates. Here, I should think, the pragmatist comes into his own, for though he may not tell us how to answer problems arising from such considerations, he can induce us to ask how we would ever know whether the problems were answered satisfactorily or not. For though the meaning of a judgment may not be equivalent to the technique of verifying it, unless one knows how to verify a judgment, one will never know whether it means anything or nothing. I confess to an inability to see why an unanswerable question should be meaningless. It is not meaningless to ask what is the square of a circle. But by now it would be foolish to try once more to answer it.

My attitude towards the question of literal statements is in part attributable to my belief that each experience is an individual, dated and localized, event. What we say about it is determined not only by what is "there," in the form of a material stimulus, but also by what we are looking for, by our linguistic habits, by our education, by the demands of other people, by ourselves as complexes of memories and habits. To find a residual experience which will be qualitatively identical with a previous experience demands a simplification of a present experience. That simplification is made not merely because of external physical pressures, but for teleological reasons, or, if one will, for pragmatic reasons. But "pragmatic" must be taken in a very wide sense. These then are the psychological reasons for resorting to metaphor. And I conclude that every common noun and adjective, every universal, is metaphorical.

That metaphors can lose their figurative meaning I have asserted on evidence from the history of language. Languages are mainly collective instruments; only very few words are invented by individuals, and most syntax is a contribution to the speech of an individual by society. De Maistre and Bonald, Reid and his disciples may have been wrong in calling language the embodiment of common sense, but the fact remains that we can still read ancient literature and understand what it says for the most part, though we probably do not have the same affective experiences in reading it as people had who were contemporaneous with its authors. But none of this allows us to infer a universal and immutable meaning common to all speech nor a collective mind common to all human beings. Whether "father" comes from an Indo-European root meaning "to protect" or not, it has come to mean a definite person standing in a definite biological relationship to a child. When it is applied to a clergyman, to George Washington, or to Geoffrey Chaucer, (Father Brown, the Father of his Country, the Father of English poetry) it acquires a new metaphorical meaning. Such extensions and retractions of meaning are common enough to be taken seriously and, as far as I myself am concerned, they seem to me to explain in part why literal statements are, as I have asserted, metaphors which have lost their figurative sense.

2. *The Concept of Society*

Though I hope that the body of the lectures has made it clear that I do not believe in social minds, souls, or spirits, what I consider society to be may not be as clear as is necessary.

First, I am thinking of societies as made up of different individuals. These individuals have had parents and ancestors, and they also may have children. They learn from the former and teach the latter. The lessons concern language and the rituals of the tribe; the right way to behave on various occasions, manners of eating, dressing, and so on. Second, in a modern society there are also specialized groups, societies with certain purposes, such as formal education and religious ritual. Sometimes the two groups are interlocking, as in Roman Catholicism and some other religious organizations. The child is thus submitted to discipline by at least the following: his parents, his siblings, his schoolteachers, his schoolmates, his ecclesiastical authorities, if he is sent to a church and Sunday School, and of course the police. The instruction received from these various individuals may or may not be discordant, but in the United States it usually is. A youngster may come from a Protestant family, be sent to the public schools where he makes friends with Catholics and Jews, learns two standards of linguistic decency, that of the home and that of his schoolmates, and soon becomes aware of the necessity of keeping part of his interests and their satisfactions insulated from home and church. Or he may come from a Catholic or orthodox Jewish family and either go to church-schools or the public schools, in either of which cases a similar conflict will arise at an early age.

Third, in the lives of adults various other social groups will claim the allegiance of the individual: his business or profession, his clubs, his play, and again his church, if any. The purposes of these groups may again be discordant to a greater or less degree. That is, there is a theoretical possibility that the ethical standards of his religion will be harmonious with those of his business organization, but it is more likely that the slogan, "Business is business," will be invoked on many occasions as a recognition of the conflict between the two sets of standards. Hence it will be rare to find an adult who has the same criteria of right and wrong at home, in business, in church, in play, or even the same criteria of the beautiful and ugly. That is, an industrial magnate may build a thoroughly contemporary factory and live in an imitation Tudor house or a replica of a French château. Or he may be a financier who is pitiless in competitive dealings with his rivals and generous to his college, church, or municipal art museum. He is neither always conservative nor always radical, assuming that such terms are significant, but conservative in some areas and radical in others. This can only be explained by invoking the influence of the societies to which he belongs, for if he alone were responsible, the variation would be inexplicable.

Fourth, each of the social groups may vary in the mutability of its standards. The fact that an industry meets new conditions of production, just to take one item, and adjusts to them, does not mean that the directors of that industry will accept the latest innovations in the arts or will attempt to renovate the dogmas of their churches. In general it may be said, I think, that no society, whether organized for economic or recreational ends, will try to commit suicide. In some cases an economic group will continue to exist even when its products are obsolete, witness the horse-business. It is true that in such cases the product is likely to satisfy new wants, that is, though the horse will no longer be bought as a vehicle, it will become an object for sport. This is common enough to cause no surprise, since many of our *objets*

d'art are obsolete instruments. Sometimes a whole social group
or institution will be retained when its original purpose is lost.
Examples will occur to anyone who reflects upon the survival
of ancient institutions and traces the mutations of their purposes.
As words and other symbols change their meanings while out-
wardly remaining the same, so social groups may retain their
names and rituals while changing their purposes. The development of the various churches in the United States is a case in point.

When I say then that a value or a standard of value is imposed
upon the individual by society, I mean by other people organized
for the accomplishment of some purpose or other, and the purpose may be simply self-perpetuation. The loyalty of a given individual to his various societies will vary, and he may often have
to choose between which he will support. Such loyalty will be
called submission; disloyalty will be called rebellion or recalcitrancy. No one to date has ever come upon a society to which
all its members are submissive, no matter how clear the "pattern
of culture" may seem to the ethnologist. Moreover there will
always be a demand on the part of some social group to be
pre-eminent. Ultramontanism, for instance, was an overt and well-
justified attempt on the part of the Church to make itself supreme
in all societies. But sometimes a group may obtain power in an
occult fashion, even while allowing the traditional institutions of
government to appear to be paramount. When Ambassador
Girard maintained that sixty families ruled the United States, he
was referring to the real power exercised by the individuals concerned through their wealth and their industrial supremacy, not
to any recognized right which they might enjoy openly. The existence of the Emperors in Japan alongside the Shoguns was an
example of real power being exercised by one group openly while
it permitted another to wield ceremonial power. In Great Britain
the Throne as against Parliament is a case where the traditional
governors are retained as symbols, and the real governors are the
political descendants of men who seized power and increased it
bit by bit by continued efforts. The differences between the English
Parliament and the Shoguns are very great, but in this context

the differences are minimized. If kings rule by divine right, then Magna Carta was rebellion.

Behind all this there must be two desires at work, the desire for conformity and the desire for non-conformity. But each desire can be strengthened through education, and the power of each social group may vary in its efficacy. Thus the fact that a man belongs to a highly authoritative church to whose demands he conforms gladly, does not permit us to infer that he will conform to the demands of civic society. Even clergymen have been known to be criminals. Moreover, a member of a proscribed group, a gang, for instance, may display invincible loyalty to the gang and at the same time be a non-conformist in many other groups. The problem then becomes that of determining why an individual is submissive here and recalcitrant there. And in such problems the residual individual has the upper hand. Traitors, stool-pigeons, informers, rebels seem to exist in all groups, and so do loyalists and conformists. I should imagine, but have found no convincing information on this point, that each of us is disloyal to some group and loyal to others, though we should probably cover up our delinquency by using appropriate language to name our behavior.

In the cognitive field social pressures and standards are just as effective as in the Army or the Church. When a way of thinking, a method of verification, the acceptance of a set of premises becomes self-justified, the philosopher has reason to believe that ritual has taken the place of personal investigation. The body of these lectures, as well as other articles of mine, has emphasized the contribution of tradition to inquiry. It may determine what problems will be investigated and also how they will be investigated. Recourse will be had to self-evidence, common sense, intuition, the *lumen naturale,* faith, experience, even Revelation as bases of such beliefs. The history of philosophy will show that in all such cases the insight produces what people have believed for some time; it seldom produces something radically new. Reforms in philosophy come about by criticising self-evidence, common sense, intuition, and the rest. The criticism is not another appeal to a non-rational or supra-rational faculty, but to internal contradictions, the perception of problems which accepted belief does not answer, the inability of the proponents of the beliefs to verify them by whatever method the critic holds to be right. But we have also seen some men who, believing in ideas which contradict other ideas which they do not want to reject, will rig up a theory of manifold truth, such that an assertion may be true here and false there. In such cases the problem is that of the strength of the beliefs which the men want to retain. What is there about them which gives them a kind of sanctity?

3. *Truth*

The position of these lectures has been that truth is the consistency of beliefs. A belief is verified when it is shown to be consistent with beliefs already held. Such beliefs are called the facts. Since this point of view is different from both the consistency theory of truth and what is traditionally called empiricism, it may be well to add a note in the hope of clarifying it.

The question boils down, I suppose, to the problem of belief. Why does a man believe one thing rather than another? We all believe that the earth is an oblate sphere, but there is no direct testimony to this. Proofs of the earth's shape are all indirect, that is, inferred from observations which corroborate assertions about its shape. Such observations are the shape of the earth's shadow during an eclipse, the circumnavigation of the globe, the way a ship at sea disappears and reappears at the horizon. They become relevant to our belief when it is seen that they would not be possible if the earth were a flat disk or a square or some other non-globular shape. This is obviously oversimplified, but in every case what is observed is discordant with belief in some shape of the earth and harmonious with belief in another, the globular. My point throughout the lectures has been that no observation is in isolation proof of anything. A judgment has to be made about it before it will "say anything," and whatever judgment is made arises out of a larger context of beliefs.

This does not mean that all beliefs actual and possible are consistent. We shall undoubtedly try to make them consistent, but the attempt is made by purging uncontrolled observation of its personal and what I can only call its historical features. This transforms judgments into logical propositions, and all logical propositions are, by the very fact that they are anti-historical, items in a theoretically consistent system. The system may not be complete and it may never be completed. But whatever the situation may be, it should be borne in mind that a single judgment, if it is true, must not be inconsistent with other judgments held to be true.

I am not denying, but on the contrary, am insisting, that the systematic complex within which a judgment is to be integrated may not be present to consciousness. I may say, "My hat is on the table," and verify it by looking and seeing it on the table. This is undeniable. But it is also undeniable that my judgment may be questioned, and someone may say, "What makes you think that it is your hat?" If I reply that I see the hat, my reply is very poor evidence. I have to have in the back of my mind, or, if the debate becomes strenuous, overtly, tests of the identity of that hat and my hat. But these tests are not themselves part of what I see. I see the hat, and I judge that it is my hat. The tests can be discussed between me and my opponent without doing any looking whatsoever, and in fact, they may be the more trustworthy if I announce them without looking. They may consist in the size of the hat, the maker's mark inside the hat, my initials which have been perforated into the sweatband. But after all I am not the only person whose hats are of the size of mine, whose hats came from that particular maker, and who has my very ordinary initials. If in reply to this one says that a combination of such events here and now is extremely unlikely, two things must be said (1) every historical event is unlikely, and (2) the tests of probability, the concordance of these marks, are neither empirically given. They arise from a technique of answering inquiry which is logically prior to their application. My judgment, "My hat is on the table," has to be consistent with that technique as well as with a number of other propositions which are not asserted.

No one would deny that if it was known that I had no hat, my judgment would be false. If it was also known that I had looked inside the hat to discover its size and initials and the maker's mark and then announced my judgment, my report on the identifying marks of the hat would be poor evidence that it was mine. For I might well be cheating. This does not deny that I am seeing something, that there is a physical hat on the table. But it is denying that the judgment in question arises spontaneously from the visual or otherwise sensory data. In larger questions than the ownership of hats and their location on tables, two people may agree beforehand on what they will accept as relevant testimony. Such tests are easily found in books on legal evidence or in manuals of laboratory chemistry or of medical diagnosis. The men who apply the tests need know nothing whatsoever of their historical origin, but nevertheless the tests have their roots in history and not in logic. They usually come out of many years of co-operative work, and their theoretical justification can be made explicit if need be. All I wish to do here is to point out that such theoretical justification exists, for when that is accepted, the relevance of a given set of observations to previously held beliefs becomes indubitable.

As early as 1854, Beauperthuy had suggested that yellow fever might be transmitted by a mosquito. In 1881 Finlay advanced the theory once more and made it more precise. In 1900 the Yellow Fever Commission, Walter Reed, Carroll, and Agramonte during their experimental research on the transmission of the disease picked up Finlay's suggestion and tried to verify it. As everyone knows, or should know, the hypothesis failed of verification when first tried. The reason why it failed, as was later discovered, was that not enough time was allowed for the bacillus to incubate in the insect host between the time of its biting a yellow fever patient and a non-immune person. The only conclusion possible at that time was that the mosquito did not transmit the disease. As simple observation, perceptual data, looking and seeing, nothing was wrong with the experiment. One had first to know something about the incubation-periods of bacilli before one could construct a fertile experiment. One can say, if one wishes, that whether the experiment failed or not, the mosquito was the host of the bacillus in 1854 as in 1900. But if one is talking about knowledge, this cannot be said. The mosquito was neither true nor false; it was an insect. Ideas, sentences, alone are true, and they cannot be true if they are not in existence. This particular idea became true in 1900. For the mere suggestion by Beauperthuy in 1854 was not the same as the whole theoretical structure elaborated by Reed and his fellows, nor is a mosquito bite the same as the injection through the proboscis of a specific mosquito of a certain number of bacilli. We often give ideas which have a certain similarity the same name, as when, for instance, we sentimentally attribute the modern atomic theory to Democritus. But this is clearly misleading. For the atomic theory of Dalton is not the simple statement that all matter is composed of little particles called atoms. Again, some historians have been known to speak of Anaximander as a proto-Darwinian, because of the fragment in which it is stated that man must originally have evolved from another animal of fishlike nature. But the Darwinian theory is a vastly more complicated set of ideas than that expressed in the fragment.

Moreover, logical consistency, the non-contradiction of two sentences, is in no way evidence of truth to fact. This is a platitude, but one which can stand repetition. (1) All triangles are human, (2) Socrates is a triangle, are both false and both consistent. Their falsity, however, is not demonstrated by looking at triangles and seeing that they are not human. At a minimum one has to know what the two terms mean before one can look and see, and one also has to know what to look for in order to see whether something is a triangle or a human being. The mere fact that no one in his right mind would believe either of my sentences does not prove that their absurdity arises like a mist from a swamp out of the symbols in which they are expressed. People who hear or read them have learned their meaning before hearing or reading them and for that reason know that they form false sentences.

But just as two consistent sentences may be false, so observations may be relevant to two inconsistent sentences. This is illustrated by any simple judgment of identification, for even if the hat on the table is mine, what of it? Its presence on the table may be proof either that I am an orderly or disorderly person, that I put it there or that someone else put it there, that it was put there at nine o'clock this morning or at noon or some other time up to now, and so on. To see a hat on a table is not in itself proof of anything except that it is on the table, until other ideas are brought to bear upon it. Orderly people hang their hats on hatracks; disorderly people leave them on tables. But, it will be said, this introduces new elements into the case: definitions of "orderly" and "disorderly." That is obvious and shows that the presence of the hat *in itself* is inarticulate until a question has been put to it. And that is what I have been maintaining since the first lecture in this series.

What now is consistency? It is customary in discussing such questions to invoke the aid of symbolic logic, and indeed such aid is always good. But we are discussing the natural history of ideas, not their formal relations. Let us then see whether we can put the matter into words. It would be tempting to say that a statement is inconsistent with another statement if the second is identical with the first in all respects except that it contains a negative in the predicate. This, however, will not work, since, "Some cats are gray," is not necessarily inconsistent with the statement, "Some cats are not gray." In this case we do not know whether the two statements are consistent or not until we have understood how the quantifier "some" is being used: that is, whether it means "some but not all," or "some, possibly all." Moreover, two affirmative statements may be inconsistent: e.g., "It takes eight minutes for light to travel from the sun to the earth," and "It takes ten minutes—or any other number of minutes except eight—for light to travel from the sun to the earth." In this case ten minutes may be interpreted as "non-eight minutes," if one wishes, but it is obvious that to say that the light from the sun takes non-eight minutes to reach the earth is not equivalent to saying that it takes ten minutes, for non-eight is equivalent to

an infinite range of numbers. No one would ever assert that an
event took place in non-eight minutes or in non-X minutes,
though he might assert that it did not take place in eight minutes.
Such a sentence as this is an historical description, not a logical
assertion, and the inconsistency appears when an observer fails
to realize his expectations. It is analogous to saying that a given
chemical substance does not contain sodium or some other element, meaning that the tests for sodium fail. Here the negative
is a symbol of our failure, not of a non-presence in some metaphysical sense. But one's expectations cannot fail unless one
has expectations, and one cannot have expectations unless one has
prior information about the normal course of history—in my
sense of "history"—and the normal course of history cannot be
determined without either previous experience on the part of the
investigator or of a group of investigators in whose experience
one has confidence. But such considerations are psychological, or
methodological, not logical.

The logical symbolism of inconsistency through contradictory
and contrary statements is based on experience in the long run,
but its formulation is not necessary in order for a man to know
what inconsistency is. P and not-P are inconsistent by the rules
of the game, and I have no doubt that the rules of the game have
been developed from what actually happens empirically. But
that does not mean that when they are developed they are a
picture of what happens empirically. To argue in that fashion
would be analogous to arguing that because two apples do not
weigh twice what one of the apples weighs, 1 plus 1 are not 2.
The kind of inconsistency which disproves a factual or existential
or historical statement is the failure of an observation to meet
one's expectations. If the expectations and the observation as
well are symbolized in logical form, then the two statements
will be logically inconsistent. Failure may be symbolized by
negation, if one wishes, but it should be noted that one cannot
observe nothing, though one may pay no attention to what one
does observe. To see the blue sky and to say, "It is not raining,"
makes sense, for usually the sky is not clear and blue when it is

raining, though sometimes a passing shower may occur in one part of the sky and not in the part at which one is looking. But one would normally say, "It is not raining," when one sees the blue sky, only if one had reason to believe that it *was* raining. There is of course a large range of possible verifications of the statement, "It is not raining"; it does not have to be verified by seeing the blue sky. Negation is a useful device for gathering together all sorts of observations or experiences which fail to meet the requirements of the problem. But failure again is far from being non-being, and no metaphysical or ontological problem is raised by its happening to anyone.

Schematically the situation is about as follows. (1) As a result of past experience, habit, I expect or look for something. (2) I find something else. (3) I am able to recognize the difference between what I expected and what I find. (4) If my expectations are called my beliefs, my set of acquired facts, then what I find is said to be inconsistent with my beliefs or the facts. On the other hand it is always possible that I will find what I expected. If I can recognize the similarity between my expectations and my findings—and I can—then I say that my beliefs have been justified, my hypothesis verified, my expectations satisfied, or what you will. No such schematization is very convincing, since our habits by their nature as habits conceal their epistemological structure. The verification of an idea frequently is made in a few moments because of the mechanism of perception as described in my second lecture. But if we are going to argue about such matters, we must formalize them, and no apology is needed for doing so.

If one has any confidence in history, one can conclude that logical systems were derived from ways of thinking and after their development acted as a corrective of thinking. No one has to learn, for instance, the possible pairs of two contrary qualities to be able to set them down. A child long before he has any knowledge of logic knows that a thing cannot be both permitted and not permitted (forbidden) at the same time. I have myself heard a child of four say with great solemnity, "Some people look nice and are not nice, some don't look nice and are nice, some look nice and are nice too." And I am confident that if she had not been interrupted by the surrounding public which laughed, she would have continued with the fourth possibility. This does not imply that the Law of Contradiction is an innate idea; it simply illustrates how at an early age a child learns that sometimes his expectations are fulfilled and sometimes not. He phrases his experience according to the rituals of language but the language is given to him by others; he does not invent it.

The expressions which I have used in these lectures and supplementary notes may unfortunately suggest to some readers that I am pleading for a kind of subjectivism, a sort of epistemological individualism, according to which every man has a right to believe whatever he will and his beliefs will therefore be true. I have purposely used psychological terms for they seem more fitting to express what I have wanted to express, and though my usage will prove distasteful to many contemporary psychologists, they do not have the associations which the traditional language of epistemology has. The unsatisfactoriness of theories has always interested me as much as their satisfactoriness. I have always wondered why some theories seemed reasonable and others unreasonable, and the answer has not been that the former were harmonious with the facts, as the data of immediate experience, and the latter not. If people do not begin as babies living in social groups, families, then most of what I have said is rubbish. If it makes sense to say that memory of my own past, my observation of babies coming into being and learning various lessons, my reading of books written ostensibly by other people, most of whom in my own case are dead, are not completely misleading, something like a dream, then some part of what I have said may be worth taking seriously, though it is hardly likely that most of it will be. If my premises seem obvious, and they no doubt will seem so to readers ignorant of the history of philosophy, so much the better. For if it is possible for certain ideas to seem obvious, then we have evidence that several people can and do hold to the same beliefs. This might of course be simply an interesting coincidence. But it might also come about because of a certain uniformity in experience. I see no reason to accept the former alternative.

INDEX

INDEX OF NAMES

428